T0394288

Arts Education

Doing Arts Thinking: Arts Practice, Research and Education

Arts Education

A Global Affair

Edited by

Bernard W. Andrews

BRILL

LEIDEN | BOSTON

Cover illustration: iStock.com/AlexLMX

All chapters in this book have undergone peer review.

Library of Congress Cataloging-in-Publication Data

Names: Andrews, Bernard W., 1950- editor. | Akuno, Emily Achieng', writer
of foreword.
Title: Arts education : a global affair / edited by Bernard W. Andrews.
Other titles: Arts education (Koninklijke Brill NV).
Description: Leiden ; Boston : Brill, [2024] | Series: Doing arts thinking:
arts practice, research and education, 2542-9744 ; volume 13 | Includes
bibliographical references.
Identifiers: LCCN 2023039816 (print) | LCCN 2023039817 (ebook) | ISBN
9789004685239 (paperback) | ISBN 9789004685246 (hardback) | ISBN
9789004685253 (ebook)
Subjects: LCSH: Arts--Study and teaching. | COVID-19 Pandemic,
2020---Influence. | Educational change.
Classification: LCC NX282 .A79 2023 (print) | LCC NX282 (ebook) | DDC
700.71--dc23/eng/20231018
LC record available at https://lccn.loc.gov/2023039816
LC ebook record available at https://lccn.loc.gov/2023039817

Typeface for the Latin, Greek, and Cyrillic scripts: "Brill". See and download: brill.com/brill-typeface.

ISSN 2542-9744
ISBN 978-90-04-68523-9 (paperback)
ISBN 978-90-04-68524-6 (hardback)
ISBN 978-90-04-68525-3 (e-book)
DOI 10.1163/9789004685253

Advance Praise for
Arts Education: A Global Affair

"*Arts Education: A Global Affair* is a timely reminder of the international reach of the arts education community and its open-hearted approach in embracing diverse experiences and points of view. The impact of the Coronavirus COVID-19 Pandemic on arts education practice is the elephant in the research room. The Pandemic shook fundamental commitments to hands-on, face to face learning and teaching. This collection critically examines the deep and profound impact of pivoting to online teaching. Importantly, this collection celebrates the 'silver linings,' the innovations, the seeking of alternatives, embracing technology, experimentation and capacity for pandemic-friendly solutions while maintaining focus on the essentially human relationships implicit in arts education. Contributors from Austria, Canada, Czech Republic, Japan, Kenya, New Zealand, Spain, United Kingdom, United Arab Emirates, and United States of America write cogently about the changed landscape, and theory and practice in the space between the real and the digital. They explore experiences in arts pedagogies informed by multi-literate worlds and the consequences of change."

– Robin Pascoe, Honorary Fellow, College of Science, Health, Engineering and Education, Murdoch University, Perth, Western Australia, Australia; Past President, International Drama/Theatre and Education Association (IDEA); Past Chair, World Alliance for Arts Education (WAAE)

"Every single chapter in this veritable cornucopia of creative solutions to educational challenges, will bring inspiration to arts educators of all sorts in many corners of the globe. The authors each address how they continued to carry on teaching and researching when the global pandemic which began in 2020 presented particular problems for arts educators to solve. The volume contains case-studies of what arts teachers can do in a pandemic and beyond. There is no doubt that the solutions they found will continue to be put to good use in new ways of constructing and construing teaching and learning in many new online and other environments for years to come. I congratulate them all for this brave response and for their work."

– Lucy Green, Professor Emerita of Music Education, UCL Institute of Education, London, UK

"Twenty chapters from scholar/practitioners from nine different countries, *Arts Education: A Global Affair* stories the state of the arts in the first half of the 21st century. Forward-moving, fast-paced and vibrant, each contribution provides a piece to our collective puzzle, providing a vision of the future that is attainable and accessible for the diverse populations that we serve. This book is sure to electrify your perspective and animate your thoughts around the future of arts education."

– **Clint Randles, Professor, School of Music, University of South Florida, Tampa, Florida, USA**

Contents

Foreword

I am honoured and privileged to write the Foreword to this publication that promises to be a must-read for arts educators desiring to move on, be it from a period of disruption or from a season of inactivity. Thank you to the editor and authors for sharing these experiences with such clear foresight.

A publication on arts and arts education taking on a global perspective will need to do at least a few several possible things:

1. Consider contextual concepts of 'art';
2. Articulate manifestations of 'art';
3. Delineate boundaries of the practice of 'arts education';
4. Demonstrate the global nature of the attributes, benefits and application of and access to arts education; and
5. Analyse the procedures and activities that are labelled and embedded in arts education

... and many more.

This publication not only delves into the elements above, but also provides a global perspective on the mitigations of and for arts education during the recent global catastrophe occasioned by COVID-19. Art is what we do. Arts education is how we develop us. Arts-based training is how we cultivate resilience and adaptability. It speaks to issues of identity formation – as cultural and professional beings. We live out our 'selves' through:

1. creative digital activities;
2. representation of our recollections, reflection and imagination through visual arts and film;
3. verbal expression of our aspirations and fear in theatre, poetry and narrative;
4. movement, gestures and formations in dance, as well as
5. vocal and instrumental sounds in music.

To do this meaningfully in ways that satisfy the actors and benefit society, education in and through the arts must forge relationships between the individual and the sum total of the environment in which they function. These relationships are both characteristic of and reflected in the arts as practised and must therefore be components of the arts as taught and learnt. Arts education therefore suits, benefits and accommodates participants of all ages and stations in life. The provision and support for meaningful experiences are crucial if learners and society are to receive high standards of and valuable learning experiences and products.

The global nature of arts education affair is exhibited clearly in this publication. The authors are drawn from diverse regions of the globe. The context of practice is cross-generational, with research outcomes of work with children, young and older learners. The learning environment accommodates both practice and school, in person and online. The art forms are diverse and often multidimensional. Education is reported to happen through, with and in the application of arts in communities. There are reflections on research that cuts across layers and dimensions of practice and policy. Research designs reported include participatory action, experimentation, surveys and case study, with strong elements of personal reflection and self-analysis. Creativity, creative processes and outcome are interrogated from diverse angles, leading to the confirmation of arts education strategies in mitigating effects of disruption, in this case, a pandemic induced one. The duality of the real and digital class is examined in various projects and learning interventions that involved in person and/or online teaching of drama, choir etc, the teaching of practical arts performance that had hitherto been accomplished during in-person presentations.

This book, in offering a glimpse of what a section of the global arts education community experienced, provides examples of how arts and arts education influence and guide human response to, and accommodation of social upheavals. The publication unveils some of the innovative uses to which arts educators put commonly accessible technology, demonstrating arts teachers' creative problem-solving tendencies and practices. This publication is a minefield of examples and reports that support arts education for all and in all environments. Indeed, it demonstrates that arts education is a global affair.

I trust that you, the reader, will, by teasing the brains of the authors as you read their reports and proposals, find solutions and mitigations for your challenges while finding support for your choices on arts education in your part of the globe. The authors' willingness to share snippets of their work makes this volume valuable. May readers find substance to support their practice.

Emily Achieng' Akuno
Professor of Music, Department of Music and Performing Arts,
Technical University of Kenya, Nairobi, Kenya
Past President, International Society for Music Education (ISME)
Past Chair, World Alliance for Arts Education (WAAE)

Preface

Arts education research has increased significantly across the globe since the beginning of the century. New forms of arts-based research, such as ethnodrama and a/r/t/ography, have arisen and made significant contributions to both the research literature and to professional practice. Researchers in departments/schools/faculties of dance, drama, music, visual arts, media studies, cultural studies and education have been successful in acquiring peer-reviewed grants from government agencies to undertake large-scale projects and disseminate the findings internationally. Moreover, teaching and research in arts education have changed significantly as a consequence of the worldwide pandemic, COVID-19. Emerging variants have exacerbated the situation and show no signs of subsiding. In response to these challenges, arts educators and researchers have developed new modes of instructional delivery and data collection. These include asynchronous, synchronous, hybrid and bi-modal online learning, and online questionnaires, surveys, focus groups, and video interviews. This peer-reviewed book, entitled *Arts Education: A Global Affair*, highlights the adaptations that arts educators and researchers have undertaken to successfully adjust to this new reality in education. This *peer-reviewed* book will provide a valuable resource for students, teachers, professors and researchers in the arts disciplines, media studies, education, and cultural studies.

Acknowledgements

Many thanks to the Past Chairs of the World Alliance for Arts Education, Robin Pascoe and Emily Akuno, for their encouragement and support of *Arts Education: A Global Affair*. I also would like this opportunity to thank all the contributors to this volume for their hard work and persistence, and to my wife, Angelie, for her patience. Many thanks also to Derya Sahingil for her proof-reading expertise.

Figures and Tables

Figures

Tables

Notes on Contributors

Emily Achieng' Akuno
trained as a performer-educator at Kenyatta University in Kenya, Northwestern State University of Louisiana, USA, and Kingston University in the UK. Her research interests veer towards cultural relevance in music education. A professor of music of the Technical University of Kenya, she is editor and contributing author of the 2019 published *Music Education in Africa: Concept, Process and Practice* as well as articles tackling issues around music and teacher education in cultural context. She is a former president of the International Music Council (IMC) and the International Society for Music Education (ISME) as well as founding chair of the Music Education Research Group – Kenya (MERG-Kenya).

Bernie Andrews
is Professor of Education at the University of Ottawa where he teaches undergraduate music certification courses and graduate arts education and creativity courses. His research focuses on educational music, interactive teaching strategies, arts education partnerships, research methods, and teacher development in the arts. Bernie has recently completed three research/creation projects in education: New Sounds of Learning: Composing *for* Young Musicians funded by the Social Sciences and Humanities Research Council (SSHRC); Sound Connections: Composing Educational Music funded by the Trillium Foundation; and Making Music: Composing *with* Young Musicians funded by SSHRC. These research/creation projects have resulted in the composition of 147 new educational pieces. He also completed The Genesis Project: An investigation of contemporary music composition funded by SSHRC which involved the commissioning of 12 new works by composers-in-residence of major Canadian symphony orchestras. Bernie is currently Principal Investigator of the SSHRC-funded Viva Voce: Composing vocal music for education in Canada study which involves the creation of new vocal music for schools. His research has been recognized with the Brick Robb Research Award (OSSTF), Partners for Change Award (OADE), Award of Commendation (OMEA), Excellence in Innovation Award (CMEA), Fred L. Barlett Memorial Award (OPSBA), and Beckwith Award (CMC), in addition to several publication awards.

Simone Arsenault-May
(MES, BA) is a community facilitator currently working with the Pointe-Saint-Charles Art School and at l'École des Saules-Rieurs.

Amy Atkinson

is a PhD candidate at Concordia University in Art Education and visual arts teacher at the upper secondary level at Canadian International School in Hong Kong. She is also the co-editor of *The Canadian Art Teacher* journal and a member of the CSEA/SCEA executive. Amy has been a secondary visual art teacher for over 15 years in Canada, online through Ontario Virtual School, and internationally. Her research interests lie in the areas of art teacher support and education, research-creation, and international education. As a practising artist and creative writer, Amy explores ephemeral connections through new materialities, sustainability, and mindfulness, grounding her practice within a philosophical and transient spirit of place.

Julianne Burgess

has taught English to adult newcomers for more than 25 years in a variety of settings. She recently completed her PhD in Education at Brock University. Her arts-based dissertation research, supported by a Social Sciences and Humanities Research Council Doctoral Fellowship, explored newcomer experiences of belonging. She is keenly interested in people and their stories. Her research interests include artistic inquiry, participatory methods, translanguaging, and the ways in which everyday literacy practices are brought to life.

Lee Cheng

is an interdisciplinary artist-teacher and researcher. His research and artistic interests include music, technology, education, computer games, immersive and interactive media, digital and sonic arts, law and policy. Cheng received his Doctor of Philosophy, Master of Law, Postgraduate Diploma in Education, Postgraduate Diploma in Music Therapy, Bachelor of Engineering and Bachelor of Business Administration from The University of Hong Kong and The Education University of Hong Kong. He is currently working as Associate Professor in Games at Anglia Ruskin University, and serving different roles in multiple organisations including board member of the International Society for Music Education, co-opted council member of the Royal Musical Association, Theory Examiner of the Associated Board of the Royal Schools of Music, Arts Education Examiner of the Hong Kong Arts Development Council, and editorial board member of the *International Journal of Music Education*.

Manuel Fernández-Díaz

holds a PhD in Arts and Humanities. He is also Biologist, Primary Education Teacher, Master's in Education and Museums, Master's in Arts and Master's in Biodiversity Management in Mediterranean Environments. He currently teaches as an Associate Professor at the University of Murcia in the Department of Didactics of Experimental Sciences. His research focuses on the teaching and learning of the natural sciences. His main research interests focus on the initial and permanent training of science teachers, the characteristics of students in experimental sciences or methodological alternatives in experimental sciences. To date he has published fifteen articles in scientific journals and has made more than twenty contributions to national and international scientific congresses. He also participates in various research projects and innovation teaching projects.

Kara Flanagan

is a PhD candidate in the Education Studies program, Department of Curriculum and Instruction, Faculty of Education at the University of Victoria. Flanagan's research focus is on acting and music education. Flanagan is the co-founder of an acting school, the Victoria Academy of Dramatic Arts (www.vadarts.com), and a theatre company, Theatre Carpe Diem. In her capacity as a curriculum developer and teacher, she is focused on developing curriculum for students at the post-secondary level to support them in school and in their professional work. She is a Canada Council for the Arts award winner.

Vendula Fremlová

(PhD) is a university lecturer at the Department of Art Education, Faculty of Education, Charles University, and at the Department of History and Theory of Art, Faculty of Art and Design, Jan Evangelista Purkyně University in Ústí nad Labem. She also works as a freelance curator of contemporary art exhibitions, art critic, theorist, author and editor of publications and articles in art periodicals. Her work focuses on visual literacy and critical approaches to images, as well as on the relationship between the dominant culture, marginalised artistic expressions and their creators. Since 2020, she has been the editor-in-chief of the magazine *Life/Život*, published by Umělecká beseda, the oldest Czech art society.

Samuel Graden

is a music teacher and trombone player specializing in jazz music. He grew up in California where he studied trombone with Tonight Show house band musician Matt Finders, then attended California State University, Chico where he earned a BA in Music Industry with an Option in Recording Arts. Sam worked for Carnival Cruise Line as a showband musician until he decided he wanted to become a music teacher and earned a PGCE with Specialist Instrumental Teaching through Manchester Metropolitan University and the Royal Northern College of Music. Sam currently resides in Abu Dhabi where he teaches music and plays trombone in the Saadiyat Big Band.

Shelley M. Griffin

is Professor of Elementary Music Education in Brock University's Faculty of Education, Department of Educational Studies, St. Catharine's, Ontario. She obtained her Doctor of Philosophy and Master of Education Degrees from the University of Alberta, and her Bachelor of Music Degree from the University of Prince Edward Island. Shelley's research interests include children's narratives of musical experiences, pre-service music teacher education, narrative inquiry, vulnerability, emotional pedagogy, informal faculty mentorship, and collaborative scholarship. Shelley presents at various international conferences and publishes in numerous journals and edited books. She has served as the co-chair for the 7th International Conference on Narrative Inquiry in Music Education (NIME7). Shelley is the 2019 recipient of the Brock University Faculty of Education Award for Excellence in Teaching. In addition to her teaching and scholarship, Shelley is an active musician in the Niagara, Ontario region, performing regularly as a vocalist with Avanti Chamber Singers.

Catherine Hands

is Associate Professor of Educational Administration and Leadership at Brock University. Catherine has worked with Canadian and American school boards, teachers' unions, and the Ontario Ministry of Education as a researcher and consultant. Catherine's research interests stem from her classroom experience as well as her work with school leaders and teachers, and include school-community relations, family involvement in schooling, educational leadership, values and ethics in education, social justice, professional learning communities, and educational reform. She maintains an active research agenda in these areas, and has presented and published her work regionally, nationally and internationally.

Jacqueline Hood

is the Head of the Drama Faculty at a secondary college in Auckland, New Zealand where she has taught drama and directed a range of school productions. Jacqueline has a degree in Drama and English from The University of Wales at Swansea, a PGCE in Drama Education at The University of Reading, England and completed her Masters at The University of Auckland. During her postgraduate study Jacqueline devised and performed *Stories of Motherhood* to a public audience over several evenings. She has co-authored the ESA (*LearnWell*) NCEA *Drama Study Guides* for students and teachers since 2012. In 2021, she played the role of Creon in Corvus Theatre Co's production of *Antigone* performed in a glass box. She is currently in rehearsal for *The Women of Troy*.

Baris Isikguner

is currently Associate Professor and Deputy Head of Cambridge School of Creative Industries in Anglia Ruskin University. He teaches the theoretical and technical dimensions of computer animation and visual effects. He is specially focused on practice-based research in procedural animation and its connections to believable character motion. Baris is a certified master level animator and has over 15 years of industry and academic experience in game art and visual effects. He was also awarded the DNIIT Certificate by the National Institute of Information Technology (NIIT). He studied BA Visual Communication and Design (3D Animation), MA Animation and has a PhD in procedural animation. Baris is experienced with Blender, Maya, Substance designer and painter, ZBrush and Unreal Engine.

Nao Kameishi

is a public elementary school teacher in Hiroshima, Japan. She received her Master's degree majoring in education from Hiroshima University in 2023. Her research interests include museum education, aesthetic education with contemporary art that fosters empathy in children, and international education through art. She has worked more than two years on a collaborative project of the Hiroshima City Museum of Contemporary Art and public elementary schools in Hiroshima. She has also participated in an international art exchange project developed by public schools in Hiroshima and schools in Indiana, USA, since 2021

Jeannie Kyungjin Kim

is an artist, educator and cultural worker based in Dundas and Toronto, Ontario. She holds a Master of Arts from Concordia University (Art Education) a Honors Bachelor of Arts and Diploma from University of Toronto Mississauga and Sheridan College (Art and Art History). Her studio and research practice fluctuates between utilizing, critiquing and teaching traditional Korean methodologies with an intercultural lens using Asian/Korean watercolours, oil painting, drawing, and video. She has taught diverse visual and digital art programs for children, youth, and adults in the Greater Toronto Area and Montréal such as the Living Arts Centre, Lakeshore Arts, the City of Mississauga, Pointe-Saint Charles Art School, and Concordia University. Her current work focuses on dismantling structural barriers and creating true inclusion for all artists and community members by developing and implementing arts programming for equity-deserving groups as the Executive Secretary at Hamilton Artists Inc. and a Board Member at Centre3 for Social + Artistic Practice.

Nadia Kuehn

was born and raised in East Berlin (GDR). At the University of Leipzig in Leipzig she studied Social Anthropology and American Literature. She worked for several years as an artistic assistant for Alba D'Urbano and at the Documentary Film Festival (DOK Leipzig) before taking the position as a production manager at the documentary production company ma.ja.de. When she moved with her family to Montreal in 2017, she briefly worked as a Video Chanel Manager before starting as a Program Coordinator and Administrator for Pointe Saint Charles Art School in 2019. At the same time, she began her creative journey in illustration, animation, painting and writing.

David LeRue

is an artist, educator and PhD student based in Montreal, Quebec. He holds a BFA from NSCAD University, and an MFA in Painting and Drawing from Concordia University. His painting practice explores the connection between landscape and the built environment, with a particular focus on how sporting events such as the Olympics permanently change their host cities. His SSHRC-funded doctoral project, tentatively titled "The Phantom Expos", explores the connection between sport, neighbourhood histories and urban development, studying a proposed stadium development in Montreal's Peel Basin. The project combines oral history, landscape painting, archive research and public pedagogy to explore the perspectives of many stakeholders in a development project. He is currently a painting instructor and collaborator with the Pointe-St-Charles art school, a part-time instructor at Concordia, and teaches occasional workshops with Ross Creek Centre for the arts in Nova Scotia.

Congmao Li

is from Sichuan, China and is a doctoral student at the Graduate School of Humanities and Social Sciences at Hiroshima University. Her research interests include children's individuality and personality development, self-expression in art activities, and Dewey's educational theory. To understand the issues regarding self-expression of Chinese children, she recently conducted an analysis based on a survey of children from the middle and upper grades in China. Referring to Dewey's theory of art, she discussed the key components and the process of self-expression. She integrated the elements that constitute self-expression into the survey sheets for a quantitative and qualitative analysis to identify the degree of children's self-expression in art activities and the impeding factors. This study aims to reveal the underlying factors that inhibit self-expression of Chinese children. The findings will inform future research and assist in the design of art courses that can cultivate children's capability of self-expression effectively.

Nancy Long

is an art and media teacher and artist from Montreal, Quebec. She has taught at the high school level for over 20 years. She is currently a university supervisor at Concordia University to undergraduate pre-service teachers and has taught seminars on university teaching. Nancy is also a PhD candidate in the Department of Art Education at Concordia. Her doctoral research focuses on high school art students and teachers developing their skills in tolerance for ambiguity and questioning prescribed outcomes and 'mistakes' made in the art room. Nancy is also interested in pre-service teacher education and cross-curricular integration of the arts. In her studio practice in painting, drawing and installation art, she examines the overlap of nostalgia and memory by reflecting on how they interact with our senses.

Jane Isobel Luton

has been a Drama teacher and Head of Department in secondary schools in England and New Zealand. She graduated with a PhD in Drama Education through creative practice from The University of Auckland in 2015 supervised by Professor Peter O'Connor. She has written several international chapters, and articles on aspects of drama education and on her playful research methodology 'Embodied Reflections'. She is the co-author of five ESA NZ (*LearnWell*) *Drama Study Guides* for Year 12 and 13 students and teachers. In 2022, Jane and her daughter Holly Luton had a chapter published in the *Routledge Companion to Theatre and Young People,* she presented her research on embodiment at the TaPRA Conference at Essex University and on teaching drama during the pandemic at the NZARE conference with her colleague Jacqui Hood. She is currently a senior lecturer for drama education at The Faculty of Education and Social Work at The University of Auckland.

Nancy Abigael Masasabi

is a lecturer at Maseno University's Department of Music and Theatre Studies, Kenya. She holds a Master of Music degree in Music Composition from Kenyatta University and a Doctor of Musicology degree from the University of South Africa. Her areas of research interest include Music Composition, Musicology and Cultural studies. Masasabi has published the book titled *Silao-sikeleko as a Process of Performance Compositional Elaboration in Bukusu Litungu Music,* among other book chapters and articles. She is the immediate former

Chairperson of the Department of Music and Theatre Studies. Masasabi is a choir director, band director, singer, music composer, choral conductor both at the university and in church. This has given her practical music experience in addition to research and academia.

Anneke Britt McCabe

is a Sessional Instructor in Brock University's Faculty of Education, Department of Education Studies, St. Catharines, Ontario. Anneke is a trained pianist and songwriter, who has taught and directed choirs, concert bands, and musical groups in a variety of Ontario public elementary schools, in Canada, over the last 20 years. Anneke appreciates the art of wearing different hats in her field and is currently a Vice Principal in the Upper Grand District School Board. In the field of music education, Anneke's research focuses on inquiring into and exploring the life-long journey of musician-music teachers, through the craft of creating music. Anneke's new album, *Evoking a Soundscape* (2023), was written as a reflective, musical accompaniment to her thesis, and can be found on all streaming platforms (e.g., iTunes, Spotify, YouTube).

Julie Mongeon-Ferré

is the Arts Education Consultant with the Bureau de l'éducation française in the Manitoba Department of Education and Early Childhood Learning. Her responsibilities include the development and implementation of curricula in Dramatic Arts, Visual Arts, Dance, and Music, from kindergarten to Grade 12. She works actively to promote arts education while developing teaching resources and supporting teacher professional learning in arts disciplines. Prior to her current position, she taught music in elementary school for nearly thirty years in Winnipeg after studying at the Vincent d'Indy School of Music and the Université du Québec in Montreal. Julie is currently a co-researcher on an action-research study in the field of arts education and multiliteracies and is working to obtain her Master in Education degree at Université de Saint-Boniface. She has also been teaching courses in music didactics at this same university.

Francine Morin

(PhD) is Professor at the Faculty of Education, University of Manitoba and leads music/arts education and teacher development initiatives. She is the former Associate Dean of Undergraduate Programs and Department Head of Curriculum, Teaching and Learning. She teaches courses in music/arts education and research methodologies. Dr. Morin conducts research aimed at improving educational experiences for children and educators. She works with field-based partners on refining a two-year induction and mentoring program for new teachers and an after-school orchestral program for children who live in high challenge circumstances. Recently, Dr. Morin completed a survey study examining pandemic impacts on singing in Canadian school music programs. Currently, she is leading a study investigating pandemic influences on an after-school orchestral program operating in two schools. Dr. Morin also collaborates with a team of Indigenous and settler researchers undertaking an exploration of anti-racist, arts-based responses to the violence described in the *Missing and Murdered Indigenous Women and Girls* report in the contexts of teacher and nursing education. Her outreach work includes serving as the Canadian Music Educators' Association's Director of Research and Publications, Editorial Board member for the *Canadian Journal of Action Research*, and on the Advisory Council for the Canadian Network for Arts and Learning.

Yasaman Moussavi

is an Iranian visual artist and educator. She is a PhD student in art education at the University of British Columbia and holds an MFA from Texas Tech University. In her art practice, she explores the socio-cultural in-betweenness as a capacity and disposition to participate in meaning-making across cultures and languages. For her, transitional spaces are the performative embodiment of spatial mapping and in-betweenness. Yasaman's arts research has been displayed and published in many national and international solo and group exhibitions. She is Currently, live and work in Vancouver.

Lucy Mugambi

is currently a PhD Candidate in Art and Visual Culture Education program at the University of Arizona, School of Fine arts. She holds a bachelor's degree in Education from Kenyatta University, a Master's degree in Primary Teacher Education, Kenyatta University, Kenya, and a Master's in Art Education from The University of British Columbia, Vancouver, Canada. Lucy is an artist/teacher/researcher interested in the use of the arts to reach marginalized groups. During COVID-9 pandemic Lucy, while in the US, used the WhatsApp as a pedagogical tool to reach out and instruct children in Kenya who were facing many challenges while locked down in their homes. Her current research focuses on the intersection between the arts and children with disabilities in the Kenyan primary schools.

Kazuyo Nakamura

is Professor, Art Education, Hiroshima University, Japan, is active in areas of aesthetic education, international education, community art teacher education, and teacher training curriculum development. She was a 2014 U.S.-Japan Fulbright Scholar whose focus of research was on international peace education through art. She has directed, in collaboration with Indiana University's East Asian Studies Center in the US of America, an international project for community schools entitled The Intercultural Eye for Art for eight years. She has served on the editorial board of the Japan national arts and crafts textbooks for elementary and junior high schools for more than ten years. She serves as a Director of the Japanese Association of Art Education and a Director of the John Dewey Society of Japan.

Snežana Obradović-Ratković

is a research officer and scholar in the Faculty of Education, Brock University, Ontario, Canada. She immigrated to Canada in 1998 as a refugee science teacher from the former Yugoslavia. In her doctoral research, Snežana explored the re-settlement experiences of refugee women teachers from the former Yugoslavia who immigrated to Canada during or after Yugoslav wars. In 2017, Snežana's research team – funded by the Social Sciences and Humanities Research Council of Canada – compiled Canada's knowledge about refugee student K-12 education and well-being. In collaboration with educators from Canada, Greece, Namibia, Pakistan, and Turkey, she has published a book chapter, Educating refugee students: Global perspectives and priorities, concluding that schools and the arts can create healing spaces for all students. She believes that safety, care, and community building with refugee students must extend beyond the classroom into institutional, local, national, and international settings and communities. Her scholarship focuses on migration and indigeneity, transnational and transdisciplinary teacher education, decolonizing and arts-based research methodologies, academic writing and publishing, generous scholarship, and well-being in higher education.

Natalie Pavlik

is a multifaceted artist, researcher, and educator in Montreal, Quebec. Currently completing her Ph.D. in Art Education at Concordia University, she holds a B.A. in Sociocultural Anthropology (University of Toronto), a B.Ed. in Junior/ Intermediate Visual Arts (University of Ottawa), and an M.A. in Art Education (Concordia University). Her SSHRC-funded doctoral research explores how artistic process as pedagogy can promote the centering of EDIA+ practices in art education across global contexts. Within her art practice, she investigates how technology can be used to harness the intersections between digital and analogue artistic mediums, and how these creative methods can support international art education collaborations. Natalie has taught art in schools and alternative learning environments in Canada, Germany, and Switzerland.

Beryl Peters

has dedicated her career to arts education, teaching in Kindergarten to Grade 12 public schools and post-secondary institutions from Texas to the Yukon. She is currently Director of Practicum and Partnerships at the Faculty of Education, University of Manitoba where she is also an assistant professor in the Department of Curriculum, Teaching and Learning. She holds a PhD in Inclusive Education (University of Manitoba) and a Master of Music (East Texas State University) with undergraduate degrees in music and education. Prior to her appointment as Director of Practicum and Partnerships in 2018, Dr. Peters was Arts Education Consultant with the Manitoba Department of Education where she coordinated the development and implementation of curricula and resources for Kindergarten to Grade 12 Dance, Dramatic Arts, Music, and Visual Arts Education. Her research and writing focus on arts education, multiliteracies, and teacher education. Dr. Peters is a past President of Carl Orff Canada and holds multiple teaching and research awards including the Canadian Arts Researchers and Teachers Society Doctoral Graduate Research Award for her doctoral research on the semiotic potential of multimodal experiences for early years readers.

Anita Prest

is Associate Professor of Music Education at the University of Victoria, Canada. Guided by multi-First Nation, Métis, and non-Indigenous partners, she engages in federally funded community-based participatory research to examine the embedding of local Indigenous knowledge, pedagogies, and worldviews in British Columbia's public school music classes. She recently was awarded a University of Victoria Faculty of Education Award for Excellence in Research. Anita teaches undergraduate music education courses to both secondary music specialist and elementary generalist teacher candidates, plus graduate research methodology courses. She is a member of the MayDay Steering Committee, and a commissioner for the ISME Commission on Policy: Culture, Education, and Media. Anita is co-founder of the International Society for Music Education (ISME) Decolonizing and Indigenizing Music Education special interest group. Prior to her appointment at the University of Victoria, she taught K-12 music for 20 years.

Maria Luz Ruiz-Bañon

is the Vice-Dean of Quality and Students and professor of Audiovisuals and Sculpture in the Faculty of Fine Arts at the University of Murcia in Spain (UMU). She obtained a PhD in Fine Arts and Master's in Education and Museums at the UMU and a Master's degree in teacher training at the UCAM, specialising in art. She received a first prize in the speciality of sculpture awarded by the Regional

Ministry of Education and Universities of Murcia. She has held a pre-doctoral research grant at the Fine Arts Department of the UMU, funded by the Spanish Ministry of Science, Research and Universities. Multidisciplinary artist who is committed to research and teaching innovation. She is a member of the Research Group Visual Studies: Images, Texts, Contexts, and of the Teaching Innovation Group Art in Construction of the UMU in which the project entitled "Graphic description of the monumental trees of the Region of Murcia" was developed. Author of different articles and chapters related to teaching innovation and art. She was the PI of the innovation project "Surrealist games as a cooperative tool in audiovisual creation for Fine Arts students".

Victoria Sánchez-Giner

is the Dean of the Faculty of Fine Arts and Professor of Painting at the University of Murcia in Spain (UMU). She holds a PhD in Fine Arts at the University of Valencia, a Master's degree in Education and Museums at the UMU, and is a visual artist. Her line of research is the ethical and aesthetic foundations of landscape, both in the field of scientific and artistic production. She alternates artistic production and teaching activity with research on landscape and art, having made numerous contributions to national and international publications and scientific meetings. She is a member of the Ecce Homo research group at the UMU. Principal Investigator of the international and multidisciplinary teaching innovation group specializing in Art, Culture and Nature called Art in Construction at the University of Murcia. Since 2007 she has been coordinating the teaching project "UM Landscape versus protected natural spaces in the Region of Murcia" for the dissemination of the Regional Parks through landscape painting.

Elmira Sarreshtehdari

is an Iranian artist, art researcher, and educator based in Canada. She is a PhD student in art education at the University of British Columbia and holds an MFA from the University of Calgary. Elmira is interested in the ways in which the performative and embodied act of participating in art making activates liminal spaces of one's encounters with the object/subject of the world and how these encounters provide a fertile space for probing, finding, making, and learning. In that regard, Elmira's recent art-based inquiry focuses on the audiences' encounter with immigrant/dis-placed art and the ways in which this aesthetic interaction could translate into a proliferating space for further communication and meaning-making between multiple cultures, bodies, mediums, traditions, places, assumptions.

Breanna Shanahan

(she/her) is an artist and educator based in the traditional Erie, Neutral, Huron-Wendat, Haudenosaunee and Mississaugas region, known by some as Hamilton. She received her MFA at Concordia University in June 2019 and was a SSHRC (Social Sciences and Humanities Research Council) recipient in 2017. She received her BFA (Hons) at the University of Toronto in 2014, and her Diploma in Fine Arts from Sheridan College the same year. Her history as a woodshop and digital fabrication technician has worked in parallel with her practice which explores cultural posthumanism as a foundational approach to artmaking, championing various technoscientific avenues in her research creation process. Shanahan often leans into material exploration hovering between silos of two-dimensional and three-dimensional practices. She has taught at Concordia University, Mount Allison University, NSCAD University and Sherdan College all levels of Drawing and Sculpture and her work has been exhibited in Italy, China, Austria, the United States of America and in Canada.

Anita Sinner

is a Professor of Art Education at Concordia University, Montreal. Her research interests include artwork scholarship, international art education, historical perspectives and community teacher education. She works extensively with stories as pedagogic pivots, with particular emphasis on artful inquiry in relation to curriculum studies and social and cultural issues in education. Anita is the lead editor of the artwork scholarship series with Intellect, and recent co-edited books include *Living Histories: Global perspectives in Art Education* (Intellect); *Provoking the Field: International Perspectives on Visual Arts PhDs in Education* (Intellect) and the companion text, *Visually Provoking: Dissertations in Art Education* (Lapland).

Danu Anthony Stinson

(PhD) is a social psychologist and Associate Professor at the University of Victoria, Canada. She is a teacher and researcher who studies the social self now, but she was an actor and playwright in her youth. Collaborating on this chapter forged a wonderful bridge between her past and present selves.

Kristina Urquhart

holds a Honours BA in Sociology from the University of Waterloo, Ontario. She is a multi-disciplinary artist who has trained broadly in photography, ceramics, printmaking, sculpture, textiles, installation, and painting. She attended the Langara College Professional Photography program and the Emily Carr

University of Art and Design in Vancouver, BC, as well as the Grennan Mill Craft School and Kilkenny College of Art and Design in Ireland. Kristina is an experienced and enthusiastic arts educator who believes that creating art in the company of others is one of life's great pleasures, and that accessible art programs have far reaching benefits for all ages.

Motoki Wada

received the Bachelor of Education in 2022 from Hiroshima University, Japan. He is currently a master's student at the Graduate School of Humanities and Social Sciences at Hiroshima University. Motoki's research interests include industrial arts education for children, maker movement, and education combining technology with art. In 2021 and 2022, he participated in an international art education project that includes collaborative work with students at Concordia University in Canada. He has been engaged in action research on manufacturing education based on concepts of the Maker movement at the elementary school in Hiroshima since 2023.

Xiong Wang

is Assistant Lecturer from Faculty of Education, University of Alberta. Her research interests focus on teachers' professional learning, online learning and literacy development in mathematics education as well as the connections between arts and mathematics.

Catherine Wells

(BFA, MA) is an art therapist, art teacher and artist, director of the Pointe-Saint-Charles Art School, and a professional member of the Association des art-thérapeutes du Québec. She has worked in the art, medical, educational, community and corporate milieus with individuals and groups of all ages for over thirty years. Presently she practices as an art therapist and teacher at the art school, and is the art therapist at Chez Doris, a women's shelter in Montreal. She also has a private art therapy practice and is cultivating her painting skills.

Michelle Wiebe

is an Assistant Professor of Art Education at the University of Victoria. Prior to joining the faculty at UVic she taught Graphic Design in Toronto, Ontario. Currently, her primary research is currently centered on building empathic capacity in art education design students and developing open, welcoming and safe studio environments for non-binary students. She has an abiding interest in the discourse of design education, creativity, and design thinking. She maintains an active studio painting practice and is a registered graphic designer.

Kari-Lynn Winters

is a Full Professor, award-winning Canadian children's author, and celebrated performer, and playwright. She currently teaches drama-in-education, dance-in-education, and language arts to teacher candidates at Brock University in the Faculty of Education. Holding degrees from UBC, OISE/UT, Brock University, and the National Theatre School in literacy education, teacher education, and the arts, her research interests include: STEAM, refugee and immigrant education, Indigenous ways of knowing, mental health and wellness, equitable education, body image, embodied pedagogies, children's literature, drama, and multimodal literacies.

Kateřina Žarnikov

is a drama teacher. For almost ten years she worked at a basic art school in Nové Město na Moravě in Czechia. Since 2018 she has been freelancing and conducting workshops in the Czech Republic, Slovakia and Austria. She is also a PhD student of the Theory and Practice in Drama Education at the Theatre Faculty of the Academy of Performing Arts in Prague. Her doctoral research focuses on drama education in basic education in Europe. During the COVID-lockdown she gathered experiences of Czech and Slovak drama teachers and created an online platform where she shares these experiences.

CHAPTER 1

Artistic Creation and Dissemination of Landscape in Hybrid Online Learning

Approach outside the Classroom through Local Arboreal Heritage

Maria Luz Ruiz-Bañon, Victoria Sánchez-Giner and Manuel Fernández-Díaz

Abstract

The interdisciplinary teaching innovation project "Graphic description of the monumental trees of the Region of Murcia" arose within the teaching innovation group of the University of Murcia "Art in Construction" during the 2020–21 academic year. Its aim was to try to solve the limitations to classroom teaching resulting from the health emergency caused by COVID-19 in Spain. Among the pandemic containment measures put in place by the Spanish government, there were physical distancing regulations and travel restrictions. This generated a widespread need to adapt university teaching from a fully face-to-face to a online hybrid scenario. This was a major handicap in eminently practical subjects, such as "Painting and Landscape" and "Design" in the Fine Arts Degree, "Teaching and Learning in the Natural Environment" or "Nature Workshops" in the Primary Education Degree at the University of Murcia. The main limitation was the impossibility of carrying out practices of direct observation of the landscape, research and graphic representation jointly in the classroom. To provide a solution to this circumstance, we proposed the usefulness of implementing a collaborative and interdisciplinary methodological action based on the autonomous work of the students with the coordination of the teaching staff developed through the virtual environment. We designed a didactic intervention based on the development of a collaborative social, pedagogical, and artistic c/a/r/tography through the direct and individual observation of the local arboreal heritage of each participant. This intervention was materialised in the publication of the book *Singular Trees of the Region of Murcia*.

Keywords

hybrid teaching – c/a/r/tography – cooperative learning – arboreal heritage

1   Introduction

Since World Health Organization characterised the public health emergency caused by COVID-19 as an international pandemic on March 11th, 2020, the Spanish government had been implementing a series of urgent measures to deal with its spread and protect the health and safety of citizens. With this objective, restrictive rules on the freedom of movement of persons and mandatory physical interpersonal distancing were established, which affected all sectors, including education and professional training. All educational establishments had to ensure the adoption of the necessary organisational measures to avoid crowds and guarantee a minimum safety distance. For this reason, various contingency plans were drawn up at the university area in which the rector's office proposed measures for action in accordance with the guidelines established at state and regional level.

As epidemiological data in Spain evolved, the central government modified the containment measures. The Ministry of Universities and the Conference of Rectors of Spanish Universities (CRUE) recommended that universities plan their teaching activity according to three possible scenarios: the first based on full face-to-face teaching; the second in which reduced and secure face-to-face teaching was combined with non-face-to-face teaching; and the third scenario in which all teaching was given in an online format. At the beginning of the first term of the academic year 2020–21, new epidemiological outbreaks appeared. This had a special impact on the Autonomous Community of Murcia, so the University of Murcia applied its Contingency Plan 3.0. After noting the exceptional nature of the virus, the impact of contagion and its unpredictable and exponential evolution, it was determined that during that academic year, classes would be held in the second scenario, i.e. in a hybrid online learning. As a result, many of the activities planned for the different degrees and subjects taught at the university could not be carried out as planned, and in many cases they had to be cancelled or delayed. In other cases, the activities were rearticulated and redesigned by the teachers, adapting them to a hybrid learning environment.

With this objective, from the multidisciplinary group of teaching innovation "Art in Construction/Ecotone" (AECE) of the University of Murcia, we developed a project entitled "Graphic description of the monumental trees of the Region of Murcia". This was aimed at teachers and students of the subjects "Painting and Landscape" and "Design" of the Degree in Fine Arts, "Teaching and Learning of the Natural Environment" and "Nature Workshops" of the Degree in Primary Education of the University of Murcia. The project was developed within the framework of the call for teaching innovation actions Innova 2020–21 of the University of Murcia (Id. 1021) (R.440/2020 of June 11th) with the participation of both faculties. The main objective of this project was to promote the design and implementation of a collaborative didactic activity to complement and dynamise the teaching-learning process in the exceptional academic environment of hybrid online learning. This project relied mainly on different tools of the virtual environment for its development. The strict limitations of mobility between municipalities in the region also imposed the necessary condition of including in its design an important component of autonomous development.

2   A c/a/r/tographic Project for a Hybrid Academic Environment

The design of the project "Graphic description of the monumental trees of the Region of Murcia" was based on the a/r/tography methodology (Irwin & De Cosson, 2004; Spinggay et al., 2008; Irwin et al., 2018). This qualitative research technique emerged in 2003 by Rita L. Irwin as a procedure capable of unifying artistic, educational and research interests through its different strategies, techniques and tools. A/r/tography is closely related to the methodological approach that arose in 1993 from arts-based research (Barone & Eisner, 2012). Although both methodologies use the representational forms of the arts as a means to pose questions, arts-based research is not so focused on the specific field of education and can be applied to other fields of knowledge. In artography, each of the letters of the acronym 'art' corresponds to the first letter of the holistic triad artist-researcher-teacher, or also of art-research-teaching, being used interchangeably in both senses. It takes the letter 'a' from artistic practices, especially community-based ones; the letter 'r' (research) reinforces the sense of instrument within an research methodology that emphasises the collaborative; and which is applied by researcher-teachers in an educational context latent in the letter 't' for teachers, to finally be represented graphically (graph) (Ramón & Alonso-Sanz, 2022, p. 537). This emphasis on personal embodiment as artist-researcher-teacher is especially relevant for how it connects with the concepts of "embodied thought" and "situated activity" or "situated cognition" that affirm that thinking is inseparable from action and from social and cultural contexts (Marín-Viadel & Roldan, 2019). As David Roussell (2019, p. 71) notes, "a/r/tography provides a way to describe, interpret and express the lived experiences of artists, teachers and researchers through praxis (doing), theoria (conceptualisation), and poiesis (making)". This meaning, "the action research as living practice" (Sumara & Carson, 1997). So, according to Irwin (n.d.):

> To be engaged in the practice of a/r/tography means to inquire in the world through an ongoing process of art making in any art form and

> writing not separate or illustrative of each other but interconnected and woven through each other to create relational and/or enhanced meanings. A/r/tographical work are often rendered through the methodological concepts of contiguity, living inquiry, openings, metaphor/metonymy, reverberations, and excess, which are enacted and presented/ performed when a relational aesthetic inquiry condition is envisioned as embodied understandings and exchanges between art and text, and between and among the broadly conceived identities of artist/researcher/teacher.

Although our project followed the postulates of a/r/tography for its development, it was designed with explicit reference to the concept of cartography. Instead of focusing on the map or the representation of its layout, we were interested in the connection of cartography with the terms art and affects (Ramon, 2021). This is why this project can be considered in line with the affective methodology that Rousell and Lasczik (2014) call c/a/r/tography. According to Lasczik and Irwin (2017), this methodology involves the use of "visual mapping as an approach to performing (rather than presenting) the interrelationships between art, teaching and research" (p. 69). C/a/r/tography adds to the concept of artography the letter 'c' from its association with social, pedagogical and artistic cartography and visual mapping (Ramon & Alonso-Sanz, 2022, p. 537). Based on the postulates of c/a/r/tography, a collaborative teaching project, to be developed in a hybrid online learning environment, was designed based on the creation of a social, pedagogical, and artistic cartography from the direct and autonomous observation of the local arboreal heritage of each of the participants.

The reason for opting for the development of this cartographic typology as a mechanism for research and innovation was because social, artistic, or visual cartography is capable of exposing reflective results related to the cultural, historical and political aspects of the territory through its two-dimensional representation. This is something that differentiates it from traditional cartography, which is purely linked to the existing physical space from which it starts. C/a/r/tographies are used to work on any subject or reality in the world, but from an exclusively visual, artistic, and symbolic viewpoint and perspective. In the process of creating an artistic cartographic representation, it is linked to the mental and emotional states and memories of the experiences of those who create it. The relevance and innovation that this methodological practice brings lies through the lens of a/r/tography, and more specifically c/a/r/tography, educational and artistic investigations become collaborative processes that, according to Davis and Sumara (2006), "expand the space of human possibility by exploring the space of the existing possible" (p. 168). According to Irwin (n.d.):

> A/r/tography is inherently about self as artist/researcher/teacher yet it is also social when groups or communities of a/r/tographers come together to engage in shared inquiries, act as critical friends, articulate an evolution of research questions, and present their collective evocative/provocative works to others.

The aim of this methodology is to open up, propose or suggest new ways of understanding the world around us through the arts and the joint exploration of teachers and students, and in this way not to lead the exploration to conclusions that close or limit the resolution of problems.

The project was adapted and configured to be carried out in an academic hybrid online learning environment. On the one hand, it was developed in the virtual space through the *aulavirtual*. This is the official virtual teaching platform (elearning) of the University of Murcia where teachers and students have various telematic tools that facilitate the development of teaching and learning processes. And on the other hand, it took place in different natural areas of the Region of Murcia, opening up and consolidating the natural heritage as a new learning scenario beyond the classroom. It should be noted that natural heritage is understood as those biological and geological formations, animal and plant habitats, landscapes and natural areas that have exceptional values from the point of view of their conservation, scientific interest, or natural beauty. We are all familiar with the formal and informal contexts in which teaching and learning processes usually take place. We tend to assume that formal education is almost always presented within a specific setting: the classroom. After the experience of the COVID-19 pandemic, was necessary to consider formal education in settings that are able to go beyond the classroom walls. When the contents belong to or are related to the area of natural sciences, as was the case for the subjects involved in this project, the work is easily transferable outside the classroom, and is also highly recommendable. In a face-to-face educational environment, working on content related to plants, animals, rocks, relief, or landscape simply from the classroom is not very effective for meaningful learning. As we found ourselves in an exceptional context where it was not possible to move the whole group of students between the different municipalities of the region, it was necessary to adapt the field practices of the subjects to an individual level so as not to lose the opportunity of learning through direct contact with nature. The main difficulty was to organise and coordinate it in order to be able to carry out the field visits independently. However, we had an advantage. In our immediate environment, the Autonomous Community of Murcia, exposure to the landscape is easy because, despite being a relatively small area, we have a high diversity of landscapes, biology, and geology, as reflected in the numerous Protected Natural Areas, Natura 2000 sites and other monumental trees, which are available to us. Therefore, the students had no problem finding a location close to their homes to carry out the activity.

Rather than this blended learning environment being an obstacle to the development of the project, this allowed all participants, teachers and students, to assume the role of researcher, artist, and educator by having to develop a part of their work autonomously from outside the classroom and another part collectively from the virtual environment. Each student developed their own research, took on peer-teaching roles through cooperative work, and developed their creative skills through their own artistic designs. The educators and the artists' practices became sites of research, and they, in turn, became researchers.

With their cartographies, the painting students developed their own images in the form of a visual diary according to their personal, subjective, and lived narrative. The emotion of the search, the enquiry and the formal discovery activated their senses, placing them in the world through creation. Nadine Kalim (2007) remarks that "art making not as a mode of representation, but also a mode of narrative inquiry that evokes self-understanding and attempts to express experience" (p. 17). Images have the capacity to tell stories and therefore help to inspire qualitative research (Denzin & Lincoln, 2005; Harper, 2005). Multiple literacies consider visual representations, such as drawings, as a legitimate way of communicating meaning (Hobbs, 1997; Richards & McKenna, 2003). Visual semiotics, the science of signs and meaning, also understands that reality can be represented through culturally agreed symbols, drawings and images (Barthes, 1972/1973, 1977/1977; Harste, 2000; Rose, 2003; van Leeuwen & Jewitt, 2001). Dual coding theory connects the symbolic system of cognition with written language and imagery, arguing that this fosters more communication options (Paivio, 1986; Sadoski & Paivio, 2001). Consequently, as Richards (2006) states, any postmodern research that relies on visual methods offers more opportunities than if we were to use written language alone (p. 39). Research is no longer perceived from a traditional scientific perspective, but from an alternative point of view, where research is a life practice intimately linked to the arts and education (Irwin, 2013). In our project this had a greater impact on the teaching-learning process as it was developed in a bidirectional way between students and teachers.

3   Methodological Development of the Project

The method used for the development of this teaching innovation project focused on the perspective of the postulates of a/r/tography, adapted to the hybrid online environment. More specifically, the c/a/i/tographic method was used for data collection based on the autonomous but coordinated experience of students and teachers outside the classroom. The project was developed during the 2020–21 academic year with 225 students at the University of Murcia. Specifically, there were 50 students from the subject "Painting and Landscape" and 50 from "Design" of the Fine Arts Degree, 75 students from "Teaching and learning of the natural environment" and 50 from "Nature Workshops" of the Primary Education Degree of the University of Murcia. The project was conceived as a compulsory activity programmed in each participating subject to replace another previously classroom-based activity, which retained the same weighting within the assessment criteria. The students were informed that this was an educational innovation project, so records were kept of the activities carried out and their results for research purposes.

This activity was supported by different virtual tools of the aulavirtual platform of the University of Murcia. Among them, students had a personal online folder where they hosted video recordings, shared photographs, notes, drawings and sketches made during their autonomous field trip. This folder was visible to all their classmates and teachers. The teachers also had a virtual multimedia gallery to store all the video lectures that had been given so that the students could access them at any time. Through the Wiki tool, students modified and created joint text and content for the subjects quickly and easily. This tool was used for the collaborative creation and revision of the draft of the book, which was then passed onto the design students for final layout. In the virtual resource folder, teachers housed all the necessary legislation and documentation related to the activity. In the synchronous videoconferences, time was set aside for focus groups, which were also divided into smaller groups in other rooms to facilitate a more participatory coordination involving more students. In the synchronous video lectures, teachers used online questionnaires via the wooklap.com platform to obtain immediate feedback. This is a dynamic tool that allows students to participate during the lesson through real-time interactions. In addition, students had a chat application and a blog at their disposal at all times where they could ask questions to teachers or classmates, or open discussion threads. With the help of all these tools, each student had to c/a/r/tograph the arboreal heritage of their locality assuming the role of artist and researcher, but also of speaker, as each student had to present and explain their findings in the virtual classroom. With the exception of the "Design" students from the Fine Arts Degree who joined the project in its final phase as they oversaw the layout of the results obtained by the rest of the students.

The objectives of the project were distributed and established according to the discipline in charge of its development. The first, common to both participating degrees, was to propose a collaborative activity of observation, study, artistic creation, and dissemination of the monumental trees of the Region of Murcia as part of its natural and cultural heritage which would contribute to the development of learning of students. This involved an initial bibliographical review of primary and secondary sources in this theoretical framework, carrying out information searches in the virtual library of the University of Murcia in its *Alba* and *Xabio* catalogues, in order to proceed to the design and implementation of activities for these students. After the autonomous field activity, a joint student-teacher review process was carried out as a final part of the cooperative activity, using the tools of surveys, blogs and focus groups.

The second objective was to generate and design didactic material in the form of a field notebook on the monumental trees of the Region of Murcia, combining the visual-artistic work carried out by the students of the Degree in Fine Arts and the scientific-didactic work carried out by the students of the Degree in Primary Education. This process also involved establishing a process of compiling the visual and textual information developed by the students, which was then to be transferred to the students of Fine Arts Degree Design to develop the graphic design and digital production of the material on their part.

3.1   *Work Plan*

In order to achieve these objectives, a work plan was developed in several phases during the first four-month period of the 2020–21 academic year. In the first phase, in the subjects of "Painting and Landscape" of the Degree in Fine Arts and "Teaching and learning of the natural environment" and "Nature Workshops" of the Degree in Primary Education, the project was presented to the students in two previous two-hour sessions carried out in blended learning format.

In these sessions, students who were able to travel to their faculties because they were in the same municipality attended the classroom in person, following all the recommended safety and prevention measures. Those who had mobility limitations, as they were unable to travel due to the reduced means of transport available, received these classes by synchronous videoconference. In these previous sessions, the teaching staff provided theoretical-practical contents, instructions, and the organisation of the practices, defining the guidelines and giving orientations to elaborate the cartography in a creative and personal way. The students had to investigate and locate the monumental or singular trees closest to their location, and then select one of them for observation and representation. Both concepts are similar and are treated and protected equally in Spanish legislation. The difference lies in the fact that the uniqueness of monumental trees has to do with their unusual size while singular trees are characterised as such by their unusual shape. No formal requirements were imposed for their selection, leaving it to their personal judgement and experimentation. These could be trees that the students were previously familiar with, or nearby but unknown trees that they could locate by researching their location.

To facilitate the research process, they were provided with the catalogue of monumental and singular trees of the Region of Murcia included in Ley 14/2016 de 7 de noviembre, de Patrimonio Arbóreo Monumental de la Región de Murcia. They were also provided through the aulavirtual websites application with several links to regional websites and publications through which they geolocated all the trees in this category close to their environment.

Thus, from their particular location, each student chose the tree or trees, located within their perimeter of free movement, which they considered to be most suitable for the project. It is worth remembering that, at that time, due to the pandemic containment regulations in force, people could not move freely between the different municipalities, and could only do so for certain justified work reasons or to attend their study centres with a safe-conduct signed by the university rector. However, it was not possible for the whole group of students to travel outside the faculty to other municipalities.

In a second phase, the students of "Painting" of the Degree in Fine Arts carried out two face-to-face sessions of drawing practices to consolidate the technique explained in the previous master classes (see Figure 1.1).

The students carried out these practical sessions in the open air in an environment close to the campus. These were supervised by the teaching staff, respecting all the necessary prevention measures in force, such as the use of masks (even in an open space), the maintenance of an interpersonal safety distance of one and a half metres, and frequent hand washing. For students who were unable to travel, synchronous videoconference sessions were set up during tutoring hours for the individual monitoring of their autonomous work and the resolution of doubts. In this first field trip, students were asked to make their drawings on A4 paper with a 4 mm black marker pen or graphite pencils to facilitate their completion (both in the classroom and autonomous format). Figure 1.2 shows an example of previous preparatory work done by the students.

In the third phase, the painting students had to apply autonomously the techniques they had learned in the realisation of the final tree. The students from the degree in Primary Education also did two field trip practice sessions to familiarise themselves with the field notebooks and consolidate the instructions received in the previous master classes. As in the previous case, students who were able to travel to the campus carried out these guided practices

FIGURE 1.1   Drawing practices (photograph by Macarena López García)

outdoors, while for those who could not, videoconference sessions were set up and recordings were made for deferred viewing.

As the project is a collaborative work that has been carried out in a coordinated way between students of the degree in Fine Arts and Primary Education, each degree had a specific weight in the development of the c/a/r/tography according to their skills. Specifically, in the case of the subject "Painting and Landscape" of the Fine Arts degree, the students travelled independently to the chosen location to make detailed drawings from life of the selected tree. In the activity, they were specifically asked to show the size of the tree in their drawing, even adding an element that would show the tree's wingspan. This reference element could be a drawing of a person, a fence, or other elements. The drawings were made in a specific format on 200 g paper and A3 size in black and white, to facilitate its later digitalisation. Figure 1.3 illustrates an example. In the case of the participating subjects of the degree in Primary Education, they also travelled to the chosen places where they made their own technical sheet of the chosen tree or trees, designing their own field notebook models. The task of each one was to design a didactic activity aimed at a primary school class. This was to revolve around a monumental tree in our region, which each student selected according to their own interests.

FIGURE 1.2   Drawing practices (sketch by Macarena López García)

After these, a fourth phase was carried out in which the different stories and individual images were collected and shared by teachers and students in the virtual environment in order to select and categorise the common defining features of c/a/r/tography. The results were then discussed with all students individually and collectively in the virtual environment.

During the final phase, once all the material had been compiled, the students of the "Design" course of the Fine Arts degree proceeded to scan, digitalise and

FIGURE 1.3   Final project: Monumental tree (sketch by Ruben Poyato Hernández)

layout it to produce a collective didactic-artistic book. The idea was to be able
to use the drawings and field notebook models to produce a physical or virtual
book that could be shared with schools in the region to be used as a teaching
and didactic resource for primary school students. A key condition in the layout was that the book should be simple, without colour, in order to facilitate
and reduce the cost of its reproduction and digitalisation.

4   Results Obtained

With regard to diferent objectives, a sequence of activities was designed
consisting of a lecture by the teaching staff to introduce the subject. The students learned about the species declared to be of interest through the document of the Law of Monumental Tree Heritage of the Region of Murcia, and
their location with the exact coordinates in order to subsequently move to

the place to carry out the practice specified in the Teaching Guide. With this information, different field trip sessions and direct observation of the local arboreal heritage were planned.

4.1   *Field Trip and Direct Observation of Tree Heritage*

The direct contact with nature was a great help to work on the methods of observation as a scientific process. Intentional, non-accidental, systematic observation allowed us to obtain qualitative or iconic data, such as a drawing, a photograph, or a video.

Field trips required prior planning to establish what we want to achieve, as detailed in Table 1.1.

4.2   *Dissemination and Awareness of the Region's Arboreal Heritage*

This activity was linked to the dissemination of the monumental and singular trees of the Region of Murcia as part of its natural and cultural heritage. Knowledge of this heritage through observation and study undoubtedly contributes to the technical and conceptual training of Fine Arts students, but above all to

TABLE 1.1   Planning the different phases of field trips

Before the field trip

Previous ideas of the students

Inform students about:

– The place to visit
– The things to see, get to know, observe, touch, etc.
– The equipment and materials needed and appropriate for the outing.

During the outing

Respect all existing security measures and restrictions.

Carry out observation and information-gathering activities.

Encourage respect for the natural environment.

Self-assessment.

After the outing

Sharing of experiences in the virtual classroom.

Reflection on the experience of the field trip in small groups and with the whole group.

Evaluation through surveys and voting.

---

the enhancement of elements that are often unknown to our students. Therefore, this project is directly linked to support and promote knowledge of protected trees and awareness for their conservation, as well as the inclusion of monumental trees in eco-educational circuits and curricula. In relation to the objective of promoting knowledge of the arboreal heritage among students of the degree in teacher training for Primary Education, the result of this activity was a set of fifteen educational proposals in which, taking a monumental tree as the central axis.

4.3   *Design of the Field Notebooks*

Another of the results obtained after the sharing of the different field trip experiences was the establishment of a consensual field notebook model made up of five work sheets, as shown in Figures 1.4 to 1.8. This model is a tool that could be used in field trips in multiple disciplines to encourage initiation into scientific practice in the field.

In these worksheets, students and teachers reflected on the teaching-learning process, as it is a reconstruction exercise that asks questions from an interdisciplinary point of view. By extrapolating and adapting this scientific instrument to the disciplines of Primary Education and Fine Arts, we offer a didactic tool that allows us to bring university and school students closer to scientific work.

Sheet 1. Tree Identification

Common name:

Scientific name:

Location of the tree:

Sketch of the tree site

FIGURE 1.4   Details of field notebook. Work sheet 1: Identification of the tree

Sheet 2. Tree Size

Height:

Trunk thickness at the base:

Trunk thickness at 1 metre height:

Appearance of the bark (colour, texture, throns, etc.):

Appearance of twigs (very dense, not very dense, straight branches, twisted branches, etc.):

Drawing of the general bearing of the tree:

FIGURE 1.5   Details of field notebook. Work sheet 2: The size of the tree

Sheet 3. The Leaves

Deciduous or evergreen tree:

Simple or compound leaves:

Leaf shape:

Leaf margin:

Nervation of the leaf:

Detailed drawing of the leaf:

FIGURE 1.6   Details of field notebook. Work sheet 3: The leaves

Sheet 4. Flowers

Isolated or grouped flowers:

Number of petals of the corolla:

Colour of petals:

Number of sepals in the calyx:

Colour of sepals:

Size of flower:

Pollinating animals:

Detailed drawing of the flower:

FIGURE 1.7   Details of field notebook. Work sheet 4: The flowers

Sheet 5. Fruits and Seeds

Fruit type:

Fruit colour:

Fruit size:

Fruit shape:

Number of seeds inside the fruit:

Seed size:

Seed shape:

Detailed drawing of fruit and seed:

FIGURE 1.8   Details of field notebook. Work sheet 5: Fruits and seeds

A field notebook such as this one makes it possible to record the observations made on field trips. It allows information to be collected in the form of drawings, sketches, annotations, as well as the collection of some natural specimens, without harming them, and facilitates their subsequent analysis in class.

4.4   *Publication of the Book* Singular Trees of the Region of Murcia
In relation to the objective of aimed at designing a didactic material, in the form of a field notebook. of the monumental and singular trees of the Region of Murcia, the visual work carried out by the students of the Degree in Fine Arts and the scientific-didactic work carried out by the students of the Degree in Primary Education were combined for the design and layout of the didactic material by the students of "Design" of the Degree in Fine Arts. The graphic design of the material and the final digital production led to the publication of a collective didactic-artistic book (see Figures 1.9 and 1.10), which in turn aims to encourage the protection, conservation, dissemination, promotion, research, and enhancement of the monumental arboreal heritage of the Region of Murcia. The book includes information sheets on 12 singular trees of the Region of Murcia of different species: Cork oak (*Quercus suber*), Casuarina (*Casuarina cunninghamiana*), Cypress (*Cupressus sempervirens*), Eucalyptus (*Eucalyptus camaldulensis*), Ficus (*Ficus macrophylla*), Fig (*Ficus carica*), Olive (*Olea europaea*), Elm (*Ulmus minor*), Ombú (*Phytolacca dioica*), Palm (*Phoenix dactylifera*), Aleppo Pine (*Pinus halepensis*) and the Shade Plane (*Platanus hispanica*). All of them were described, including details of flowering and fruiting, ecology, geographical origin and curiosities. Guidelines and sheets for guided observation and collection of information on the trees were also included.

5   Conclusions

The aim of this project was to design an innovative teaching activity where students could learn in a hybrid online environment and not lose their social ties between students and teachers, as well as the two-way teaching-learning relationships in the classroom. The aim was to break down the limitations that this may entail in their perception and learning, provoking curiosity, and surprise among the students. For this purpose, the usefulness of implementing a methodological action based on the autonomous but coordinated work of the students outside the classroom by means of individualised instructions was considered. The aim was to overcome the limitations that a blended learning situation could entail compared to face-to-face teaching, while at the same

Árboles singulares
de la Región de Murcia
Innovación docente transversal desde el arte, la ciencia y la educación

FIGURE 1.9   Book holder of *Singular Trees of the Region of Murcia: Transversal Teaching Innovation from Art, Science and Education*

time allowing the competences of the different subjects involved in the experience to be fulfilled.

With this project, the students were able to broaden their capacity to perceive the ecosystem around them, and from this experience they created a joint c/a/r/tography through the graphic representation of the different local monumental trees. This is a collective experience that was completed and

Cork oak

Quercus suber   **Familly:** *Fagaceae*

Description

Monoecious evergreen tree that can reach a height of 20 metres.
Its crown is globular and dense. The trunk and main branches are
covered with very thick, greyish, cracked bark. The leaves are
oval, with a strong coriaceous consistency and a serrated and
somewhat curved margin on the underside. The upper side of the
leaves is dark green, while the underside is greyish due to a
tomentose covering of very fine hairs. The flowers appear on
hanging stalks called catkins. The fruit, when ripe, is a dark brown
acorn, about 4 or 5 centimetres long, covered by a husk or dome
with soft scales.

Flowering and fruiting

The flowering period is between April and May. Acorns ripen
during autumn and winter.

Ecology

It is a tree typical of Mediterranean environments. It grows from sea
level to altitudes of around 1000 metres. It does not tolerate frost or
areas with an extremely dry climate, requiring a minimum annual
rainfall of 400 mm. In addition, it only grows on acid soils, it is not
found in limestone soils.

Geographical origin

Its natural distribution is limited to the western area of the
Mediterranean region. It is found in Italy, France, Tunisia, Algeria, and
Morocco, with Portugal and Spain being the countries with the largest
areas of cork oak groves.

Curiosities

The cork oak is known for the use that man makes of its outer bark:
cork. In many rural areas of Spain and Portugal the cork industry is an
important economic engine. This material is used for various purposes
such as insulation, cork stoppers, footwear, etc.

In the Region of Murcia its origin seems to be the plantation,
however, it is a protected tree species. It can be found in some parts of
the Sierra de Carrascoy, Yecla and Molina de Segura.

8

FIGURE 1.10   Example of the book's inner content

shared with the rest of the students through cooperative artistic work. One
of the results was the publication of a book entitled *Singular Trees of the
Region of Murcia.* This innovative experience was perceived and experienced
in a very positive way by the students, highlighting their involvement and the
good results obtained in the evaluation of these tasks in all the participating disciplines. The satisfaction of the students was so outstanding and the
academic and artistic results so satisfactory that this activity has been repeated

and consolidated in the following academic year 2021–22. It is planned to repeat in the next academic year 2022–23, although adapting it to a potential hundred percent face-to-face environment. In these new editions, we are faced with the new challenge of taking this project to a geolocalised environment using an application such as google map, thus increasing its coverage and effectiveness.

To sum up, the design of this project helped to overcomes the limitations of blended learning and facilitated, through direct contact with nature, the connection and relationship of concepts with its reality in an enjoyable and entertaining way, promoting active and meaningful learning. By considering the results obtained from the implementation of this project, we can determine that the characteristics of c/a/r/tography make it a very useful visual methodology for teaching and artistic research in this educational field.

References

Barone, T., & Eisner, E. W. (2012). *Art based research.* Sage.

Barthes, R. (1973). *Mythologies* (A. Louves, Trans.). Paladin. (Original work published 1972)

Barthes, R. (1977). *Image-music-text* (S. Heath, Ed. & Trans.). Fontana. (Original work published in 1977)

Davis, B., & Sumara, D. (2008). *Complexity and education: Inquiries into learning, teaching, and research.* Routledge.

Denzin, N., & Lincoln, Y. (2000). *Handbook of qualitative research* (2nd ed.). Sage Publications.

Harper, D. (2005). What's new visually? In N. Denzin & Y. Lincoln (Eds.), *Handbook of qualitative research* (3rd ed., pp. 747–762). Sage Publications.

Harste, J. (2000). Six points of departure. In B. Berghoff, K. Egawa, J. Harste, & B. Hoonanc (Eds.), *Beyond reading and writing: Inquiry, curriculum, and multiple ways of knowing* (pp. 1–16). National Council of Teachers of English.

Hobbs, R. (1997). Literacy for the information age. In J. Flood, S. Heath, & D. Lapp (Eds.), *Research on teaching through the visual and communicative arts* (pp. 7–14). Simon & Schuster Macmillan.

Irwin, R. L. (n.d.). *A/r/tography. An invitation to think through art making, researching, teaching and learning.* https://artography.edcp.educ.ubc.ca/

Irwin, R. L. (2013). La práctica de la a/r/tografía (D. García, Trans.). *Revista Educación y Pedagogía, 25*(65), 106–113.

Irwin, R. L., & De Cosson, A. (Eds.). (2004). *A/r/tography: Rendering self throught arts-based living inquiry.* Pacific Educational Press.

Irwin, R. L., LeBlanc, N., Yeon Ryu, J., & Belliveau, G. (2018). A/r/tography as Living Inquiry. In P. Leavy (Ed.), *Handbook of arts-based research* (pp. 37–53). Guilford Press.

Kalin, N. (2007). *Conversations on teaching and learning drawing: Drawn toward transformation* [Doctoral dissertation]. University of British Columbia. https://open.library.ubc.ca/media/stream/pdf/831/1.0055228/1

Lasczik, A., & Irwin, R. L. (2017). Walkings-through paint: A c/a/r/tography of slow scholarship. *Journal of Curriculum and Pedagogy, 14*(2), 116–124. https://dx.doi.org/10.1080/15505170.2017.1310680

Marín-Viadel, R., & Roldán, J. (2019). A/r/tografía e Investigación Educativa Basada en Artes Visuales en el panorama de las metodologías de investigación en Educación Artística. *Arte, Individuo y Sociedad, 31*(4), 881–895. https://dx.doi.org/10.5209/aris.63409

Paivio, A. (1986). *Mental representations: A dual coding approach.* Oxford University Press.

Ramon, R. (2021). The narrative, visual and artistic fiction as a pedagogical research practice of the urban, social and cultural environment. In R. Abeledo (Ed.), *Art, culture and economy to democratize society* (pp. 119–130). Tirant lo Blanch.

Ramon, R. y Alonso-Sanz, A. (2022). La c/a/r/tografía en el aula como instrumento de desarrollo creativo, visual y de pensamiento complejo a través de las artes. *Revista Kepes, 19*(25), 531–563.

Richards, J., & McKenna, M. (2003). *Integrating multiple literacies in K-8 classrooms: Cases, commentaries, and practical applications.* Lawrence Erlbaum.

Richards, J. C. (2006). Post-modern image-based research: An innovative data collection method for illuminating preservice teachers' developing perceptions in field-based courses. *The Qualitative Report, 11*(1), 37–54.

Rose, G. (2003). *Visual methodologies.* Sage.

Rousell, D. & Lasczik, A. (2014). Echoes of a C/a/r/tography: Mapping the practicum experiences of pre-service visual arts teachers in the 'Visual Echoes Project'. *Australian Art Education, 36*(2), 69–82.

Sadoski, M., & Paivio, A. (2001). *Imagery and text: A dual coding theory of reading and writing.* Lawrence Erlbaum.

Spinggay, S., Irwin, R. L., Leggo, C., & Gouzouasis, P. (Eds.). (2008). *Being with a/r/tography.* Sense Publishers.

Sumara, D. J., & Carson, T. R. (Eds.). (1997). *Action research as living practice.* Peter Lang Inc.

van Leeuwen, T., & Jewitt, C. (2001). *Handbook of visual analysis.* Sage.

CHAPTER 2

Community of Practice in Game Art and Design Education with Discord Application

Lee Cheng and Baris Isikguner

Abstract

Arts education in the 2020s has seen a drastic change in the modes of instructional delivery and learning as a consequence of global pandemic, which put into practice various kinds of online learning tools and approaches on a large scale. With different video conferencing and social communication platforms not originally designed for educational use being applied in the teaching and learning contexts, discourses on their educational affordance have been unfolded for best practices in the realm of arts education. This chapter presents the adoption of Discord application, an instant messaging social platform originally built for gamers, as a single-platform solution for teaching and learning activities in game art and design programmes at higher education levels. It illustrates the system design that facilitates remote learning, virtual classroom structure, dynamics and social interactions among students and teachers, and the educational affordances beyond general communication. The blurred borderline and proper balance between formal and informal learning have also been discussed, which help build a more democratic community of learning among teachers and students as suggested by Dewey (1916). It helps resemble the flow of the physical schooling experience implemented in the virial space where learning is unbounded and immersed in social presence, where students enjoyed a new nuance in arts learning and be prepared for any further transformative changes in arts education. Suggestions on how this approach could be applied in the teaching and learning of other arts disciplines are provided.

Keywords

game design education – game art education – Discord – community of practice – educational affordance

1 Introduction

The outbreak of COVID-19 pandemic did not only pose challenges to the public health systems globally, but also had unprecedented effects on education. Educational institutions have to make immediate changes from traditional face-to-face to remote modes of learning, which drastically affected the normal functioning of school systems at all levels (Nickerson & Sulkowski, 2021). The digital transformation has been a painful process for both the teachers and students, yet it also served as a positive catalyst that drives the sustainable development of the education sector and teachers' professional training to cope with the changes and unforeseeable challenges in the future. It makes available informal and incidental learning within the rigid education system (Watkins & Marsick, 2021), which opened up opportunities for democratising the teaching and learning process by keeping a proper balance between the informal and the formal, the incidental and the intentional, modes of education (Dewey, 1916).

In arts education, new forms of delivery and expression not being widely adopted before have now been put into practice in the virtual environment. For example, live streaming in social media and video sharing platforms has now been recognised as an authentic way for performing arts students to share their creative outputs; online gallery and virtual tour have been a viable alternative to replace the actual, in-person exhibitions for arts and design students' presentation and dissemination of artistic creations. The changes faced by the educational process have been more challenging, as many teaching and learning activities in arts education rely heavily on multimodal sensory and auditory-motor interactions. Some attempts have been made for innovative pedagogical approaches to emerge (e.g., Desai et al., 2021; Koh & Kan, 2021; Li et al., 2021), which gradually shifts the paradigm of arts learning to become more constructivist and autonomous (Hildebrandt, 2021; Simamora, 2020).

Depending less on auditory-motor interactions, the educational change of those newer forms of arts such as design and new media art seem to be less painful than those traditional ones. Different types of online learning and innovative approaches have been practised effectively in the teaching and learning of those art forms (e.g., Antunes & Barreto, 2021; Kultima et al., 2021), which involve the use of information and communication technology for emergency remote teaching in arts education. With different video conferencing and social communication platforms not originally designed for educational use being applied in the teaching and learning contexts, discourses on their educational affordance have been unfolded for best practices in the realm of arts education.

In this chapter, we present the adoption of Discord, an instant messaging social platform originally built for gaming communities, in the teaching and learning of game art and design programmes at higher education levels. The proximity of this application with gaming communication has made it easily adoptable for gaming teachers and students, which forms the backbone for more experimental and innovative pedagogy to flourish that facilitates the digital transformation in arts education. The authors declare no conflict of interest in writing this chapter, including financial or consultant support from any software service provider.

2   Discord in Educational Settings

Discord was initially released in mid-2015 (Ardiyansah et al., 2021). Originally developed for gaming communities, the platform has gradually been used generally for many other kinds of communities. Similar to other instant messaging platforms, its standard features allow one-to-one messaging and group chat, voice and video call over the internet, file sharing and viewing, and profile setting-up. It also runs on mobile smartphones, tablets, desktop computers and web browsers. What makes it different is the features that cater the needs of computer gamers. The most important one is live streaming. Discord users are allowed to share their entire screen or a specific application simultaneously, and others in the same channel or group chat can watch the streaming and communicate at the same time. This is similar to most of the social media platforms, but is made for a small audience base and allows multiple users to share their screens at the same time. Another important feature is the availability of channels that users within the same server could join in different channels and communicate at any time, including offline messages and real-time interactions. Application programming interface (API) was also introduced to allow game developers directly integrate Discord into games that facilitates live streaming and communication among game players. Internally, Discord server administrators can create their own bots, an embedded software application that runs automated tasks such as virtual agent services, to regulate the users' activities and the daily operations of the server. These grounded options have made Discord popular in the gaming industries and social gaming communities, which also appeal to other non-gaming uses especially in the education sector.

Discord could be applicable in non-gaming educational contexts to maintain social links, create dynamic learning environments, and engage students in active learning through gamification (Arifianto & Izzudin, 2021;

Di Marco, 2021). Students could make use of Discord to socialise, form study groups, moderate collaboration and teamwork, and participate in community-building activities, while teachers could benefit from the logging functions that help audit and monitor students' learning achievement (Lacher & Biehl, 2018; Mock, 2019). Kruglyk et al. (2020) conducted a comparative analysis among different digital communication platforms and surveyed university teachers and students about their views for the feasibility of using Discord in online teaching. They revealed the competitive advantages of Discord over other platforms and its effective features for quality communication and distance learning in the schooling context. A similar study was conducted by Dayana, Andre and Andrade-Arenas (2020), who adopted a design thinking methodology to conduct the comparison and conducted a survey with sciences and humanities students. The study result yielded similar results for the effectiveness of applying Discord in online teaching, which provides a comfortable study environment and makes available a virtual social space for students to interact beyond the classroom context.

In-depth research about the educational use of Discord in different subject matters and educational levels could also be found in previous studies. Wahyuningsih and Baidi (2021) interviewed primary school teachers and students about their use of Discord for religious and moral education. They found that Discord could be a viable alternative for primary school educators as a digital learning platform during the emergency remote learning in the pandemic period, which creates an interesting and enjoyable learning environment for students. Odinokaya et al. (2021) conducted a pre-post-test study to examine university students' acquisition of English as a foreign language. The findings revealed better use of vocabulary and performance in speech for students who participated in English learning with Discord than those taught conventionally with an instructional approach. They concluded that Discord could reinforce in-class tasks and activities, and encourage communication within the learning community. Di Marco (2021) surveyed midwifery students about their views on the use of Discord for online teaching at the pandemic period, who confirmed its adaptiveness and effectiveness in different learning contexts but not for practical work. The review conducted by Arifianto and Izzudin (2021) explored literature students' experience of using Discord for learning purposes. The findings suggested that Discord can create a dynamic, fun, and gamified atmospheres for students as if they are playing online games, which facilitates teaching and learning in the virtual medium.

The use of video conferencing and social communication platforms for game arts and design has also been documented in previous literature, in which students were found to be more positive and comfort about remote learning when compared to their peers in other disciplines (Franco et al., 2021). Reynolds and Chiu (2013) investigated the effects of formality (formal vs. informal) on student engagement and self-efficacy in a game design project, in which students made use of social media and other information resources for game design and implementation. Kapralos et al. (2015) developed a course on serious game design, which made use of online video sharing and conferencing platforms for students' self-learning learning and discussion. McDaniel and Telep (2021) described their approach in the implementation of video design course and best practices during pandemic lockdown. They made use of various platforms for different teaching and learning activities, such as Zoom for lecturing and presentation, learning management system for students' brainstorming, online forum for discussion, Google Docs for collaborative writing, and Wiki page for documentation. Their students also made use of Discord to communicate through, text, image, links, and voice chatting, in which staff members helped to host and create chat channel for them. Other than this, no other literature has been identified that investigate the use of Discord for game art or design education.

3 Setup and Implementation in Game Art and Design Education

When the COVID-19 pandemic turned into a global crisis in early 2020, various measures were adopted by educational institutions to implement teaching and learning under the social distancing rules posed by local governments. This is also the case of the Computer Games Unit at Anglia Ruskin University in the East of England, where face-to-face instructions and in-person teaching activities had been prohibited across the country. The teaching team was in need of a diverse tool to deliver teaching materials and communicate with students, and most importantly, to teach effectively and alternatively in the online space. While the learning management system that the university employed had been doing part of the work, most of the other units at the university relied heavily on existing or emerging video-conferencing software for their real-time synchronous instruction such as Zoom, Webex, Microsoft Teams, and Google Meet. These platforms are capable of serving the purpose of online teaching, despite some limitations when it comes to performing arts education (Simamora, 2020). The widespread use of Discord in the gaming community is of the unit's interest because of the relevance to computer games students' daily life. As an art form contextualised in computer games, the challenges faced by students and teachers were not only limited to the lack of multimodal sensory and auditory-motor interactions in remote learning, but also the technical complexity and artistic excellence in making successful game arts. The teaching team considered that the flexibility and proximity of Discord to the gaming computer may be able to compensate for the lack of interactions in online teaching, and therefore decided to pursue the use of Discord in the teaching and learning of game art and design.

Once the university announced the complete shift from face-to-face to online learning towards the end of 2019, the unit has started preparing and setting up the Discord server dedicated to the teaching and learning for all computer games students. The initial stage comprises setting up of the server, rules, and automations that facilitate the teaching process and prevent overloading staff members for administrative matters such as patrolling and security check. The administrative team has set up bots to ensure internal security, facilitate task management, and control the use of language such as filtering out foul languages by keyword matching. The modules from all computer games programmes are managed within categories, each consisting of announcement, text, and voice channels (see Figure 2.1).

Module leaders or tutors can deliver important messages through the announcement channel, which is read-only and commerce with notifications to alert fellow students. A text channel is where conversations could happen among students and teachers in the same module at any time; emojis, sticks and memes in the format of animated GIFs are available to facilitate media-rich communication. Voice channel is the virtual classroom environment where synchronised teaching is conducted. Students join the voice channel according to their timetable and teachers usually share their computer screens to deliver the lectures. Both the teachers and students are allowed to turn on or off their microphones and cameras for discussion or other kinds of interactions.

While it is imperative to provide students with effective teaching and learning through the use of Discord, it is equally important that they are also provided with a monitored and safe social virtual environment. A variety of channels for social and networking as well as collaboration and productivity are created for them to communicate with their peers, exchange knowledge and get up-to-date information from the industry. These include channels for social and networking, group projects, meetings, seminar talks, technical support, one-to-one consultation and other cross-level collaborations. The private rooms, for example, allow the teachers to provide individual and personal support for students who lag behind in the lecture or encounter difficulties dealing with the assignment; the social and networking channel comes with bots that automatically follow relevant news feeds and post the news to update students with latest developments in the industry.

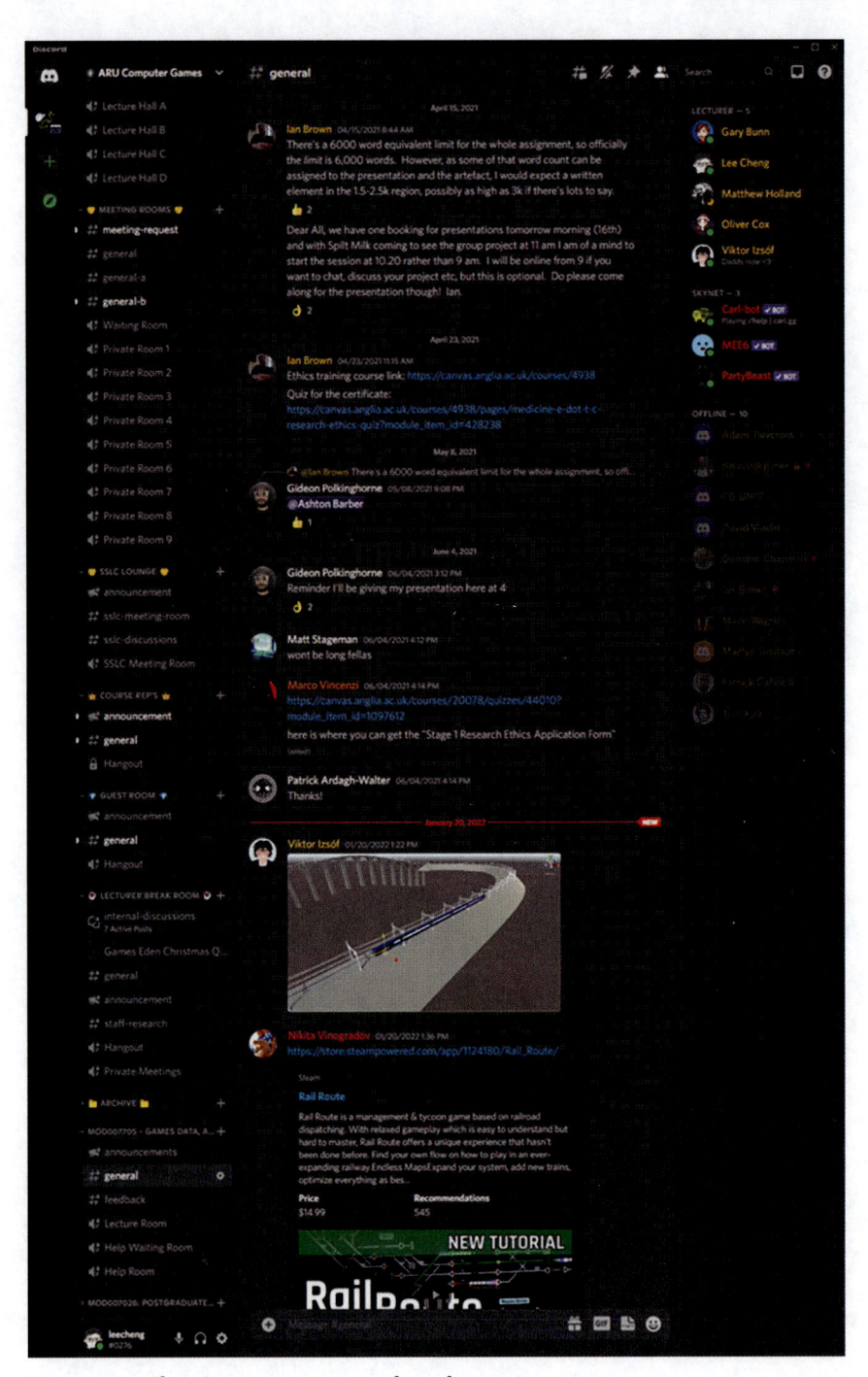

FIGURE 2.1   Classroom management on discord server

Except the requirement to set their full name as the username for the purpose of classroom management, students are free to personalise their profiles such as setting up their profile pictures and subtitles. They were also assigned with different roles that indicate their corresponding programme and year of study, which could be recalled and notified easily for public announcements. A briefing session has been conducted to all students at the very beginning, who were mostly satisfied with the arrangement and appreciated the choice over other platforms. Since most of the students were familiar with instant messaging platforms and some were current users of Discord, the migration was generally smooth. The use of Discord outperformed other video-conferencing software and added value to the teaching effectiveness. It not only solved the issue of emergency remote learning, but also brought transformative changes to game art and design education.

4 Teaching and Learning Effectiveness

Discord outperforms other video-conferencing software in terms of its effectiveness in remote learning in many ways. It provides a single platform for the education governance for all formal and informal learning activities to take place (Robinson, 2022). Instead of looking for the hyperlink and password from learning management systems or emails, the integrated platform makes available a hyperlink-free experience with access to all the virtual classrooms. The ad-hoc switching mechanism allows students to switch from one classroom to another smoothly without re-opening the application. This walk-in classroom arrangement resembles the flow of the physical schooling experience implemented in the virtual space where learning is physically unbounded and immersed in the social presence (Park & Kim, 2022). The foreground teaching and learning activities happening in Discord could synergise with the structured backend support of the learning management systems, which take care of formal processes such as assignment submission and assessment.

The use of remote learning through the use of Discord has also sustained beyond the social distancing period. When the university campus reopened after the peak pandemic season, the hybrid mode of learning was adopted in which teachers delivered the lecture to students in both the physical and virtual classroom on Discord. While students are required to attend the lectures on campus after the relaxation of social distancing measures, the hybrid mode helped to cater those who may not be able to go back to the campus, such as overseas and infected students. In case of unforeseeable circumstances other than the pandemic, such as extreme bad weather or regional traffic issues, the unit could switch to online teaching with a quick announcement. Since students and teachers are already familiar with remote learning, the teaching and learning effectiveness could be guaranteed which adds value to the current schooling system.

5   Student-Teacher Relationship and Social Interaction

The enhancement of student-teacher interaction and the facilitated community of practice are the main competitive advantages of Discord over other similar platforms for remote learning. Since the same platform was used for teaching, learning, gaming, and social life, students' and teachers' communicate more often than before. Their interactions are no longer limited to either academic matters or social communication, but a mixture of both; for example, students would share their artwork design with others not limited by coursework, while teachers could provide comments and feedback for their self-improvement. The teachers were less reluctant replying to students' inquiries through instant messaging on Discord after office hours. By setting up the virtual classroom on a social platform, the borderline between formal and informal learning has been blurred in which students and teachers learn and socialise in the same space. It helps build a more democratic virtual space by incorporating informal and learning into the institutionalised educational structure, one that is often considered as overly rigid, linear, and hierarchical. The virtual space gradually becomes a learning community that nurtures student-teacher and peer interactions, which echoes with the tendency of decentralised and student-centred participatory learning through social media and web-based technologies (Czerkawski, 2016; Greenhow & Lewin, 2016).

6   Individual Learning Needs

Other than the participatory learning and the community of practice, the improved relationship among students and teachers also improved the catering for individual learning needs. Similar to the findings of McDaniel and Telep (2021), students preferred voice catting to full video conferencing to retain privacy. They were not required to turn on their camera during live streaming, which also cater introvert and mentally retarded students who may have negative feelings showing their faces. As administrators, teachers also kept an eye on students' interactions and daily activities to ensure a safe, fair, equal, and caring virtual learning environment.

Although office hours were assigned to teachers for individual student consultation, the time was often not well-utilised due to the inflexibility of the consultation settings and the weak student-teacher relationship (Fitzsimmons et al., 2021; Wilson et al., 2011). The flexibility afforded by Discord and the aforesaid improved student-teacher relationship could help remove the barriers for students to reach out to their teachers for guidance and support. Students and teachers could meet at a more flexible time and ad-hoc manner unbounded by the physical location, which makes available extra time and chances for the consultations to happen. The setting up of the private rooms in the Discord server allows students to make consultation appointments at any time upon the teachers' availability and makes available multimodal interactions within the virtual medium. Students could engage in direct conversation with the teacher through voice call, or share their computer screen showing their design or artmaking process for teachers' comments and feedback. The improved responsiveness and the allocation of extra time enhanced students' learning beyond the classroom and lecture hours, and catered for the learning differences among students through individual guidance and support.

Students with learning difficulties are particularly benefited from the individual consultation in the virtual space. The multimodal interaction within the Discord space allows students to express their ideas in different ways. While students with dyslexia could be overwhelmed in understanding or elaborating complex concepts wrapped by composite sentences (Tancredi, 2020), they could supplement their inquiries with a combination of text-based conservation, voice call, and live streaming of the workflow. The virtual appearances of users on Discord promotes equality and social inclusion, where everyone could touch up their own profile according to their preference. Students who felt socially excluded in the physical learning space within the schooling environment could gain confidence by 'hiding' behind the screen, which encouraged them to engage in learning activities and thereby promoting positive learning behaviour (Machado & Almedia, 2013).

7 Limitations

Despite the competitive advantages of Discord over other instant messaging and video conferencing platforms, there are limitations that deteriorate its effectiveness in remote learning as a result of its characteristics and features for educational purposes. The improved student-teacher relationship and social interaction are beneficial to students' learning, yet it also implies a threat to the work-life balance of the teachers. Students who do not engage in the workplace before may assume teachers' instant replies at any date and time, yet teachers have no obligations to respond to students' inquiries after office hours. They could be confused about their roles, especially for those who do not devote themselves to social and new media like their fellow students. The conflict between students' preferred communication methods and the institutional communication tools has been revealed since the rise of social media (Shelton, 2017), which also has an impact on the structure of teacher work engagement. While the transformative change of the teachers' roles within and outside the classroom catalysed by the involvement of emerging technology has been undergoing, how educational institutions could manage such changes and how teachers could cope with the tension between their personal and professional identity in online space remains a challenging task in the post-pandemic future (Fox & Bird, 2017).

The institutional technological infrastructure and the system design of Discord may pose challenges to its smooth adoption for teaching purposes. Because of its relevance with computer games, information technology services at university level or school technicians may ban the use of Discord on campus computers and some negotiation may be needed. Unlike other video conferencing platforms that are dedicated for synchronised meetings, Discord is more for social gathering of the gaming community that does not have recording function and cloud storage. A teacher then has to rely on third party software to archive a lecture for students' revisiting purposes. There is an absence of a file management system in Discord as in most other video conferencing platforms. While a simple graphic or text file could be sent in an ad-hoc manner, the platform is completely separated from and disconnected with any learning management systems. Although the formality provided by the learning management systems could synergise with the flexibility afforded by Discord, a better file management system would help for the easier access of bulky game art and design prototypes.

8   Discord for Broader Arts Education

The aforesaid implementation of Discord in game art and design education has found an effective solution for emergency remote teaching and facilitated the transition from face-to-face to remote learning. While the teaching and learning of game art and design may be different from the delivery of other art forms, some heuristics could be taken away and applicable to the broader arts education which has been largely disadvantaged due to the lack of sensorimotor interactions during the pandemic period. The multiple screen-sharing feature of Discord could be used to simulate the synchronised learning environment where student-teacher interactions take place. Dance and music students, for example, could take turn to live stream their pre-recorded or live performance and invite comments from the others; arts and design students could simultaneous share their screen to showcase their artmaking and design process; and teachers could arrange practice sessions during the lecture and dropped into the shared screens of individual students for guidance and support. The combined functions as an instant messaging, video conferencing and social communication platform of Discord could also benefit the arts education by cultivating a community of practice among teachers and students, which help to facilitate the instructional transition and support students for the challenges they encountered during the pandemic (Carey et al., 2020; Poss et al., 2022).

9 Concluding Remarks

This chapter presented the adoption of Discord in game art and design programmes at higher education levels that helped to facilitate sudden change for the emergency remote during the outbreak of COVID-19 pandemic. Best practices for the adaptive use of Discord are presented, together with the details of implementation that cultivates a community of practice among teachers and students in the virtual learning space. The flexibility afforded by the platform and its proximity with students' daily life allowed the teaching team to accomplish a smooth transition for remote learning during the pandemic period and beyond, which forms the backbone for more experimental and innovative pedagogy to flourish that facilitates the digital transformation in arts education.

While the transformative changes brought by the pandemic seem to be endure after getting back to 'normal', the near future of arts education comes with both positive implications and negative consequences. Whatever the situation goes, upskilling of educators, and top-down efforts such as continuous policy review and curriculum reform are necessary to ensure the relevance and effectiveness of teaching and learning in arts education. Further research from the approach attempted in this book chapter includes empirical research that examines the differences among various video conferencing platforms for online teaching and learning purposes, and the in-depth analysis of its teaching and learning effectiveness from the perspectives of students and teachers.

References

Antunes, S., & Barreto, S. (2021). Design education: The impact of COVID-19 pandemic. In D. Raposo, J. Neves, & J. Silva. (Eds.), *Perspectives on design 11: Research, education and practice* (pp. 147–160). Springer.

Ardiyansah, T. Y., Batubara, R. W., & Auliya, P. K. (2021). Understanding Discord to facilitate students in teaching learning process during COVID-19 outbreak. *Journal of English Teaching, Literature, and Applied Linguistics, 5*(1), 76–78.

Arifianto, M. L., & Izzudin, I. F. (2021). From gaming to learning: Assessing the gamification of Discord in the realm of education. In *Proceedings of the 7th international conference on education and technology* (pp. 95–99). Institute of Electrical and Electronics Engineers.

Carey, L., B., Sadera, W. A., Cai, Q. V., & Filipiak, S. (2020). Creating a community of practice for educators forced to transition to remote teaching. In R. E. Ferdig, E. Baumgartner, R. Hartshorne, R. Kaplan-Rakowski, & C. Mouza (Eds.), *Teaching, technology, and teacher education during the COVID-19 pandemic: Stories from the field* (pp. 251–255). Association for the Advancement of Computing in Education.

Czerkawski, B. C. (2016). Blending formal and informal learning networks for online learning. *International Review of Research in Open and Distributed Learning, 17*(3), 138–156.

Dayana, Y. E., Andre, O. M., & Andrade-Arenas, L. (2021). Design of the Discord application as an e-learning tool at the University of Science and Humanities. In M. M. L. Petrie, L. F. Z. Rivera, & C. Aranzazu-Suescun (Eds.), *Proceedings of the 18th Latin American and Caribbean Consortium of Engineering Institutions international multi-conference for engineering, education and technology* (Vol. 9, pp. 1–7). Latin American and Caribbean Consortium of Engineering Institutions.

Desai, S., Stahl, I., & Chamorro-Koc, M. (2021). Global design studio: Advancing cross-disciplinary experiential education during the COVID-19 pandemic. *Design and Technology Education: An International Journal, 26*(4), 165–181.

Dewey, J. (1916). *Democracy and education: An introduction to the philosophy of education*. Macmillan.

Di Marco, L. (2021). User-centered evaluation of Discord in midwifery education during the COVID-19 pandemic: Analysis of the adaptation of the tool to student needs. *European Journal of Midwifery, 5*, 51.

Fitzsimmons, W., Trigg, R., & Premkumar, P. (2021). Developing and maintaining the teacher-student relationship in one to one alternative provision: The tutor's experience. *Educational Review, 73*(4), 399–416.

Fox, A., & Bird, T. (2017). The challenge to professionals of using social media: Teachers in England negotiating personal-professional identities. *Educational and Informational Technologies, 22*(2), 647–675.

Franco, D., Fonseca, M., & Luz, F. (2021). COVID-19 and remote teaching: Challenges for post-pandemic teaching? In L. Gómez Chova, A. López Martínez, & I. Candel Torres (Eds.), *Proceedings of 13th international conference on education and new learning technologies* (pp. 4617–4623). International Academy of Technology, Education and Development.

Greenhow, C., & Lewin, C. (2016). Social media and education: Reconceptualizing the boundaries of formal and informal learning. *Learning, Media and Technology, 41*(1), 6–30.

Hildebrandt, M. (2021). Creativity and resilience in art students during COVID-19. *Art Education, 74*(1), 17–18.

Kapralos, B., Fisher, S., Clarkson, J., & van Oostveen, R. (2015). A course on serious game design and development using an online problem-based learning approach. *Interactive Technology and Smart Education, 12*(2), 116–136.

Koh, J. H. L., & Kan, R. Y. P. (2021). Educating the artist with technology: COVID-19 and beyond. In J. H. L. Koh & R. Y. P. Kan (Eds.), *Teaching and learning the arts in higher education with technology* (pp. 191–209). Springer.

Kultima, A., Park, S., Kankainen, V., Aurava, R., Piispanen, L., & Kauppinen, T. (2021). Expert-driven (online) game jams for (game) design education. In *Proceedings of the sixth annual international conference on game jams, hackathons, and game creation events* (pp. 64–68). Association for Computing Machinery.

Kruglyk, V., Bukreiev, D., Chornyi, P., Kupchak, E., & Sender, A. (2020). Discord platform as an online learning environment for emergencies. Ukrainian *Journal of Educational Studies and Information Technology, 8*(2), 13–28.

Lacher, L., & Biehl, C. (2018). Using Discord to understand and moderate collaboration and teamwork. In *Proceedings of the 49th ACM technical symposium on computer science education* (p. 1107). Association for Computing Machinery.

Li, Q., Li, Z., & Han, J. (2021). A hybrid learning pedagogy for surmounting the challenges of the COVID-19 pandemic in the performing arts education. *Education and Information Technologies, 26*, 7635–7655.

Machado, A. C., & Almeida, M. A. (2013). Identification of academic and behavioral performance of children with learning difficulties to participate in a consultation program. *Revista Psicopedagogia, 30*(91), 21–33.

McDaniel, R., & Telep, P. (2021). Game design tactics for teaching technical communication in online courses. *Journal of Technical Writing and Communication, 51*(1), 70–92.

Mock, K., (2019). Experiences using Discord as platform for online tutoring and building a CS community. In *Proceedings of the 50th ACM technical symposium on computer science education* (p. 1284). Association for Computing Machinery.

Nickerson, A. B., & Sulkowski, M. L. (2021). The COVID-19 pandemic as a long-term school crisis: Impact, risk, resilience, and crisis management. *School Psychology, 36*(5), 271–276.

Odinokaya, M. A., Krylova, E. A., Rubtsova, A. V., & Almazova, N. I. (2021). Using the Discord application to facilitate EFL vocabulary acquisition. *Education Sciences, 11,* 470.

Park, S., & Kim, S. (2022). Identifying world types to deliver gameful experiences for sustainable learning in the metaverse. *Sustainability, 14,* 1361.

Poss, B., Gregory, S., & Marotta, M. (2022). Voices from the field: A journey to build a community of practice during the COVID-19 pandemic. *Assistive Technology Outcomes and Benefits, 16*(1), 75–83.

Reynolds, R., & Chiu, M. M. (2013). Formal and informal context factors as contributors to student engagement in a guided discovery-based program of game design learning. *Learning, Media and Technology, 38*(4), 429–462.

Robinson, B. (2022). Governance on, with, behind, and beyond the Discord platform: A study of platform practices in an informal learning context. *Learning, Media and Technology.* Advanced online publication.

Shelton, C. (2017). Giving up technology and social media: Why university lecturers stop using technology in teaching. *Technology, Pedagogy and Education, 26*(3), 303–321.

Simamora, R. M. (2020). The challenges of online learning during the COVID-19 pandemic: An essay analysis of performing arts education students. *Studies in Learning and Teaching, 1*(2), 86–103.

Tancredi, H. (2020). Meeting obligations to consult students with disability: Methodological considerations and successful elements for consultation. *The Australian Educational Researcher, 47*(2), 201–217.

Wahyuningsih, E., & Baidi, B. (2021). Scrutinizing the potential use of Discord application as a digital platform amidst emergency remote learning. *Journal of Educational Management and Instruction, 1*(1), 9–18.

Watkins, K. E., & Marsick, V. J. (2021). Informal and incidental learning in the time of COVID-19. *Advances in Developing Human Resources, 23*(1), 88–96.

Wilson, K., Li, L. Y., Collins, G. (2011). Co-constructing academic literacy: Examining teacher-student discourse in a one-to-one consultation. *Journal of Academic Language and Learning, 5*(1), 139–153.

CHAPTER 3

Adapting Acting Education for Pandemic-Friendly Mediums

A Play about Self-Preservation and Self-Presentation

Kara Flanagan, Danu Anthony Stinson and Anita Prest

Abstract

When an educator drastically changes the physical learning environment, there is a potential for a psychological change in a student's focus and will. Psychological changes can naturally manifest in one's presentation of energy, behaviour, and appearance. With traditional classroom settings being converted into online and significantly different in-person training environments, the potential for a parallel transformation by actors and teachers in adjusting to these new environments can be expected. In self-presentation theory, an individual can control the self-image presented to others (Leary, 1983). But what if the new self-image is: survivor? Online classrooms have unique challenges in adapting traditional actor training methods, and educators should be alert to the impacts on students' commitment by observing their changes in energy, behaviour, and costuming because self-presentation impacts not only the characters being portrayed, but more importantly, the actors. Our success as educators is largely determined by how well our students learn and what kind of actors they become. Self-presentation theory can be used as a lens through which to observe students' focus, and it can be applied to reimagine the roles of the students and teachers. This chapter is written as a play, enabling you, our readers to take on a role. The question for our readers is: what role does self-presentation theory play for students and teachers in adapting actor training education into pandemic friendly mediums: online, in-person indoor and in-person outdoor classrooms?

Keywords

acting education – arts-based research – a/r/tography – self-presentation theory – teaching acting online

1 A Comedy in Two Acts

1.1 *Characters*
The following characters will shape and enact our play:
- Puck: an instigator, much like Coyote and Raven (Cole & O'Riley, 2010), any gender
- Researcher: an arts-based researcher, any gender
- Drew: an acting teacher, she/her
- Lysander: a not very tech savvy acting student, irritable, he/him
- Hermia: a classical acting student, loves Shakespeare, follows protocols, she/her
- Demetrius: a natural actor of the stage, jokester, he/him
- Helena: acting student, suffers from migraines, loves British acting culture, opinionated and obsessive, think *Mean Girls* (Waters, 2004), she/her
- Phone: Drew's cellular voicemail, any gender
- TV: Drew's TV, usually displays classic films, any gender
- Mirror: a magical, interactive mirror in Drew's living room, any gender
- Professor: a drama educator, theatrical, she/her

2 Prologue

Puck: "To hold, as 'twere, the mirror up to nature; to show virtue her own feature, scorn her own image, and the very age and body of the time his form and pressure" (Shakespeare, 1603/2007a, 3.2.15–17).

Researcher: Dear artists, researchers, teachers, professors, students, and fellow thespians, thank you for coming to our play, a living embodiment of a changing world. "A world remembered", in the words of Shakespeare. His world was constantly shaken by the threat of plagues (Greenblat, 2020). Our world today is not so different than his. Our ability to innovate to find solutions is a common key trait in our societies in forming the way we live and educate in the wake of the pressures we face today. And for educators, we need to adapt our teaching pedagogies according to the learning environment to enable our students to also adapt.

3 Act 1: Dressed to Impress or Hold the Mirror up to Nature?

3.1 *Scene 1: Wings of Change*
A dimly lit actors' studio is encased by red brick walls and long black curtains. A group of acting students meander through the rows searching for their habitual

places. They stare at that dark stage, waiting nervously. This is no ordinary class. This is no ordinary world. A door swings open and a cold breeze passes among the class. The stage lights go up. It's bright. Almost too bright for them to take in the scene.

Drew: Actors. Thank you for coming. I've told you that the key to success is showing up. But that was then. This is now. Our government has asked us to shelter in place. The studio will be closed. Please go home. We have new technology. We're going online. I'll email you details.

Lysander: I don't have a laptop.

Hermia: You can use your smart phone.

Demetrius: How can we act online?

Drew: Instead of a purely theatre class, think of it like stage to screen. Acting on camera.

Hermia: Shakespeare on screen? Like Kenneth Branagh's Shakespeare? Or Trevor Nunn or –

Helena: RSC?

Lysander: Stratford?

Helena: England!

Lysander: Ontario!!

Demetrius: Can't we just stay in the theatre, but stay far, far away from each other?

Drew: Do you want to be a working actor?

Demetrius: Yes.

Drew: Then consider this useful experience in learning how to act on film.

Helena: I don't like film lights. It gives me migraines.

Drew: How about rose-tinted glasses to cut out the light? *Helena and Demetrius groan.* Yellow? *Helena shakes her head.* See you online in one hour.

The stage lights dim, and a cold breeze rushes through the wings and into the studio, pushing the students out. The lights grow darker, and the stage appears to shrink until all that is left is a small lit digital screen.

3.2   Scene 2: Tech Tech Tok
A meticulous condo. Posters of plays and films adorn a long hallway into the living room where Drew paces, flicking her fingers by her lips. She wonders why she quit smoking. A message pops up on her laptop. Fifteen minutes to install the application. Uggghhh. She opens a drawer to grab a lighter, running the steel by her thumb, and promptly puts it back in the drawer. She grabs her wallet, keys, and exits.

3.3   Scene 3: Ritual
Blossom trees form a canopy over the sidewalk, as Drew walks briskly to a coffee shop. Her usual order. Exiting the coffee shop, she hears the door lock behind her. It's dark. The sign in the window jostles. Closed. The world is shutting down. Her world. She walks fast ... faster, feeling a coldness and weight in the air around her, until – home!

3.4   Scene 4: Moment before
Back in her living room, the computer is bright, ready to launch a new online class. But is Drew ready? Her phone is alight with messages.

Drew: Casting? *She clicks voicemail.*

Phone: Drew? Drewww??? I'm so sorry you didn't get the part. And yes, I *never* call to say that. But maybe casting directors should call actors back? Right? Maybe I should be reachable? To you. To our peers. Did I just say that? Did I just call actors my peers? Oooohh ... I had to cancel the casting session. Everything's canceled. I don't know what to do? And then I thought about what you said about teaching online. How? How will you do that!? How can you just carry on? With work? Drew ... ? Did you pick up? Oh, sorry. My cat. I thought maybe you picked up. But you didn't? ... Eh hem. Just in case you're wondering, I'm doing okay, just fine really. But your students? They must be struggling, right? Like I'd like to know how they're handing this, you know. Just wanna be supportive of you know, people. Actors. Right? I love people. But where did they all go? Dreeewww! If you get this message, it would be great to ah – hear from you and maybe I don't know. You need someone to teach these people how to get hired. Maybe I should share my knowledge. Because what if I'm dead tomorrow? Oh, god. We could all be dead tomorrow. And I'm sorry I've never ever called you back before. Or hired you for that union film. I'm sorry I told you were too tall, too Canadian, or maybe too theatrical. Yes, I think that was it –

Click. Game time. Drew smiles, rolls her eyes, and catches a glimpse of herself in the mirror. She pats her cheeks and smiles awkwardly into the mirror. Thumbs up.

Drew: You've got this. You have to! The world may crash around you, but if you don't keep standing, then neither will your students. *She darts a glance at her cabinet drawer.* And you don't need a cigarette. *Her phone lights up and dances.* If one of the top power houses in the industry can't handle change, then this is just the beginning of a cataclysmic shake-up. Addictions? Mental illness? Addictions. *She looks longingly at the drawer holding her cigarettes.* No, no. I've got this.

Mirror: Remember your training.

Drew: I hope the fact my mirror talks to me is not a bad sign? Artists, we just have finer sensory abilities. (*laughs*) I think. Yes ... Mirror, mirror ... ? Ack ... I have two minutes to get ready and then inspire a class of young actors. I need, ah, a character. Michael Chekhov's psychological gesture? Hmmm ... mirror, my mind is blank. Blank! *She snaps her fingers.* Amy Cuddy's power pose (Cuddy, 2012; Cuddy, et al., 2015). *Drew grips her hips, elbows pointed out, raises her chin and adopts a steely gaze, and thinks of Wonder Woman. A true power pose. She holds for two minutes ...* I got this!

3.5   *Scene 5: Welcome to the Zoom Room*

Two classes and two weeks later. The Zoom acting room is lit up like The Brady Bunch (Schwartz, 1969-1974) with Drew and a dozen students. Cameras flick on and off, heads rotate sideways and upside down. The sound of pets, roommates, and toilets flushing, as students multi-task their way into the new room.

Drew: Welcome actors. Okay for starters, please mute yourself when you're not talking, or acting. When your mic is unmuted, we can hear you, wherever you are – your bathroom, kitchen, private roof deck with your roommates. I know this is new, but now you've had two weeks to work through the kinks. Lysander, you're horizontal.

Lysander: Sorry, camera phone. *He adjusts his phone.*

Drew: And people, please. Don't come to class in robes. You may be in your bedroom, but this is not a pajama party. I am not sixteen, and we aren't going to be talking about which boys we like. Wear what you would wear in class. And be prepared. Keep to your rituals. Before class, I would go to the same coffee shop and order the same drink and walk the same path to class. I start my focus two hours before. I make my notes. And long before that I make sure I'm dressed the part. I don't think, well, I'm not going to shave again, shower, or wear trousers. No. I'm going to do exactly what I did before. I'm going to get a coffee – maybe make my own coffee. Maybe my dry cleaning is delayed, and I have to iron. This is like working on set. You may be filming in an unfamiliar location, working with people you don't know, surrounded by a language you don't speak. Keep your rituals. That's what will keep you in the work. Your rituals will keep you sane. So, I'm going to stop the class for ten minutes, so you can get in your actor clothes. If you want to go to a sweet sixteen slumber party, this is not the occasion. Your success, as an actor, is defined by the habits you create for yourself. If you can't learn this now, you will burn your chance for success. See you in ten.

3.6   Scene 6: Afterburner

Four hours later. Drew's living room. Drew watches The Philadelphia Story with a large bowl of microwaved popcorn. Celebrity gossip magazines form a collage on top of her coffee table. She's wearing her favourite pink Hello Kitty bathrobe.

TV: "Has your mind taken hold again, dear Professor?" (Cukor, 2017, 1:16).

Drew: (*imitating James Stewart*) "Well, it's a good thing, don't you agree?"

A steely eyed Professor appears in Drew's mirror, dressed in a 1940's suit.

Professor: How many times have you watched *The Philadelphia Story?*

Drew: Lay off, Professor. It's research. I've been trying to teach my students how important it is to dress up for class. Just because it's online doesn't mean that they have to stop trying. Look at those costumes. Look at the way Katherine Hepburn's dress sparkles like a constellation. Amazing! I wish they made clothes like that now. *They* had class.

Professor: You're worried that if your students give up on their appearance, they'll give up –

Drew: On their habits and ultimately their work. If it's one thing that educators can instill in students, it's work ethic.

Professor: Or as Dewey (1916) would say: a focus and willingness to learn.

Drew: Yes. That's the thing that will keep them working beyond the classroom and in the real world. Whatever and wherever that is, Professor. Online classes can work, yes. But the comfort of working at home is changing their habits. *Drew pounds her fits on her couch, as soft pink tufts fly off her sleeves.* Their way of presenting themselves, their –

Professor: Accountability.

Drew: Yes. The authority instilled in a classroom setting with peers keeping each other in check helps create a sense of community and a standard. I don't know how to recreate that online.

Professor: Yes, you do. You're an actor.

Drew: And you're a figment of my imagination.

Professor: In self-presentation theory, an individual can control the self-relevant images that they present to others (Leary, 1983, p. 60). So, you just have to get your students to create a role for themselves. To be the very best acting student they can.

Drew: Can you create a character with potentially different behaviours, attitudes, and costuming?

Professor: Yes.

Drew: So, I just need them to be good acting students on top of being good actors?

Professor: We all play roles (Schechner, 2004).

Drew: "And one man in his time plays many parts" (Shakespeare 1623/2007b, 2.7.145).

Professor: They just need to be accountable to their roles and to themselves.

Drew: Thank you, Professor. Now if you don't mind, I'd like to get back to my movie.

The Professor vanishes and Drew continues to study The Philadelphia Story with great concentration and admiration. Drew drifts off and falls asleep on her couch.

4   Act 2: Online vs. In-Person, Film vs. Theatre, Student vs. Teacher

4.1   *Scene 1: What Dreams May Come*
A year later. In the early hours of the day, Drew awakens to hear the voice of the Professor – stationed again in the mirror. The Professor speaks as though she's delivering the news, albeit to an audience of one.

Professor: Indoor classes – with masks and routinely sanitized hands and socially distanced students and teachers – present a controlled image of self-preservation. In tandem, an outdoor acting environment with optional masks and actors six feet apart presents another image of self-preservation, albeit with less control. In contrast, an online class without masks presents a class with a more relaxed self-image, fewer protocols, and sometimes with pajamas. *The Professor breaks her newscaster act to speak informally.* Psst, hey! Which class format will you be teaching, Drew?

Drew: (*waking up*) What? In-person? Umm ... Online ... Both?

Professor: (*back in newscaster mode*) Creating a safe and respectful learning environment during a pandemic while maintaining a high standard of teaching with impactful learning is likely one of the most significant challenges of the last two and a half years.

Drew: Hybrid learning?

Professor: Schebetta (2022) advocates for hybrid approaches to teaching performing arts: online and in-person.

Drew: Well, it looks like I've got it.

Professor: But Cox (2021) says students don't know how to use zoom. They could end up sideways, zooming from the bathroom.

Drew: It can be a problem, yes.

Professor: Our success as educators is largely determined by how well our students learn and what kind of actors they become. *The Professor breaks her newscaster act again.* What kind of actors are your students, Drew?

Drew: Well, some are working actors, some are balancing multiple jobs.

Professor: But how did they do in the pandemic? What was their experience? Dewey (1916, 1938) predicts that students are profoundly influenced by their experience. Dewey (1916) argues that a person's success in education is related to their focus and willingness to learn, and that the body and mind have important roles in the interpretation of experience. Moreover, Dewey (1938) highlights how the quality and continuity of experiences that educators provide their students can affect students' motivation to learn. Self-presentation is one way in which you can see how these experiences impact them. But their inner experience matters too. So, Drew, what are their experiences in learning across different formats?

Drew: Well, Professor, it's a bit of a blur, but I think it went something like this …

Mist enters Drew's apartment. She falls back asleep.

4.2   Scene 2: Stand-in

Pre-pandemic. Drew is teaching a scene from On the Waterfront in which Terry Malloy accuses his brother, Charley, of not looking out for him. Helena (playing

Terry) and Lysander (playing Charley) sit on two chairs, moving as though they're driving in the back seat of a taxi. Lysander, frustrated, stands.

Drew: Lysander, you just put your head through the roof the cab. Are you imagining it's a convertible?

Lysander: I can't do this scene.

Drew: It's a difficult scene.

Lysander: I mean I can't play it without my scene partner. Where's Demetrius?

Helena: Sick.

Lysander starts to pace.

Drew: Please sit down. If this were a film set, you would have ruined the prop car and put a couple of set designers out of work.

Lysander sits reluctantly.

Drew: You know Rod Steiger said the same thing when Marlon Brando left and his stand-in – *Drew draws a blank look.*

Helena: Helena.

Drew: When Helena, or Rod's stand-in, replaced Marlon, Rod was so mad, he thought he couldn't act the scene (Kazan, 2013). But it was his anger that fueled his delivery and helped make that scene so iconic.

Lysander: Oh. So, I should use that feeling?

Drew: Right.

Lysander: But whatever happened to the rule that your only excuse to not show up on stage or onset is when you're dead?

Helena: Industry standard. I had to work through the most awful migraine. The lights. I had to wear sunglasses through –

Lysander: Demetrius and I rehearsed this scene, and now that we're filming my take, he's gone.

Drew: No director is going to say, okay, you're allowed to quit because it's difficult. They'll hire someone else. They'll hire – *blank look.*

Helena: Helena.

Drew: Right. She'll get both parts.

Helena: *I'd kill both parts.*

Lysander: Can we start again?

Drew: It's your scene.

Lysander sits down and nods to Helena.

4.3   *Scene 3: Take 2*

1 year later in a pandemic. Film lights illuminate Lysander and Demetrius, who sit on chairs six feet apart on the stage. They take their masks off and mimic they're in the back seat of a cab, perhaps a limo. Lysander and Demetrius are playing Charley and Terry from On the Waterfront. The classroom is sparse. Students sit far apart and eye each other suspiciously, keeping their masks on. Drew takes a read on the class.

Drew: Action.

Hermia presses the record button on the camera. Lysander, frustrated, stands.

Drew: You put your head through the roof the cab.

Lysander: I can't do this scene.

Drew: What happened?

Lysander: I can't play it with him.

Drew: Why not?

Lysander: He's sick.

Drew: What?

Demetrius: (*coughs*) It's nothing.

Drew: We have a ten-page health and safety guide to avoid these situations. Page one. Don't come in if you're sick. Page two. Don't come in if you're sick. Page ten. Don't come in if you're sick! Demetrius?!

Demetrius: It's allergies.

The class wide-eyed stares at Demetrius.

Demetrius: Really.

Drew: Temperature check.

Hermia drapes herself in a scarf and walks slowly over to Demetrius and points the thermometer at his forehead.

Hermia: It's ... normal.

The class sighs with relief. Lysander starts to pace.

Drew: Back to the top.

Lysander sits down reluctantly, darts a look at Demetrius.

Demetrius: I thought the only excuse for not showing up is if I were –

Helena: Oooohh ... don't say it.

Hermia: Times have changed. Theatre has changed. The rules –

Demetrius: And dark humour is out, along with my asthma. I get it.

Lysander wiggles in his chair.

Lysander: It's my film take, people. And now I've lost the will to act ... I'm really annoyed with all of you.

Drew: Do you think Charley would be annoyed at Terry for saying he never looked out for him? For not being the kind of brother he wanted him to be? Like the kind of classmates you want them to be? You think you'd be okay with that?

Lysander: No. Of course, not. I wouldn't.

Drew: Then use that.

Lysander: Hmmm ...

After a long pause, Lysander nods to Hermia. She adjusts the camera's focus.

Drew: Action.

Lysander and Demetrius wiggle on their chairs as if the taxi is moving at a fast clip. Lysander looks at Demetrius with a mixture of fear and annoyance. They begin the scene.

4.4   Scene 4: Take Three
A year later. The class is on Zoom. A matrix of actor heads lights up on Drew's computer.

Drew: Welcome to the Zoom Room. Or should I say zoo room? Hah no animal exercises today. We're revisiting scenes. First up ... (*checking her list*) Lysander.

Demetrius: Lysander, you coulda been a contender, if you could ever finish this scene.

Lysander: Shut-up.

Drew: Actors, you're unmuted, when you should be muted.

Lysander rambles, but muted.

Drew: You want to be unmuted for your scenes. Muted for snide remarks. Start again.

Lysander: (*unmutes his mic*) I can't do this scene.

Drew: Are you going to make me ask you why?

Lysander: I can't see Demetrius. I see Helena eating an ice cream sundae. Hermia's painting her nails. I can see everyone but Demetrius.

Helena: (*unmuted*) Try the next screen.

Lysander: How?

Helena: Press the arrow on the right.

Lysander: Okay.

Drew: Start again.

Lysander prepares. Frustrated he throws his script.

Lysander: I can't do this scene. He's too small. It's like I'm talking to a leprechaun. I can't. How many films do you think I'm going to do talking to a leprechaun?

Drew: If you book a film with leprechauns, Lysander, I would say you would be very, very lucky.

Lysander: Demetrius doesn't give me much as a reader to begin with. Now he's five pixels. I can't.

Helena: You have to pin him to your screen.

Lysander: What?

Helena: Click the pin button, so that he's full screen.

Lysander clicks the pin button his screen.

Drew: Again.

Lysander picks up his script, studies it carefully, and then puts it down. He stares intently at the screen. His eyes dart around.

Lysander: I can't.

Drew: Because?

Lysander: I can't act with a computer. It just doesn't feel real. There are only two dimensions. I need a third. I need to see his depth.

Helena: (*chuckling*) Ha! Good luck with that!

Demetrius: Well, if that isn't the pan calling the kettle shallow.

Drew: Okay actors. Here's a teaching moment. We have an actor here that for all intents and purposes is in the same scene that he's played –

Lysander: Twenty-six times.

Drew: And what's different?

Lysander: Well, this time I'm playing after dinner whereas last week, I hadn't eaten.

Drew: No. What's different versus in-person?

Lysander: Well, the room. I'm in my den, and I know I'm not in a cab. And I'm with a leprechaun.

Drew: So, let's move on from the leprechaun motif for a moment.

Drew's mirror lights up. The Professor appears.

Professor: (*whispers*) Talk about state-dependent memory (Zarrindast & Khakpai, 2020).

Drew: Actors, something we're dealing with here is state-dependent memory. Meaning ... meaning?

Professor: The space that you rehearse in contributes to you learning the scene.

Drew: Got it. The space that you rehearse in contributes to you learning the scene. So, one way to tackle this is to continue to rehearse in the same space. Lysander, where did you rehearse?

Lysander: In my tree in the backyard.

Drew: Oh, no.

Lysander: I can bring my laptop there ... just a moment. *Lysander's camera clicks off.*

Drew: While Lysander sets up ... I'd like to say that another way to manage your learning process is to actually keep changing your rehearsal environment so you don't become too reliant on a space for your own recall and comfort of working.

Lysander's camera clicks on. He's sitting on a low branch in an oak tree.

Drew: And Lysander, what about your costume? Do you think the Blue Jays were around in the forties and fifties?

Helena: No. They were established in 1977 ...

Drew: The choices you make, as an actor, impact your work. Try a costume that makes you experience that world.

Lysander: Okay.

Lysander's camera clicks off ... Lysander reappears wearing an old tweed jacket from his cupboard.

Drew: Next. What can you change to make it feel like you're in the scene?

Lysander: Well, I could bounce on this branch like I'm not wearing a seat belt in the back of a cab.

Drew: Good. Okay you've got your inner world working with your outer world. And you look the part of a 40s gangster.

Lysander continues to bounce on the branch. Crack! Thud!!

Lysander: (*off camera*) I'm okay!

Drew: Helena? Want to sub in?

Helena: Actually, I'd prefer to do a scene from Darby O'Gill and the Little People.

Drew: That's time. 'Night, class.

Drew closes her laptop and turns towards her mirror.

Professor: If they can change their habits and rely less on state-dependent memory, they could act anywhere, anytime.

Drew: Oh, so you're going to lecture me on Dewey (1916) and how if my students were more –

Professor: Malleable. You know, if they had a certain plasticity to their grey matter –

Drew: Right. Then they could form new habits –

Professor: Correct. And learn faster.

Drew: Professor, you're welcome to takeover my class. Please.

Professor: No, no. Just an observation.

The Professor vanishes in the mirror. Drew stares at her twitchy fingers, and picks up her remote.

Drew: On the Waterfront.

Drew smiles as Leonard Bernstein's score rolls off the trailer.

Drew: If only, I could make them (my students) like them (trailblazing actors). Eh, Professor?

The mirror glistens with a wave of light.

Professor: No comment.

The room darkens and the smell of popcorn inhabits Drew's living room.

4.5   *Scene 5: Ready, Set, Action*

Six months later. An outdoor film set. A taxicab. Film crew putter around putting up lights and setting up a camera. Students hover around, curious. Hermia, the COVID officer, takes people's temperatures, enforces mask wearing to non-performers, and piles on sanitizer to any dry hand she passes.

Demetrius: I had my temperature checked already.

Hermia: That was yesterday. I'm following all UBCP/ACTRA COVID safety guidelines, consistent with WorkSafeBC, the BC Motion Picture Industry guide, and Actsafe.

Demetrius groans, while Hermia takes his temperature. Lysander squirms in his seat.

Helena: Quiet on set. Camera rolling.

Drew: Action.

Lysander: I forgot my line.

Demetrius: Oh, no.

Drew: Lysander, this is your tenth take.

Lysander: Remember what you said about state-dependent memory?

Drew: Yes?

Lysander: I can only remember my lines in a tree. I can't perform in a cab. I need my tree.

Drew: You may have missed the part when I said to overcome state-dependent memory issues, you should rehearse in a variety of settings. Not just trees.

Lysander: I think that's when I broke my branch. I missed that.

Drew: Where's your costume?

Lysander: Oh, yeah. I thought it was too hot for tweed. I have my lucky jersey on.

Drew: Couldn't you wear that under the tweed? Okay, people, we're going to take five.

Helena: There's an old oak there. I think I could use some visual effects if we put the green screen behind it so it will look like the cab.

Drew: Great idea. Lysander, climb that tree.

Lysander: Sir.

Lysander climbs the tree. His jacket snags on a branch and after making his way up, his hair becomes disheveled. He sighs with relief as he sits on a thick branch and mimes driving in a cab.

Drew: Okay, Lysander, this is it. It's the final take of the last day and the last time we ever work on this scene. Got it?

Lysander: Please refer to me by my character name, Charley.

Drew: Okay, Charley.

Helena: Quiet on set ... Camera rolling.

Drew: Action.

Lysander delivers a great rendition of Charley Malloy, several years in the making, and his delivery shows a grace and charisma fitting of Hollywood royalty. Drew sheds a tear.

Drew: (*whisper*) Well, Professor, maybe learning is a compromise?

Crew clap. Lysander and Demetrius awkwardly shake hands, and Hermia is quick to sprinkle on drabs of sanitizer. Helena checks the gate and nods to Drew. The take is good. Drew's work is done – for today.

4.6 Epilogue

Puck: "We know what we are, but know not what we may be" (Shakespeare, 1603/2007a, 4.4.42–43).

Researcher: Dear artists, researchers, teachers, professors, students, and fellow thespians, thank you for embodying our play, a memory of our inconstant world. A world remembered by us in these words, in your words, and the words of Shakespeare. It is not just our ability to innovate that allows us to shape education – our society. Adapting our classes to the pandemic presents new challenges, whether we are working in-person or online. For example, students' experiences are influenced by their learning environment. These environments impact students' ways of relating to their scene partners and their ability to recall their lines. Students' presentation of their self-image and the characters they represent are also impacted by their learning environment. Changes in a student's focus and motivation to play a role indicate challenges that can be overcome with the teacher identifying the problem and finding an alternative approach for the student. As educators, we need to adapt our teaching pedagogies according to the learning environment in order to support and empower students in their work and be the best actors they can be.

References

Barone, T., & Eisner, E. (2012). *Arts based research*. Sage.

Chekhov, M. (2002). *To the actor: On the technique of acting* (M. Powers, Ed.). Routledge. (Original work published 1953)

Cole, P., & O'Riley, P. (2010). Coyote and Raven (p)re-visit environmental education, sustainablility and runaway capitalism. *Canadian Journal of Environmental Education, 15*, 25–46.

Cox, K. (2021). A lesson in Zoom: Teaching students how to learn remotely. *Nineteenth-Century Gender Studies, 17*(1).

Cramer, D. S. (1975–1979). *Wonder woman* [TV series]. Warner Bros. TV.

Cuddy, A. J. C. (2012, June). *Your body language may shape who you are* [Video]. TED Conferences. https://www.ted.com/talks/amy_cuddy_your_body_language_may_shape_who_you_are?language=en

Cuddy, A. J. C., Wilmuth, C. A., Yap, A. J., & Carney, D. R. (2015). Preparatory power posing affects nonverbal presence and job interview performance. *Journal of Applied Psychology, 100*(4), 1286–1295. https://doi.org/10.1037/a0038543

Cukor, G. (Director). (2017). *The Philadelphia story* [Film: DVD]. MGM. (Originally published 1940)

Dewey, J. (1916). *Democracy and education. An introduction to the philosophy of education*. The Macmillan Company.

Dewey, J. (1938). *Experience and education*. Macmillan Company.

Elliott, S. N., Kratochwill, T. R., Littlefield Cook, J., & Travers, J. (2000). *Educational psychology: Effective teaching, effective learning* (3rd ed.). McGraw-Hill College.

Gordon, R. (2006). *The purpose of playing: Modern acting theories in perspective*. University of Michigan Press.

Greenblat, S. (2020, May 7). What Shakespeare actually wrote about the plague. *The New Yorker*. https://www.newyorker.com/culture/cultural-comment/what-shakespeare-actually-wrote-about-the-plague

Kazan, E. (Director). (2013). *On the waterfront* [Film: DVD with audio commentary]. Columbia Pictures. (Originally published 1954)

Leary, M. R. (1983). *Understanding social anxiety: Social, personality and clinical perspectives*. Sage Publications.

Leary, M. R., & Tangney, J. P. (2012). *Handbook of self and identity* (2nd ed.). Guilford Press.

Schebetta, D. (2022). Re-making rehearsal and performance: Intersections of collaboration and accessibility in a hybrid Romeo & Juliet. In J. Higgins & E. Clark Halpin (Eds.), *Teaching performance practices in remote and hybrid spaces* (1st ed., pp. 134–144). Routledge, Taylor & Francis Group.

Schechner, R. (2004). *Performance theory*. Routledge Classics. https://doi.org/10.4324/9780203426630

Schwartz, S. (Executive Producer). (1969–1974). *The Brady Bunch* [TV series]. Paramount Television.

Shakespeare, W. (2007a). *Hamlet* (J. Bate & E. Rasmussen, Eds.). Macmillan Publishers. (Original work published 1603)

Shakespeare, W. (2007b). *As you like it* (J. Bate & E. Rasmussen, Eds.). Macmillan Publishers. (Original work published 1623)

Springgay, S., Irwin, R. L., & Kind, S. W. (2005). A/r/tography as living inquiry through art and text. *Qualitative Inquiry, 11*(6), 897–912. doi:10.1177/1077800405280696

Stanislavsky, K., & Hapgood, E. R. (2004). *An actor's handbook: An alphabetical arrangement of concise statements on aspects of acting*. Routledge. (Original work published 1936)

Stevenson, R. (1959). *Darby O'Gill and the little people* [Film]. Walt Disney Productions.

UBCP/ACTRA. (2021, May 1). COVID-19 FAQs – safety on sets. https://www.ubcpactra.ca/wp-content/uploads/2021/06/Covid-Safety-on-sets-052021.pdf

UBCP/ACTRA. (2022). https://www.ubcpactra.ca

Waters, M. (Director). (2004). *Mean girls* [Film]. Broadway Video.

Zarrindast, M. R., & Khakpai, F. (2020). State-dependent memory and its modulation by different brain areas and neurotransmitters. *EXCLI Journal, 19*, 1081–1099. https://doi.org/10.17179/excli2020-2612

CHAPTER 4

A Rack for Memories

Between Theory and Praxis, the Real and the Digital

Vendula Fremlová

Abstract

This chapter describes the starting points, the duration, and the results of the pilot year of the course entitled The Contexts of Art, taught at the Department of Art Education at the Faculty of Education, Charles University, and oriented towards visual production by art education candidates within the context of contemporary art. The course was taught in the summer semester of the academic year 2021/22 by lecturers Vendula Fremlová (curator of contemporary art) and Michal Sedlák (sculptor). The topic of this year's course was the duality of the digital and real worlds, demonstrated by means of the visual depiction of memories and sharing it online on social media. The chapter interprets selected works of art created during the course, as well as the final exhibition that offered a comprehensive presentation of the students' works. It situates the students' works within the context of the current post-digital trend in art, additionally establishing a connection between these interpretations and selected observations and theoretical studies from the field of visual studies, social psychology, sociology and the theories of communication and online interaction. It focuses primarily on Goffman's performance metaphor and Hogan's exhibition metaphor, which offer not only a framework for grasping the ways in which social media operate and are used, but also new opportunities for thinking about the role of art, exhibitions and curatorship.

Keywords

visual art, post-digital trend in art, online social media, memory, remembering, digital footprint, performance, exhibition, curator

1   Introduction

'Since we were born with a cell phone in our hand, amputating it could be dangerous for our psyche' (Sokołowska, 2021), wrote the Polish artist

Sokołowska (born in 1996) in a text accompanying the exhibition *The Pathology of Normality* by Young Talented Sexy Collective, which she is a member of. Thus, she aptly describes the mode of perception and art production significant for this art group, but first and foremost, a characteristic of generations born into the digital setting who are also referred to as digital-native (Barlow, 1996; Prensky, 2001). Her introspective statement, endowed with a certain amount of humour, illustrates the notion that for generations of young people, technologies and social media are extensions of their sense organs. In a similar spirit and a more general vein, Nicolas Mirzoeff sums up the main ideas of his book *How to See the World*. According to Mirzoeff (2015), 'our bodies are now extensions of data networks, clicking, linking and taking selfies. We render what we see and understand on screens that go everywhere with us' (p. 14).

The above statements regarding the nature of our relationship with technologies naturally concern also current university students. They impact on them – members of the (neo) digital-native generation – on many fronts: as more or less active everyday users of mobile devices, digital networks and social media; as creators of a visual statement (as part of regular communication, as well as attempts to produce art); and last but not least, as future art teachers who ought to be aware of changes in the area of visuality and visual perception associated with the need for visual and digital literacy.

In this chapter, I describe the starting points, duration and results of the pilot year of the course entitled The Contexts of Art, taught at the Department of Art Education at the Faculty of Education, Charles University,[1] and oriented towards visual production by art education candidates embedded within the context of contemporary art. The course was taught in the summer semester of the academic year 2021/22 by lecturers Vendula Fremlová (curator of contemporary art) and Michal Sedlák (sculptor). The topic of this year's course was the duality of the digital and real worlds, demonstrated by means of the visual depiction of memories and sharing it online through social media. In this chapter, I interpret those works of art that emerged during the course, as well as the final exhibition *A Rack for Memories*[2] held at the Artivist Lab Gallery[3] in Prague that offered a comprehensive presentation of the students' works. I establish a connection between these interpretations and selected observations and theoretical studies from art theory, visual studies, social psychology, sociology, as well as the theories of communication and online interaction, which offer a framework for grasping the ways in which young people perceive and coexist with technologies.

2   The Broader (Not Only) Artistic Context

The pandemic situation promoted and enhanced the use of the digital setting, which is becoming – in line with the Polish artist's statement – our second nature. Restricting direct interpersonal communication and interaction and diverting them into a socially distanced, online form in the years 2020 and 2021 was entirely unprecedented. This is also demonstrated by the ever-increasing numbers of social media users: 'Social media user numbers continue to grow faster than they did pre-pandemic, with the global total still increasing at a rate of almost 13½ new users every second' (Hootsuite Inc., 2022). However, the increase in the amount of time spent in the digital setting and by means of communicating through mobile devices and social media is not a new phenomenon. On the contrary, we have been able to watch this ever-increasing trend for many years now. A 2018 study stated that '(e)ach day, people share almost 5 billion posts on Facebook, 500 million tweets on Twitter, 70 million pictures on Instagram, and 12 years' worth of video on YouTube' (Tamir et al., 2018, p. 161).

Therefore, it is only natural that this dimension of our lives, even more exacerbated by the pandemic experience of the on- and offline worlds, gets reflected in contemporary visual art. The duality of the physical and the digital, the real and the virtual becomes the theme of individual works of art and of topical exhibition projects, including major world shows. A good example may be the exhibition HISTORYNOW by the eminent British artist Marc Quinn (born in 1964), presented at this year's Venice Biennale,[4] as a parallel event, which reflected this trend as well. The project HISTORYNOW, which the artist has been working on since 2020, is based on working with screenshots on the artist's iPhone. Their blow-ups become the basis for additional, very diverse painting interventions: that is, for classical hanging pictures. The use of screenshots 'presents a familiar, first-person account of the daily updates and viral stories that we consumed – and which consumed us [...]' (Marc Quinn studio, 2022). 'The screenshot remains a constant, evoking both the enduring permanence and timely ephemerality of news and technology in our lives' (Marc Quinn studio, 2022) despite the aforementioned diversity of the painter's rendition.

Marc Quinn's approach illustrates well the current trend of freely combining analogue media with digital ones, though the distinction between the analogue and the digital is effectively very lay and inaccurate,[5] as pointed out by Cramer (2014). Nevertheless, it is precisely in this free use of the media available to us, in their interconnectedness and permeability, where we find a key trait of the post-digital approach in art. The prefix 'post' does not mean that the digital era has been surpassed: rather, it means that it is a new stage of the digital era. Artworks often acquire the form of a classic artefact, into which lived experiences of the digital world, amplified at present by the radical experience of pandemic lockdowns and social isolation, are projected.

3 The 'ZET Rack' and 'Post-Digital Intimacy' Exhibitions

The specific thematic focus of this year's course was based on exhibitions shown at exhibition halls and institutions in Prague (Czech Republic) in spring 2022 that the students were able to see in person. While both exhibitions were related to the duality of the real and the digital worlds, each did so from a different viewpoint.

We first went to see the exhibition entitled *ZET Rack*[6] by the Czech sculptor, performer and multimedia artist Martin Zet (1959).[7] His exhibition related to the themes of self-presentation and leaving traces, or footprint in the digital world. However, in this case, this notion was conceived of the other way around. The artist does not project himself actively into the public (hence the virtual) space, nor does he leave traces of his own activities: on the contrary, he seeks random – as it were – footprint, or projections of himself. During lockdowns, the artist undertook thorough research of the internet, buying up goods that had ZET in their title: that is, a designation identical to the artist's surname. The resulting gallery installation, which deliberately looked like a designer show room, gave the visitors an opportunity to see a peculiar assemblage of miscellaneous objects. The only linking element of this otherwise heterogenous objects was the connection between the title and the artist's name. Finding and exhibiting them then functions on the basis of the notion of ready-made, where the artistic method is additionally enriched by the duality of the real and digital space. Nevertheless, finding and assembling miscellaneous objects of the same name would have been practically unfeasible without a globalised internet network and its browsers.

The exhibition *ZET Rack* also related to the topic of commodifying ourselves. By projecting himself into many objects by means of his name, the artist pointed to the notion that even our identities, memories, needs and preferences – or our sensitive personal data – become a marketable commodity. For our presence and functioning in the online space are closely associated

FIGURE 4.1   View of the exhibition Martin Zet – ZET Rack. Nevan Contempo, Prague
(photograph by Martin Polák)

with the commercial use of our digital footprint, control and surveillance by social media companies and internet browser operators, contrasting with the seeming freedom of movement in the digital world.

The international collective exhibition *Post-digital Intimacy*[8] presented contemporary positions in relation to the issue of the post-digital approach (Cramer, 2014) in visual art, with a focus on 'describing physical estrangement and the loss of self in the endless sea of the internet' (Blažíček, 2022). The exhibition was an excellent reflection of the current comeback of drawing, painting, print, sculpture and object into art, newly altered by the digital experience. A remarkable feature of the exhibition was its material form and presence, which were in stark contract with the topic of disrupting physical autonomy by means of the immaterial, digital, virtual. The themes of the body and disrupting bodily and mental integrity occurred in the works of all the artists presented (Darja Bajagić, Ivana Bašić, Louisa Gagliardi, Lola Gonzàlez, Daiga Grantina, Rachel Maclean, Pakui Hardware, Viktor Timofeev and Tenant of Culture), each time in a different form and on a different level. The highlight of the exhibition, Rachel Maclean's spectacular film 'Feed me', works with themes such as one's own multiplication, the 'switching' of identities, evoking a false sense of contentment and happiness and unethical trading with these

FIGURE 4.2   View of the exhibition Post-digital Intimacy, National Gallery Prague 2021.
Rachel Maclean, Feed me, 2015 (photography by Katarína Hudačinová)

fragile entities. The title 'Feed me' expresses a need and a dependence, where the boundary between the physical and psychological planes is similarly hard to grasp, just like in the virtual world.

4   Curatorial Approach

We presented the reflections outlined above – and mirrored through the exhibition projects – to our students as part of joint discussions about the duality of the virtual and the real worlds, the visual depiction of memories and the process of sharing them on social media. We presented them as a basis for the students' own artistic investigation and rhizomatic thinking (Deleuze & Guattari, 2010); and for thinking not only about how 'visual art keeps up with the ever-increasing pace at which the structures of the physical and virtual worlds permeate one another and get interconnected with global networks and processes' (Hlaváčková, 2022, p. 8) but also how each and every one of us copes with this mutual permeation and interconnectedness. Thus, the thematic focus of the course functioned as an invitation to reflect critically on the issue that is inseparable from the self-reflection of one's own communication strategies and habits; from realising what contents I communicate, what forms I choose to communicate them in, what image of myself I create. It is also inseparable from realising how the tools of mobile devices and the algorithms of social media – in this case primarily Facebook – impact on and form these contents and the types of self-presentation, communication, memory and remembering.

Gradually, the drafts of the students' artwork were shaped by our discussions and consultations with the students. During these discussions and consultations, depending on the focus of each of the projects, we would try to recommend to them additional resources and inspiring works of art or approaches in contemporary art and art theory; or we would offer our own opinions informed by our own experience as curators, artists, teachers and, last but not least, as spectators. The culmination of the course – a fortnightly exhibition of all the completed works of art held at the Artivist Lab Gallery in central Prague – was a source of immense motivation for the students. This was primarily because they succeeded in finishing their semestral projects, turning them into a presentable work that enters public space instead of remaining in the insular community of the university only. At the same time, the students were faced with the challenge of thinking about the final presentation as a whole: that is, thinking of the exhibition as a specific artwork where the task is not only to present isolated artistic approaches but rather to show mutual connections both in terms of content and form, and to try to formulate them through the exhibition installation determined by the actual space, its properties and facilities.

Given this conception of the course, our roles changed from lecturers to curators,[9] but not in the sense of an authority that is often hidden, selects works of art and imposes a certain hierarchy on them; an authority whose socio-cultural orientation, as well as professional and personal interests often remains hidden behind archives, collections and specific exhibitions. Here, by curators, I mean primarily people and activities representing a creative link between the theory and praxis of art and, simultaneously, motivating critical thinking. An important aspect, associated with the original meaning of the word 'curator' (from the Latin 'curare') is care – in our case, it refers to taking care of students, their work and the final exhibition. The way we tried to lead the course is related to direct communication and personal involvement, through which new pathways to artistic expression are sought and new meanings emerge. Simultaneously, it is precisely care and ethics that become an important aspect of such an approach (Tronto, 1998).

The following sections will attempt to describe the themes and motifs resonating within the students' works of art, which I find to be of interest and characteristic. I will add my reflections on the process and the resulting artistic production by the individual students.[10]

5 A Rack or a Machine for Memories?

The title of this year's course and of the final exhibition – *A Rack for Memories* – is a metaphor that refers to the notion of the interconnected nature of the real and the digital worlds. Besides the pairs 'external – internal', 'object – subject', 'material – mental', the title implies the pair 'activity – passivity' and many more.

Considering memory, remembering and recording memories, it is helpful to take into account the transformation of the scale 'activity – passivity'. Recording memories in the form of a written text, a journal, for example, or by means of classic photographs and photographic albums etc. is not new. Even these types of memory media can be seen as a sort of 'racks for memories': they are carriers that serve as memory extensions: that is, they have been devised with a view to being used as external sources of memory (cognitive augmenting) (Eliseev & Marsh, 2021). Still, the form and circumstances of the activities and personal involvement that people used to undertake in order to capture, as well as to evoke memories is markedly different compared with the present:

> Memory retrieval can be voluntary, driven by an individual's search through memory, or involuntary, in response to environmental cues. Many apps and social media platforms provide such cues; for example, Facebook Memories periodically prompts users to review past memories (e.g., a photo from 3 years ago). (Eliseev & Marsh, 2021, p. 1076)

Magdalena Machalická's work entitled *Facebook Intervention of Memories* relates to the phenomenon of algorithmic memory retrieval and, to an extent, to an unsolicited and automatised evocation of memories on social media. A mysterious rotary object that the student created using black fabric, a hanger, a set of minute engines and a strip light illuminating images from her own Facebook profile is reminiscent of a 'black box' on a plane, but also of funfair attractions and didactic exhibits. The student described it as follows:

> Have you ever experienced a situation where a "memory" that Facebook offers you evoked unexpected emotions in you? A memory of one's own

life, selected by an unknown device, an algorithm that we do not really understand and whose existence we are not often aware of ... , an algorithm that can very realistically influence our life. (Machalická, 2022)

Turning a sophisticated invisible algorithm into an imperfect mechanical DIY (do it yourself) machine gave the spectators a sense of humorous distance and perspective. The combination of pseudoscientific and intuitive approaches the student employed was a fitting metaphor for the way we unproblematically include these external and systemic incentives into the spectrum of our livelihood and experiences; and how our remembering, as well as the reverse process – forgetting – thus change. The term 'retrieval-induced forgetting' refers to a situation where it is apparent that

> [a]lthough sharing events on social media can benefit memory, there may be consequences for events that are not chosen for sharing. The larger literature makes clear that retrieving a subset of events is often at the expense of memory for related non-reviewed events ... (Eliseev & Marsh, 2021, p. 1077)

FIGURE 4.3   Magdalena Machalická, Facebook intervention of memories, rotary object, 2022. View of the exhibition, Artivist Lab Gallery (photograph by Adriána Vančová)

In the future, are we going to remember only those moments and situations that we share with others and that we will be notified about?

What differs is not just the forms and circumstances of evoking memories and the process of remembering itself that is becoming automatised by social media to a certain extent, though. Apart from memory carriers changing from analogue to digital, a key change is 'the sheer number of memory cues (i.e. records) stored externally [...] and accessibility of those cues, given the convenience of smartphones and the synchronization of records across devices (e.g., via cloud storage)' (Eliseev & Marsh, 2021, p. 1077). In connection with the character of social media and the accessibility of our records, compared to the past, what has seen a fundamental change is also the size of the audience, thus shifting the scale 'intimate – public'. Family pictures that used to be meant for viewing by a maximum of tens of individuals during special – often even ceremonial – occasions are now ordinarily publicised and consumed by hundreds, if not thousands of people online. The large volume of digital records we share with others and, additionally, we are regularly reminded of begs the question of what to do with past records that we may see as outdated after some time. '(T)here is an uneasy relationship between people and their past data when the data becomes detached from their original context' (Zhao et al., 2013, p. 2). We may see the former context as entirely distant or, alternatively, it may not fit at all with our current self-presentation, which may lead to the so-called 'profile pruning' where people delete old posts and untag themselves from photos (Eliseev & Marsh, 2021, p. 1075). Exploring the changing context, Eliška Císařová traced these changes using her own Facebook posts dating back 7 years. In her work *Statuses* (2022), the student accompanied old posts with critical commentaries, in which she spells out the conflict in terms of the permanency of posts and the changing nature of social bonds, memories, our perception of others, as well as of ourselves:

> With hindsight, in some cases I do not even remember in what contexts the photos and statuses that I am part of on social media were created. When thinking about social media, I often come back to this moment – the context that is necessary in order to understand the photos is missing. The ever-changing nature of memories, relationships and realities is not mentioned. (Císařová, 2022)

In her work, she responded through a subversive use of the tool and properties of social media; at the same time, for purposes of the exhibition, she anonymised the photographs as well as her friends' posts. In a similar vein, she also commented on a publicised photo of a specific place. In her comment, she reflected on the lifelong process of forming a relationship to a place, in which even memories that keep changing over the course of one's life play a significant role.

FIGURE 4.4   Eliška Císařová, Statuses, print, 2022. View of the exhibition *A Rack for Memories*, Artivist Lab Gallery (photograph by Adriána Vančová)

6   A Mask, a Wig, a Hollow Head: The Self-Portrait and Its Different Forms in a Time of the Selfie

In connection with the post-digital trend in art, it is only symptomatic that while elaborating on the topic of the course, most of our students chose the form of a classic material artefact. The most frequent media were object, sculpture, and installation; digital outputs were represented only in a minority of cases. However, even some of the digital outputs were based on classic drawing, for instance; or they contained multiple conversions from analogue to digital media and vice versa. A frequent motif that appeared in the students' works was the human head, be it in an anonymised form or a concrete form, or in various possible transitions between the two. In fact, this is not exactly a surprise. Social media and their contents are seen as platforms for self-presentation, equipped with the specific corresponding tools. In this setting, we adjust our own activities to the spectator's external perspective: an occurrence naturally stemming from the social character of these media (Zhao et al., 2013). This external perspective can be read most prominently in the format of the selfie. Pointing to the growing trend of making selfies, Nicolas Mirzoeff establishes a link between the popularity of this format and the classic portrait, or the self-portrait. These formats used to be meant only for a very small group of high ranking or very talented individuals, though they started to be accessible for an ever-growing number of people thanks to technological progress. According to Mirzoeff (2015):

> The self-portrait showed to others the status of the person depicted. In this sense, what we have come to call our "image" – the interface of the way we think we look and the way others see us – is the first and fundamental object of global visual culture. The selfie depicts the drama of our own daily performance of ourselves in tension with our inner emotions that may or may not be expressed as we wish. (p. 31)

Yet, during their own art production, the students barely worked with the classic format of the selfie in a direct manner. Reflections on working with the portrait or the self-portrait appeared more often, impacted by the aforementioned post-digital hybrid approach, where an awareness of the existence of the selfie is present and implicitly contained. At first glance, the staged self-portraits edited in postproduction, which became the basis of student Lukáš Kohl's video, are a far cry from the selfie's essential formal traits – that is, from a detailed photograph of one's own face, often taken from above. Selfies

often serve or may serve as 'memory "trophies" that document one's accomplishments (e.g., finishing a marathon) or experiences (e.g., visiting the Eiffel
Tower)' (Eliseev & Marsh, 2021, p. 1078). On the contrary, these are fantasy portrait scenes, in which laboriously prepared masks and costumes, influenced by
the student's interest in popular culture, primarily in film at that time, played a
principal role. His video entitled *Manifold* is a memory of his secondary school
studies, during which he took photos of his temporary changes or the dou-
bling, multiplication of his own identity:

> Costumes, photomontages, dreams ... I have had many looks and identi-
> ties. And I shared them with others. *The video Manifold* goes back to some
> of them, reflecting on the human urge to hide behind masks – material,
> immaterial, social. Are we aware of our masks? And why is showing our
> real face the hardest thing at times? (Kohl, 2022)

Lukáš Kohl's video is an example of the unflagging permeation of the digital
and material worlds, so characteristic of post-digital art. It utilises photographic
material obtained from the student's own social media profile, which was created by using real costumes. The profile pictures from different time periods
were converted into classic linear drawing. The drawings were then digitalised
again for the purposes of the video, in which they mutually intersect and permeate one another, creating the impression of an ever-accelerating, cyclical
metamorphosis, culminating in a cathartic revelation of his face. Simultaneously, the video *Manifold* is also an apt reflection on self-presentation and

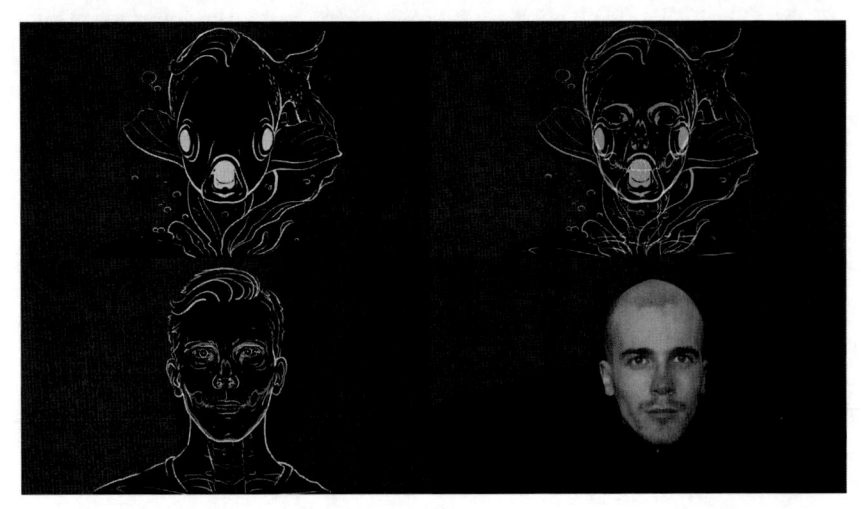

FIGURE 4.5   Lukáš Kohl, Manifold, 1 video shote, 2022

FIGURE 4.6
Zuzana Trojovská, Profile pictures, installation, 2022. View of the exhibition *A Rack for Memories*, Artivist Lab Gallery (photograph by Adriána Vančová)

image creation, on seeking and creating one's own identity, on the need (not) to fulfil society's expectations, or, as the case may be, to (momentarily) step out of them.

In her work *Profile pictures,* Zuzana Trojovská worked with self-portraits, as well as conversions of a material artefact into a digital form and back. These were classic self-portrait drawings, watercolours, and the artist's plaster self-portrait, too. At certain point in time, the student used these works of art, or more precisely, photographs of them, as her profile pictures on Facebook:

> The album of profile pictures on social media is a record of self-presentation over time. Apart from the digital collection, I also assemble a physical collection in a drawer. What both have in common is an intentional or random deformation (Who shows reality in full?). Some of the pictures have become part of my digital footprint, so it is not enough to just close the drawer. (Trojovská, 2022)

Her drawer installation of individual artefacts refers to the phenomenon of private archive. We assemble and hide objects that are significant to us, our own or other people's notes, photographs. In a material form, such a private archive may take the form of a journal that we hide somewhere, or a drawer that we close or open depending on our needs. On social media, it is not so easy though. The private and intimate plain is antithetical to the nature of social media that focus on social interaction and on sharing current events. But what happens to the data that we amass over the years?

The motif of the head appeared in the students' works in the form of a wig as a trophy and as an abstract object a few times. Anna Hůlková used the head as an archetypal object – a sphere or an ovoid – that has both an exterior, as well as an interior. What the student created was an almost surreal pending object – an anonymous plaster head, reminiscent of a hollow eggshell

FIGURE 4.7
Anna Hůlková, Identity, hanging object, 2022.
View of the exhibition *A Rack for Memories*,
Artivist Lab Gallery (photograph by Adriána
Vančová)

containing a fragment of a broken mirror inside. This 'cave' functioned first as a metaphor for inner life, i.e., of memory, too; or using the current vocabulary, of an internal 'network' or 'data storage'. At the same time, such a notion evokes the vision of external storage, and hence also the shift from the human to the technological. The spectator's reflection in the mirror inside the plaster head shows us another human, without whom interpersonal interaction and communication would not be possible. Their temporary or seeming presence then evokes the vision or a direct, remote form of communication.

7   Performance, Exhibition, Invisible Curator

Let us now try consider various forms of interpersonal interaction on social media and the digital footprint that we leave and amass over the years, through the metaphors of *performance* (Goffman, 1959) and the *exhibition* (Hogan, 2010). The issue of showing off and of showing one's own image relates to the format of the selfie and global visual culture in general – i.e., to online social media, too. 'Each selfie', according to Mirzoeff (2015), 'is a performance of a person as they hope to be seen by others' (p. 62). Self-presentation and showing off assumes the presence of a spectator or an audience, of someone for whom we stage our behaviour, for whom we 'perform'. Thus, we find ourselves engaging in reflections about forms of interpersonal interaction comparable to a theatre performance, as suggested by Erving Goffman (1959) in his influential book *The Presentation of Self in Everyday Life*.

Despite the concept being over 60 years old, it is precisely thanks to its focus on the phenomenon of self-presentation as a theatre performance that Goffman's dramaturgical approach at the interface of sociology a psychology is still very inspirational for reflections on online media and online interaction.[11] According to Goffman (1959), this takes place in a specific space and a specific time, which is identical for both the actor and their spectators. In a performance, we can differentiate between *frontstage* and *backstage*, where *front* refers to 'that part of the individual's performance which regularly functions in a general and fixed fashion to define the situation for those who observe the performance' (p. 22). By contrast, *backstage* or the *back region* is a place where we can step out of the role. Thus, it is 'a place relative to a given performance, where the impression fostered by the performance is knowingly contradicted as a matter of course' (Goffman, 1959, p. 112). The idea of everyday self-presentation as a situationally embedded theatre performance and its most visible *frontstage* corresponds very well with the character of online social media, mainly with their focus on the present and present events. 'It matches well with the fact that behaviors in social media are socially embedded and observed, activating concerns about others' expectations' (Zhao et al., 2013, p. 1).

In relation to social media, Hogan (2010) widens Goffman's metaphor of performance with the metaphor of the exhibition in order to distinguish between 'the sorts of on-line spaces where actors behave with each other ("performance" spaces or behaviour regions) and "exhibition" spaces where individuals submit artefacts to show to each other' (p. 377). At the same time, Hogan defines an artefact as 'the result of a past performance and lives on for others to view on their time' (Hogan, 2010).

Social media are oriented towards societal interaction and towards the context of this interaction, which is by its very nature temporal, temporary. Thus, it is evident that it is precisely the dimension of temporal currency and the present, along with embedding the actor and the spectators in a given time, that are pivotal for each performance. If we record a performance, its character changes: it becomes a reproducible data footprint, or an artefact that we can view repeatedly, asynchronously, outside its original context. In the suggested exhibition approach, Hogan (2010) also considers the role of a third party: i.e., the role of a social media operator who provides space for an exhibition (that is, the space of a database, data storage) and who also provides a virtual curator for the artefacts. This invisible curator[12] who orders, newly organises and redistributes past data footprint, or exhibits it for us is an algorithm us. 'The role of the curator is to manage the preexisting content on behalf of the submitters' (Hogan, 2010, p. 382). Yet, apart from this invisible systemic curator, social media users themselves actively construct their own identities through self-presentation and thus function as curators of their own data footprint (Zhao et al., 2013). The metaphor of the exhibition therefore works also in the sense of the long-term and intentional creation of our own image, where we play an active curatorial role. We conceive of self-presentation on social media not only as narrating a story for others but also for ourselves, so that the individual posts match the coveted narrative or scheme.

8   Conclusion

Thus, we come back to the students' works of art and the topic of the course – the duality of the digital and real worlds, demonstrated by the visual depiction of memories and through sharing it on online social media. Using specific examples, we have been able to see that a characteristic trait of the current students' artistic production is a preference for material forms of an artwork, while various transitions between the material and the digital are reflected in its genesis. This hybrid, post-digital approach points to a mutual permeability of both spheres – experiencing the physical world is now inseparable from experiencing the digital world. This applies also to memory and remembering – those aspects are now also interconnected with digital and social media, whose tools we have included into the spectrum of living and experiencing. Data footprint from a more or less distant past are incentives to remember.

Reflections on the topics of temporal self-presentation and algorithmic, hence automatised redistribution of past data footprint naturally appeared in the students' works. The course's focus on the medium of exhibition – in the form of introductory initiation moments, their interpretation and most importantly, in the form of a final presentation of the students' works in a classic gallery space – motivated the students to reflect on this medium, to look at the topic retrospectively and to establish a connection between self-presentation in the digital and real space.

The metaphors of performance, exhibition, curator and artefact, used in order to describe the course and the different forms of interaction on social media, employ terms characteristic of disciplines in fine arts. Thus, they transfer schemes found in certain practices and theoretical thinking from one field to another, and, above all, apply the schemes common to the physical world to the digital world so that we can better understand it. Seen from this angle, thinking about art, exhibitions and curatorship becomes very topical; in fact, all the more topical since the current exhibition and curatorial practices offer an opportunity to develop trends in critical thinking and institutional critique: something that is very much needed in the digital world. Ultimately, what such a curatorial approach – in the sense of a creative intersection of theory and praxis, in the sense of creating and developing critical thinking, and, most importantly, in the sense of taking care of production, distribution and redistribution of both material and digital artefacts – offers is a new conception of an art teacher's role and approaches.

Notes

1   This study is a part of an reasearch project AMASS – Acting on the Margin – Arts as a Social Sculpture, Horizon 2020, Grant agreement ID: 870621. The AMASS project has been approved by the department of Science and reasearch at the Faculty of Education for realisation and data protection. Full description including security measures are described in the Directive No. 16/2018 available at https://cuni.cz/uken-804.html

2   The exhibition *A Rack for Memories* took place from 3 to 15 June 2022. A total of 16 students from the Department of Art Education at the Faculty of Education, Charles University: B. Bestajovská, S. Bobková, E. Císařová, P. Dusilová, A. Hůlková, M. Jonášová, P. Koberová, B. Koblasová, L. Kohl, M. Machalická, H. Mladá, J. Němec, K. Novotná, N. Petříková, A. Šikutová, Z. Trojovská. The exhibition curators were lecturers Vendula Fremlová and Michal Sedlák. The exhibition was accompanied by a printed text – a short exhibition catalogue with abstracts relating to the individual students' works of art referenced in this chapter.

3   Artivist Lab Gallery is non-state institution, led by artist and curator Tamara Moyzes. The gallery focuses on contemporary socially and politically engaged art. More information can be found on https://www.artivistlab.info/

4   Not as an official collateral of the Venice Biennale.

5   According to Cramer, a digital medium is one that transfers an impulse into a system of quantifiable units, e.g., in this sense, even a classic typewriter is a digital, not analogue tool.

6   The exhibition ZET Rack took place from 8 January to 2 April 2022 at Nevan Contempo Gallery in Prague.

7   The students had an opportunity to meet the artist in person and he gave them a tour of the exhibition.

8   The exhibition Post-digital Intimacy took place from 11 November 2021 to 10 July 2022 at the National Gallery in Prague (Trade Fair Palace). See https://www.ngprague.cz/en/event/3182/post-digital-intimacy

9   Novotná and Fremlová (2021) investigate the intertwined roles of the teacher and the curator.

10   Due to capacity issues, out of the 17 presented works produced by 16 students, we are limiting ourselves only to a number of selected works of art.

11   In the chapter referenced herein, Bernie Hogan offers a list of texts that have applied Goffman's dramaturgic approach to interaction in the setting of online media.

12   Nowadays, digital curatorship is a term describing to the work of an expert as part of research v databases, e.g., libraries. Similar to Hogan (2010, pp. 384–385), intentionally, I do not use this term here as it does not concern the issue of self-presentation on online social media.

References

Barlow, J. P. (1996). *A declaration of the independence of cyberspace.* John Perry Barlow Library. Retrieved June 23, 2022, from https://www.eff.org/cyberspace-independence

Blažíček, M. (2022). Blízkost, intimita, a co na to diváci? [Proximity, intimacy, and what about the spectators?] *Artalk.* Retrieved July 11, 2022, from https://artalk.cz/2022/01/03/blizkost-intimita-a-co-na-to-divaci/

Císařová, E. (2022). *Statuses* [Artwork]. Artivist Lab Gallery.

Cramer, F. (2014). What is 'post-digital'? *A Peer-Reviewed Journal About, 3*(1), 10–24. https://aprja.net//issue/view/8400

Deleuze, G., & Guattari, F. (1987). *A thousand plateaus: Capitalism and schizophrenia.* University of Minnesota Press.

Eliseev, E. D., & Marsh, E. J. (2021). Externalizing autobiographical memories in the digital age. *Trends in Cognitive Sciences, 25*(12), 1072–1081. https://doi.org/10.1016/j.tics.2021.08.005

Goffman, E. (1959). *The presentation of self in everyday life.* Anchor Books.

Hlaváčková, J. (2022). Úvod do věštění v postmediální době [An introduction to fortune-telling in post-modern times]. In J. Hlaváčková (Ed.), *Věštění z noční oblohy. Role fotografií v postmediální době* [Telling fortune from the night sky: The role of photographs in postmodern times] (pp. 8–39). House of Photography.

Hogan, B. (2010). The presentation of self in the age of social media: Distinguishing performances and exhibitions online. *Bulletin of Science, Technology & Society, 30*(6), 377–386. https://dx.doi.org/10.1177/0270467610385893

Hootsuite Inc. (2022). *DIGITAL 2022: A global overview report.* https://blog.hootsuite.com/social-media-statistics-for-social-media-managers/

Kohl, L. (2022). Manyfold. *A rack for memories. An exhibition of DAE PeF CU student works from seminars Workshop II – The contexts of art* [Catalogue sheet]. UNP.

Machalická, M. (2022). Facebook intervention of memories. *A rack for memories. An exhibition of DAE PeF CU student works a from seminars Workshop II – The contexts of art* [Catalogue sheet]. UNP

Marc Quinn studio. (2022). *Marc Quinn. HISTORYNOW* [Exhibition guide]. Museo Archeologico Nazionale di Venezia.

Mirzoeff, N. (2015). *How to see the world.* Penguin Books Ltd.

Novotná, M., & Fremlová, V. (2021). Neviditelní, kteří ukazují a vyprávějí [The invisible ones who show and narrate]. *Výtvarná výchova. Časopis pro výtvarnou a obecně estetickou výchovu školní a mimoškolní* [Art education: A magazine for curricular and extra-curricular art and general aesthetic education], 1–2, 6–30.

Prensky, M. (2001, October). Digital natives, digital immigrants Part 1. *On the Horizon, 9*(5), 1–6. https://doi.org/10.1108/10748120110424816

Sokołowska, M. (2021). Young talented sexy. Pathology of normality. Retrieved June 11, 2022, from https://u-jazdowski.pl/en/programme/project-room/mlodzi-zdolni-seksowni

Tamir, D. I., Templeton, E. M., Ward, A. F., & Zaki, J. (2018). Media usage diminishes memory for experiences. *Journal of Experimental Social Psychology, 76*, 161–168. https://doi.org/10.1016/j.jesp.2018.01.006

Trojovská, Z. (2022). Profile pictures. *A rack for memories. An exhibition of DAE PeF CU student works a from seminars Workshop II – The contexts of art* [Catalogue sheet]. UNP.

Tronto, J. C. (1998). An ethic of care. *Generations: Journal of the American Society on Aging, 22*(3), 15–20. https://www.jstor.org/stable/44875693

Zhao, X., Saleshi, N., Naranjit, S., Alwaalan, S., Voida, S., & Cosley, D. (2013). *The many faces of Facebook: Experiencing social media as performance, exhibition, and personal archive* [Conference paper]. CHI 2013: Changing perspectives, Paris. https://dx.doi.org/ 10.1145/2470654.2470656

CHAPTER 5

Music Technology and the Hybrid Classroom Model

Samuel Graden

Abstract

Technology is becoming commonplace in school curricula. The effectiveness of the digital music software GarageBand and BandLab for Education was evaluated in general music hybrid classrooms (simultaneous in-person and online learning) during the COVID-19 pandemic. Students both in-school and online accessed the music learning platforms equally well. The visual nature of the music technology helped students grasp musical concepts and identify musical changes. Both software can be accessed on a variety of electronic learning devices that both in-school and online students have available to them. No prior skills or knowledge are needed, and learning topics such as layering, form, editing and dynamics can be introduced and explored. This was a successful teaching method and outlet for student creativity and problem solving.

Keywords

music technology – loops – chorus – composition – layering

1   Introduction

> The answer is music technology. (Heeley, 2020a)

In September 2021, my school, like countless others worldwide, adopted a hybrid learning classroom model to accommodate in-school and online students equally during the COVID-19 pandemic. All staff and students had to reimagine how a typical 'classroom' operates, and the current music curriculum would have to change to accommodate the hybrid setting. Issues of synchronicity and lag on the Google Meet platform used by our school, the lack of instrumental resources available to online students, and the inability to directly interact with one another meant that music lessons could not continue as normal. To provide meaningful music instruction during hybrid learning, we needed to redesign the music curriculum to accommodate synchronous (real-time) and asynchronous (flexible time) learning and the needs of students across a range of locations and using a range of personal devices. We chose to focus on and incorporate music technology that was accessible to students, did not require formal musical skills, and could be accessed anywhere. The idea was that students could still make personal, meaningful music in compliance with school hybrid learning and curriculum expectations.

2   Process

> Learning is the residue of experience. (Swanwick, 1999)

The use of music technology was evaluated for two months with approximately two hundred forty Grade 6–8 students aged 11 to 14 at a private international school in the United Arab Emirates. Students at the school were segregated into boys and girls classes (in accordance with school protocol) with an equal number of boys and girls learning the same music technology lessons. Music classes met once a week, were taught by the same teacher, and were of mixed musical ability with less than 5% of the students taking private music lessons outside of school; most did not read any kind of formal music notation; and they had never used a DAW (Digital Audio Workstation) like GarageBand or BandLab before.

All students had access to personal electronic devices (either iPads or Chromebooks) which either came with the GarageBand IOS app (iPad) or were used to access the BandLab for Education website (Chromebook) depending on their device. Students working remotely joined the Google Meet for live instruction during music lessons and had access to video tutorials and PowerPoint instructional slides made by the teacher. These videos and PowerPoints were also available to in-school learners as a supplemental learning tool for asynchronous learning.

To facilitate learning and enable access for students of all ability levels, we followed the programmes 'Teaching Music with GarageBand for iPad' by Ben Sellers (2017) and 'BandLab for Absolute Beginners' by Phil Heeley (2020b). Both programmes start with and focus on loops to compose music. Loops are pre-recorded instrument samples that can be played automatically by touching them (in GarageBand IOS) or clicking and dragging them (in BandLab for Education). Loops cycle for a count of 4 or 8 beats in perfect time (see Appendix 1) and come in various loop packs with high-quality sound samples for 'hundreds of different instruments you wouldn't normally find in the classroom or at home' (Wardrobe & Heeley, 2019).

Our loops-based composition tasks were designed so that students without any prior musical skills or knowledge could make music and learn composition techniques such as layering (adding or subtracting different sounds on top of each other over time), editing tracks in the Mix Editor window (see Appendix 2), simple form structure of a Beginning/Middle/Ending or 'Intro/Chorus/Outro', and changes in volume or 'dynamics' (see Appendix 3). Higher ability students could add 'breaks' in their song, explore sound effects and compose longer form structures.

Students engaged in weekly composing tasks with loops to demonstrate their understanding of layering, editing, form, and dynamics. During class, students listened to and verbally reflected on each other's work, and the teacher documented these comments onto Google Classroom. The teacher also provided weekly feedback privately to the students via Google Classroom which students could respond to privately. Some of these private student comments are presented in Section 3 of the chapter.

The Final Project served as a culmination of the topics learned and included 'Required' and 'Encouraged' features to support and challenge the students (see Appendix 4). 'Required' features were to compose a 1 to 2-minute piece using the app to demonstrate a clean start and layering (see Appendix 2) with a fade-out at the end. Students had total creative freedom in terms of which loop instruments and genres were used, and they could add as many or as few loops as they wanted provided they met the 'Required' features of 1 to 2-minute time length, clean start, and layering. 'Encouraged' features were to include a fade-in at the beginning of the song, demonstrate use of Intro/Chorus/Outro form, adjust volumes so nothing was too loud or quiet, and ensure that sounds worked well together. The 'Encouraged' features aimed to help students structure a well-balanced and dynamic composition although the last feature 'sounds work well together' was very subjective, and the grading considered both the teacher's and students' opinions.

3   Outcomes

> I can't read any music ... but through technology I can get the music in me out. (Heeley, 2020a)

Students both in-school and online accessed the learning platforms equally well. Students effectively used loops to create songs demonstrating layering, form, and dynamics. The visual nature of the music technology helped students grasp the concepts. Students were very keen to give feedback to classmates, and this discussion affected composition revisions as well as the final grading. Sellers (2017) notes that:

> We find [that] a system of peer evaluation focuses minds and gets the best results from pupils ... Pupils seek feedback from their peers and if necessary change their composition in response.

When reflecting on classmates' work, students were able to identify when sounds changed and when they stayed static. Students complained when the song 'sounded the same all the time' and complimented when the song 'had good changes' reinforced by the graphic presentation of the loop tracks in the Mix Editor window (see Appendices 2 and 3).

Instrumental loops and style choices were very broad, ranging from Hard Rock, Trip Hop, Rhythm and Blues, and Orchestral. Heeley recommended four instrument requirements for beginners: drums, bass, melodic instrument and 'free choice' (Heeley, 2020b). Initially, we followed these guidelines, particularly the drums and bass instrumentation, but as time went on the students favored more open-ended instrumental choice.

The grade marks amongst in-school and remote learners were very consistent, and neither group showed a higher inclination toward music technology or loops-based composition than the other. However, boys' classes scored higher marks than girls' classes in all but one class, and the boys showed more enthusiasm in general toward music technology and the genres presented. Boys responded that these genres represented the type of music they would listen to casually in their free time, and it was clear that this impacted the students' music making in line with Lucy Green's informal learning philosophy (Green, 2008) which puts students' identification and relationship with music and genres at the heart of their music making. Girls did not comment on whether they related to the styles of music represented in the loop packs.

Overall, students enjoyed the ability to create their 'own music' and demonstrated an ownership in their music lessons. They were enthusiastic about making revisions and improving their work:

> Mister, I think I need to fix my automation, and change [the song to] make some sounds different. (Student X)

They also showed an interest in the music making process regardless of the grade they would receive:

> I like the extra bit, also if I get a low mark, I have another song (as a) backup. I added in the music as the FX (and) the radio sound to make a good intro and outro. (Student I)

Several students opted to continue working with music technology long after the unit finished:

> I made this song and I thought you might have a look at it and give feedback since I like doing it in my free time. It has nothing to do with the assignment. (Student I)

Technical issues were prevalent with both in-school and online students. Some were unavoidable (e.g., GarageBand IOS and Google Meet cannot run at the same time) and some merely required the user to restart the app or device, or to delete some other apps to make more storage space for their music. Technical issues provided problem-solving opportunities for students:

> Mister my GarageBand [wasn't] working so [I] did BandLab. I tried it [and] I hope you like my song. (Student A)

They also allowed opportunities for students to demonstrate their learning:

> Mr idk how to do this on GarageBand but I clicked ... Wait [Mr] I'll do a video and show u how I fixed it. (Student H)

Some students displayed completely independent learning when neither GargeBand IOS nor BandLab for Education worked on their device, and they resorted to other software:

> Mr this App [Ableton Learn] it's very [different] from GarageBand but see if it [is] nice. I made beats. (Student S)

4 Discussion

We found that music fundamentals can be successfully taught using readily available technology. The successful use of technology to facilitate music instruction has been documented in the literature. In an assessment of 'How an Educator uses BandLab in the Classroom' and 'Teaching with GarageBand for iPad', Heeley (2020b) and Sellers (2017) concluded that the visual natures of the software, ease of use and high-quality sounds engaged students to compose music that they identified with and related to.

The observation that boys performed well with the use of technology is consistent with other research findings (Stade, 2021; Fuller, 2014; Upitis, 1998; Lawry et al., 1994). Boys need practical, hands-on learning (Stade, 2021; Upitis, 1998) and the technology we used, with its visual graphics, animation, and touch-screen interaction, is a powerful kinesthetic tool (Stade, 2021; Upitis, 1998; Lawry et al., 1994). Girls typically do not engage with electronic music as well as boys and there are fewer women working in the electronic music industry than men (Le Vay, 2012).

Opportunities could have been made for more student project collaboration and, based on research, it is presumed that this approach would work well for both boys and girls classes (Lawry et al., 1994; Inkpen et al., 1999; Upitis, 1998). Ruthmann (2007) advocates a collaborative workshop approach in which listening to and analysing music serves as the building block for student composition and peer feedback.

Ruthmann's (2007) and Sellers' (2017) compositional requirements and use of technology were very similar to the process evaluated in our school: use loops to create interesting introductions and clear endings, refine transitions between sections, and explore contrast both instrumentally (different loop sounds) and dynamically (volume changes). Ruthmann (2007) also encourages an exploration and understanding of panning (left and right stereo sound placement).

Heeley's instrumental recommendations of drums, bass, 'melodic instrument', and 'free choice' (Heeley, 2020b) may have provided more structure for students, especially for those with lower ability that struggled to begin the task. Drums and bass provide the 'groove' and foundational harmony, and they are easily searchable in the BandLab for Education and GarageBand search engines. However, the 'melodic instrument' offers a greyer area of interpretation. Heeley suggests using instruments such as 'synths, keys, guitar or arp' (Heeley, 2020b) but these instrumental loops gear more towards harmonic accompaniment or 'background figures' that give the user no pitch or rhythmic control. We could offer instead a mixture of required instruments (drums and bass) and 'free choice' instruments as well as an exploration of MIDI (Musical Instrument Digital Interfaces) instruments where users have total control over the notes and rhythms they want to compose with.

The Final Project Rubric (see Appendix 4) was aimed at assessing students' technical capabilities with the software and demonstration of form and dynamics. Most students were keen to include 'Encouraged' features in their work (e.g. Fade-in at the beginning; Intro/Chorus/Outro form) because they were achievable, earned a higher mark, and helped the song sound more musical. However, the rubric can fall into the 'more is better' trap that Swanwick (1999) warns of where more 'Required' features or more 'Encouraged' features lead to a better grade without carefully considering the musicality of the song. For example, a student could compose a piece of music that starts with a 5 bar drum track, add bass at bar 17, add guitar at bar 18, take out guitar at bar 25, take out bass at bar 34, and fade out with drums at bar 37. S/he has met all five 'Required' features (time limit, clean start, layering, fade out, and recorded) and may have met 'Encouraged' features to earn an A*. But does this composition demonstrate musical understanding and musicality? Does it demonstrate phrasing, control of textures and sonorities, stylistic awareness, or use of silence as a compositional tool (Swanwick, 1999)? These are important questions that Swanwick (1999) challenges us with to mold our assessment framework away from the 'more is better' approach (or 'simple to complex') and focus more on musical understanding.

5   Concluding Remarks

Music technology is a viable educational tool for hybrid model music lessons and allows music educators to devise a modern curriculum that is accessible and interesting to students. Software programmes like GarageBand iOS and BandLab for Education are free to use and can be accessed on a variety of electronic learning devices that both in-school and online students have available to them. Loops-based music is accessible to learners across a wide range of learning styles and can be differentiated to challenge and support both high and low ability learners equally. No prior skills or knowledge are needed, and learning topics such as layering, form, editing and dynamics can be introduced and explored. Finally, creativity and technical problem-solving skills will prepare students to succeed in a technology-driven culture in the future.

References

Fuller, A. (2014). *Teaching boys*. Andrew Fuller. https://andrewfuller.com.au/wp-content/uploads/2014/08/Teaching-Boys.pdf

Green, L. (2008). *Music, informal learning and the school: A new classroom pedagogy* (1st ed.). Routledge.

Heeley, P. (2020a). *How a music educator uses BandLab in the classroom* [Blog]. BandLab. https://blog.bandlab.com/how-a-music-educator-uses-bandlab-in-the-classroom/

Heeley, P. (2020b). BandLab for absolute beginners: #1 Start making music today. *Inclusive Music*. https://www.youtube.com/watch?v=2LklV9EAvuI

Inkpen, K., Upitis, R., Klawe, M., Lawry, J., Anderson, A., Ndunda, Mutindi., Sedighian, K., Leroux, S., & Hsu, D. (1999). We have never-forgetful flowers in our garden: Girls' responses to electronic games. *Journal of Computers in Mathematics and Science Teaching, 13*(4), 383–403.

Lawry, J., Upitis, R., Klawe, M., Anderson, A., Inkpen, K., Ndunda, M., Hsu, D., Leroux, S., & Sedighian, K. (1994). Exploring common conceptions about boys and electronic games. *Electronic Games for Education in Math and Science, 14*(4), 439–459.

Le Vay, L. (2012). It's different for girls: Women in dance music. *Attack Magazine*. https://www.attackmagazine.com/features/long-read/its-different-for-girls-women-in-dance-music/2/

Ruthmann, A. (2007). The composers' workshop: An approach to composing in the classroom. *Music Educators Journal, 93*(4), 38–43.

Sellers, B. (2017). *Teaching music with GarageBand for iPad* (2nd ed., pp. 16–34). Independent Publisher's Network.

Stade, L. (2021). *4 Powerful ways to help boys with learning at school*. Linda Stade Education. https://lindastade.com/teaching-boys/

Swanwick, K. (1999). *Teaching music musically* (1st ed.). Routledge.

Upitis, R. (1998). From hackers to luddites, game players to creators: Profiles of adolescent students using technology. *Journal of Curriculum Studies, 30*(3), 293–318.

Wardrobe, K., & Heeley, P. (2019). *The music tech teacher podcast: MTT97: Inclusive music making with Phil Heeley*. Music Tech Teacher. https://musictechteacher.libsyn.com/mtt97-inclusive-music-making-with-phil-heeley

Appendix 1

Instruments are shown pictorially on the left-hand column and the loops are shown as blue or yellow ('smart drum') squares. The user touches loops to start and/or stop them, and loops cycle a count of 4 or 8 beats in perfect time. The user can play many different loops at a time and 'layer' them into the song but can only play one loop per instrument at a time (e.g. one guitar loop, one drum loop, one bass loop).

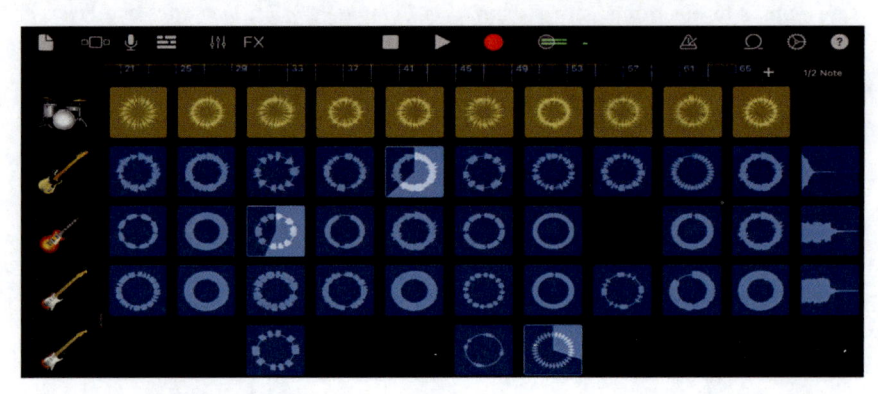

FIGURE 5.1   Loops in garageband

Appendix 2

Once Loops are recorded, they appear as blue or yellow ('smart drum) tracks in the Mix Editor. These can be dragged, copied, shortened, lengthened, or split.

An emphasis was made in the criteria that students should have 'clean starts' with the first track lined up to 'beat 1 of bar 1'.

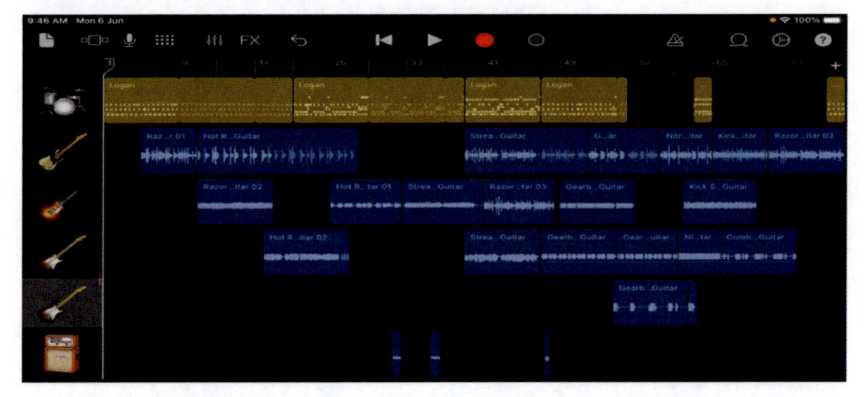

FIGURE 5.2   Garageband mix editor

Appendix 3

The user 'unlocks' and enables volume changes (top-left icon) and clicks, drags, and adds points (yellow dots) to the volume automation lines (yellow lines). When the automation line goes up, the volume increases; when the line goes down, the volume decreases; when the line stays horizontal, the volume stays the same.

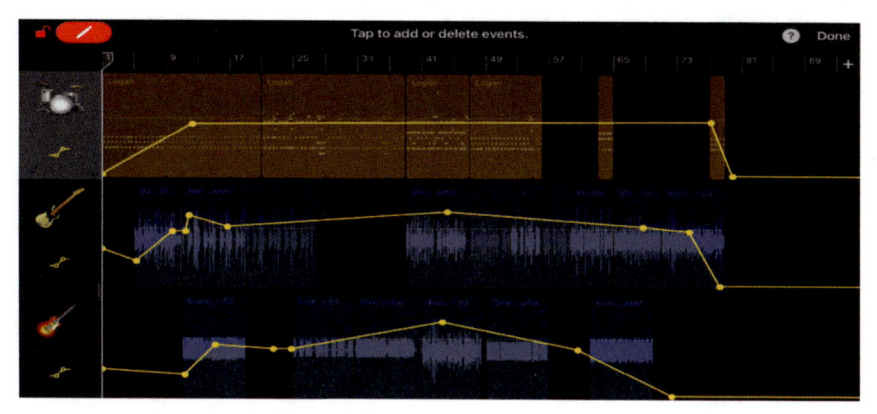

FIGURE 5.3   Automation volume control

Appendix 4

These guidelines were made by the teacher to help support and challenge students. Grades were based on the inclusion of 'Required' and 'Encouraged' criteria (layering, form, editing, dynamics) and on student critiques and feedback during the lesson.

Create a 1 to 2-minute song using GarageBand Loops and/or Smart Instruments

Required:
- *Recorded* in app (so you can edit and add *Automation*)
- *Clean start*: music starts on Beat 1 of Bar 1
- *Layering*: adding and subtracting sounds over time
- *Automation*: fade-out at end
- *Time: 1 to 2 minutes* (about 35–50 bars of music)

Encouraged:
- *Automation*: fade-in at beginning
- *Form*: Intro/Chorus/Outro (use *Layering* to *build your song up* to Chorus then *take away sounds to* Outro)

– *Adjust volumes* so nothing is too loud or too quiet
– *Sounds work well together!* (What will your classmates think when they hear your song?)

TABLE 5.1   Final project rubric

0 (0/10)	C (> 5.5/10)	B (6–7/10)	A (8–9/10)	A* (9.5 < 10)
Did not submit	Very little criteria met	Some criteria met	Most criteria met	All criteria met
	Has 1 or 2 *Required features*	Has 3 or more *Required features*	Has 4 or 5 *Required features*	Has 5 *Required features*
			Has 1 or more *Encouraged features*	Has 3 or more *Encouraged features*

CHAPTER 6

Community-Based Art Education in a Pandemic World

Maintaining and Building an "Art-Home" in a Time of Isolation

David LeRue, Catherine Wells, Kristina Urquhart, Jeannie Kyunjin Kim, Breanna Shanahan, Simone Aresnault-May and Nadia Kuehn

Abstract

Art educators have faced significant challenges in reaching their students during the COVID-19 pandemic, and this challenge has been doubly difficult in community art schools where participation in classrooms is voluntary and financial precarity is the norm. In this chapter, teachers and administrators from the Pointe-Saint-Charles Art School in Montreal, Quebec, will discuss how the pandemic has affected and changed our community art school, which aims to offer affordable and free high-quality art instruction to artists of all ages and social, linguistic and economic backgrounds. Considering this, we will describe the challenges and successes of adapting our in-person art school to meet restrictions that required physical isolation, and societal conditions that required re-thinking the role of art in the lives of our students. We will discuss how our mission to build an "art-home", meaning a place where artists of all levels and interests can come and develop their practice and share their insights in a community, guided our decision-making process, leading to adapting and creating in-person, online and informal programming, including exhibitions, outdoor arts activities, online classes and the launching of a community art therapy program. We will also consider how lockdowns challenged the administrative structure of the school, and how the pressure of the pandemic required working through competing visions and pressures for our staff members. We will conclude with some greater lessons we have gleaned from these challenges, and how these will implement the vision of the school going forward.

Keywords

arts administration – art therapy – community-based art education – online learning – pandemic learning

1   Introduction

Art educators have faced significant challenges in reaching their students during the COVID-19 pandemic, and this has been doubly difficult in community
art schools where participation in classrooms is voluntary and funding is often
precarious. The Pointe-Saint-Charles Art School has historically relied on volunteers and fees collected from students to cover our costs, but the COVID-19
pandemic and associated lockdown forced us to re-imagine our role in offering
art education to the community built from years of an in-person presence. This
chapter aims to give an honest re-telling of our school's triumphs and struggles
throughout the pandemic lockdowns of 2020/21. We begin by introducing our
school and its values, and what sustained our growth before the pandemic. We
will then consider how COVID lockdowns forced us to re-imagine our role in the
world and how we innovated out of necessity to move both outside and online
during lockdowns which led to building an online art community and developing regular and periodic outdoor programming. Coincidental to the lockdowns
was the implementation of our art therapy program, which as we will explain,
was a critical service for the many we were able to serve during lockdowns.
Later, we will consider how the administration adapted, grew and struggled
to overcome emergent challenges brought on by the moment, including navigating funding, relationships strained by the moment and diverging interests
within our school. We will close by discussing how the experience of the pandemic has influenced our offerings moving forward toward a post-pandemic
world.

2   School Background and Values

Our school was founded in a small storefront in 2015, aiming to give affordable,
high-quality art classes to students of any artistic level in Montreal's Sud-Ouest.
The Sud-Ouest was built up over the industrial period to house workers and
their families, many of whom at the factories spread along the Lachine Canal,
a shipping corridor that opened in 1825 that handled all boat traffic headed
in and out of the Great Lakes. After the dredging of the St. Lawrence Seaway
in the 1960s, the canal closed while most factories moved offshore, leaving
the Sud-Ouest economically depressed for decades. While nearby neighborhoods in the Sud-Ouest changed drastically through urban renewal projects,
activist citizens of Pointe-Saint-Charles, particularly women, fought for the
preservation of the neighborhood while fighting for the critical social services

needed for a vibrant community (Hammond, 2016). The spirit of activism and solidarity continues today and influences the foundations of our school. We are housed in a restored industrial building called Bâtiment 7, which had initially been sold to build a casino and entertainment complex at the edge of our neighborhood (Bisson, 2008). Some long-time residents feared the social impact of a casino in their neighborhood and thought the building could go to better use in the hands of the community. After over a decade of activism and struggle by community activist organisation 7 À Nous, possession was turned over in 2017, with the first phase of development that included the art school opening in 2018.

Our school was formed organically through conversations about what art offers to a community, and what it means to develop a community of like-minded artists. Our mission is to bring arts programming to as many people as possible, aiming to create an "art-home", meaning a place where those interested in art can come and feel stimulated and fulfilled in meeting their artistic goals with others who share their vision. This has led to ongoing programming for all ages, and a recurring community of individuals from a variety of social, linguistic and economic backgrounds. Our goal is to make all our programming accessible or free to those without the means to pay, and as such, we offer free workshops fulfilled by volunteers or funded with grant money and have partnered with many educators and academics to offer classes to the community. We also have regular exhibitions featuring student, community and instructor work in our own spaces and in other spaces loaned or leased to us within the city. These exhibitions have provided an opportunity to feature student work to the community, and to have moments of gathering to celebrate the accomplishments and practices of our teachers and students.

2.1 Onset of the Pandemic

Like many community-run organisations, the pandemic put our very survival at stake. When the shutdown first happened, we closed completely for a planned two weeks with hopes for a quick return to normal. It became clear however that pandemic regulations would make a return to in-person learning impossible for at least a few months, halting our classes and costing us our primary form of funding and engagement. Fortunately, there was pandemic support from the federal government meant that meant we could afford salaries and rent, with funding from grants that made up the difference. But given that our teachers work on a commission of the fees collected, many of them lost income. Our school could survive in this context administratively, but financial survival is not the same as maintaining a vibrant community and surviving past the initial pandemic aid required us to re-develop our programming.

3 Pandemic Programming

Our mission guided us and informed the re-development of our programming after we initially struggled to reach our community in the digital world. Our re-development focused on moving outside and moving online, which was conjoined with some in-person programming which quietly continued at reduced capacity with regular long-time students. Both online programing and the outdoor club began to develop sub-communities within our school which continues today. Additionally, our Art Therapy program was scheduled to open in fall, 2020, but incidentally became a critical part of our online offerings. In this section, we will elaborate on the successes and complications of each of our offerings and discuss how they have informed the school moving forward.

3.1 *Art Therapy*

Our art therapy program began online in 2020/21, moving to a hybrid online and in-studio offering in 2021/22. It has long been a vision of our co-founder Catherine Wells, herself a certified Art Therapist, to build an art therapy program at our school to address the needs for therapy she believes our society is lacking. For her, art therapy can provide the means for productive self-reflection through artmaking, leading to personal growth and emotional well-being. She believes a key concept of art therapy is that images can help when words are hard to find. We found that being able to support mental health in our community through visual art was an additional way for us to fulfill our mission to bring art to everyone. This included private sessions, where one or two participants worked with a therapist, and group sessions, where seven or eight people gathered, with a therapist to lead the session. Generally, participants reported that the sessions were helpful to combat the isolation and anxiety from the pandemic, and that mental well-being improved. Furthermore, a representative of the school would deliver art materials to the door, which seemed to humanise the otherwise impersonal online interactions. While art therapy is necessarily separated from many of our other offerings, this has still led to cross over – many of our students took art therapy, and many in art therapy took classes in our school. While the timing of the implementation of this program was coincidental, it helped us to contribute to our community's mental health and wellbeing during the pandemic isolation while contributing to our engagement and relationships within our neighborhood. The art therapy program also strengthened our connection with Concordia University, who were supportive of our initiative and provided interns to our site. We are working with them in partnership to develop our program further.

3.2   *Moving Outside*

We began developing outdoor programming when we learned that outdoor transmission of the virus was less likely, making it safer for our school's older population to come together and make art. This led to the creation of the Outdoor Club and short to medium length outdoor workshops. The Outdoor Club was developed by Wells, who was reading about artists who maintain outdoor studio practices year-round, which many in our community found inspiring given the punishingly cold winters. Wells remarked on the tricks plein-aire artists use when working outdoors, such as how watercolourists mix water with Vodka to keep it from freezing. The club met once a week in a predetermined location in the city, choosing sites such as local heritage buildings, museums, waterways and lookoffs, where participants would continue self-directed learning in a community of other artists. Sometimes sessions would go on for many hours, with participants developing drawings over longer periods of time that they would then turn into paintings in the studio. In moments of extreme cold, the sessions might last 20 minutes because the air made fingers hurt almost immediately, although one student remarked on the liberating and creative effect of drawing with gloves on! A core group developed that met in all weather, huddled underneath awnings on rainy days or in glass bus stops in the cold Montreal snow. It has allowed us to visit local locations and has made the school more visible to the public, who often happen upon the group and ask questions. The Outdoor Club invigorated a love for landscape and on-site

FIGURE 6.1   Left: Students sketching in the outdoor club, 2021; right: Student figure drawings from outdoors, 2020 (photographs by Nadia Kuehn)

artistic practices among our students, continuing to generate a variety of artworks of our neighborhood in all seasons.

Most of our partnerships and funding developed over COVID focused on outdoor art activities, allowing us to offer free outdoor classes and workshops dealing with everything from ecology, landscape, drawing, watercolour, knitting, urban landscape and mending to name a few. These workshops ranged from one-offs to workshop series, and were taught by both our own instructors, art therapists and guest instructors and academics undertaking their own work. These workshops often blended aspects and were generally well attended and received, attracting students of all levels, ages and backgrounds to our school who otherwise did not have the means or the time to attend regular ongoing classes. This began with a series of workshops led by our art therapy interns that conjoined therapy and ecology, leading to our instructors to further experimenting with what the outdoors can offer art, such as Well's class *Breathing with Trees*, where students attending the workshop conjoined mindfulness and sketching practices, or co-author Kristina Urquhart's *Middle Summer Sun Lantern* workshop, where students created a keepsake from the summer to remind them of warmth in winter. These initiatives also brought access to students who were uncomfortable with being indoors during COVID, and by making things in places the public gathers anyway, welcomed an encounter with the arts from people who might never step foot in our school. Moving outside helped to ground our school and our human presence within the built environment and made art programming an unavoidable part of the neighborhood.

3.3 Online Offerings and Classes

Moving online was no small feat for our school, as our long-time participants tend to be older adults with less experience with technology. We had initially feared how this might prove difficult but given the overall societal familiarity with software like Zoom, we decided to try it starting small. Our first online offering was an Open Studio, which started early in the pandemic but has anchored our online presence through to today. Students from our school, community members, our admin and some of our teachers meet weekly to work on guided or personal projects over Zoom, which created an avenue for open exchange that touched on projects assigned in our classes, in collective making of a similar image or from participants working on their own projects. Early in the pandemic the environment on these calls was generally one of excitement and care, creating a unique opportunity to buoy the community of the art school during the early days of the pandemic. The aversion to Zoom we had feared seemed to dissipate after a couple sessions, with participants doing weekly check-ins with each other that ranged from the artistic to the personal. The atmosphere gave participants and the school some semblance of a community, offering a weekly gathering place to hone artistic identities.

In October 2020, intern David LeRue (2023) launched a free online class called *Landscaping the City*, which was focused on applying landscape principles and frameworks to students' neighborhoods. At that point of the pandemic, there were still backed-up supply chains, which meant that even the most basic materials could not be expected from the students. While students were welcome to use whatever materials they had, the class required only a sketchbook and pencil, which in turn were the materials the instructor used for demonstrations. This class attracted about 15 participants of various ages, backgrounds and abilities. Class met weekly for two hours and thirty minutes and discussed one or two drawing exercises that would build toward optional homework for the week, which often sent students out into their neighborhood to gather images or to draw on site. Exercises taught drawing skills while asking students reflect on how they relate to the social and aesthetic aspects of their neighborhood. The final weeks of the class culminated in a final project, where the students took elements they found interesting from the earlier portion of the class and developed it into a single or multiple artworks.

The Power of Possessions ran for five weeks in the fall of 2021, building on the momentum of open studio and *Landscaping the City*, welcoming many of the same students into our online learning community. The class was taught by artist and educator Jeannie Kyunjin Kim (2020), who turned elements of her research-creation master's thesis on chaekgeori paintings, which is a Korean still-life painting genre depicting a scholars' collection of unique and original items in stacked, flat compositions (Figure 6.2). According to Cho and Lee (1990), this flatness led to distorted perspectives and pictorial choices such as no backgrounds further abstracting and marking the medium. After reviewing traditional and contemporary chaekgeori paintings, students were asked to gather objects meaningful to them and work through drawing exercises to develop compositions that formed the basis of a final class project in a medium of their choosing. Students were invited to interpret these principles freely and project their own practices into their projects. The in-class activities were designed to ensure instruction translated effectively online in the form of simple prompts, and for student engagement to be possible. For instance, the activity for Week 1 was to workshop the definitions of the terms possession, book and tool. Kim first asked them what comes to their minds when they hear these words, and then while sharing my screen, she directly edited a PowerPoint presentation

FIGURE 6.2   Example of chaekgeori painting (Jeannie Kyunjin Kim, 2020; Untitled [painting and digital photograph]; collection of the artist)

with their answers. For the term 'tool', the words and phrases students thought of were: Helpful, facilitation, making things easier, ingenuity (creating something to help us), and utilitarian. She then wrapped up the activity by stating the importance of not letting textbook definitions restrict our knowledge, especially what constitutes a scholar's tool, and the significance of stepping out of traditions to find true meaning within our possessions and tools. For Kim, this posed an interesting moment to engage in cultural appreciation, and to share this style and method of Korean painting with a group of non-Korean students from our community.

Daily Art Practice was taught in fall and winter 2021/2022 by artist and educator Breanna Shanahan, who developed the class out of her own experiences trying to maintain an artistic practice during the pandemic. For many artists, the pandemic was isolating, so Author 5 and others got together to socialise and to challenge each other to fulfill timed art prompts in quick succession. She drew inspiration from artists like Ed Pien (n.d.), who made many three-minute drawings in quick succession over many years so that he might make millions in his career like the greats such as Jonathan Borofsky. Like Pien, Shanahan found that this method of drawing encouraged artists to be intuitive, and

FIGURE 6.3   Example of 30 minutes of 3-minute drawings (Breanna Shanahan, 2021, Untitled
[watercolour and ink]; collection of the artist)

to cycle through many ideas in short order. This informed the structure and layout of the class, which was designed to encourage students to be focused and prolific in their practice. Each *Daily Art Practice* began with 30 minutes of three-minute drawings, followed by a thematic weekly lecture that would be meant to give some background into contemporary artists and techniques and practice, such as collage, music and writing prompts. The themes likewise would take on contemporary questions and issues, such as AI being developed to create drawings, or different machines artists would develop to make marks. These lectures would inform and inspire new processes and ways of working that were taken up in exercises until the end of the class.

3.4   Successes and Challenges with Online Learning

Online pedagogy challenged what we thought might be of interest within community education, with our students rigorously engaging with three unique and challenging courses. *Landscaping the City* interjected questions about urban development into the community classroom and asked how students could take up complicated questions about their neighborhoods and make quality projects drawing on their own lives. Some of the work became a publication, with many pieces submitted to in-person exhibitions from the school. *The Power of Possessions* pushed students to experiment with other visual cultures and brought research-creation scholarship into the community classroom. Although sharing brief lessons of chaekgeori paintings was feasible, for Kim, there were limitations to instructing art techniques online as students naturally worked independently throughout the creation process, gaining ownership of their practice and mediums. *Daily Art Practice* ran three times and counting, helping to elevate our online programming for students hoping to develop contemporary art practices. The class demanded a lot from students but grew a large following of new and accomplished artists who created many complete artworks. Shanahan also mounted a virtual vernissage in software called ArtSteps, which brought the three-minute creations into a virtual white cube gallery. For the students, this elevated their greatest hits – over 80 works in total – into a space where they could invite their friends and family to experience the work, garnering even further interest in our classes.

Online programming consistently encountered the limits of teaching art through screens, with our instructors having to find workarounds to explain concepts and teach skills. In a classroom, instructors can circulate and check up on students, making corrections or conducting on-the-fly adjustments as necessary. Online workarounds were sometimes small such as asking students to hold work up to their camera to share with the instructor or classmates or using videos to show basic techniques. Some instructors developed camera set-ups to demonstrate techniques so they could explain them in real-time. Additionally, conventional wisdom for drawing pedagogy is that working from life is preferable to photography. According to the often-referenced drawing instructor Betty Edwards (2012), our eyes capture more depth, detail and colour than photographs, with photographs making critical decisions such as composition and cropping for us. In this view, drawings are about documenting our own perception as much as they are about rendering, and thus our growth as artists is expedited by working from life. In *The Power of Possessions* and *Landscaping the City*, students were encouraged to draw from observation when possible, the former asking students to use objects to create compositions in their own homes. In *Landscaping the City,* students were asked to draw outdoors from life outside class time, but in-class lessons used images shared through Zoom to practice the lessons of the day. Nevertheless, students demonstrated growth in applying these techniques to real life without much apparent trouble. The transmissibility from the screen to reality has some basis in emerging research around 2D art practices. For example, the Drawing Lab at the Nova Scotia College of Art and Design has studied the habits of many artists by having them either drew directly onto screens or draw from screens without much trouble after some initial practice (Burk et al., 2022). In LeRue's view, working from life is preferable, but students nevertheless demonstrated growth after working from screens.

As most of our offerings have moved to in-person, we maintain our online footprint. Many of the same students signed up for the online classes, developing a community of learners living in other neighborhoods and other provinces who might not ordinarily have time to travel to the school for class or art therapy. Furthermore, there are others who choose to remain online for either preference or fears of COVID. This has created a sub-community within the school that has helped us to grow in an area we never previously considered. It has fostered the experimentation that has helped our school to grow to this point, challenging our teachers to push their pedagogical approaches. Challenges remain with online programming, however, such as finding ways to make it financially sustainable. Initially, classes were free before switching to a pay-what-you-can model, which netted only a fraction of the true value of the classes. Eventually, we began to advertise the full value of the class, which did increase donations to levels that make the paycheck worthwhile for the teachers. Overall, the school considers online learning a surprisingly successful endeavor, with classrooms being jovial and warm environments even through the filter of Zoom.

4   Decision Making and Administration

Before COVID-19 lockdowns, our administration was largely organic, with decisions often made collectively during the many hours individuals shared the physical space of the art school. While writing this chapter, there was romantic reflection on the time before COVID, as decisions seemed to come over the course of conversations and did not feel rushed or urgent. Being physically present also meant that we had more volunteers who would come and go from the school without needing to necessarily be introduced to our ways of doing things. Lockdown however created urgency in our decision making and began to ask for a lot more mental space from employees and volunteers alike. In the first eight months of lockdown, we grew from three paid part-time employees to six on increased available funding from grants and pandemic benefits. While we lost more casual volunteers, we gained some who took on more substantial roles in the school. This still proved difficult, as the school administration to this point has relied on a shared love of art and community. When many of our staff and volunteers were dealing with other life stresses from the pandemic, work at the school became less prioritised.

Issues were compounded by our attempt to reach sustainability, as we took on more grants and programming which was a testament to our reputation and our growth, but also challenged our capacities and decision-making models. Taking on more made it clear that our processes for making decisions were incompatible with Zoom meetings, and many of our core members were exhausted with keeping up with the constant meetings needed to maintain the administrative load. For the first time since our founding, decisions became contentious which made meetings stressful. At various points, members of our administration took time away, and further discussions were needed to resolve conflicts that began to arise between members who developed seemingly competing visions for our school's priorities. This became most pronounced when we began to meet again in-person, after the pandemic supports ended and our money dwindled. The pandemic supports meant we could grow larger, but we failed in achieving an organisation that could sustain the number of salaries and projects. We had said yes too often and to too many things, which stretched many members thin. We have mutually agreed that to maintain our love for art, the school and each other, we will have to be more deliberate in what we seek out and say yes to going forward.

5   Greater Lessons and Future Plans

The successes of our online and outdoor content have shown us how important it is to foster a community within our school, and to maintain our principle of creating an art-home for our students and staff. However, over lockdown the various pedagogical and administrative aspects of our school became siloed, which caused tremendous stress on our school as we moved past lockdown causing us to become overextended as we maintained our various components. This has caused us to keep in mind the workloads we are taking on and can organically sustain, but also work to create cohesion among our various elements. In the past year, we have made efforts to connect these parts by hosting four large-scale exhibitions, one in Bâtiment 7 where we are housed and three others at a loaned storefront in a nearby tourist area. These have helped to make our mission feel connected, to bring together current students, volunteers and staff of the school and to show the products of our classes and initiatives to the greater community. We have become keenly aware of how our art school is interdependent on layers of community – the Community of our shared industrial development, neighboring non-profits, the greater area of our neighborhood and the art world of our city and beyond have worked together as an ecosystem which without each part we might not have survived.

We realise that the structure of the art school that we long for from before the pandemic may never return, as the changes we have gone through over lockdown are also symptomatic of our growth. In reflecting through this writing, we believe it is more important than ever for community art education initiatives such as our school to persist. The belief that art is for everybody is shared by most in community-based practice, but holding this value does nothing to build the social infrastructure needed to deliver it. Rather, making art accessible requires the love, sweat and tears that go into a venture as precarious and rewarding as ours – it requires procuring quality professionals such as therapists and teachers, the resources to pay them and the space to gather. It requires approaching our community with dignity, and actively working to break down the walls that have been built accidentally through a lack of education and understanding about art in the public school system, and intentionally through a lack of access and elitism that persist in many art spaces. While the last years have challenged our resolve, we believe that we have a lot of space to grow, believing now more than ever that the mission of our art school will resonate long into the future.

References

Bisson, B. (2008, October). AMT: projet de 168 millions à Pointe-Saint-Charles. *La Presse.*

Burk, A., Christie, J., Fedak, T., Klein, R. M., Liu, G., Maycock, B., Reichertz, M., & Wong, J. (2022). *Researching the teaching of drawing* (R. M. Klein, Ed.). Vernon Press.

Cho, C., & Lee, U.-H. (1990). *Traditional Korean painting: A lost art rediscovered* (1st ed). Kodansha International.

Edwards, B. (2012). *Drawing on the right side of the brain* (4th ed). Tarcher/Penguin.

High, S. C. (2022). *Deindustrializing Montreal: Entangled histories of race, residence, and class.* McGill-Queen's University Press.

Hammond, C. (2018). The keystone of the neighbourhood: Gender, collective action, and working-class heritage strategy in Pointe-Saint-Chales, Montreal. *Journal of Canadian Studies/Revue d'études Canadiennes, 52*(1), 108–148.

Kim, J. K. (2020). *Korean Chaekgeori paintings: A research-creation approach to intercultural art education and heuristic thinking* (Doctoral dissertation). Concordia University.

Pien, E. (n.d.). *Image bank 3-minute drawings 1996–* [Artist's website].
    https://www.edpien.com/3minutedrawings
LeRue, D. (2022). Landscaping the city: Place-based online learning in the time of pan-
    demic. *Canadian Art Teacher, 19*(1), 7–11.

CHAPTER 7

"Drama Education in the Distance, Really?! ... Really!"

Ways of Adapting Drama Education in Czechia and Slovakia in the First COVID-19 Lockdown in Spring 2020

Kateřina Žarnikov

Abstract

During the first COVID lockdown in spring 2020, Czech and Slovak drama teachers had to cope with the immediate transition to distance learning. This research seeks to find out how they adapted their teaching to that situation. The research focused on getting a general overview of the teaching practices and map changes in them. To get a general overview, I conducted surveys with 148 Czech and Slovak drama teachers. The study found that almost three quarters of them continued to teach during the first lockdown, but many of them reduced the number of lessons. To identify changes in practice, I analysed the responses and lessons that some drama teachers shared with me. The findings suggest that the choice of drama strategies, creative process, focus, and tasks seems to have changed. Creative writing and theatre performance analysis came to the fore. The creative process was often enriched with new art forms – film, radio play, etc. The focus of the lessons tended to change from theatrical aspects to group and personal well-being. Adapting lessons to distance learning usually led to a reduction in the complexity of the tasks. One of the main outcomes of this research is the website and Facebook group where Czech and Slovak drama teachers could share their lessons and experiences and find inspiration for distance learning in the school year 2020/2021. In that school year, the choice of methods and the focus of the lessons continued to change and seemed to return to the pre-COVID theatrical aspects of drama education.

Keywords

drama education – teaching practice – distance learning – COVID-19 – learning format

> This situation encourages a transformation or an inner shift. This takes place on two levels – in the self, in the life of the educator, and in her or his professional activity. It is intertwined and influential. Perhaps it also gains more flavor if she or he finds herself or himself in a halt, or a professional crisis, or a strange undefinition of herself/himself. Just cleansing.
>
> RESPONDENT P25

•
• •

1   Introduction

When the COVID-19 first hit Czechia and Slovakia, I was a PhD student of Theory and Practice in drama education. I focused on the current situation in the Czech and Slovakian drama education in primary and lower secondary education, mapping whether drama education is offered as a subject, and if so, what kind of subject it is. I looked into the grades, for which it is designed, the main learning outcomes, drama strategies, and teacher profiles. All of a sudden, from March to June 2020 the entire education sector (along with many others) had to move into virtual space. That new reality fascinated me. I decided to conduct research into how Czech and Slovak drama teachers were coping with this situation. I focused on a general overview of the teaching practice, e.g. the scope of teaching, motivation, organisation, challenges and problems.

Although many teachers were overwhelmed by this unprecedented situation, the response to my initial survey was unexpectedly high and informative. 148 Czech and Slovak drama teachers participated, and what is more, many of them were willing to share their lessons prepared for distance learning. This abundance of new data allowed me to expand on my research and map the changes in their teaching practice. The key questions that emerged from the responses, shared materials, and lesson plans revolved round the following areas: Which methods of drama education were used more/less frequently in distance learning? What were the main changes in the creative process, lesson aims, and tasks? How did the teachers perceive the connection with the participants? Was the transition to distance learning only perceived negatively or as something potentially beneficial?

Although it may still be too early to piece together the mosaic of how the pandemic affected drama education around the world, a number of studies have offered the first insights into this topic. During the transition from face-to-face teaching to virtual environment, drama teachers had to learn and use

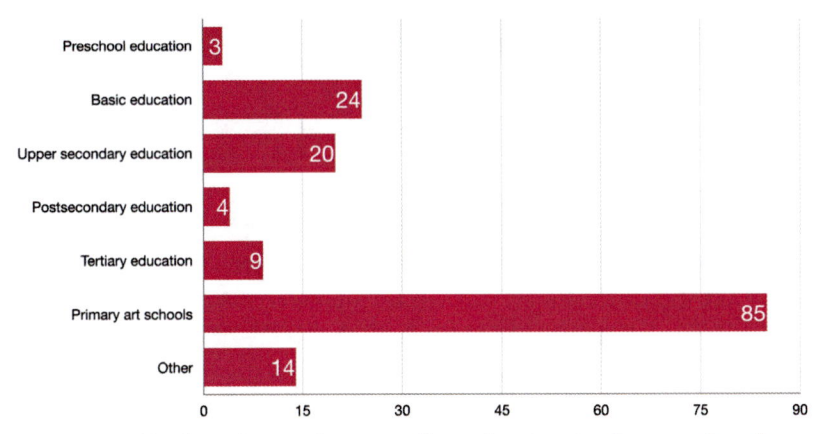

FIGURE 7.1   Numbers of respondents according to the educational sectors where they work

globally distributed digital and online technology tools (Davis & Phillips, 2020; Karaosmanoğlu et al., 2022) and find ways to use them effectively to support the teaching process (Cziboly & Bethlenfalvy, 2020; Donohoe & Bale, 2020). Drama strategies and exercises had to be transformed for distance learning because the online environment did not offer the same quality of contact and communication (Karaosmanoğlu et al., 2022). What these studies seem to have paid less attention to so far is a deeper analysis of changes in teaching practice during distance education, in particular, how and why teachers adapted drama strategies to online environments, and what these changes might entail for drama education in the future. My research could bring about a small piece of mosaic to this missing analysis.

2   Methodology

To collect data I created a questionnaire with both open-ended and multiple choice questions. The questionnaire was distributed online using Google Forms at the end of March 2020.

Out of 519 active members of the Czech and Slovak Creative Dramatics' Association who were contacted via email and social media, 148 (28.9%) participated in the research between March and June 2020.

The cohort mirrors the educational sectors where Czech and Slovak drama teachers operate, with the majority teaching in the primary art schools. These art schools stand outside of regular primary and secondary schools offering long-running art education for five to 19-year-olds exclusively in four art fields – music, dance, fine arts, and drama education. Arts education is accessible to many children for two main reasons. First, the network of primary art schools is very large; there are 525 primary art schools in the Czech Republic and 380 in Slovakia. They are supported by the Ministry of Education, follow the national curriculum, and offer classes in the afternoon so that they do not interfere with regular school hours. Second, as primary art schools are mostly financed from state and municipal budgets, parents pay relatively low school fees.

Drama education in primary art schools focuses on cooperative learning in groups, starting from spontaneous role-playing. Children gradually develop the ability to express themselves independently, distinctively and naturally. At the same time, they get training in social and artistic communication and cultivate their vocal techniques, body language, gestures, writing skills, or work with puppetry. Teaching progresses from simple improvisations to the staging process, from the creation of small literary works to the creation of scripts, etc. Individual work with selected material (poetry, prose, monologue, dialogue, theme, subject) is also an integral part of the teaching, taking into account the pupil's development.

The second largest group represented in my research were drama teachers in basic education (primary and lower secondary education). In this sector, drama education is offered as a subject or as a method in other subjects.

Drama teachers in upper secondary, postsecondary, and tertiary education often teach drama education as a subject or course in teacher training schools (in programmes for drama teachers or for preschool or primary school teachers). In addition to the acquisition of practical skills, the subject or course covers the didactic of drama education.

Drama teachers in preschool education use drama education mostly as a method. The group "Other" includes freelancers from different fields of teaching and theatre.

Having combined quantitative and qualitative methods, I employed frequency analysis to examine the responses to multiple choice questions, and content analysis to interpret the open ended questions. The content analysis was also used for the lessons that the Czech and Slovak drama teachers were willing to share. Teachers' answers and content of their lessons were categorised as follows: 1) delivery of the lesson; 2) methods used in the lessons; 3) changes in the creative process; 4) focus of the lessons; 5) cooperation with participants; and 6) experience with distance learning.

3   General Overview

3.1   *To Be or Not to Be*
When the first lockdown started, the crucial questions for all Czech and Slovak drama teachers were if, how, and to what extent they could continue in their

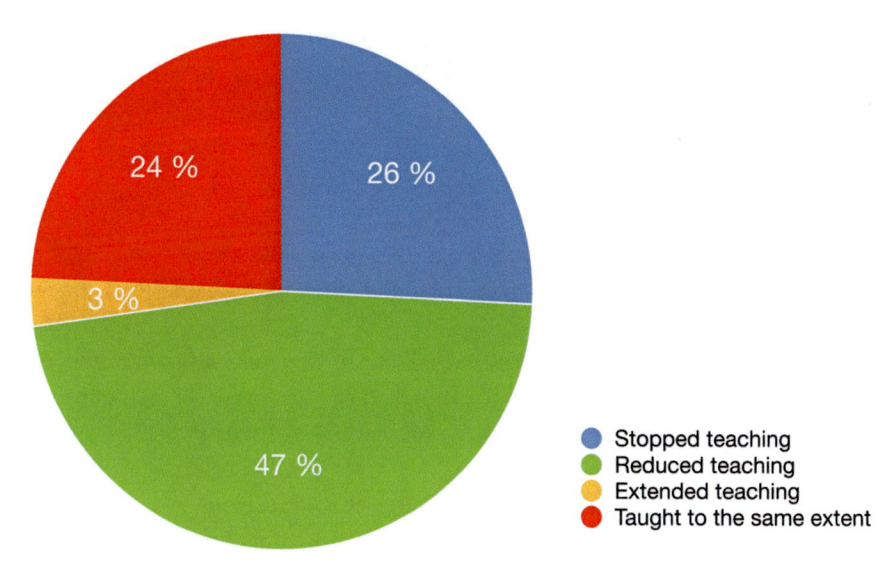

FIGURE 7.2   Drama teachers' reactions to the lockdown in terms of the scope of teaching

teaching practice. The decision-making about the scope of teaching depended on several factors, starting from logistics and management attitudes held by the institutions; furthermore, it was necessary to consider the availability of equipment and teaching materials in the online space, the load of students in other subjects, and the tech skills of teachers and students. As can be seen in Figure 7.2, nearly a half of the respondents reduced their teaching, and only a fraction (3%) extended their practice. Approximately a quarter of the respondents stopped teaching completely, while the remaining quarter maintained a similar study load.

The reasons why almost half of the respondents reduced their teaching are varied. Most respondents said that they did not want to increase the study load which the pupils had to face in other main school subjects. Drama teachers were often required to design more generic creative tasks suitable for all participants (without any age or group limitation), and the completion of the task was optional. For instance, respondent P45 describes his situation as, "drama education is an experiential, immediate and contact subject which is now 95 percent cut". Some drama teachers reduced the number of the lessons because the distance learning did not allow group work. Others did not want to discriminate against participants who had no options to connect to online distance learning, e.g., respondent P55 states that "It is impossible to be in direct contact with students".

The respondents who taught their lessons to the same extent worked mainly in primary art schools and secondary schools focused on teacher training. Primary art school drama teachers highlighted the need to maintain the creative process, help students stay in contact, thus preventing them from falling into social isolation and apathy. On the other hand, drama teachers in pedagogical secondary schools found it important to pass on knowledge (and partly experience) to prepare participants for practice, as is apparent from the following commentaries:

> Students need to gain knowledge and at least partial experience of the subject in order to be prepared for further study in the field. (P52)

> I wouldn't like the pupils to either fall out of their accustomed mode, or lose contact with each other. During distance learning, we create repertoire we could use once everything returns to "normal". (P104)

> Schools continue with distance learning, and so it seems logical to me – because we are also a school and part of the education system in the country – to continue to teach the best we can. Distance learning is naturally very different from face-to-face teaching, but it offers, on the contrary, layers and areas that are not given as much time and attention in face-to-face teaching. (P70)

Several drama teachers stated that they had extended their teaching. It was mainly thanks to theatre productions that could be watched online and explored in the light of the contemporary context. For some drama teachers, extending the teaching meant that they were more involved in the preparation of the lessons. For instance, respondent P25 explained the extra workload as follows: "Teaching young children now takes more of my time because I record poems and stories on audio and add fun little tasks by email".

The respondents who stopped teaching reported that this was for two main reasons: the institution where they worked remained closed due to the coronavirus measures, or, the management of the primary or secondary school decided to cancel drama education in the summer term of 2020. In some cases, they could not connect with the participants for technological reasons or teacher's beliefs. For respondent P26, who completely stopped teaching the group of 13-year-olds, it was both the reasons: he needed physical contact in this age group and lacked technological equipment for collective online work in the countryside (P26). The inability to adapt drama education or theatre performance to an online space was reported by other respondents, for example, P2 mentions "the inability to organize online meetings". Last but not the least, some institutions decided not to overload pupils: according to respondent P84, "the reason for stopping classes was the headmistress' instruction not to burden the children with arts education".

3.2   Tools

During the first lockdown, drama teachers had to, among other responsibilities, explore the possibilities of distance learning tools. Most of them had no previous experience and lacked a clear instruction of which tools to use in terms of security and suitability for diverse ways of distance learning. Although the Ministry of Education and various educational initiatives created a number of web signposts, they dealt with the topics in general terms. Thus, in the first phase of preparation for distance learning, many drama teachers had to not only find tools that would suit the learning and teaching objectives in their groups, but also learn how to use them.

Most of the drama teachers opted for one dominant tool of communication (email, video conference or chat), which was further supplemented by other channels (e.g. cloud storage, Facebook groups, telephone calls, etc.). Their choices often depended on their own technical skills, technical support from the institution, their participants' communication tools, and the learning format.

Regarding synchronous learning, drama teachers usually worked with MS Teams or Zoom; only a few mentioned Skype. These results are consistent with the findings of Karaosmanoğlu et al. (2022) and Davis and Phillips (2020) and other studies into the global distribution of these communication tools.

Regarding asynchronous learning, the main tool was email. Via email communication, the participants or their parents received instructions and tasks, summaries, reflections of their work, or brief notifications about new creative tasks and offers on the cloud. Fewer teachers used internal school systems. To collect the tasks and share them amongst participants, drama teachers often used cloud storage, mainly the Google Drive. Clouds were also used to share supplementary teaching materials.

3.3   Learning Formats

In Czechia and Slovakia, the transition to distance education was very sudden. Drama teachers (as other teachers) switched to distance learning literally overnight, most of them without any previous experience. They were looking for an effective learning format on the fly, in the process of trial and error.

Nearly a half of the drama teachers decided for asynchronous distance learning. According to Ali (2021), asynchronous classes appear to be a better alternative for students with poor internet connections because they lower

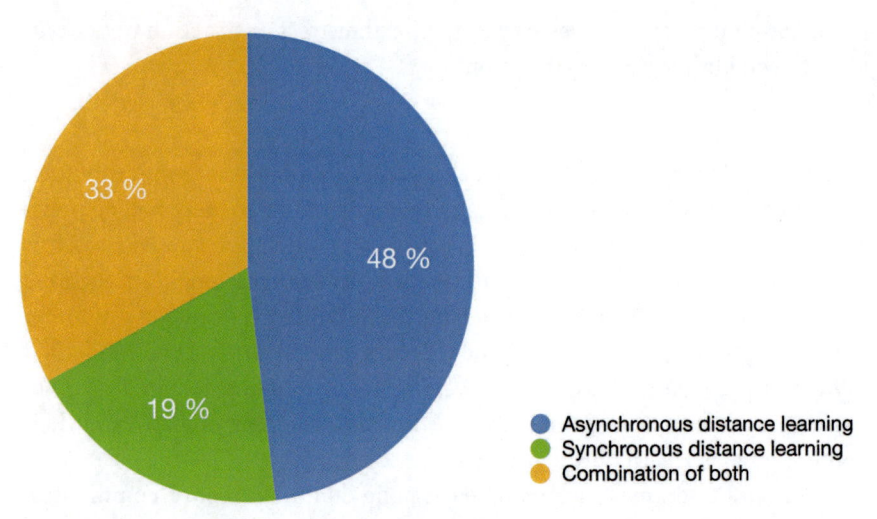

FIGURE 7.3   Learning formats chosen for distance learning

their level of frustration if they cannot fully participate in online learning. A similar reason for choosing asynchronous format can be observed in my study. Most respondents mentioned that the decision for asynchronous learning was influenced by the quality of the Internet connection, technical equipment, and the IT skills of both teachers and learners. Some drama teachers chose asynchronous learning to give students their own time to study and keep them off the screen. Materials for asynchronous learning ranged from lessons in written form with teacher's notes to journals or worksheets on a selected topic (often creative writing or the theory and history of theatre). These were accompanied by creative tasks. Some drama teachers created video or audio materials for their lessons (how to use voice and body language, make puppets, etc.). However, some of them also mentioned that their creative efforts sometimes did not receive much response.

The second most common learning form was the combination of synchronous and asynchronous learning. Live online classes often represented a starting point or reflection on participants' independent homework. The asynchronous element often consisted of a summary of the online lesson, supplemental materials on the topic, videos, and/or audio recordings, etc.

The number of drama teachers who used only synchronous distance learning and created interactive drama lessons was the lowest of all. The reason may be the short time it takes to transition to distance learning. Only a few teachers were able to quickly transform teaching in class to teaching online in the sense of not only adapting methods to online environments but also mastering the technical aspects of online learning.

4   Changing Practices

4.1   *Drama Strategies Used in Distance Learning and Creative Process*

Strategies that came to the fore were creative writing and the reception and reflection on theatre performance.

Creative writing was mainly chosen because it is easily adaptable to distance learning, especially in asynchronous form. It does not depend on the participation of the whole group and respects the individuals' pace. The focus on creative writing allowed teachers to take advantage of interesting texts, encourage reading, and explore language resources. Working with different literary genres, participants wrote short stories, fairy tales, poems, and diaries (e.g., their own diary written in the future); letters (e.g., a letter to my older self); or, short dialogues and dramatic texts (e.g., a dialogue between two characters depicted in a photograph). This was seen mainly positively by the respondents, for instance, P57 wrote: "Students are more engaged in creative writing. This is an area that has been somewhat marginal in our department".

Paradoxically, the greater emphasis on watching and reflecting on theatre performances was a positive knock-on effect brought by the global lockdown. Although live theatre performances and festivals were cancelled in many countries, many streamed their performances and sometimes offered follow-up discussions with the creators or worksheets for schools. Theatre performances by amateur groups were available, too, thus enabling drama teachers to work with the resources that are not normally available. Theatre performances were also used to teach theatre theory and history. In this way, participants not only learnt about interesting productions, but also received additional material and activities on various aspects of theatre which gave them insights into dramatic

FIGURE 7.4   Word cloud with strategies used in the lessons

texts in different historical contexts. These new areas of focus were seen very positively by most of the respondents:

> With the older students, I've been doing things I haven't had time for in a long time. Top performances from around the world are now available. We watch them together, I record audio lectures about the period of the play, the play itself, the director, the concept, etc. (P25)

> Normally we don't have time to analyze theatre performances, we don't devote ourselves to it at all. It's interesting that the kids are enjoying it and it pushes them. (P19)

The creative process was often enriched with new art forms – animation, radio play, or video instructions. Some drama teachers used the potential of newly available technological tools to guide learners on how to create videos or audios. Participants would make videos reflecting on quarantine, as well as short fiction or animation films based on given topics or inspired by stories. Many of the videos were based on texts with which the participants worked in solo performances. The text was translated into work with body movement, sound or music. Several audio forms were also created, for instance recordings of recitation. Drama teachers worked with participants in radio production, enriching the texts they had worked with by sounds and music, creating fictional radio broadcasts on given themes or radio plays. These new forms were used not only by students, but also by some drama teachers who prepared their own video or audio production. These new forms offered new ways of communication and an opportunity to learn specific film or radio language, as one of the respondents described:

> With the younger children we have started to create a "radio play" – they have chosen fairy tales for 3–4 children, I will now dramatize it and we will create sound effects with objects and instruments children will find at home. Older students have started making a "film" of experimental poetry – we're picking out different poems and figuring out where they could be performed and how, and we still want it to be "cinematic" – which we can't do, but we're trying. The students not only film but also edit. (P40)

Many drama teachers exploited video calls. They guided learners on how to work with framing of the "scene", play with the distance from the camera, or walk with the camera to find the right place at home for the topic of improvisation. Some drama teachers worked with the possibility of changing the background. Cziboly and Bethlenfalvy (2020) mentioned that changing background did not work well in the online process drama because the props blended into the background. Respondents of my research did not mention such issues, perhaps because they used the changing background only in short improvisations developing acting skills rather than for situations in process drama.

4.2   Keep It Simple

Adapting lessons to distance learning usually consisted in reducing the complexity of the tasks. Many drama teachers claimed that there were two reasons for this reduction: to avoid a study overload and exploit only materials that the participants are likely to have at home. Some drama teachers mentioned problems with timing and pacing their lessons in an online space, where everything took longer. Drama teachers who used asynchronous distance learning often reduced the complexity and number of tasks to simplify instructions and avoid further explanation.

This in turn forced drama teachers to be more precise in their teaching approach and lesson staging. Many drama teachers came back to the basics of drama education, taking inspiration from a playbook of games and improvisations that had been tested over the years. Going back to the basics helped many drama teachers to enhance their teaching skills and step out of their comfort zone and regular teaching practices:

> I am learning better, more concise wording (e.g., questions) because I am preparing lessons in written form. (P21)

> I have learned that less is more; there is no need to overwhelm students with tasks, observations, suggestions. (P46)

> I am currently dusting off the Playbook Games for the five senses by Hana Budínská, which, apart from a few exercises, I have never been able to use properly. (P118)

4.3   Let Them Unwind

As Davis and Phillips (2020) mentioned in their study, many drama teachers were mainly concerned with students. To overcome loneliness of separation, most respondents tended to switch their focus from theatrical aspects to group and personal well-being. They felt the pressure that the participants had to face due to other school obligations and wanted to lower the stress level in their classes, as one of them explains: "I really think kids are overloaded and drama education should offer them mainly an active break from online activities" (P108).

In their lesson plans, many drama teachers included stages specifically aimed to check how participants were feeling and opened space for discussing the current situation. They also offered activities that brought fun to the group, not only drama games and improvisation, but also games and quizzes about drama groups and performances they had prepared. Some drama teachers wanted to compensate for screen time by offering activities to be done outdoors or offering unusual explorations of participants' homes:

> Everything is new, our values are changing, our view of the world is changing, our friends are changing ... we are a place that can be incredibly helpful. More than ever, we can be partners, mentors, and helpers to children. (P25)

4.4   *Togetherness*

Paradoxically, the lockdown facilitated deeper connections between students and their drama teachers. For instance, respondent P97 became "much more aware of the relationship between student and teacher and how mutual support is essential". During distance learning, teachers received support in solving technical issues not only from their more experienced colleagues and acquaintances, but also from their students, who were often more technologically proficient. Some students even created websites or edited videos. A common virtual space for sharing student work across groups allowed for more cooperative learning and exchange of inspiration: "We keep the materials together. We share work across groups, we continue to work with materials that have been created, we are not isolated and limited by study groups" (P136). Moreover, drama teachers had the possibility to look into the participants' homes and meet parents, siblings, or pets. For instance, respondent P104 appreciated "the opportunity to get to know the pupils, their learning opportunities, and backgrounds", which helped her to better understand the participants' learning environment and circumstances.

"I'm trying to get other family members involved and keep the good mood at home, because it's not easy at all right now", writes respondent P22. Similarly to other drama teachers who worked with young participants, she often needed the help of the parents or older siblings. The whole family was involved, either as partners in role plays or as those who documented small performances. Sometimes, the "family ensembles" were formed and they shared their homemade creations with each other, way beyond the assigned task. Sometimes the siblings became regular participants of the lesson and enrolled in the drama class. It was a great opportunity for families to directly experience drama education and realise the positive effects on their children's well-being.

4.5   *Opportunity to Learn*

Although most drama teachers focused on describing the challenges posed by distance learning, some were also able to name the benefits.

Breaking away from the routine often allowed for reflection on teaching practices which helped to identify the essentials for their teaching, in particular effective communication with students and creating a good group atmosphere: "I see the advantage in being able to slow down and reflect on my work from a distance. To choose and focus on what makes the most sense to me" (P4). Thanks to distance teaching, teachers could see their learners from a different perspective, discover some of their hidden potential, and learn how to enhance group's cooperation. One of the respondents finds a special value in "the opportunity to get to know a child's personality in a slightly different way. Children are also becoming more aware, thanks to the emergency, of values that they took for granted" (P72).

Some drama teachers appreciated learning about or deepening their use of technology and web-based tools: "It's a time for improving technical skills, breaking out of the mundane routine, adding to your own "stack" of games, exercises and lessons, new impulses and thinking about how to move forward not only in this situation, but also after it" (P17). They have expanded on their use of resources, adapted them in their teaching, and refined their means of expression. They discovered ways to archive and share students' ideas and work.

5   Discussion

In order to determine how Czech and Slovak drama teachers coped with the distance learning during the first COVID-19 lockdown, I looked at the scope of teaching, tools, learning formats and changes in their practices. It can be argued that despite the negative impacts caused mainly by the abrupt switch to the distance learning, the response of the drama teachers in Czechia and Slovakia was in many ways successful, in that it strengthened the rapport with students and opened space for reflection, creativity, and new ways of student and teacher development. One of the main downsides was the reduction in teaching. Many teachers were forced to teach less, or stopped teaching completely. According to a report from the UK, such a reduction is likely to result in deficiencies not only in practical skills development but also in interpersonal skills of participants as a group (Bradley, 2021). Although these deficiencies need to be explored more thoroughly in the Czech and Slovak context, in terms of the development of practical theatrical skills, my research suggests that students could not develop in this area with the same intensity as before. This might be partially given by the reduced opportunities for group work. On the other hand, with reduced teaching, drama teachers focused usually on developing skills that were less emphasised in face-to-face learning, e.g., creative writing, reflection on theatre performances, and rehearsing solo performances.

My findings also shed more light on the form of distance learning that most teachers opted for. Asynchronous distance learning was the most popular for those who continued teaching.

While this may be in conflict with the basic principle of drama education – group work in one time and space, Czech and Slovak drama teachers were generally able to exploit the possibilities that asynchronous learning can offer in conventional education. Asynchronous learning proved to be an effective way of blended learning, particularly in the areas of methodology, didactics and theory of drama education. It also provided a solution for students who could not attend synchronous learning. On the other hand, there were drawbacks, such as loneliness when completing the tasks, impossibility of immediate consultation with the teacher, and lack of peer interaction.

Moving to the positive side-effects, it was mainly the change in drama strategies, creative process, focus, and tasks that triggered good outcomes. The shifted attention to areas that had been marginalised in face-to-face learning, in particular creative writing and theatre performance analysis, enhanced students' and teachers' creativity. The creative process was often enriched with new art forms – film, radio play, etc. This allowed participants and also drama teachers to develop new skills and show the possibilities of creative expression in a different form using the skills learned in drama lessons.

The main feature of lesson adaptations to distance learning was a reduction in the complexity of the tasks, not in the sense of making the learning easier, but as a return to the basics of drama education. It was an opportunity for the participants to deepen their basic skills. At the same time, the simplification allowed for a greater precision, concise instructions, thus contributing to an effective design of the lesson.

Perhaps the most remarkable consequence of the first lockdown was the enhanced rapport and interpersonal connections between teachers and students. The distance learning allowed drama teachers to see their students in a broader context – at home, as technical experts, talented in other areas than drama and theatre. Many Czech and Slovak drama teachers reflected on creating deeper bonds with students, which positively affected students' motivation and participation. It could be argued that closer rapport is likely to have a positive effect on the future learning, whether it will take place online or in face-to-face teaching.

Last but not least, similarly as in Cziboly and Bethlenfalvy's study (2020), where the lockdown is seen as an opportunity to reconsider the effectiveness of their teaching and their role as educators, Czech and Slovak drama teachers appreciated their professional development: engaging in reflective practice, identifying the essentials for their teaching, as well as improving their technological skills.

My study only looked at the first lockdown period when teachers were looking for ways to swiftly adapt to the change in teaching.[1] These platforms built the bridge between the theoretical recommendations of the Ministry of Education and the teaching practices by providing examples of materials, step-by-step lesson plans, tools, and methods. These resources served as inspiration for distance learning in the school year 2020/2021 and motivated drama teachers to further enhance their teaching skills. The preliminary findings of my follow-up research into the lockdown that followed suggest that it was partially thanks to these platforms (among other resources) that many drama teachers found the courage to use new digital tools and switch from asynchronous to synchronous distance learning. More attention still needs to be paid to teaching drama education in distance learning in other lockdowns.

6   Conclusion

In this research I investigated how Czech and Slovak drama teachers adapted their teaching to distance learning during the first COVID-19 lockdown in spring 2020. I analysed the questionnaire completed by 148 drama teachers and lesson plans that some of them were willing to share.

The main drawbacks of the abrupt switch to distance learning was the reduction in teaching which may have resulted in less intensive development of practical theatrical skills. On the other hand, the adaptation of Czech and Slovak drama teachers to distance learning was successful in many ways, as it strengthened the rapport with students and opened space for reflection, creativity, and new ways of student and teacher development.

My research brought a small piece to the mosaic of analysis of how the pandemic affected drama education. There is still a deep need to explore the adaptation of drama education to distance education, to analyse how drama strategies work in virtual space and what challenges and opportunities they present, and whether and what drama teachers have transferred from distance education during the lockdown to face-to-face teaching.

Note

1   One of the main outcomes of this research outlined in this chapter is the website https://dramadistancne.blogspot.com and the Facebook group "Dramatická výchova online" (translated from Czech – Dramatic education online) https://www.facebook.com/groups/739750146561387 where Czech and Slovak drama teachers shared their lessons and experiences.

References

Ali, M. A. (2021). Students' learning experiences in introduction to drama theatre classes during COVID-19. *Journal of Cognitive Science and Human Development, 7*(1), 123–133. https://doi.org/10.33736/jcshd.3040.2021

Bradley, C. (2021). *National drama COVID impact study* [Online]. National Drama. https://www.nationaldrama.org.uk/wp-content/uploads/Outcome-of-National-Drama-Covid-Impact-Study.pdf

Cziboly, A., & Bethlenfalvy, A. (2020). Response to COVID-19 zooming in on online process drama. *Research in Drama Education: The Journal of Applied Theatre and Performance, 25*(4), 645–651. https://doi.org/10.1080/13569783.2020.1816818

Davis, S., & Phillips, L. G. (2020). Teaching during COVID 19 times – The experiences of drama and performing arts teachers and the human dimensions of learning. *NJ: Drama Austria Journal, 44*(2), 66–87. https://doi.org/10.1080/14452294.2021.1943838

Donohoe, P., & Bale, M. (2020). To Zoom or not to Zoom: Adapting educational versions of Shakespeare's plays for an online platform during the COVID pandemic. *Scenario, 14*(2), 116–124. https://doi.org/10.33178/scenario.14.2.7

Karaosmanoğlu, G., Metinnam, İ., Özen, Z., & Adıgüzel, Ö. (2022). Can drama lessons be given online? Perspectives of drama teachers during the COVID-19. *International Online Journal of Education and Teaching (IOJET), 9*(3), 1249–1272. https://www.researchgate.net/publication/361664664_CAN_DRAMA_LESSONS_BE_GIVEN_ONLINE_PERSPECTIVES_OF_DRAMA_TEACHERS_DURING_THE_COVID-19

CHAPTER 8

Teaching Is about Human Relationships

Art Education Graduate Students as Teachers and Learners in the Pandemic

Nancy Long, Amy Atkinson and David LeRue

Abstract

COVID-19 pandemic lockdowns significantly changed how art education is received and delivered, moving from the tactile environment of an in-person studio classroom to isolated online video conferencing classes. As doctoral students, artists, and educators who teach student teachers, the authors found themselves in the unique position of teaching and learning on both sides of the screen. The authors share a programme and a home university, with each having a different focus on teacher training – one is focused on pre-service teachers, one on high-school in-service teachers and one on teachers in informal and community settings. In this chapter, the authors examine their teaching and learning, elaborating on how they cultivated human relationships and built communities of learning as both students and teachers. They recount how they negotiated the intricacies of sharing ideas, artwork and teaching strategies in the applied field.

The authors also consider bridging the digital and in-person environment: the tangible ways they adapted creative learning to the online environment and how the online environment has informed the recent return to in-person learning. They also consider how this experience inspired their pedagogical practices going forward, and what kind of ethics, approaches and wisdom they aim to integrate as we move into a post-pandemic world. Finally, the authors offer a visual metaphor, using a Penrose tiling as an artistic response to their shared situations.

Keywords

pedagogy – community – student teachers – online – high school – Penrose tiling

1 Introduction

During the incursion of online learning brought on by the COVID-19 pandemic, we, the authors of this paper, found ourselves in a unique position: we were each teaching art at various levels and in varied contexts while attending courses to fulfil the requirements of our graduate education programme. David LeRue attended to community settings, while Nancy Long to pre-service teachers and Amy Atkinson to in-service teachers, in addition to each teaching an undergraduate course in our university's department of Art Education. Despite this, we found ample commonalities in our individual situations and responses to online teaching: translating the tactile world of visual art to the digital realm, adapting to new technologies with little preparation, and our students' heightened anxieties about assessment, grades, and creating under exceptional conditions. In this paper, we discuss our experiences teaching in different contexts while adapting to extraordinary circumstances, deducing the lessons we learned about both artistic and pedagogical practices we will take forward as we move past lockdowns. We invoke a Penrose tiling first as a metaphor for our shared but separate situations before concluding the paper with the creation of our own Penrose tile design to give artistic form to our experiences.

2   Penrose Tiling

Our experiences diverged frequently and were defined by entanglements with our students as well as those of the material world of online platforms and digital and physical spaces. Subsequently, we acknowledged tenets of Barad's (2014) diffractive processes to expose these entangled situations beyond simply reflecting on them.

Diffraction invokes physics, where waves pass through an obstacle, bend and head in numerous different directions. For Barad, a diffractive methodology is an ontological approach to the material world wherein social researchers' perspectives on phenomena continuously evolve when faced with new contexts and material engagements. In our exploration of our teaching and learning circumstances surrounding the COVID-19 pandemic and where they can lead us, we concurred with Barad's (2014) resolution on diffractive practices: "there is no moving beyond, no leaving the 'old' behind. There is no absolute boundary between here-now and there-then. There is nothing that is new; there is nothing that is not new" (p. 168). We moved forward from our experiences and became steadfast in the belief that they are ever-evolving.

As art educators who resonate with visual stimuli, we envisioned diffraction using Penrose tiling as its metaphor to describe how our unique individual experiences, given similar constraints, cascaded outward, unfolding into the unknown while influencing each other and welcoming infinite possibilities. In this sense, a Penrose tiling also works as a visual metaphor to show that even though COVID lockdowns and online teaching might be thought of as a single phenomenon, the situations and subsequent effects for teachers like us developed in ways that were seemingly infinite. Despite the infinite reactions, we found our individual cases also interconnected, much like the interconnected shapes of a Penrose tiling.

The discovery of Penrose tiling is credited to and subsequently refined in the 1970s by mathematics research fellow, Roger Penrose, now Emeritus Rouse Ball Professor of Mathematics at Oxford University. Penrose's more famous tile set occurs with the kite and dart shapes. These two symmetrical, quadrilateral shapes, when placed side by side with a specific constraint, can yield an endless aperiodic configuration. In other words, the patterns produced can never be predicted, and the possibilities are infinite (Barss, 2014). Though we noted this often occurred in our day-to-day teaching, we felt this particularly resonated with teaching during the pandemic. With online learning, our experiences began to diffract in ways that represent a Penrose tiling. We all adopted the digital tools and spaces, but we operated and proceeded in different directions, "revealing how infinite variation could emerge within a highly ordered [even recurring] environment" (Barss, 2014, n.p.). Furthermore, as we explored and compared our circumstances, we learned and borrowed from each other and noticed that, like a Penrose tiling, this created infinite teaching and learning outcomes that we could not predict and could never repeat. As art educators, we felt compelled to express ourselves creatively using this tiling system for inspiration. Like our online experiences, we devised our artworks using similar tools, but each of us took our creative work in different directions (Figures 8.1–8.3).

3 Moving Online

When the world began locking down between February and mid-March 2020, we were each actively teaching at different levels of education. LeRue and Long were first-year students in their PhD. LeRue worked as a tutorial leader at the university with plans to integrate community teaching into his dissertation. Long worked at a city high school teaching art and elective courses with plans to integrate art classroom practices into her research. Atkinson was teaching at an international school in Shenzhen, China, which shut down while on holiday during Chinese New Year, meaning many instructors and students were on vacation in other countries and did not have ready access to computers and technology. At the same time, China imposed visa restrictions, which meant many expatriate teachers had to find new living situations in various

FIGURE 8.1   David LeRue, 2022, Penrose Tiling, digital collage

FIGURE 8.2
Amy Atkinson, 2022, Penrose
Tiling, marker and ink on paper,
80 cm × 80 cm

FIGURE 8.3
Nancy Long, 2022, Penrose
Tiling, acrylic ink, white
charcoal on polyfilm,
23 cm × 30 cm

parts of the world so that they could see their classes through to the end of the semester, in an abridged form. This was similar for LeRue and Long, whose PhD courses abruptly ended as their instructors were tasked to restructure their assignments and grading schemes. As teachers ourselves, we were asked to do the same for our students. While everyone adjusted to this new mode of teaching and learning, there was much trial and error and highly experimental moments. We quickly realised that, in the years behind us as students and teachers, we took for granted the benefits of classroom community and in-person transactions.

4 Technological Possibilities

Distance learning during the pandemic was mediated by the available technologies, and in the early days, there were extensive discussions about the possibilities these technologies offered. Some of our colleagues began experimenting with video game-like software, quiz software, online galleries, and asynchronous streaming. In the early days, it seemed like these technologies could revolutionise classrooms and activate our students' imaginations. It appeared these technologies could liven traditional methods of learning and find resonance with our students in an age characterised by devices and software.

In our experience in the COVID-19 context, the uptake of technology posed many issues for both instructors and students. As art instructors primarily working with physical media and tasked with teaching assignments built on these foundations, we each found the basic functions of Zoom and Moodle – our university's online course management system – to be challenging. We struggled to learn more complicated technologies and had difficulties imagining how we would implement them into our teaching as well as adopt them as part of our coursework as students. We also believed that the technological ask for all instructors was immense, falling generally outside of the confines of our training as educators. For some students, the injunction of new technologies also raised problems of access. This included limited bandwidth being shared by multiple family members also in work-from-home situations, outdated or inadequate technologies for certain functions, lack of space for some families to study/find quiet time, and for others, there was difficulty navigating even basic functions such as e-mail or Zoom. In LeRue's community classes, these problems were compounded since students came from a wider range of situations and the school did not have the same resources as a public school or university to help navigate technologies.

Despite such complications, we acknowledge that moving online allowed some to feel included in ways they had not previously been before (Ansuini et al., 2022), and accommodated students who needed to provide childcare, students with long commutes, students who lived in other places, and students who overall preferred learning online. In general, this scenario privileged students with access to technology and technological know-how, while requiring instructors to spend more time familiarizing other students with technology and etiquette. In our view, this created additional stress for the latter.

For us, the discourse around technology boiled down to novelty versus utility, and what we could realistically implement in our given situations. In our online classrooms, the uses of technology became pared down to the most basic: Teleconferencing software (e.g., Zoom) file organizing software (e.g., Moodle), presentation software (e.g., PowerPoint), and web-based collaborative applications (e.g., Google Docs). These essentially mimicked through Zoom what we delivered in a standard classroom pre-pandemic. While we believe under other circumstances that technological evolution has its place in our classrooms, we found that we and our students were undertrained and lacked the energy to explore these possibilities.

5   Building Community Online

By autumn of 2020, schools and universities had implemented plans for online learning, and during that academic year, each of us taught at various levels online while enrolled in our PhD programme. LeRue and Long were teaching at the university level, Atkinson for a secondary school, and LeRue also for a community school. By this time, it became clear that the pandemic lockdowns were in effect for the whole semester, and that we would have entire classes where we had only ever met the students through online conferencing software. The struggles of this time have been well documented, with students, in general, having a difficult time with the lack of human contact, and with their overall production (Kee, 2021; Watermeyer et al., 2020). As we became aware of how our students were feeling in our classrooms, we adjusted our strategies and approaches for teaching online to ensure that we were deliberately building social cohesion and community among our students. In this section, we unpack some of the pedagogical and social changes that took place in our online classrooms during this moment. As well, we reveal what we observed their effects to be on student learning and classroom cohesion.

The immediate aftermath of the lockdown required leniency in evaluations and given the noted state of many students during this lockdown period, leniency in one form or another continued throughout. Initially, this was a way to get students over the shock of lockdown, but as the reality of a semester online sunk in, we realised that in general, students were less productive and less able to concentrate for long periods. This was an effect we noticed in ourselves, with our own projects, forcing a shift in our habits as teachers in relation to lockdown.

We each took a more empathetic approach in accepting late coursework and with students not fully equipped with the various technologies we used to communicate our expectations. We found that students often submitted projects not only well past deadlines, but also submitted incomplete work to platforms and e-mails we were not monitoring regularly. In the community school setting, students were more engaged and organised, but some students demonstrated similar frustrations in completing projects and lacked the energy to do so. However, these students generally attended class weekly and in verbal feedback to the instructor said they found social and pedagogical value in simply listening to course material and discussions. In the high school settings, both Atkinson and Long observed a general lack of screen presence, low attendance and low participation compared to that in their undergraduate courses. Finding methods to engage students proved difficult, given that there was a subset of students in every classroom who would turn off their cameras and never respond to course content, even if their engagement through assignments was exemplary. We suspect that the students engaged in "cyberslacking" behaviours, exacerbated because of the missing teacher figure in the room (Mumu et al., 2022) and the lack of accountability to the classroom dynamic that comes from the weekly in-person interactions and from working alongside classmates. These factors likely contributed to a lack of engagement during class time. When lecturing or demonstrating to a group of students in a physical classroom, we could read faces and body language, more readily able to decipher disinterest from confusion. The feedback in person is immediate, while in the digital realm the feedback felt flattened to student engagement with technology. Group discussions and questions felt more forced and formal through Zoom.

Long and Atkinson then each noted a surge in their students' need for more one-on-one attention, thus intensifying their workload and corroborating Watermeyer et al.'s (2020) findings that professors had to deal with an increase in students contacting them due to anxiety. For Long, this was a turning point. As a graduate student during the pandemic, Long was determined to maintain some sense of control over her coursework by adhering to strict deadlines and production of quality work. The leniency, extra one-on-one time, and help she easily afforded to her students were not being observed or sought out by herself as a student. Why was there such a marked divide between the two? The exhaustion of failing to find balance and the feeling of lacking self-efficacy registered deeply (Pressley & Ha, 2022). Long resigned from her twenty-year career as a high school teacher, with insights that she brought to her university teaching, explored later in this text.

Overall, we found that the moment called for leniency, but this may have also diluted the content we delivered, and the students' learning outcomes. This created an opportunity for LeRue, however, who found that some of his students in the community setting thrived with having permission to explore things with more self-direction, even if certain aspects, such as skill-building, were given less prevalence. For instance, in a studio environment, teachers can be specific about directives on a project, so it seems an easy ask for a student to make an oil painting in a ventilated studio. This is unlikely, however, if they are sharing a one-bedroom apartment with many family members. To address this inequity, we welcomed students to tinker with projects so that they might use what they have available to the best of their ability. Interestingly, for LeRue's students in the community setting, things like craft and collage became more common than that in the pre-pandemic time, and more students began to share aspects of their identity and family handicrafts in ways that felt genuinely important to them. LeRue's classes focused on the landscape of students' respective neighbourhoods, and he developed assignments that encouraged independent insights into materials of students' choosing. He found that with some encouragement, students created exceptional projects that were fulfilled using their existing skills, demonstrations in class, and online tutorials.

For Long and Atkinson in the high school setting, such free use of available materials in students' homes bore fruition only once very specific guidelines as to what to make were established. They found that their students struggled with work that had more open-ended parameters. Students were inclined to complete highly structured work more thoroughly, possibly because there was organisation within the uncertainty of the outside world. As well, it seemed that without in-class guidance from the teacher and without peer feedback, many students expressed a lack of confidence in their skills or ideas. They doubted their abilities and took much longer to complete projects. As a result, Long and Atkinson often compensated with detailed step-by-step guidelines, leaving little room for independent exploration.

We noticed that the ways and conventions of gathering online were different from physical learning environments. Our former physical learning environments had many opportunities for discussions between students and professors, and for conversations between colleagues in the hallway, while in a Zoom classroom, only one person can speak at a time and it is challenging to have organic conversations. Furthermore, it was difficult for our students to establish the usual social relationships developed while meeting in an art studio or a lecture hall. Both Long and Atkinson observed, however, a sense of community among teachers developing during this time. Perhaps it was the forced increase in digital use that encouraged digital confidence or provided a new communicative convenience among teachers, or perhaps teachers too felt isolated, but during the past year, Long joined different weekly or bi-weekly teacher check-in sessions with teachers from her former school and with current colleagues. Atkinson found herself sought out through her online presence with requests of personal online tutoring from teachers, and online workshops were frequently requested. Before the pandemic, Atkinson was commonly sought out by students for online support, but the influx of teachers seeking validation and encouragement was notable.

To compensate for the challenges of the digital classroom, we used basic functions in Zoom to help build community and cohesion among our students. Group activities became more common in our classrooms, specifically those which put students into Zoom breakout rooms for discussions and building familiarity that was impossible when the whole class was connected at once. Course material was occasionally considered through online quizzes or games, to inject some laughter into what often felt a little bleak. Not only did this work to build rapport among individual students and mimicked something like the proverbial 'conversation in the hallway', but it seemed to also help students to feel connected to others learning in the same way. Thus, we allowed more time than usual for students to talk and break the ice every class.

6   Pedagogical Impediments of Online

Moving from the tactile environment of a physical classroom to online required that we completely overhaul our approach to teaching art. In our view, the physical classroom engages our physical bodies, and as teachers, we learn to be sensitive to the energy and feeling in a room while teaching, which is far more difficult to cultivate and gauge through Zoom. While none of us pre-ferred online teaching, our time was characterised by experimentation to find what worked to reach our students in lockdown. In this section, we analyse our specific observations of teaching and learning at this time, and how we overcame some of the challenges brought on by the moment. We build toward pointed strategies we developed online, and how they will inform our teaching practices in a post-lockdown world.

For each of us, 2-D and 3-D media were the foundation of our training and our practices, which had to this point been the baseline of our classroom teach-ing. In physical classrooms, we often circulate and help students throughout the process of making, suggesting subtle technical adjustments for artworks that are best received throughout the creation process. On Zoom, work is often examined by holding in-progress work up to a camera, and we are often unable to pinpoint issues students are facing in their process, since the work translates through the screen as flat, without a clear sense of texture or an accurate sense of the scale of the work. Even digital works felt less impactful, as teachers and students experienced these works through different monitors and at differ-ent scales, meaning works that might have a presence in a theatre or a gal-lery appeared to us as no different than YouTube videos. Despite offering guidance on work, it was often challenging to explain without tactile demon-stration, which can readily make apparent the physicality of materials such as paint thickness, colour mixing, graphite blending, the handling of glues, and the tangible elements of sculpting material like clay and plasticine. It was possible to develop elaborate teaching set-ups to give students a better sense of these materials digitally– LeRue had arranged an easel and a camera for live demonstrations – but he would often have to explain more than usual and sensed he did not reach students as clearly as he did in person. Furthermore, the online environment thwarted important learning and growth we usually witnessed during physical circulation. Instances of the teacher seeing immediate problems students are encountering, mixing paint for a student to help them find a specific colour, showing different techniques to be achieved with pencils and erasers, or pointing to inconsistencies in a drawing that might cause problems down the line, could not occur. This meant that we were often catching students' difficulties far later in the artistic process, hence skill building could no longer be centred in our classes.

An important component of our teaching is looking at the artworks of fellow students in the form of critiques and exhibitions, and of professionals through trips to galleries and museums. We were able to look at each other's artworks through screen sharing on Zoom for live critiques, and on Google Classroom, where students could upload works to give a-synchronous feedback. In-person exhibitions were forbidden; therefore, students took to creating online exhibitions, either with software, through publications or on websites where work could be accompanied with text. For in-class examples, we took advantage of online offerings from public galleries and arts organisations across Canada,[1] which listed online exhibitions, tours and talks of various kinds that allowed some access to contemporary art. As instructors, we noticed the impact of the lack of physicality in these instances. LeRue noticed students expressing more ideas-based analysis of work; the material aspects usually prevalent when viewing art in person was not given as much consideration by students. Atkinson noticed the limitations of sharing work online. When Atkinson first went online, it was with a class that had previously established in-person connections, so there was already a comprehension of students' work habits, interests, and inspirations. When meeting students in a fully digital creative learning environment, Atkinson felt connections with and among her students lacked depth. When viewing online work, it was challenging to understand scale and details, and the artist's hand became less apparent when works were translated into digital photographs. For Long, since the chosen online exhibition platform only allowed for one curator, the end-of-year graduating student exhibition lacked the collaborative student voice in decision-making. As well, the conviviality, shared encouragement, and pride commonly occurring at this culminating event were lost.

7   Returning to the Classroom

Returning to the classroom allowed us an opportunity to translate what we learned about the fundamentals of teaching in the digital realm to in-person learning. Coming out of lockdown, LeRue began teaching regular courses in the community art school in the Fall of 2021, while all three of us had university teaching assignments later in the Winter and Spring. LeRue and Atkinson taught a mandatory community education class with student internships and Long supervised students in their final high-school teaching internship placements and taught a graduate seminar in university teaching. Winter 2022 was the first semester our department returned to in-person teaching, though we remained online for three weeks with the Omicron wave of COVID-19. While in those three weeks, some students expressed initial hesitation to return, it became apparent by the first day in each of our courses that there was an exciting dynamic in the face-to-face classes, and by the second class, students were exclaiming their appreciation for seeing each other in person. This enthusiasm for the class and each other continued throughout the semester and their energy fed ours.

The return to an in-person model was not and is still not without some trepidation and remaining fears, from worries about lifted mask mandates to a return to a potentially less accommodating format for those whose needs were better met online. What we gleaned from our online teaching practice is ongoing and we are learning from it as we implement its lessons within our in-person classrooms.

We felt the positive sentiment among many of the teachers and students during the first foray back into the classrooms, however, as the return gains traction and in-class learning develops solidity, it exposes concerning challenges to the long-term growth of student and teacher development. As Atkinson returned to full in-class secondary teaching in international schools, a said challenge lay in what she and Mumu et al. (2022) observed as a learning deficit occurring with students during extended Zoom classes. LeRue noticed that as community classrooms have slowly returned to in-person, the extracurricular nature of the classes has meant that when government messaging shifts on COVID-19, attendance drops, making regularity in the week-to-week schedule difficult to maintain. When Long faced her first in-person undergraduate class, she perceived in many adult students what she had seen in her high school students, that is, a need for order and very clear guidelines towards specific end products. Long hoped her adult pre-service students (future art teachers), having just delved into the ambiguous territory of creating in a pandemic, could explore more willingly their capabilities of creating with no right or wrong. In this way, perhaps they could promote with their future students, student-centred individual discovery in experimentation.

The ambiguity proved too ambiguous and creating this way, Long realised, needs to be nurtured and developed as a skill in its own right. This could explain why Long's students in this formal course setting were far more concerned with their performance and their perceived "right" way to do things than her non-graded seminar students, who threw themselves into all kinds of ambiguous learning activities with little hesitation. Although no assignment was formally graded, there was still much anxiety about the quick turnaround of the nature of the course and the lack of gestation time with ideas, even with flexible and personalised deadlines.

8 Collective Insights

Overall, there appears to be general exhaustion and depression among both teachers and students and a dramatic increase in concerns for mental wellness to contend with (Jones et al., 2021; Key, 2021; Pressley & Ha, 2022). As we come out of the pandemic, what we think is important is that we are not trying or hoping to return to a specific place of pre-COVID. Instead, we are moving through COVID and taking the following collective insights to heart:

- Increasing the forgiving temperament and leniency to ourselves and to our students while developing and implementing facets of slow pedagogy, through prolonged gestation periods and enhancing skills in tolerance for ambiguity in the creative process;
- Regularly promoting the classroom as a collective and considering the communication needs of both teachers and students;
- Re-thinking grading schemes and university expectations. Our undergraduate students are operating in a competitive programme where only those meeting high grade-point averages, among other criteria, are chosen for the teaching specialisation. They are in some form of competition with each other based on university expectations. How can we remove as many barriers as possible and build a sense of community?

We are confident that in exploring these insights, we will make strides in moving away from a goal-oriented desire to 'get good grades' to a perspective aimed more toward collective learning.

We are certainly not alone in questioning and revising our pedagogical approaches at this juncture towards a more humanised approach (Ansuini et al., 2022; Bozkurt & Sharma, 2021; Zhao & Watterston, 2021). Our collective takeaways are not new ideas. As Zhao and Watterston (2021, p. 4) pointed out, we have the "rare opportunity" now to accomplish the student-centred pedagogical goals that existed prior to the pandemic, but that were perhaps not "gaining traction". The authors furthered that this moment of pedagogical uncertainty is "the opportunity for educators and children to come together to rethink the education we actually need as opposed to the inflexible and outdated model that we are likely to feverishly cling to" (Zhao & Watterston, 2021, p. 4).

Penrose tiling inspired us as we met to discuss our different circumstances and prepare this chapter. As one shape shifts and a pattern seems to develop, the configuration bares no predictable outcome. LeRue's reflective musing on his teaching through the pandemic as "one of the most formative teaching experiences I ever had, and I never want to do it again", echoes our collective sentiment and celebrates the aperiodic nature of our joint experiences. In our discussions connecting our practices with the metaphoric tiling, we challenged ourselves to buttress our writing with art making (Figures 8.1–8.3). Our creative responses were informed by our own narratives of the pandemic. Just as our individual teaching realities revealed, though all our circumstances originated with the same tools, our responses were diverse and unpredictable, and serve as tools for infinite possibilities for our teaching practices. Through this, we found the Penrose tiling to be an apt metaphor for our changing circumstances, and for the new patterns we had to invent on the fly to maintain the human relationships we argue are intrinsic to teaching and learning.

In each creating our own tiling system, the numerous design configurations appealed to us immediately, and Atkinson pointed to the tiles' potential as a teaching tool. Atkinson recently left Penrose tile pieces out on a spare table for her students to play with (Figure 8.4). At first, students were intrigued and found it akin to playing with a puzzle. They chatted lightheartedly as they joined the shapes and created patterns. Eventually, the patterns wouldn't fit together, and gaps were left, and students returned to their other creative projects. Atkinson realised that, by looking for common or instinctual patterns and trying to join the kite and the dart shapes in predictable formations, one would always be left with gaps or extra shapes that didn't fit anywhere. Atkinson and her students researched the Penrose tiling in more depth and then configured the shapes with the recommended vertex constraints (Figure 8.5), thus creating more opportunities to connect the shapes into cohesive groupings. But it was only when they gave up on creating definitive patterns that the shapes would begin to join consecutively, revealing an infinite aperiodic cluster of geometric shapes.

FIGURE 8.4
Students configuring Penrose tiles
(from Atkinson, 2022)

As we embraced the Penrose Tile with only surface information, similarly, in our involvement with teaching and learning during the Coronavirus pandemic, we found ourselves out of depth and with an unshakable feeling that both we and our students were missing specialised knowledge and scopic understanding. Yet, like an infinite Penrose tiling is created with some constraints, our individual teaching realities revealed that though all our experiences originated with the same tools, our responses were diverse and unpredictable, and serve as means for infinite possibilities for our teaching practices. Re-building and considering our situations post-pandemic reminded us of how important interconnections between colleagues as teachers and students are critical to success even at the best of times, and how human relationships have been integral to our own growth as students and teachers. By reframing the move online to connect humans in a community, we have in turn re-framed our ongoing relationships with teaching and learning.

Finally, with our artistic and pedagogic use of the Penrose tiles, we are reminded of the relevance of embracing the diffractive parts of our whole endeavour as we work through our past and present towards a familiar ambiguity, in a kind of "iterative repatterning" (Barad, 2014, p. 169). We find ourselves well equipped with accounts of our collective narratives and commitment as not only dedicated, adaptable teachers, but as ever-evolving students.

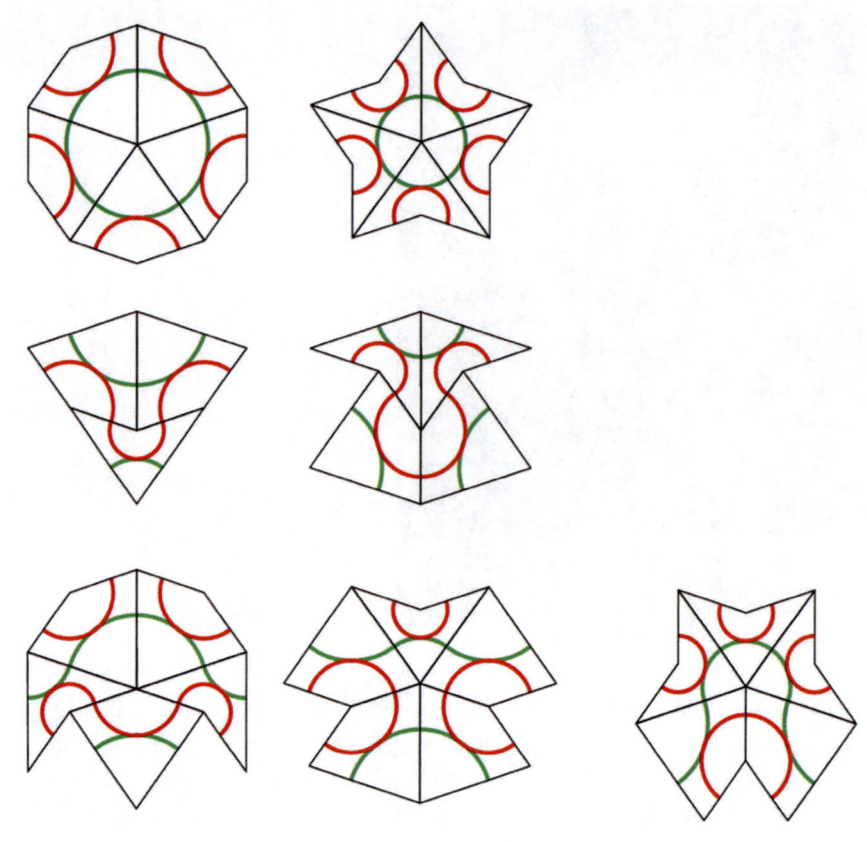

FIGURE 8.5   Kite and dart placements considering vertex constraints (from Glassner, 1998, p. 79)

Note

1   Such as the website www.fieldtrip.art

References

Ansuini, A., Castro, J. C., Greer, G. H., & Castro, A. P. (2022). Rethinking what it means to return to normal. *Art Education, 75*(2), 46–48. https://doi.org/10.1080/00043125.2021.2020036

Barad, K., (2014). Diffracting diffraction: Cutting together-apart. *Parallax, 20*(3), 168–187. https://doi.org/10.1080/13534645.2014.927623

Barss, P., (2014, April 25). Impossible cookware and other triumphs of the Penrose tile. *Nautilus Quarterly.* https://nautil.us/impossible-cookware-and-other-triumphs-of-the-penrose-tile-rp-234895/

Bozkurt, A., & Sharma, R. C. (2021). On the verge of a new renaissance: Care and empathy oriented, human-centered pandemic pedagogy. *Asian Journal of Distance Education, 16*(1), I–VII. https://doi.org/10.5281/zenodo.5070496

Field trip: Art across Canada. (n.d.). Retrieved November 21, 2021, from https://www.fieldtrip.art/

Glassner, A., (1998). Penrose tiling. *IEEE Computer Graphics and Applications 4*(18), 78–86. https://doi.org/10.1109/38.689670

Jones, A., & Bennett, R. (2017). Reaching beyond an online/offline divide: Invoking the rhizome in higher education course design. *Technology, Pedagogy and Education, 26*(2), 193–210. https://doi.org/10.1080/1475939X.2016.1201527

Jones, S. E., Ethier, K. A., Hertz, M., DeGue, S., Le, V. D., Thornton, J., Lim, C., Dittus, P. J., & Geda, S. (2022). Mental health, suicidality, and connectedness among high school students during the COVID-19 pandemic – Adolescent behaviors and experiences survey, United States, January–June 2021. *MMWR Supplements, 71*(3), 16–21. https://doi.org/10.15585/mmwr.su7103a3

Kee, C. E. (2021). The impact of COVID-19: Graduate students' emotional and psychological experience. *Journal of Human Behavior in the Social Environment, 31*(1–4), 476–488. https://doi.org/10.1080/10911359.2020.1855285

Mumu, J. R., Connolly, R., Wanke, P., Azad, M., & Kalam, A. (2022, January 4). *Understanding cyberslacking intention during COVID-19 online classes: An fsQCA analysis* [Paper]. 55th Hawaii international conference on system sciences, Hawaii, USA. https://hdl.handle.net/10125/79692

Pressley, T., & Ha, C. (2022). Teacher exhaustion during COVID-19: Exploring the role of administrators, self-efficacy, and anxiety. *The Teacher Educator, 57*(1), 61–78. https://doi.org/10.1080/08878730.2021.1995094

Watermeyer, R., Crick, T., Knight, C., & Goodall, J. (2020). COVID-19 and digital disruption in UK universities: afflictions and affordances of emergency online migration. *High Education, 81*(3), 623–641. https://doi.org/10.1007/s10734-020-00561-y

Zhao, Y., & Watterston, J. (2021). The changes we need: Education post COVID-19. *Journal of Educational Change, 22*(1), 3–12. https://doi.org/10.1007/s10833-021-09417-3

CHAPTER 9

Are Talking Heads the Only Answer?

Remote and Hybrid Drama Education in a New Zealand Secondary School

Jane Isobel Luton and Jacqueline Hood

Abstract

This chapter explores the digital and classroom-based experiences of two drama teachers in a secondary school in Auckland, New Zealand, during the COVID-19 pandemic. They discuss ways in which Drama, an embodied art form, was facilitated in a disembodied space, while acknowledging the problems and challenges, this paradox has provoked. As one of the four Arts subjects in the New Zealand curriculum, Drama plays an important role in the cultural life of New Zealand schools, developing critical thinking, creativity, and knowledge, using voice, body, and movement and space. When the pandemic, brought national lockdowns and home isolation, closing schools, drama studios were transformed from figurative to literal 'empty spaces', replaced by digital learning platforms. Lively spaces of exploration, experimentation, and embodied learning were reduced to a set of 'talking heads' and icons on a screen. Drama teachers confident in a 'real' space of creativity, surrounded by organised chaos, had to adapt to this 'digital' space. After two and a half years of remote and hybrid teaching, and amidst the frustrations and disappointments, we begin to acknowledge moments of success. However, our experiences render us sceptical that teaching drama remotely can ever be as truly effective as when it is enacted in the live space.

Keywords

drama education – embodied learning – teacher voice – digital learning

1 Introduction

1.1 *The Authors*

This chapter written by two secondary school teachers each with over 25 years' experience as drama and theatre specialists gives voice to some of the challenges and successes, experienced teaching drama during the COVID-19 pandemic with students as young as thirteen. Jacqui Hood has a Masters in Theatre and has been the Head of Department at a secondary school in Auckland, Aotearoa New Zealand for several years. Jane Luton has a PhD in Drama Education and was a prior Head of Department at the school, returning in 2021 for one year to teach Year 9 classes, and Year 11. Together we explored our positive and negative experiences of teaching drama remotely and in hybrid forms as part of our self-reflection to improve our practice.

1.2   *The Pandemic and Learning*

Although the COVID-19 pandemic was still affecting lives internationally, 2021 began in a near normal state in New Zealand, with only a few days of lockdown occurring early in term one. However, on August 17th all schools were closed, and Auckland plunged into what would become a nearly four-month lockdown. All teaching, including drama, moved online.

In 2022, Jacqui Hood continued teaching as the Omicron variant spiked. The situation became more challenging as teaching was no longer just 'in the classroom', or 'only online' but took on a variety of hybrid forms.

1.2.1   Bring Your Own Device

New Zealand schools have adopted a bring your own device [BYOD] policy which expects all students to have a laptop or tablet available for daily school use. Our school is a Microsoft school which uses Teams as the shared platform. However, while we have embraced a range of technologies in performances and lessons, Drama remains fundamentally an embodied practice. Students are encouraged to work in practical and collegial ways within one of the two main drama spaces often referred to as "the empty space" (Brook, 1968, p. 11). During the pandemic it was a shock to become reduced to a set of 'talking heads' on a screen.

1.2.2   Talking Heads

'Talking heads' describes a head and shoulders shot of a television presenter. It epitomised our sense that we no longer seem to inhabit whole bodies while teaching online. Many 'memes' have arisen from this aspect of the pandemic suggesting that those working from home dressed only in their corporate attire from the waist up (Todorov, 2022). While the school mandated that all students should use their cameras in class, most junior drama students refused, and were identifiable only by their chosen icon. Those who did appear often hid themselves from full view by angling their cameras or in one case showing the air vent on their bedroom wall. Psychologists have suggested that "observing your perfect double as a body-in-action remains, for most people, distracting and awkward" (Dunphy-Lelii, 2020, para. 2). It certainly limited the possibilities for us to communicate and feel a sense of community:

> We leant closer to the screen exaggerating our facial expressions and gestures attempting to make eye contact, ignoring the video feedback of ourselves. Even in intense moments of frustration, we presented a positive front. Alongside our attempts to educate through this electronic medium, we were conscious that everyone's mental health and wellbeing must be a priority. (Luton, & Hood, 2022, p. 42)

This pandemic has been a particularly challenging time for drama teachers attempting to teach an embodied performative art form through the medium of digital platforms, remotely, in a disembodied world. In the following narrative we will discuss the context of drama education in New Zealand, how it is addressed in our school and the arts-based approach we took to generate our stories of pandemic drama teaching. We will look at the concerns we have had and some of the solutions and successes we experienced.

2   Drama in New Zealand Secondary Schools

Secondary schools in New Zealand teach students from Year 9 to Year 13. The National Curriculum, which was introduced twenty years ago, lists Drama as one of four Arts subjects valued because:

> students learn to work both independently and collaboratively to construct meanings, produce works, and respond to and value others' contributions. They learn to use imagination to engage with unexpected outcomes and to explore multiple solutions. (Ministry of Education, 2014, para. 3)

Senior students at Year 11 to 13 can study Drama as one of their National Certificates of Educational Achievement (NCEA) which contributes towards a university entrance qualification.

2.1   *Drama in Our School*
The school is an urban state co-educational secondary school. It is well-resourced, with a modern learning environment. At Year 9, Drama is a mandated subject at the school. All students participate in three, hour-long

classes a week for one term. At Year 10, Drama is offered as a year-long optional course. At Years 11 to 13, students can opt to study Drama for NCEA Level 1, 2, and 3. A few students opt to undertake the Scholarship examination, a "portfolio of recorded performances and oral justifications, with supporting evidence" (NZQA, 2022) live to camera. Extra-curricular opportunities are offered during the year including a school production.

The World Economic Forum (2016, Exhibit 1) advocates for the skills of creativity, communication, and collaboration to be foremost in education to prepare students for life in the 21st century. This, and the knowledge that drama lies at the heart of a society where imagination is key to helping us to work collectively and "cooperate flexibly in large numbers" (Harari, 2011, p. 27), helps us to promote drama as a vital learning experience.

3 Using Arts Based Research

Early in the pandemic, Davis, and Phillips (2020) sought "to ascertain how teachers were making sense of the COVID-19 restrictions, the impact upon teaching and learning, and how their understandings influenced their practices" (p. 67). Their motivation for conducting the research was the "relatively low-profile given to teacher voices about how they were experiencing these extraordinary changes" (p. 66). As drama teachers researching our own practice, we too were questioning how we could better facilitate our embodied subject via hybrid and synchronous means. We decided to explore our own stories from the 'coalface' of the drama classroom.

We are informed by arts-based researchers, including Lynn Fels (2012) who articulated Performative Inquiry to inquire "into what matters as we engage in drama or theatre activities" (Fels, 2012, p. 51), and Peter O'Connor and Michael Anderson (2015), who remind us that "we know the world through all our senses, through our bodies" (p. 26). Arts-based researchers, and particularly those who focus on drama, inspire us as they embrace narratives, personal experience, emotions, performative, and intuitive responses as valid aspects of research. We juxtaposed our stories with our previous experiences of teaching drama and recognised our emotive responses to the changing times. Our shared discussions took place remotely and face to face, often in the immediate moments after lessons when our joys and disappointments were at their highest level. Writing this chapter, and a previous article (Luton & Hood, 2022) has helped us to reflect further on how, and even whether, drama can truly be effectively taught in secondary schools when we cannot meet in the actual and live space. Throughout this experience our question has always been 'how can we create learning tasks to generate more than just talking heads'? So, during the pandemic lockdowns of 2021, and 2022, how did this online engagement realise some successful outcomes?

4   The Concerns of Teaching Drama Remotely

4.1   *Like Nailing Jelly to a Wall*
Davis and Phillips' (2020) findings regarding the "shared challenges" (p. 67) of drama teachers during the pandemic confirmed that we were not alone in attempting to teach an embodied subject remotely. We have described our experiences of teaching in this pandemic as like 'nailing jelly to a wall' (Luton & Hood, 2022b) or Sisyphus rolling his rock uphill (Luton & Hood, 2022).

Gallagher et al. (2020) consider that "in an exclusively digital realm where the live drama classroom has temporarily fallen away [...] traditional understandings of 'embodiment', 'participation' and 'ensemble' no longer apply" (p. 641). Teaching in this remote world has certainly made us question whether our work can still be called 'Drama' when we cannot be embodied and collegial. The digital world *appears* to bring us all together when in fact we are just disparate icons and talking heads on a screen.

4.2   *The Virtual Only Drama Classroom*
In the 'real' drama classroom, learning takes place through group activities, exploration, improvising, and devising. Much of this collegial learning is lost in the virtual space, because each student sits alone in their own environment with their own set of circumstances. We found that many students disengaged from being part of the online classroom. Instead of turning on their camera students appeared as an icon on the screen what Gallagher et al. (2020) call an "absent presence" (p. 639). They chose to type responses rather than using the microphone or camera to join discussions. Many did not join online lessons at all for which teachers had little recourse. Despite our attempts to maintain a sense of a supportive and positive community there was instead a sense of disconnection and lack of collaboration – the antithesis to the skills and practice of an embodied drama classroom. This was disheartening and frustrating, denting even the most positive pedagogues after weeks of disengagement.

4.3   *Remote and Hybrid Configurations of the Drama Space*
As the pandemic progressed, so did the challenges and possible configurations of the drama space. Some of these are given in Table 9.1.

TABLE 9.1   Remote and hybrid configurations of the drama space

Teacher	Student
Pre-COVID-19 teacher teaches in the live space of the classroom/drama studio During COVID-19 Teachers teach remotely from 'home' via an online platform. Everyone is in the remote space.	Pre-COVID-19 students learn in the live space of the classroom/drama studio Students learn remotely from 'home' via an online platform. Everyone is in the remote space.
Some year groups attend school. Teacher is in the live space of the classroom but teaches some classes through the online platform.	Some year groups have classes in the real space of the classroom and can be embodied. Some year groups learn remotely from home. They are in the remote space.
Teacher must isolate. They teach remotely from 'home'. They are in the virtual space, seen on a screen in the live classroom. The teacher uses two screens for a panoptic view of the live space and one for breakout rooms.	Some students are embodied in the real space of the classroom responding to the teacher who appears on a screen in the classroom. A relief teacher must be present for health, safety, and management requirements. Isolating students learn from home joining their working groups in the classroom via breakout rooms set up by the teacher where they can share ideas.

5   The Logistical Problems of Teaching Drama Remotely

We encountered several problems during remote and hybrid teaching including both tangible, pragmatic issues, and those of a more aesthetic nature.

5.1   *Inequity*

Firstly, despite the BYOD policy and support available for students especially from lower socio-economic circumstances, not everyone had access to working technology or fast broadband. As Gallagher et al. (2020) highlight from other studies, "differences in access to tools and habits of use complicate the assumption that young people have an innate affinity for all things digital" (p. 642). The students who did attend classes online often struggled to participate despite teachers' best efforts to engage them. Fear and embarrassment, along with a lack of working technology and private places at home to learn, proved to be a hindrance to drama lessons being actively embodied (Luton & Hood, 2022). This was exacerbated by the digital registration system which by default marked all students as attending online learning. This meant follow up for non-attendance was difficult.

Secondly, Microsoft Teams is designed for sedentary subjects and meetings. Students and teachers sit in front of a screen situated on a desk whereas in a drama classroom we are active in an empty space. Teams allows us to communicate, but we can only *pretend* to be together on screen, face to face, enhanced by breakout rooms and 'Together' mode which is designed to "mimic[s]the way humans interact" (Microsoft, 2022, para. 4) and to "replicate the experience of physically gathering together" (para. 17). But in the online space we miss much of the subtlety of actual direct human interactions including gesture and eye contact.

5.2   *Classroom Management and Safety*

For drama teachers it has been particularly difficult to facilitate lessons *remotely* while the students are in the *actual* space of the classroom. For health and safety reasons, junior and senior students cannot be left unattended in classrooms and a 'reliever' must be present to cover for an absent teacher. Classroom management is vital for successful outcomes in drama. Good working practices must be established including "structure and control" (Cowley, 2007, p. 5) that keep children both physically and emotionally safe and "willing to work with anyone and everyone" (p. 5). Prior to the pandemic, teachers needing to be absent sent in appropriate 'quiet' lessons, but now there is an expectation that teachers will continue to teach students from home, beaming into the classroom via a screen.

Mobile phone use is banned from the live classroom to protect students from being filmed or recorded when creating and experimenting with ideas. During online classes, teachers found they had to carefully monitor chat features sometimes muting students. However, we were unable to monitor the 'behind the scenes' communication via text messaging and other forums which happened during class making some students feel unsafe.

Coming directly from intermediate schools (Years 7 & 8) where drama is often not taught, Year 9 students are apprehensive and nervous of working actively together in groups. They are unsure of the processes, and drama aesthetics as taught in the drama curriculum. They struggle at first to generate and share ideas. This was problematic when attempting to use Microsoft Teams 'Breakout Rooms' with junior students. This feature enables a teacher to divide the class into small online groups. Unfortunately, unlike working in a real classroom where both the teacher and student groups interact physically, digital rooms can only be monitored when the teacher 'enters' each digital space. This difficulty was also encountered by Adam Cziboly and Adam Bethlenfalvy (2020) using Breakout rooms to work with tertiary drama students as they:

> did not have an overview of 'what is going on in the four corners of the room'. [They] could follow only one group or pair at a time, and [they] needed to trust that the others would adhere to the task. (p. 647)

As teachers of junior students, we also found Breakout rooms had the potential to be an unsafe space where the 'rules' of mutual respect and support cannot be easily monitored.

5.3 *Establishing Community*

Although we are limited by the number and length of lessons, one of the aims of drama in school is to establish a community. Community is developed by being together in the space, working on a shared purposeful project, and by encouraging and sharing ideas supported by positive critique. Everyone can see everyone, and the teacher can quietly offer support where necessary to individuals and groups. As Davis and Phillips (2020) suggest, "considerable effort is required by the teacher to create and maintain a sense of 'teacher presence' within and across online spaces, and to generate feelings of warmth and a sense of community" (pp. 75–76). This helps to allay the natural fears that students face when working and sharing their ideas with their peers. This, we feel, led to the students hiding behind their icons or limiting their appearance to a talking head. Regrettably, this sense of community was lost to us during this time of fear and confusion.

5.4 *Working with the Aesthetic*

In the real classroom space, guided by the teacher, students develop a familiarity with the aesthetics of drama and theatre, its conventional and spatial forms, and how to develop, understand, and communicate meaning through the art form. The Techniques (the use of voice, body, movement, and space), Elements (including focus, action, time, tension, role, mood, and symbol), and Conventions (for example using still images, or thoughts spoken aloud) offer myriad possibilities for exploration and shaping of narratives. Students might also play with technologies such as costume, lighting, and sound. As Luton (2021) describes:

A teacher might facilitate contrasts of sound and silence, movement and stillness, light and dark to encourage student creativity [...]. For the most part, students tend to collaborate, in groups developing and demonstrating how to take advantage of a space, as well as listening, speaking, taking turns, or experimenting with ideas. (p. 90)

As students develop and share their work they learn with, and from each other. At its very heart, drama is primarily a live, spontaneous and interactive medium, each iteration unique when shared with an audience. Teaching drama in a digital space removes much of what makes drama aesthetically interesting, collegial, and immediate. The shared embodied experience that relies heavily on non-verbal communication was sometimes by necessity replaced by script reading, writing or solo performances to camera.

5.5   *Technology*

Another difficulty of teaching online is the limited view of the class offered by a laptop screen. In the real space of a drama classroom empty of desks and chairs, the teacher moves freely, their eyes keenly aware of the students and activities that surround them, controlling the space with just a look, the epitome of 'eyes in the back of their head'.

Faced with this problem, Jacqui purchased an extra screen to help facilitate remote lessons which became a 'godsend'. One screen showed the entire class, the second was used for the breakout rooms. The two screens allowed Jacqui to watch the whole class while interacting with small groups and individuals ensuring a better control of health and safety.

FIGURE 9.1   View of the drama studio with device and screen for hybrid teaching

Sharing drama work online using Teams brought other problems including poor sound quality, the delay making it almost impossible to speak in unison. This is due to variance between individual microphones, digital connections, computer speakers and broadband. All of this detracts from the potential impact of using aesthetics like chorus, music, and sound effects.

6   Solutions and Successes of Teaching Drama Remotely

Amidst the problems of teaching drama remotely and in hybrid forms, in this time of disconnection, there were glimmers of hope and sparks of engagement that shone brightly. This was evident with the senior students who had experienced drama in the pre-pandemic era, several having participated in school productions and drama festivals. They knew each other well, had a shared history of working on various drama projects and assessments, and were a cohesive unit prior to entering lockdown. Many had been together since Year 10 and progressed through NCEA drama classes where group work is essential. The students knew they could rely on one another when completing 'high-stakes' assessment and were therefore much more willing to be vulnerable, creative, and playful within the virtual space. As a result, a range of impactful, creative work was developed by these senior students.

6.1   *Using Breakout Rooms with Senior Students*

Jacqui created breakout rooms for Year 13 students who were automatically assigned to work in smaller groups of two or three. They were tasked with creating a practical embodied response to the 'live' drama, the Royal National Theatre's production of *Jane Eyre*, viewed as part of their course. The response had to relate to the mood, meaning, and impact the scene had on them as viewers. They were asked to find objects and scenography in their own home that would support their embodied response. Students discussed and explored their ideas creatively before sharing the work with the rest of the class onscreen.

When it came time to share ideas to the class, the audience muted their microphones. Unlike a film, the students performed their piece live and in continuous action to their watching peers who showed appreciative expressions, receiving their verbal feedback once microphones were unmuted. One student focused on the scene where Thornfield House burns to the ground. On a baking tray in their kitchen, close to a water supply, a little model paper house sat which the student carefully lit with a match. Another student spoke some lines from the play as the little house was enveloped in flames and red embers lifted into the air before falling again on the tray. This would not have been possible in the drama studio at school! The performance demonstrated the imaginative possibilities that some students discovered, although constrained by the pandemic.

6.1.1   Positive Outcomes

There were clear positive outcomes from this task. The improvised nature of the initial exploration was like the classroom experience. The principal difference was that all the students were working within their own digital and 'real' spaces of home. This inspired new creative possibilities when a range of household resources were repurposed as props, costumes, characters, and sets for scenes. The students thought inventively and theatrically. The use of coloured items to symbolise and represent themes and costumes, which transformed into characters mid-scene, were all examples of their creative thinking. The students' creative energies impacted everyone involved as they recognised the originality of each other's work appreciating the ways that each group had explored their chosen moment. There was a renewed sense of community and interactive engagement.

6.2   *Using Resources to Devise Theatre Online*

NCEA drama at Year 13, seeks to challenge students to think critically about issues within New Zealand and to respond to them by devising work inspired by theatre practitioners and local resources. As part of this process, students were given a photograph of an art installation *14* by Bernie Harfleet (2022), that Jacqui had been impacted by when visiting a Sculpture Park. Fourteen pine caskets represent the lives of the "14 women [who are] killed in NZ by a member of their family each year" (Harfleet, 2022). The social issues raised by the artwork were initially discussed in an online class led by Jacqui. The task was complex. Students were asked to explore and devise drama arising from the issues, informed by the work of theatre practitioner Antonin Artaud, whom they had studied previously. Firstly, students brainstormed words that came to mind in response to the various resources. They then created a short, devised piece using a variety of movement and vocal styles including unison, canon, mirroring, repetition, exaggeration, and variations of pace, to support their chosen words. Students performed their responses to the class each appearing individually but working as a group in the digital space.

One of these groups juxtaposed the public face of a relationship with the private reality. Two actors held out their hands to the camera repeating "I love you" while another actor pummelled a pillow just off camera, breathing heavily. Two of the actors moved closely towards the camera whispering "help,

I need help". Hysterical laughter could be heard offscreen from the third actor as the others withdrew from the camera and resumed their original positions. The students were enthusiastic and brave in their responses to the resources and the piece created an impact. It demonstrated that emotion and context could be communicated in the digital space extremely successfully when students were willing to work without worrying about how they appeared on their camera feedback. The shared ideas generated further conversations about the issues raised. This work continued to be developed over several lessons and was eventually performed in the 'real' performance space. This hybrid model created initial impetus during lockdown, as students equated working online from their bedrooms, locked away from the world, to the image of the fourteen caskets each standing alone in the external space.

6.3 Encouraging Solo Work with Junior Students

Teaching remotely constrained us from doing group work with Year 9 students so we developed opportunities for solo presentations using only the resources available at home.

6.3.1 Pretending

Jane asked a class of Year 9 drama students to imagine that they were television reporters, and to invite any whanau [family] members to participate as interviewees in their area of expertise during the pandemic. The interviews had to be filmed on their cameras and uploaded to Teams for review by the teacher. Not only did students develop interesting interviews filmed in their gardens and different locations within their homes, but family members including parents, siblings, and grandparents made appearances. Insightful questions were asked, enabling us to hear about the difficulties being faced by many of front-line workers of the pandemic, from nurses to wholesalers. This activity gave us the opportunity to see individual students engaging with ideas creatively. The students thought about role and settings for their scenes, while their interviewees stepped into the imaginative space to pretend that they were speaking with a reporter. There was a sense of pride in the work presented by students and one can only hope that this might have offered a positive project that families could engage with.

6.3.2 Using Imagination

Another solo project done with Year 9 students was the preparation and presentation of a poem *as if* to small children. They were given a video resource from a children's writer explaining how to present to a young audience. The task offered possibilities for students to be playful and enthusiastic in their delivery. One of the vital aspects of drama is the use of the imagination and the willingness to accept "as if" situations. We increasingly found that if tasks were expressed in terms of "imagine that …", students seem to embrace the task more fully, having a purpose for their work. Many of the students did indeed record and upload their poem to be seen only by the teacher via Teams Assignments. These solo tasks accomplished by students gave us a closer insight into their abilities and hopefully allowed them the chance to pretend and have fun.

6.4   *Directing through the Screen*

As Jacqui was isolating with COVID, she was able to continue directing a fifteen-minute scene entered for the national Shakespeare festival. The small group of students from Year 9 to 13, gathered in medical masks in the large performing arts centre to rehearse the performance. The lead student placed a laptop on a central table and set up the meeting via Teams. Jacqui was able to see the entire group and give direction from home. This process worked well as the students were mature and some had experience in being part of a school production. Once again, a teacher needed to be present in the space to ensure health and safety protocols. The students were able to accept teacher and peer direction working together successfully, eventually winning first place in the local heats. After lockdown they subsequently travelled to the capital city to meet other successful competitors for workshops and training. Davis and Phillips (2020) suggest that:

> The community of the classroom, the energy, interchange and dynamics is part of what makes drama and performing arts teaching worthwhile, the human dimensions are fundamental. (p. 83)

This particular use of technology to rehearse a play came close to those human dimensions as the students were able to interact, work collegially, and create together in the real space. Jacqui was able to maintain the relationships previously developed, albeit directing from home. However, this did rely on a mature response from the students willing to take direction and committed to working together towards a common goal.

6.5   *Seeing International 'Live Theatre'*

Prior to the pandemic, senior students were required to see 'live' theatre to discuss and demonstrate their understanding of a performance for their drama examination. This required students to travel to a venue to see theatre during the year of examination. During the pandemic the National Qualifications Authority [NZQA] instead allowed students to watch productions that had been filmed 'live'. Schools throughout the country embraced national and international performances such as those from the Royal National Theatre in London. Students experienced a wide range of theatrical possibilities, and they could watch, and re-watch selected scenes to develop their eye for detail. All students in a class had access to the same production ensuring equity for those who may have previously struggled financially and logistically to attend a theatre production.

A participant in Lisa Siciliano's (2021) research suggested they did not watch a National Theatre Live production because "it's just an experience that cannot be equalled in a platform that wasn't meant to house it" (p. 3). However, for drama teachers working in secondary schools, productions like these are highly valuable, captured live, in a 'real' theatre space with an audience present that can be seen and heard. The play running continuously, including the interval. This provides a different theatre experience to that offered by pandemic digital performances where plays have been presented via Zoom with actors appearing at home in their own 'talking head', sometimes presenting a read performance rather than an enacted one. While the students cannot experience the spontaneity of live performance themselves, sharing the space with the actors, they can watch and re-watch the show identifying and discussing the aesthetics in detail as per the examination specifications. One of the positive outcomes from this has been an improvement in written examination results. This was noticeable when examining the data since 2019 for the department. Together the teacher and students created extensive notes through focused online discussions which were then collated and further developed when they returned to school.

7   Conclusions: New Challenges and Celebrations

7.1   *New Challenges*

Davis and Phillips (2020), and Cziboly and Bethlenfalvy (2020) have acknowledged these teaching times as difficult and full of new challenges. Researchers are determined to find ways to "create innovative drama pedagogies that can respond to an unpredictable future" (Gallagher et al., 2020, p. 640). Siciliano asks whether it is "possible to possess two conflicting realities at the same time – one of holding fast to what theatre was before the pandemic and one of embracing the new ways of doing things" (2021, p. 6).

Throughout the pandemic we have tried to find ways to engage our students, experimenting and remaining flexible in our teaching approaches. We watched online theatre performances created during the pandemic to draw inspiration and while we could applaud their successes, we recognised that Year 9 and 10 students do not want to be seen online let alone participate without the tangible support of their peers and teacher in the real space. Although there have been successes in remote teaching, particularly among the senior students, they have in reality all been variations on 'talking heads' with solo performances. When viewed together on the screen these give some sense of a group presentation.

Unfortunately, the downside of students studying remotely in disrupted classrooms since the pandemic began is the ongoing negative effect it has had on attendance rates with percentages that "sit below attendance levels in other comparable countries" (Education Review Office, 2022). This in turn has had a devastating effect on the number of students choosing to study drama. This is particularly sad as the school has had many years of highly successful student engagement, examination results, and school productions. Without the live interactive experience, students have missed out on the excitement and challenges of creating drama in the real space with their peers. Students who continue to study drama are mainly the ones who have previously experienced the excitement of embodied interaction. This gives rise to new challenges of how to retain and increase numbers to ensure students can develop their creative and communicative skills as part of a community while having fun.

7.2   *Returning to Normal?*

On our return to school in 2021, after the long lockdown, we decided to team teach our junior classes and bring them together in the larger performing arts space. We banned all digital devices except one to project images and text onto a large screen. We used challenging material. Although we were masked, we were together, we could see everyone, and we could model and encourage activities. Students moved and used their voices, they shared ideas to create responses, they made eye contact with their peers, and by the end of each lesson had a sense of achievement shared tangibly and together. However, 2022 forced teachers to once again find innovative ways to engage drama students in various hybrid situations. New Zealand academic Gavin Brown, has suggested that:

> Given the evolution of humans as social beings, ... interacting with others helps with our thinking, emotions and physicality.
>
> There's something about being human that requires us to live and interact with others that I fear a de-schooled society, using only computers would deprive our children of. (cited in Poland, 2022, p. 11)

Drama teachers know this only too well. But for now, Teams remains a constant in the lives of both students and teachers while life slowly begins to move towards a new normality. Teams may provide a useful platform for learning, but we argue that it only provides 'talking heads', while teachers and students remain for the most part, disembodied. Although we have acknowledged some success with students, we remain sceptical about teaching drama remotely, and suggest that drama is most effective when we are being creative together, face to face, in the shared, tangible, and embodied space.

References

Brook, P. (1968). *The empty space*. Penguin.

Cowley, S. (2007). *Getting the buggers into drama: practical strategies for using drama across the curriculum*. Continuum.

Cziboly, A., & Bethlenfalvy, A. (2020). Response to COVID-19 – Zooming in on online process drama. *Research in Drama Education, 25*(4), 645–651. https://doi.org/10.1080/13569783.2020.1816818

Davis, S., & Phillips, L. (2020). Teaching during COVID 19 times – The experiences of drama and performing arts teachers and the human dimensions of learning. *NJ: Drama Australia 2020, 44*(2), 66–87. https://doi.org/10.1080/14452294.2021.1943838

Dunphy-Lelii, S. (2020, August 1). The weirdness of watching yourself on zoom. *Scientific American*. https://www.scientificamerican.com/article/the-weirdness-of-watching-yourself-on-zoom/

Education Review Office. (2022, November 10). *Missing out: Why aren't our children going to school?* https://ero.govt.nz/our-research/missing-out-why-arent-our-children-going-to-school

Fels, L. (2012). Collecting data through performative inquiry: A tug on the sleeve. *Youth Theatre Journal, 26*(1), 50–60. https://doi.org/10.1080/08929092.2012.678209

Gallagher, K., Balt, C., Cardwell, N., & Charlebois, B. (2020). Response to COVID-19 – Losing and finding one another in drama: personal geographies, digital spaces and new intimacies. *Research in Drama Education, 25*(4), 638–644. https://doi.org/10.1080/13569783.2020.1816817

Harari, Y. (2011). *Sapiens: A brief history of humankind*. Vintage.

Harfleet, B. (2022). *14* [Art installation]. The Sculpture Park at Waitakaruru Arboretum, Waikato, New Zealand. https://www.sculpturepark.co.nz/exhibitions/autumn-winter-gallery/sculptures/14--15

Luton, J., & Hood, J. (2022, August 3). A Sisyphean task? Doing drama online with year 9 students in a COVID-19 lockdown. *Teachers and Curriculum [Special Issue: The*

arts will find a way: Breaking through and moving forward], 22(1) 39–45.
https://www.tandc.ac.nz/tandc/issue/view/48

Luton, J., & Hood, J. (2022b, November 13–15). *Like nailing jelly to a wall! Using performative inquiry to reflect on teaching drama in a lockdown* [Paper]. New Zealand Association for Research in Education (NZARE) Te aonui: The mighty triangle [Online
conference].

Luton, J. (2021). The space of possibilities: The drama classroom as the first innovative
learning environment. In E. Khoo & N. Wright (Eds.), *Pedagogy and partnerships in
innovative learning environments: Case studies from New Zealand contexts*. Springer.
https://www.springer.com/gp/book/9789811657108

Microsoft. (2022). *Bringing us together: How Microsoft built a new way to meet online –
and changed the world of work in the process*. https://www.microsoft.com/en-us/
worklab/bringing-us-together

Ministry of Education. (2014, March 25). *The New Zealand curriculum online: Why
study the arts?* https://nzcurriculum.tki.org.nz/The-New-Zealand-Curriculum/The-
arts/Why-study-the-arts

NZQA. (2022). *New Zealand scholarship drama* [Webpage]. https://www.nzqa.govt.nz/
qualifications-standards/awards/new-zealand-scholarship/scholarship-
subjects/scholarship-drama/

O'Connor, P., & Anderson, M. (2015). *Applied theatre: Research: Radical departures*.
Bloomsbury Methuen Drama.

Poland, O. (2022, May 16). Beyond lockdown learning: Lessons for the future. *Waipapa
Taumata Rau University of Auckland Ingenio Alumni Magazine*.
https://www.auckland.ac.nz/en/news/2022/05/16/Ingenio-education-in-
lockdown-lessons.html

Siciliano, L. (2021): Is online theatre really theatre? Teaching and researching during
a pandemic. *Teaching Artist Journal*. https://doi.org/10.1080/15411796.2021.1958220

Todorov, G. (2022, May 25). *37 funniest work from home memes that are so true in 2022*.
https://thrivemyway.com/work-from-home-memes/

World Economic Forum. (2016, March 10). *Ten 21st-century skills every student needs:
Exhibit 3: A variety of general and targeted learning strategies foster social and
emotional skills*. https://www.weforum.org/agenda/2016/03/21st-century-skills-
future-jobs-students/

University Students' Experiences Using Digital Technology in Choral Music Performance

A Case of Maseno University Choir Members

Nancy Abigael Masasabi

Abstract

The use of Technology in teaching became more profound as a result of the COVID-19 worldwide pandemic. Social distancing and lack of group gathering became the norm that we all had to follow. University students were to perform two songs and it was difficult to bring the students together for choir rehearsals and performance. It was agreed that a guiding music track be prepared and given to each student for rehearsal. The students used their cell phones to listen to the pre-recorded music, practice, and to record their final part video-performance. The video recorded performances were then put together into one performance having all the voice parts synchronised using Kinemaster.

This study aims to show how available digital technology can be utilised in the practice and performance of choral music in an informal music learning set up. Moreover, the study sought to answer the question: what were the students' experiences during learning and performance of two songs using digital technology? The study targeted sixty choir members of Maseno University. Out of this, thirty-five were able to actively participate by handing in their recorded performances. The thirty-five students were interviewed through video calls and face to face. Emerging themes were analysed by employing elements of found poetry (written by the researcher and two interviewees) and analytical observations. The use of found poetry as an art-based method illuminated interviewee experiences. The findings provide another lens through which arts education using digital technology can be elucidated and actualised.

Keywords

choral music practice – music performance – digital technology – poetic inquiry – found poetry

1 Introduction

> The prizes of life are at the end of each journey, not near the beginning; and it is not given to me to know how many steps are necessary in order to reach my goal. Failure I may still encounter at the thousandth step, yet success hides behind the next bend in the road. Never will I know how close it lies unless I turn the corner. (Mandino, 1997, p. 38)

Increase in the use of technology in various facets of everyday life continues to be a defining factor of the contemporary world. The younger generation have embraced the internet so much and they spend a considerable amount of time in it and other social media platforms. Burnard (2001, p. 38) avers,

> the internet, for example is their new playground and creates different social rooms for them. In addition, many young people are already high-end or passive consumption-bound users and consumers of music technology, mass media and the production technologies when they come to school. They are often motivated by out of school experiences of music technology.

In education the use of music technology, which is "the use of technologies for musical purposes" (Ferreira, 2007, p. 23), have found their way in the formal teaching and learning environment. Here technology has rapidly been used in various areas of music teaching and learning including music composition, musicianship training, and music theory. Scholars have discussed the place of technology in the teaching and learning process in the music classroom from various viewpoints (Creech, 2012; Macedo, 2013; Stowell & Dickson, 2014; Pignato, 2017; Upitis, 2014). Moreover, there has been an improvement of access to education through technology. Whereas there has been significant attention to music technology in the formal music learning setup, there has been little attention paid to the use of technology in choral music rehearsal and performance outside the classroom setup. Johnson (2018) has discussed the use of technology in choral rehearsal of secondary school students in America from the viewpoint that students do not practice effectively out of classroom in order to improve their performance in the classroom.

In Kenya, there has been scholarly attention on the role and need to use technology in the secondary school level classroom (Achola, 2007). In essence the use of technology in the informal music learning environment has received little attention, especially where choral practice and performance is concerned.

The use of Technology in teaching became more profound as a result of the COVID-19 worldwide pandemic. Social distancing and lack of group gathering became the norm that we all had to follow. This set up affected both the formal and informal learning of music. University students were invited by the Permanent Presidential Music Commission (PPMC) to perform two songs in a national event and it was difficult to bring the students together for choir rehearsals and performance. What would the choir director do? It is this scenario that prompted this study as the researcher/choir director had to create an alternative way to circumvent the situation and achieve the objective of having a choral performance.

2   Background of the Choir

Maseno University is a public university in Kenya which started as a constituent College of Moi university in 1990. At the moment it is a full-fledged university having received its charter in 2013. At its inception Maseno University created a department of Music which formulated the University choir. The growth of the choir over the years has been attributed to its role as a laboratory where students put into practice what is taught in class in terms of composition and performance. Since the choir is accommodated in the department of music, it has been imperative to consider a high level of musicianship in its performance. The choir has participated at the Kenya Music Festival, national state functions, Agricultural Society of Kenya functions in Kisumu, and Graduation ceremonies within the institution. The choir started participating at the Kenya Music Festival, in 1994 and continues to do so to date. Its exemplary performance has been recognised in that, "In August 1995, the choir was invited by the Kenya Music Festival committee to perform at State House as a representative of universities choral groups" (Adwar, 2010, p. 63). In addition, the Maseno University choir has been invited several times by the Permanent Presidential Music Commission (PPMC) to perform alongside students from other universities in a mass choir. The PPMC in Kenya is a body that organises entertainment at all national state functions. The formation of this mass choir gives students an opportunity to practice and share experiences with their colleagues from various universities. In 2020 the PPMC requested the performance of two anthems: the national anthem and the East African anthem, by university choirs. This was to be done virtually.

By 2020 the university choir had a team of ten students referred to as the technical team. It was made up of the chairperson of the choir, a chairperson of the team and two members from each voice, thus two from soprano, two from alto, two from tenor, and two from Bass. This team was made up of students taking a Bachelor of Education or a Bachelor of Arts Music degree at the department of Music and Theatre studies where the choir is based. These students were good at sight reading and therefore assisted in the training of musical pieces in the choir on a day to day basis under the supervision of the choir director. The group would meet with the choir director on a weekly basis to determine what was to be trained and assess the progress of the choir

Students had to use technology in a way that they had never done before. The use of modern technology has been adopted at various degrees. Whereas there are a number of applications and softwares available for performance such as Flipgrid, Google form, Accompanist app and Acapella among others, the students used their cell phones to listen to the pre-recorded music, practise, and to record their final part video-performance. The video recorded performances were then put together into one performance having all the voice parts synchronised using Kinemaster.

3   Methodology

This is a case study of Maseno University choir members. The study targeted sixty choir members of Maseno University. Out of this, thirty-five were able to actively participate by handing in their recorded performances. The thirty-five students were interviewed through video calls and face to face. A group of ten students who took part in self-assessment was made up of two voice part representatives and two overall coordinators of the team. The technical team was engaged in a focused group discussion and finally the researcher engaged in observation of the entire process. Thematic and narrative analysis was done. Emerging themes were described and presented in prose. Narratives given by the respondents were analysed by employing elements of found poetry (written by the researcher and two interviewees). Found poetry is an art-based data presentation form that has been discussed by a number of scholars (Prendergast 2012; Richardson 2002). Janesick (2016, p. 31) explains that, "the use of found poem, that is poetry found in ... the interview transcripts ... offers another way of viewing, presenting, and making sense of data". This study used the steps given by Schrauben and Leigh (2019, p. 2051) to come up with the poems from interviews which are:

Step 1 is to select interview data from which clarification is needed ...
Step 2: reread participant interview data and highlight ... recurring ideas

that occur in the transcript … Step 3: underline I-statements in an effort to establish the participant's voice … Step 4: arrange the signature lines and I-statements into stanzas that make sense and have reader flow … Step 5: invite the participant to read the PIP …

The use of found poetry as an art-based method illuminated interviewee experiences.

4   Findings and Discussion

This section combines the findings and discussion of those findings. The songs chosen were anthems which had been performed several times earlier synchronously thus it was assumed that students were conversant with their parts. However, having stayed home for some months without choir practice, most students had forgotten their parts and their voices were out of shape. There was no direction given on how long they were to practice. Whereas some students practiced for only one day before recording, majority had to practice for five days to ten days before recording their parts (see Table 10.1). Those who practiced for long periods complained of having forgotten their parts, thus they required more time to remind themselves of their parts. It was noted that some students confessed performing well when singing in a group but were unsteady when they had to sing on their own. Those who practiced an hour to recording were those in the technical team. Since they were conversant with all parts as a result of their training skills, they found it very easy to go ahead and record. There was a sense of self-regulation and self-assessment by the students as they strove to accomplish the tasks assigned to them. The students had a goal to achieve and this was a motivating factor to them. Parkes (2022, p. 112) affirms that, "self-regulation includes processes such as goal setting,

TABLE 10.1   Total number of practice days

Practice days	Student responses
7–10	15
4–6	9
1–3	6
Below 24 hrs	5

meta-cognition, and self-assessment". These processes were present during the practice moments by students.

To assist the students, instructions were given to them through a WhatsApp forum for choir members. Here a guiding instrumental track with the vocal line for each voice part was supplied. The students had to listen to the track containing their vocal line. Sopranos used the soprano track and so on for both songs. All students used the appropriate guiding track that was provided and cited that it was very useful to them. Bendall 2020 refers to a traditional face to face choir as a synchronous choir. He further explicates that while synchronous choir performances make use of a conductor, a virtual choir makes use of a guiding track. Galvan and Clauhs (2020) also highlight the importance of having such a track which they refer to as a reference track. A virtual choir or a virtual vocal ensemble according to Cayari (2016) is

> an ensemble whose performances are comprised of multitrack recordings. *Multitrack* is a vernacular term used to describe a recording that is created by layering audio-visual tracks. Often virtual vocal ensembles contain multiple audio-visual tracks layered together to create a performance. (p. 4)

The guiding track provided was useful to the students in that it set the tempo, key of performance and cued the entries. With no further instruction given on tempo, the track gave room for the students to use a unified tempo and tonality. It was not easy to have a synchronous rehearsal thus rehearsal was asynchronous. Having a unified tempo would then make it easy to align the various video tracks. It was noted that even after providing the guiding track, some students had some practice sessions without it. The reason given for this is to find out whether they could manage to sing accurately. In so doing the students were carrying out self-assessment.

Students were instructed to use any available gadget for practice and recording. It was noted that thirty-three (94.2%) out of the thirty-five students exclusively used their cell phones to play the given guiding track during their rehearsals. Attached to their phones some used earphones while others used Bluetooth speakers to amplify the sound. The other two students used both laptops and cell phones. Johnson (2018) also notes the overwhelming use of cell phones in listening to music recordings during the students' individual rehearsal sessions. The overwhelming use of cell phones is attributed to the fact that cell phones are handy.

TABLE 10.2   Issues encountered during rehearsal

Issues	Number of students
Difficulty in rehearsing alone	4
Poor vocal quality	10
Interference from family	35
Power outage	5
Forgotten parts	12

4.1   Emerging Issues Encountered by Students during Rehearsal

Choir rehearsals for a long time were done as an ensemble. Even during the learning of every voice part, the students had the opportunity of singing together. The scenario set before them was different. Rehearsal was individual. It was upon every student to decide the best time of rehearsal thus some sense of responsibility was expected of them. This process was faced by a number of issues (see Table 10.2) which are explained in the following sections.

4.2   Difficulty in Rehearsing Alone

Rehearsing is a crucial facet of every musical performance experience. This session enables a musician to focus on areas that are problematic to them. Such areas may include pitch accuracy, rhythm accuracy, articulation, diction, phrasing and the like. On one hand, some students seemed to enjoy the entire process while on the other hand some struggled with the idea of practicing individually. Singers who cited this as a challenge did not seem to know how to go about their practice. "where do I start from?" was a common phrase among them. As an eye opener for the researcher, such students do not have a culture of individual practice. The over reliance on synchronous practice was evident here. Thus, the singers here would have preferred further instructions on how to rehearse. However, they proceeded to do what they could.

4.3   Poor Vocal Quality

In order to have good vocal quality it is important for one to have regular vocal exercises. As a result of the COVID 19 pandemic, most of the choir members were out of practice. This affected their vocal quality. It became necessary for the students to use some of the vocal exercises that are used during synchronous practice sessions to improve their vocal quality. This meant that more time would be required to clear up their voices before having a good solo performance.

4.4   *Interference from Family Members*
The environment in which the students found themselves was not very conducive for practice. Finding themselves in a home set up, there was no reserved space for musical practice. It was difficult to detach themselves from family members and family activities. As a result, there was a lot of interference from the rest of the family. All students mentioned this as a main challenge for them. One student cited an incident where her mother called her during one of her rehearsal sessions to go and buy some groceries. She could not decline since in her community, it is a serious offence to disobey one's mother. Another could not go on with rehearsal since the mother requested her to take care of a younger sibling who could not just be quiet. In addition, complaints of them making noise to family members and neighbors became common place. Consequently, they had to sing softly. Another had to go out in an open field and practice there.

4.5   *Power Outage*
This is a common occurrence in Kenya that can take hours to days. In some instances, this interfered with the practice sessions that required a powered equipment whether a phone or laptop. Hence, practice sessions were delayed and picked up at a later time.

4.6   *Forgotten Parts*
Those who had forgotten their parts and used to rely heavily on others in their voice part really struggled. Any wrong pitch or rhythm would stand out in their recordings. Therefore, they had to learn the correct pitches before the final recording. Moreover, some of the students had forgotten the lyrics of the second and third stanza of the East African Anthem. The guiding track was able to remind them of the lyrics.

The individual performance of students revealed the weaknesses of some students. These are those who were unable to sing correct pitches and heavily relied on others to sing. The long absence of practice was a challenge for the many who could not organise solo rehearsals yet they had forgotten their parts. Whereas there were a number of obstacles facing their practice most students did not give up. Their sense of commitment and fulfillment pushed them to soldier on and accomplish the task set before them. In addition, the choir members had a sense of communal responsibility and a sense of belonging that was a driving force.

4.7 Emerging Issues Encountered during Video Recording

After some amount of rehearsal was done it was time for the students to video record their performances. At the onset instructions given included recording with a plain background and with a good quality camera. Only the upper body part was to be recorded while singing. It was up to the students to determine their dress code. They agreed to use a white shirt or blouse. Before the videos were submitted to the technical team each singer tried to comply with the set requirements. The technical team at the point of recording and submission carried out quality checks using the choir WhatsApp forum. There were two levels of quality checks. The first level was at the voice level, for example soprano, where the two persons in charge would listen to the other soprano singers and decide whether the melodic lines were accurate in pitch, rhythm, diction and lyrics. This was so for all the other voices, alto, tenor and bass. The second level was where the entire technical team would look into video background, video quality in terms of picture, lighting and sound. At this level members of the team had an opportunity to critique each video that was submitted. Feedback was given to every choir member who submitted their recording. Those that were found wanting were returned to the singer with comments on where the problem was so that they could rectify. The researcher who was the choir director followed the process, also giving feedback and approving every stage of the quality checks. The final recordings were handed to the choir director who worked with the chairperson of the choir to synchronise the videos.

This process was not without technical, social and environmental issues (see Table 10.3). I will hereby address each one of the ten emerging issues together with their extenuations.

TABLE 10.3   Issues encountered during video recording

Issues	Number of students
Loud track volume	3
Noisy environment	34
People walking in	10
Lack of internet	4
Power outage	4
Getting a good background	10
Poor video quality	11
Poor lighting	5
Poor recording microphones	3
Phone memory	2

The first issue noted here was having a loud track volume in the recording. This affected a few singers 8.6%. The students were unable to control the volume of the guiding track as they sung. The feedback given was to have the students lower the track volume so that their voices could be heard.

The second issue was having a noisy environment interfering with the sound. This affected almost all singers 97.1%. The home environment was not very conducive for the students. With the presence of other family members their recording sessions were greatly interfered with. For instance, some of the interferences included: laughing, shouting and talking from the next room, moving vehicles, animal sounds in the background such as cock crowing, cows mooing, and being called by parents during the recording process. Such scenarios interfered with the sound quality and prompted the singers to have recording sessions elongated. Some singers resorted to recording late in the night when all others were asleep or making requests to have some quiet time in order to accomplish the task.

The third issue had to do with interference of the video picture. As the singers were in the recording process someone would walk in, especially young children. In some cases, stubborn siblings would want to be part of the recording by trying to peep in. This affected 28.6% of the students.

Lack of internet for some students hindered them from downloading the track in good time. This delayed the onset of their practice and affected those who stay in areas without good internet connectivity. Not every part of Kenya has good internet connectivity. Students were forced to travel to some place where they could download the given track and send the recording online. In relation to this was lacking data bundles. Even in cases where internet connection was available, some students lacked the data bundles to enable them send their recording. So, they had to borrow phones from friends and parents to achieve this.

Power outage in Kenya is a frequent occurrence. This affected 11.4% of the students. "I had just managed to get everyone quiet in the house to record then there was a power outage, and my phone had no charge" said one student. It was frustrating but they had to wait until a later time in order to proceed with their recordings.

It was a requirement for the student to record against a plain background. This meant that they could record against a wall or use a sheet of cloth as a background. 28.6% of the students found it difficult to get such a background. Outside recording had audio interference and a lot of colour from the environment (see Figure 10.1). In-house recording had some singers move some furniture so that the required background was possible. One student complained of having a sheet of cloth as a background that fell while recording revealing a

FIGURE 10.1   Poor background for video recording

bed which was not required. For another, "the background was to be plain but I captured the roof". As a result, they both had to start recording again.

The seventh issue was poor video quality and poor audio as a result of poor recording microphones. Each student had their own mobile phone and some had laptops. These gadgets were all of different makes and quality. It was not possible to supply them with the same brand of mobile phone. Consequently, their audio capacities and video qualities differed greatly. Whereas some video recordings were of good quality some recordings had very dull images and poor sound. One had to strain in order to hear. 8.6% of the students had issues with poor sound while 31.4 had issues of poor video quality. One student explained that, "the angle of recording was not good. The picture captured was small because I was far from camera". The student had to adjust the camera position. Such instances had the technical committee return the recordings to the affected students for another recording attempt. They had to borrow mobile phones with better video quality.

For one to get a clear video lighting is of essence. Since not all students are competent videographers some did not consider the amount of light in their environment while recording. The images were dark. 14.3% of students had this problem and had to re-record following the advice given.

A few students 5.7% reported having lack of enough memory on the phone. The video recording required enough disk space. This forced the students to borrow a mobile phone.

The following poem titled "Again and Again", captures sentiments of students who had to record several times as a result of the issues discussed above.

Again, and Again

I take to practice five times a week
The guiding track is there
Helpful it is
It provides the key
It provides the tempo

But I have forgotten some pitches
I have forgotten some lyrics
The track helps me remember
Oh! My phone has no charge
There is a power outage
I borrow a phone
So, I practice again and again.

I look around
Where do I record from?
I go to the bedroom
It is quiet
I place a plain sheet as a background
As I record the sheet falls
So, I record again and again.

It is quiet
I proceed with the recording
Ha! Ha! Ha! I hear laughter
Be silent! Like the wheel my head spins
So, I record again and again.

Finally, it is done
I submit my video recording
No! Your picture is too small
No! Your tempo is not steady
No! Your lighting is dull
So, I record again and again.
(Nancy A. Masasabi)

There were various challenges that the students faced but they were mitigated in different ways as discussed under each challenge. Having a mobile phone looked like the norm. However, this project shed light on the fact that not all students could afford their own mobile phones. Some of those who had the phones had poor quality video cameras. Whereas some students never gave up and kept moving, there were some that gave up after several attempts in video recording.

For every scenario, there are two sides to a coin. The students did not only record challenges but also positive experiences. There was a high level of commitment noted by the technical team. Despite some having to video record several times they did not give up. This was a definite show of commitment to the task (see the poem "It Was Well"). Having a sense of belonging and unity was a driving force that kept the students going. They did their best not to let each other down.

This Ended Well

The songs were now at my fingertips
One hour was enough practice
As a voice trainer, I considered all the nips.
The warm-up made my voice pleasant through my lips
Through the guiding track, the tempo was up for keeps
I swallowed all the keys like sweet sips
Now all I needed was a mobile phone.

Observing were my brother and sister, my sibs
Seated quietly and savvy near the cribs.
All along I honed myself into proficiency
I found one room with a befitting background
To think of the lighting, splendorous
It went in tandem with my white shirt.

Time came for video recordings
Oops! My mobile phone, out of charge
Oh! And there was a power blackout
And now my phone could not help me, low memory
The onlookers became the savior
I used my brother's phone and called it wraps
Amidst all that, this ended well
And, I enjoyed it!
(Joseph Theuri & Nancy A. Masasabi)

Students enjoyed the whole process. One stated that, "I enjoyed myself because it was a challenging task". At the end of the process the students were happy with what they saw. This reiterates what Hallam and Bautista (2012) postulate that, "learning is most enjoyable when what is to be learned is challenging (not too easy or too difficult) and there is a sense of achievement when it has been mastered". The students learnt to rely on themselves in organising practice sessions. It was something new but manageable as exemplified in the poem, "A New Dawn".

A New Dawn

Sing some songs
It all began
A gentle breeze upon my face.

I sing once, I sing twice
The lyrics on my lips
A gentle breeze upon my face.

I sing and listen to my voice
Sounds like the song bird
A gentle breeze upon my face.

Who can sing with me?
Voices of the choir are in my head
My conductor is a recording

To video record I need
What do I use? Where do I stand?

Where do I start? Where do I stop?
My conductor is a recording

I have a mobile phone
Not very good
I borrow another, and another
My conductor is a recording

My photo I take
My voice I record
Is it good?
Tranquility all around
A gentle breeze upon my face.

What a task!
Can I sing again?
With a conductor as a recording?
Yes! I made it so I can
A gentle breeze upon my face.
(Nancy A. Masasabi)

In addition, there was a sense of satisfaction and self-efficacy among the students. Self-efficacy is defined "as the conviction that one can successfully execute the behavior required to produce the outcome" (Bandura, 1997, p. 79). A similar definition to this is that of McPherson (2006, p. 326) who argues that, "Put another way, self-efficacy thoughts refer to a person's beliefs about the extent to which she or he can do a task in a particular situation". This position by students was evident in their ability to look for solutions on their own. Moreover, the students learnt to self-assess.

The technical team members played the role of both student and teacher. As students they participated in video recording and as teachers they were providing feedback to the others. It enabled them to continue sharpening their listening skills, placing value judgement and identifying video recording errors. The team members were of the opinion that a similar project be carried out by them since it was viable.

Finally, the students had some good quality outputs (see Figure 10.2). These had accurate melodies, good backgrounds, good video quality and good sound quality. "We are proud of ourselves", was a comment from one student. They were content with the final products of their work. Following are concluding remarks from the technical team captured in the poem:

FIGURE 10.2   Some of the final products

It Can Be Better

To get better audio and video quality
There is need for a professional ability
Different types of recording equipment
Cameras and microphones spoil the entertainment
Making it hard to Merge and edit

There is way where there is will
It can be done as long as we are skillful
Gear and heart might be too much to ask, but is the way
From participants divided by distance
Some of whom might be off-line for instance

Assume that all the participants
Had a good mobile phone of same model
With a good camera and good mouth piece
And an environment of quiet and still peace
To allow them to record with ease
Together with good guidance on how to practice

It could be close to how it was needed
Not just doing because it was needed
But well done because they wanted
It could not have been taken for granted.

United we stand and divided, well we understand
That music done together is better
And in a distance scenario we'd better
Use an advanced technology
Which will not spoil the harmony
(Josephat S. Anabwani & Nancy A. Masasabi)

5   Conclusion

From the onset it seemed obvious that all young people have mobile phones and were able to record their parts in order to consolidate a choir. Resulting was a situation that was two thronged. On one hand, there were various challenges that faced the students during their practice and recording sessions. On the other hand, there were wonderful video recordings done by students. The reality is that not all students had mobile phones and access to internet connectivity. Those mobile phones that were used, were of different qualities thus the video outputs were of different qualities. The struggles of students to get things done were evident. However, their resilience is worth noting, showing a great level of commitment to the task assigned to them.

The use of digital technology was effective to some extent. It is worth noting that, in order to enhance the output of digital choral performance, students should have more or less the same recording equipment and better recording environments. Therefore, even though we may not be sure when such a scenario may present itself where students are to use digital technology to put up a choral performance, it is evident that with the right equipment, direction and assistance students can put up a virtual choral performance. This study motivated some students to think of investing in recording studios that can aid the recording and virtual performance of choral music. Moreover, small ensembles of both choral and instrumental performance have emerged from some of these students, where they perform and record using their mobile phones, posting their virtual performance on YouTube for others to appreciate.

References

Achola, M. A. (2007). *The role of technology in music education: A survey of computer usage in secondary schools in Nairobi province* [Unpublished PhD dissertation]. Kenyatta University.

Adwar, H. A. (2010). Moi and music performance in public and private Universities: A case of Nairobi, Moi, Egerton, Kabarak, Kenyatta and Maseno Universities. In M. N. Wanyama et al. (Eds.), *Music in Kenya: Development, management, composition and performance*. Kabarak University.

Bandura, A. (1997). *Self-efficacy: The exercise of control*. Freeman.

Bendall, C. (2020). Defining the virtual choir. *The Choral Journal, 61*(5), 69–77

Burnard, P. (2007). Reframing creativity and technology: Promoting pedagogic change in music education. *Journal of Music, Technology and Education, 1*(1), 37–55.

Buswell, D. (2006). *Performance strategies for musicians*. MX Publishing.

Cayari, C. (2016). *Virtual vocal ensembles and the mediation of performance on YouTube* [Unpublished PhD dissertation]. University of Illinois.

Creech, A., & Gaunt, H. (2012). The changing face of individual instrumental tuition: value, purpose and potential. In G. E. McPherson & G. F. Welch (Eds.), *The Oxford handbook of music education* (Vol. 1, pp. 694–711). Oxford University Press.

Ferreira G. (2007). Crossing borders: Issues in music technology education. *Journal of Music, Technology and Education, 1*(1), 23–35.

Galvan, J., & Clauhs, M. (2020). The virtual choir as collaboration. *The Choral Journal, 61*(3), 8–19.

Hallam, S., & Bautista, A. (2012). Processes of instrumental learning: The development of musical expertise. In G. E. McPherson & G., Welch (Eds.), *The Oxford handbook of music education* (Vol. 1, pp. 658–676). Oxford University Press.

Janesick, V. J. (2016). Poetic inquiry: Using found poetry and identity poetry to transform qualitative data. In A. B. Reinertsen (Ed.), *Becoming earth: A post human turn in educational discourse collapsing nature/culture divides* (pp. 31–40). https://brill.com/display/title/36676

Johnson, M. K. (2018). *High school choral students' perceptions of their use of technology in their independent choral practice habits* [Unpublished MA thesis]. Eastern Washington University.

Macedo, F. (2013). Teaching creative music technology in higher education: A phenomenological approach. *Journal of Music, Technology and Education, 6*(2), 207–219.

Mandino, O. (1997). *The greatest secret in the world*. Bantam.

McCombs, B. L. (2000, September). *Assessing the role of educational technology in the teaching and learning process: A learner-centered perspective* [Paper]. The Secretary's conference on educational technology, Alexandria, VA.

McPherson, G. E., & McCormick, J. (2006). Self-efficacy and music performance. *Psychology of Music, 34*(1), 322–336.

Nielsen, S. (2001). Self-regulating learning strategies in instrumental music practice. *Music Education Research, 3*(2), 155–167.

Parkes, K. A. (2022). Self-directed learning strategies. In G. E. McPherson (Ed.). *The Oxford handbook of music performance* (pp. 106–122). Oxford University Press.

Pignato, J. M. (2017). Pondering an end to technology in music education. In A. Ruthmann & R. Mantie (Eds.), *The Oxford handbook of technology and music education* (pp. 137–141). Oxford University Press.

Prendergast, M. (2012). Education and/as art: A found poetry suite. *International Journal of Education and Art, 13*(2), 1–19.

Richardson, L. (2002). Poetic representation of interviews. In J. F. Gubrium & J. A. Holstein (Eds.), *Handbook of interview research: Context and method* (pp. 877–891). Sage

Schrauben, J. E., & Leigh, S. R. (2019). Revisiting interview data through a Post I-Poem. *The Qualitative Report, 24*(8), 2048–2058.

Stowell, D., & Dixon, S. (2014). Integration of informal music technologies in secondary school music lessons. *British Journal of Music Education, 31*(1), 19–39.

Upitis, R. (2014). Transforming independent music teaching with digital tools. In *Collected work: Music and media-infused lives: Music education in a digital age* (pp. 89–106). Canadian Music Educators' Association.

van Manen, M. (2007). Phenomenology of practice. *Phenomenology and Practice, 1*(1), 12–28.

CHAPTER 11

Inside the Online Location

Inquiring into Musical Narratives through PhD Mentorship

Anneke Britt McCabe and Shelley M. Griffin

Abstract

This research highlights the synchronous and asynchronous learning journey of a PhD student and supervisor as they entered the relational work of narrative inquiry in music teacher education during the COVID-19 global pandemic. Despite the challenges of unplanned distance learning, the *online location* became a pivotal space of guidance about teaching and learning. This collaborative research came about through an invitation from a doctoral supervisor to a PhD student (in the spring of 2020) to observe teaching an 18-hour, face-to-face, general music education course (Grades 4–10) for teacher candidates at a southwestern Ontario university. As the face-to-face course quickly shifted to the *online location* during COVID-19, so did the *place* of interaction. The *landscape* became defined and confined to the glow of computer screens, rising and setting through Microsoft Teams. This research draws on shared dialogue as a guide to exploring the three-dimensional framework of narrative inquiry's commonplaces – temporality, sociality, and place (Connelly & Clandinin, 2006). The synchronous nature of this collaborative research allows experience, analysis, and synthesis to become a place of understanding. Findings revealed three thematic threads: online location, mentorship, and vulnerability as a pedagogical process. Music educators are encouraged to find new ways of conceptualising teaching and learning by considering the online location as a place or a medium that affords unique possibilities for collaboration. What began as a possible limitation of not being able to experience teaching and learning face-to-face becomes a rich space for inquiring into learning through the three-dimensional framework of narrative inquiry.

Keywords

narrative inquiry – PhD mentorship – musical narratives – global pandemic – synchronous/asynchronous – collaborative research

1   Anneke's Narrative Beginnings (COVID-19 Lockdown, March 2020)

I am at home under quarantine, due to COVID-19, when I hang up the virtual chat with Dr. Griffin (Professor). I have just learned that the face-to-face, on-campus elementary general music education course for teacher candidates has moved to being offered completely online for the duration of the 6-week course, and we have decided to move forward with our collaboration. Dr. Griffin is encouraging, and I follow her lead. It is time to trust the process. I am in a similar teaching situation with my own music classes; we have also moved to the *online location* for public school. I take a deep breath, feeling a flow of nervous energy, like it is the first rehearsal. Imagining my advisor as a choir conductor, Dr. Griffin is tender with the music, and disciplined with the techniques of musicianship. Dr. Griffin demonstrates care in the way she mentors, at times coming alongside me, as we listen for how to best blend our voices, as soprano and alto. Awakening this momentary daydream are the sounds of my children, right on cue, flooding the foreground with reality. I quickly transition from online to real-world and return to the family band.

2   Locating Possibilities

Positioned as a Faculty of Education PhD student in music education, under the advisement of Dr. Griffin, at a southwestern Ontario university, I engaged relationally, learning about narrative inquiry, both as experience and the phenomenon under study (Clandinin & Connelly, 2000). Working as an elementary school music teacher (Grades K–8) in Ontario for the past 20 years (and during the time of this research), I am inspired to share my experiences of teaching in Ontario classrooms with new preservice classroom teachers (i.e., teacher candidates), as well as reflect on my own practice. Our collaboration for this research came about through an invitation from Dr. Griffin to observe her university teaching in a Junior/Intermediate (Grades 4–10) face-to-face music education class in the spring, 2020. The course I was invited to observe is designed for generalist classroom teachers (not preservice music specialist teachers), who are obtaining a Bachelor of Education Degree. Within the degree, the beginning teachers engage in coursework in various subject areas, including an 18-hour music education course, which occurs over 6 weeks, 3 hours of weekly instruction, for approximately 25–28 students.

The music course is designed to help introduce classroom teachers to the beginning knowledge and musical skills necessary for guiding students towards successful music experiences. Promoting and fostering a learning environment that encourages active participation, teacher candidates engage in weekly reflection, ongoing critical thinking, and shared discussion. Some of the learning objectives include: exploring how personal music experiences shape teaching practices, becoming familiar with languages and traditions of music-making, building an understanding of music pedagogy, developing teacher musicianship, and becoming familiar with the Ontario Curriculum The Arts (1–8) as a guide to shaping creative and critical thinking, planning, and assessment and evaluation.

Considering that my area of doctoral research focuses on inquiring into the musical narratives of music teachers who are practising musicians, it is fitting to explore our collaborative research topic through the methodology of narrative inquiry (Barrett & Stauffer, 2009, 2012; Smith & Hendricks, 2020). My future goal is to teach at the post-secondary level, so I was eager to learn from Dr. Griffin. She and I were also curious about how our experience might contribute to sharing our teacher perspectives, as we came to know each other, relationally. Our collaborative writing evolved from this process.

Prior to the Bachelor of Education music education course beginning in April 2020, I had solidified details for my observation, and was being mentored by Dr. Griffin, when suddenly, we found ourselves amid the COVID-19 global pandemic. We were quickly placed under quarantine in Canada. Without warning, learning all over the world switched to online platforms, and students were distance learning from home due to the quarantine measures. Both of our teaching worlds, in the way we knew them, were challenged, as we both had to respond to these emergency measures. Elementary students, in my case, had to respond to the new challenges of learning from home, supported by their teachers, parents, and in some cases, other family members. Post-secondary students (beginning teachers) found themselves with heightened anxiety regarding the university forced closure of face-to-face learning, with an emergency transition to online learning.

Through our shared learning, we discovered that this experience drew on our resiliency as teachers and learners. Through our craft as music educators, we continued with the teaching and learning process together, allowing our shared dialogue and autobiographical reflection (Clandinin, 2013; Freeman, 2007) to guide us in exploring the three-dimensional (3D) framework of narrative inquiry's commonplaces – temporality, sociality, and place (Connelly & Clandinin, 2006). The synchronous nature of our collaboration allowed for the experience, analysis, and synthesis to become a place of shared understanding.

3   Narrative Beginnings: Engaging Theoretically

Providing the theoretical framework for this research are the three common-places of narrative inquiry. Connelly and Clandinin (2006) borrow the notion of commonplaces from Joseph Schwab's four commonplaces – teacher, learner, subject matter, and milieu, and identify the three commonplaces of narrative inquiry: "temporality, sociality, and place" (p. 479). When under study, events are in "*temporal* transition" (Connelly & Clandinin, 2006, p. 479), meaning that they are always moving and shifting. "*Sociality* in narrative inquiry involves paying attention to the personal conditions and the social conditions, mean-ing: the feelings, hopes, desires, aesthetic reactions and moral dispositions of the inquirer and study participants" (Connelly & Clandinin, 2006, p. 480). *Place* in narrative inquiry refers to the physical place and "the sequences of places where the inquiry and events take place" (p. 480). The three common-places distinguish narrative inquiry from other qualitative research method-ologies and are central to the theoretical and conceptual thinking for narrative inquiry (Caine et al., 2022; Clandinin, 2013).

In our partnership, exploring the three commonplaces allowed us to draw on the experience of learning about narrative inquiry in music education at the same time we were living through it. With mentorship guiding our relational approach, we remained flexible in our positionality as teachers. The forward and backward temporal movement edged us to embrace risk-taking. When the uneasy feeling of new learning created tension, we drew on a shared commit-ment to care for, and humanise the mentoring process (Malen & Brown, 2020). Recognising the importance of self-reflection as part of professional learning in graduate studies, Dr. Griffin ensured there were opportunities for my reflec-tion, in written form, as well as through meaningful, relational conversation (Felder et al., 2019).

To support my personal motivation and excitement for learning, it was instrumental that Dr. Griffin engaged with me by providing frequent meet-ings that were timely in relation to the teaching and observation experience of the music education course. Researchers Sverdlik et al. (2018), who study the doctoral experience, draw attention to the necessity of honouring the lived experience of doctoral students to support their well-being. Dr. Griffin's view of the best mentoring relationships are those that honour the reciprocity of shared learning, including the times when the roles reverse, as the "mentee becomes the teacher and the mentor becomes the learner" (Griffin & Beatty, 2012, p. 264). Our intention in this research was to engage collaboratively, shar-ing our teacher perspectives to deepen and broaden awareness of experience

(Clandinin, 2013). Drawing from Smith and Hendricks (2020), we remind ourselves that narrative inquiry calls for research that is "intimate, relational, and situated" (p. 11).

4   Guiding Research Questions

These theoretical conceptions guided us to inquire into the following research questions which became key to our research puzzle:

1.   What important aspects of narrative inquiry emerge from engaging in the relational work of teacher observation and reflection between a doctoral student and supervisor in a music teacher education context?

2.   Following a shift to online learning (due to the emergency 2020 global pandemic of COVID-19), how might the phenomenon and method of narrative inquiry support learning in the online location?

5   Research Design

Considering that narrative inquiry is both a phenomenon under study (theoretical) and the study of our experience (methodological), we grounded our reflective process with these underpinnings. Throughout this research, we shared a sense of uncertainty (Caine et al., 2018) and allowed for a transparent mentorship to evolve and guide our synchronous dialogue. At times, our responsibility to the collaboration awakened us to listen closely to what each other had to say (Caine et al., 2018; Clandinin, 2013) while simultaneously handling the learning with care.

As the face-to-face course quickly shifted to the *online location* due to constraints by COVID-19, so did our place of interaction. Our landscapes became defined and confined to the glow of computer screens, rising and setting through Microsoft Teams. Inside the online location, we were instantly captured, both in process and place, transitioning between teacher, learner, researcher, participant, and audience member.

Woven within our method for inquiring into this collaboration, are the twelve touchstones for narrative inquiry (Clandinin, 2013). The following sentence highlights the three touchstones with which we connected: "In the midst" of a pandemic, we tended to our "relational responsibilities", negotiating a collaborative entry to the field, and engaged with our "narrative beginnings" (p. 212). It is from this place, that we begin to point out the various methodological choices that informed our collaboration.

Using Microsoft Teams and the university's learning platform, I observed Dr. Griffin teaching her 3-hour, synchronous general music (Grades 4–10) classes each week. Following each class, Dr. Griffin and I would meet immediately on Microsoft Teams to reflect, through raw conversations that we video recorded. These video recordings, which we labelled *synchronous reflections*, served as our data, which Clandinin (2013) refers to as field texts. Video recording our synchronous reflections allowed us to capture our conversations immediately following the teaching. As well, we would synchronously watch the video recordings later, as part of our analysis of the experience itself. As we moved through the process of watching ourselves, we restoried (Caine et al., 2022; Clandinin & Connelly, 2000) our narratives from our shared experiences and stories of past teaching.

6 Analysis: Synchronous Reflections

Approximately 6 weeks following the completion of the course, we began the analysis process. Dr. Griffin and I met daily on Microsoft Teams, to re-watch each of the six video recordings, one from each 3-hour class. The following photo captures us meeting in Microsoft Teams, during one of our recording sessions (see Figure 11.1).

During the analysis of the six video recordings, Dr. Griffin and I positioned the conversations within the three-dimensional (3D) framework of narrative

FIGURE 11.1   Shelley Griffin and Anneke McCabe, Microsoft Teams Meeting, April 24, 2020

inquiry. The analysis of each video recording was approximately 2 hours per video. During the process, we paused to transcribe important parts of the conversation, video record new conversations, and engage in discussions about literature to support the findings. As we proceeded with the analysis process, we found our rhythm centred *in the pocket* of sharing stories, from current and past teaching experiences. Many of our synchronous reflections drew a pause, and further exploration of our *personal practical knowledge*, described as, "a particular way of reconstructing the past and the intentions for the future to deal with the exigencies of a present situation" (Connelly & Clandinin, 1988, p. 25).

As we discussed what was observed during the online teaching time, our synchronous reflections were housed in a chart we created in Microsoft Word. The chart included four categories: topic of discussion, video time stamps, threads (themes), and 3D framework. Therefore, as we collaboratively moved into dialogical reflection, threads of the analysis were written down, by identifying common themes, situated within the 3D framework. Each time we situated our analysis within temporality, sociality, and place, we recorded the time stamps that corresponded to the exact moment in the video recording. The details of the chart became our interim texts (Clandinin, 2013), our initial writing about the experience as we began to interpret the field texts.

Figure 11.2 offers insight into the analysis content of the chart. Here, two days of analysis are highlighted. As we collaboratively moved into dialogical reflection (column 1), threads of the analysis were written down (column 3), situated within the 3D framework: temporality, sociality, and place (column 4). Each time we situated our analysis within the 3D framework, we recorded the time stamps (column 2) that corresponded to the exact moment in the video recording.

7   Moving toward Research Texts

In this section, we intend to be chronological in the way we share the data through various quotes from our synchronous reflections. We highlight the threads that emerged as the strongest resonances in the data. We use quotes to show how our thoughts are woven together in the following three threads: online location, mentorship, and vulnerability as a pedagogical process. We begin by looking at the *online location* as a focused thread in our analysis.

7.1   *Digital Space as an Online Location*
The online location became an integral space of guidance about teaching and learning. This thread was focused on specific learning about *place*, one of the

Third Day of Analysis July 9, 2020 11:45-1:45pm

Edit 4: May 1: J/I Class 8P14 D7S7

Discussion	Time	Analysis/Threads	3D Framework
• Teaching becoming a "practise" in and of itself, as a well-oiled machine of sharing a teaching space, once we have taught 4 classes together • What makes a synergy when people are working together? • Anneke: trust, Anneke's desire to be mentored by Dr. Griffin and also learn from her • Dr. Griffin: Balance, similarities in personality and that's why we have the desire or draw to work together, Dr. Griffin believes in the lifelong journey of learning, maturity in your practice means that you realize that you still have lots to learn	0:51		Sociality

Reflection

Conversations that emerge during the analysis that are related to our teaching experience, but not necessarily to the process of this analysis. Sharing stories that contribute to telling stories about our teaching. Resonance in narrative work, one story can lead to another story. (Conle?) Still talking about teaching and learning.

Discussion	Time	Analysis/Threads	3D Framework
• Anneke talks about inviting student voice is a practice in teaching	1:36	Voice Philosophy of teaching, how approach learning	Sociality

Sixth Day of Analysis July 15, 2020 *9:45am-11:30am

Guest Lecture: April 27th: J/I Class 8P14 D7S7

Discussion	Time	Analysis/Threads	3D Framework
• Discussion in the beginning about trust and jumping in to guest lecturing during synchronous learning	Start (1:03)	Mentorship Place Voice	
• Thinking developmentally about the continuum in the learning of the curriculum (sound to symbol, symbol to notation, and then the learning within the scope and sequence of the curriculum)	2:45	Curriculum and teaching	Dr. Griffin and Anneke had a shared understanding
• Honest discussion about how we see ourselves engaged as teachers • Anneke commenting on how Dr. Griffin takes her time with the teaching and learning and how Anneke is more coming from the elementary school level so they have a different approach and pacing • Anneke self-judgement from watching herself	4:03	How we view ourselves in different teaching contexts	Sociality
• Anneke's learning developing video content for the adult learners, teaching with tech	4:43		Place
• Anneke sharing the desire to show and share her own teaching challenges, by layering in the Grade 6 learning as part of the teaching, taking a risk	5:16	Creating the synchronous learning system or environment	Place

FIGURE 11.2 Synchronous reflections: 3D framework chart (3rd and 6th days of analysis pictured)

central tenets of the three-dimensional inquiry space of narrative inquiry. Here, the learning for me (Anneke) was focused on how place may be metaphorically connected to the digital space in which we found ourselves. The focus here was less about music teaching and more about the *place* of interaction. Up until this point, we found that based upon our prior few weeks of synchronous learning, we interacted with our students via the internet as a digital space, not fully contemplating our virtual engagement with the experience as a *place* until our collaboration allowed us to look more deeply at this specificity of our individual teaching. Engaging with the place as it relates to one of the three-dimensional inquiry spaces, allowed us the opportunity to begin to think more specifically about the digital space as a physical location, which we have termed the *online location*. I pointed out how we might think about this unique location as it relates to the temporal nature of experience. In one of our video conversations, I noted:

> Would we have done this if we weren't forced to? How rich will this data be to look back on, when we have grown in our practice, through this experience … We will become stronger teachers in a new way. (Anneke, July 6, 2020)

Dr. Griffin candidly spoke of how she was feeling, having lived through her first online music teaching experience: "I feel like I'm almost like a news reporter … it's like a media class or something … '*And today's weather*'" (Dr. Griffin, July 6, 2020).

Throughout our many conversations, we realised that our *entire* experience of collaboration was housed *inside* the online location. Through contemplating the various steps in our collaboration, Dr. Griffin's words spoke to the interwoven layers of complexity of the digital space as an online location.

> There are so many layers. What comes to mind right now when we are talking would be just … Is it the piece about health? Is it about connecting with everybody? Is it about student engagement … teacher engagement … using online tools? How do you engage with music curriculum? (Dr. Griffin, July 6, 2020)

Some of these thoughts are fractured, constantly shifting, as the online location created so many additional factors affecting the ebb and flow of the online teaching and learning context. At this time, there were limited professional development opportunities for teacher educators who had to suddenly pivot without any prior online teaching experience. Despite the stresses and unknowns involved with this sudden, global shift in education, I began to think about the broader possibilities that the online location might afford. A comment that I made during one of our videos pointed to this: "I wonder if there is a way with this whole medium ..." (Anneke, July 14, 2020).

It was during this time that I began to contemplate the physical nature and feeling of being online. The *online location* had become a daily place of interaction and meeting with people, and so I thought of the online place of Microsoft Teams as a medium, or an *online location* as being in a virtual location. Through inquiring into the aspects of how the online location shaped the teaching and learning for both of us, our conversations led us to a heightened awareness of our mentoring relationship and the possibilities that the experience provided for mentorship.

7.2 Mentorship through Generosity

At the core of entering collaborative, relational work in narrative inquiry, Dr. Griffin's supervisory vision for me included engaging in meaningful experiences that would broaden my knowledgebase as a PhD student. Through learning about narrative inquiry as twofold – both the theoretical phenomenon and method of research design – Dr. Griffin discussed possibilities for analysing the collaborative experience through the 3D framework lens. Pedagogically, Dr. Griffin anticipated that doing so would be an optimal way to set up a recipe for my success as a PhD student and future academic.

It was also critical for Dr. Griffin to extend an invitation for me to see how she integrated narrative inquiry practices within her music education courses. Observing Dr. Griffin teaching allowed me to have a glimpse into the ways that she embodied emotional pedagogy and vulnerability as a music teacher educator with beginning teachers. Little did we know, however, that this would all occur, in the online location, due to the global pandemic. Throughout our conversations, I noticed that Dr. Griffin's teaching was framed through the lens of *generosity*. Recognising this allowed me to reflect on our mentoring relationship. By the second day of re-watching our synchronous reflections, we began to discuss the nature of our relationship, as mentor and mentee, positioned as two musicians, music educators, engaged in an online performance of teaching and learning, as participants, as well as audience members. I described my interpretation of generosity in teaching as the ability to capture moments of invitation with kindness – anytime there is an invitation to the learner to share an experience. The medium of the online location, and then watching each other teach, added a component of performance to the teaching. As musicians and teachers, teaching inside the online location illuminated the performative aspect because we were communicating through a screen. To help us understand the ways we moved between our roles, we enact a genuine curiosity of how we can learn from each other, in a caring way.

We draw on Prendergast's (2019) conceptualisation of *intimate generosity* through performance. As we discussed the value that we placed on the appearance of continued generosity, during our sustained online performances of teaching and learning, we connected in a similar manner in which an audience would have an experiential exchange with a performer. The more we learned from each other, the more connected our synchronous reflections became, thus increasing our ability to be vulnerable with each other. As we developed our fluency with generosity, we believe we created "a positive sense of anticipatory consciousness" (Prendergast, 2019, p. 111) in each other. One of the video conversations captured my thoughts about learning from Dr. Griffin through the process:

> This is where I could really learn from you. This is more meaningful than writing a letter, this taping we're doing, because the learning is online and then we tape our online discussion after. I feel like it's a really nice mirror of the experience ... when we can have this fluid-like ... *'Here we are again'* ... back in the medium. (Anneke, July 14, 2020)

Dr. Griffin invited my teaching contributions in the course by asking me to be a guest lecturer in one of her classes focused on teaching pitch to elementary students. In discussing this with Dr. Griffin, I explained my comfort level with guest lecturing, due to the feeling of generosity from her. The following words capture my description of the experience:

> I have felt this has been such a natural vibe between teaching together. It makes me wonder if online is a barrier. And I said this a couple videos ago, you're a generous teacher, so because you're generous, you have generosity in your teaching. I feel a lot of what we say is seamless ... I feel it is good vibes. (Anneke, July 10, 2020)

As Dr. Griffin continued to think about mentoring me, she invited me to consider the vital necessity of classroom teacher engagement in learning about music in post-secondary contexts, being immersed as an instructor, rather than solely focusing on student engagement. Based upon the first half of their initial class of having beginning teachers analyse her teaching practice, Dr. Griffin reflected:

> It is important for me, for them to be able to share their perspectives ... the good ... the challenging ... I'm open to hearing it. That's why even in the first class I asked them to analyse me ... I mean it's part of that vulnerability piece that I believe in. (Dr. Griffin, July 8, 2020)

In later conversation, Dr. Griffin reflected on how she built upon these ideas when she directed the question to her students:

> Where are *you* in the engagement? If you held a mirror in front of you, what are you, as the teacher, bringing to the engagement of student learning? (Dr. Griffin, July 9, 2020)

While contemplating this question, I began to reflect more deeply on my own experience as a classroom teacher, as well as an educator, moving toward post-secondary teaching. In this light, the generosity was not only extended to the teacher candidates, but also to me as a PhD student – an opportunity to critically think and learn about engaging teaching as a necessary component to successful music teaching practices.

7.3 *Vulnerability as a Pedagogical Process*

As conversations about Dr. Griffin's and my pedagogical processes were analysed, so were our teaching approaches. Together, we engaged in an exchange about what we were noticing in each other's teaching. An example of this is shared below, when I noticed the way Dr. Griffin modelled while teaching the Primary/Junior/Intermediate level teacher candidates:

> The minute you are teaching your P/J/I class, you model. This is a really incredible thing to watch online. Because ... that is a huge difference ... I think that it is interesting watching you – that you've held on to that, because you would do that "in person". (Anneke, July 9, 2020)

During the pivot to online learning, Dr. Griffin expressed many times the importance of teacher candidates connecting to learning *through* music, as well as learning *about* music. By this, she reflected upon the notion that being in a face-to-face classroom, participating in musical activities such as playing pitched and non-pitched percussion instruments, singing, improvising, or creating rhythmic patterns, allows for greater experiential learning that is not hindered by technical delay or a lack of in-person community for music-making. She recognised the importance of beginning general music teachers being able to increase their confidence *through* participatory music-making prior to applying theoretical applications. However, in the online learning context, Dr. Griffin noted that there was an increase in more learning *about* music as opposed to *through* music.

I quickly articulated a difference that I had observed regarding how the teacher candidates shared their thinking while participating in the online location. We observed that the students were hesitant to learn in the online platform of Microsoft Teams, often preferring to keep their cameras off. Many times, with in-person learning, the opportunity to get out of a chair, or perform in front of other people, is a motivator for some teacher candidates' extroverted learning preferences. I noticed: "In the synchronous learning environment, students are 'accountable for their talk' in a different way than when we learn in a live setting" (Anneke July 8, 2020).

The students shared that the music class was the class they participated in the most compared to other online courses within their Bachelor of Education degree. They felt the learning was the most engaging because it was an "arts" class. During the initial lockdown of the COVID-19 pandemic, there was a global outcry for the arts, and in particular, music – the engagement that music may provide – to virtually bring people together, fostering the ability to make humanistic connections (Lewis & Mass, 2022). This idea brought me to reflect on the resilient nature of music teachers during this time-period. I felt that during the pandemic, with the change to online learning, music teachers and musicians all over the world creatively shifted, to keep hope and music alive everywhere. I shared:

> You are online and you are thriving and it's because you're honed in on your teaching practice. I think it's a music thing. I don't know if all subject areas have to do that ... because they are not forced to all the time. (Anneke, July 15, 2020)

8   Delving Deeper into Our Shared Narrative

Throughout our discussion, we moved temporally, with backward and forward flow, as we shared stories from our observations, in relation to our pedagogical processes, and how our practices grew and evolved over time. Many important aspects were highlighted during the synchronous reflection recordings, contributing to important threads that emerged from inside the 3D framework, for analysis. We noticed that our analysis process allowed us to unravel and inquire into our individual and shared experiences. Our discussion prompts us to think carefully about the questions that guided our inquiry:

1. What important aspects of narrative inquiry emerge from engaging in the relational work of teacher observation and reflection between a doctoral student and supervisor in a music teacher education context?

2. Following a shift to online learning (due to the emergency 2020 global pandemic of COVID-19), how might the phenomenon and method of narrative inquiry support learning in the online location?

The online location opened a doorway to our relational work and allowed us to situate the learning in a place of trust. A curiosity of mine was whether we would have been engaging in this work if we had not been forced to. Dr. Griffin confirmed that there were many layers to consider: making connections with teacher candidates about their well-being, considering the need for engagement for both teacher and students in a virtual setting, navigating new online tools, and the challenges of making music in an online space.

Our uncertainty brought us to a place of mutual reliance for support, and our generosity encouraged us to draw on each other's strengths, in a manner that allowed our voices to sing, during a challenging time in the world. Reflecting upon sociality as one of the tenets of the 3D framework allowed us to attend to both the personal and social conditions at play in our collaboration. As we not only listened, but heard one another, we entered a new place of understanding, where our vulnerability was exposed. The following three sections highlight the real conversations about pedagogy and practice that emerged, which propelled us forward to learn about narrative inquiry as a methodology, while learning about ourselves.

8.1   *Changing Keys: Shifting to Relational Work in the Online Location*

The opportunity to take a risk, during the emergency lockdown of COVID-19, while continuing with our collaboration in the online location, was a decision that resonated with both of us. Approaching our collaboration from a learning stance opened a free-flowing dialogue between us that allowed room for mentorship and trust to grow. Dr. Griffin's invitation for me to guest lecture in her course allowed me the opportunity to work alongside her in a teaching context, reinforcing our collegial relationship. Simultaneously, I was able to bring my current, elementary school teaching experience into a post-secondary teaching context for beginning teachers to experience the reality of music teaching during the global pandemic. It became apparent that throughout the time we engaged in this research, we learned about each other, as teachers, and as supervisor and PhD student, experiencing a relational narrative inquiry. Our pedagogy and pedagogical processes were linked along a curriculum continuum of music teaching and learning, which helped to drive our conversations, urging us to dig deeper into our personal practical knowledge as music educators. It became natural for us to feel the sentiment of giving, as we both extended a genuine openness.

8.2   *Mentoring through Phenomenon and Method*

As I learned about narrative inquiry, through the experience of this collaborative research, I acknowledge the importance of mentorship during this time. Dr. Griffin's focus on spending time connecting our experiences to teachable moments had a significant impact on my learning. As we created our analysis chart, utilising the 3D framework, watching our Microsoft Teams recordings, we paused to contemplate not only on our data, but to enable a space for learning to take place. For example, as we discussed the theoretical notion of experience as the phenomenon under study, we were immersed in it – narrative inquiry as both phenomenon and method. This allowed our entire process to be experiential and invited many discussions about place. As we moved temporally, Dr. Griffin would highlight important threads about time and space, and how it related to connections that were being made in our personal practical knowledge, and the ways we were experiencing and living our inquiry. Together, we agreed on video footage that connected to temporality, sociality, and place. For example, it was pivotal for me to experience how Dr. Griffin facilitated the process of body mapping with the beginning teachers. Through sharing her own journey toward becoming a music teacher and teacher educator, I was able to see the importance of how temporality, sociality, and place, were woven together in her teaching practice.

8.3   *Observing and Reflecting on Vulnerability*

The more in-tune we became with our voices, the rawer our conversations sounded, as we began to take risks in discussing some of the challenges and successes that we had faced in teaching, over the years. Our discussions formed connections between our elementary school experiences, and our curiosity about how to design learning for young children and their teachers. Dr. Griffin shared with me how important it is to embody the process of music-making through modelling musical engagement with children. For example, this modelling may be through singing with students, demonstrating a rhythmic pattern, or showing a playing technique on an instrument such as a xylophone. The analysis of these musical experiences, nestled in the 3D framework of narrative inquiry, invited us to not only examine our restorying process, but also to inquire into new layers of understanding from conversations that were temporally located in encounters of the past.

9   Transpositions and Transformations: Limitations and Implications

As we ponder ways to move forward, we are drawn to also consider the possible limitations of our relational research experience. One limitation has been that the initial plan to observe Dr. Griffin teach, face-to-face in her music room with beginning teachers, quickly came to a grinding halt – a non-negotiable pivot to an online, web-based platform. At this time, we were not the only professionals making a shift to learning and working online, the entire world had to shift. Upon reflection, we have been curious if the state of emergency positioned us to take a risk, and if our positionality during this time propelled us to think more deeply about the temporal nature of our teaching roles, considering how they have shifted or changed.

This research occurred entirely in the online location; thus, it may be seen as a limitation. Although this space afforded a controlled environment and provided consistency in terms of a virtual setting, it did not compare to the organic nature of teaching music in person or seeing each other in person. As well, the online location did not provide a rich place for the auditory experience of real live sound, so our conversations centred on music, rather than living through music, or the experience of music itself.

Another limitation of this research may also be that we are reflecting upon, and analysing ourselves, while engaged in similar teaching situations. The similarities in our teaching positions, as music educators shifting to online learning, assisted us to find common ground in the online location. Therefore, we shared a similar focus as we drew upon our mutual resiliency.

10   A New Composition

Whether a limitation, or an enhancement for possible further research, we embraced finding new ways to conceptualise teaching and learning despite the challenges at this point in global history. Due to this learning experience as a narrative inquirer, I approached learning about the methodology with wonder and curiosity. I reflected on the possibility that this was why I experienced the online location as a place or a medium. I am curious about how other learners experienced virtual meeting spaces as places, and whether being online for longer durations of time, and more consistently throughout the day, contributed to a sense of comfort, and familiarity of a location. What began as a possible limitation without being able to experience observing Dr. Griffin in a face-to-face environment, became a pivotal point in my learning journey as I experienced the three dimensions of narrative inquiry within the online location.

As a PhD student, through this collaboration, I feel that it was an incredible learning experience for studying the phenomenon and methodology of narrative inquiry in music education. I encourage future PhD students to embark on a risk-taking adventure, of inquiring into teaching and learning, together with their supervisor, as part of the journey of a narrative inquirer.

As we moved through the process of having to re-learn much of our music teaching practice, to the musical stage of online learning, we were confronted with the immediate need to embrace risk, and to trust each other. Future music teacher educators might consider the importance of risk-taking. By doing so, it could create an opportunity to examine vulnerabilities they may have regarding successes and challenges in their teaching practice. This might create a needed space for building resiliency in music teacher education.

As we move toward our exit out of the research process, we are drawn to mull over various integral aspects enfolded within the relational ethics of narrative inquiry (Caine et al., 2022; Clandinin et al., 2018). What have we learned through our relational work? What is unique about this research experience? No matter how distant we are apart, engaging relationally through narrative inquiry is what allowed us to be "in the same music room". Thus, we advocate for the necessity of continued scholarship in narrative inquiry – for the study of experience affords deep engagement with its unique theoretical and methodological tenets – both phenomenon and method.

References

Barrett, M. S., & Stauffer, S. L. (Eds.). (2009). *Narrative inquiry in music education: Troubling certainty.* Springer. https://doi.org/10.1007/978-1-4020-9862-8

Barrett, M. S., & Stauffer, S. L. (Eds.). (2012). *Narrative soundings: An anthology of narrative inquiry in music education.* Springer. https://doi.org/10.1007/978-94-007-0699-6

Caine, V., Clandinin, D. J., & Lessard, S. (2022). *Narrative inquiry: Philosophical roots.* Bloomsbury.

Caine, V., Steeves, P., Clandinin, D. J., Estefan, A., Huber, J., & Murphy, M. S. (2018). Social justice practice: A narrative inquiry perspective. *Journal in Education, Citizenship and Social Justice, 13*(2), 133–143. https://doi.org/10.1177/1746197917710235

Clandinin, D. J. (2013). *Engaging in narrative inquiry.* Routledge.

Clandinin, D. J., Caine, V., & Lessard, S. (2018). *The relational ethics of narrative inquiry.* Routledge.

Clandinin, D. J., & Connelly, F. M. (2000). *Narrative inquiry: Experience and story in qualitative research.* Jossey-Bass. https://doi.org/10.1177/1321103X060270010301

Connelly, F. M., & Clandinin, D. J. (1988). *Teachers as curriculum planners.* Teachers College Press. https://doi.org/10.1177/019263658907351318

Connelly, F. M., & Clandinin, D. J., (2006). Narrative inquiry. In J. L. Green, G. Camilli, P. B. Elmore with A. Skukauskaite & E. Grace (Eds.), *Handbook of complementary methods in education research* (pp. 477–487). Lawrence Erlbaum. https://doi.org/10.4324/9780203874769

Felder, P., Kline, K., Harmening, D., Moore, T., & St. John, E. (2019). Professional development and moral reasoning in higher education graduate programs. *International Journal of Doctoral Studies, 14,* 383–401. https://doi.org/10.28945/4274

Griffin, S. M., & Beatty, R. J. (equal authorship). (2012). Hitting the trail running: Roadmaps and reflections on informal faculty mentorship experiences. In M. S. Barrett & S. L. Stauffer (Eds.), *Narrative soundings: An anthology of narrative inquiry in music education* (pp. 251–273). Springer.

Lewis, J., & Mass, A. (Eds.). (2022). *Music education on the verge: Stories of pandemic teaching and transformative change.* Lexington Books.

Freeman, M. (2007). Autobiographical understanding and narrative inquiry. In D. J. Clandinin (Ed.), *Handbook of narrative inquiry: Mapping a methodology* (pp. 120–145). Sage. http://dx.doi.org/10.4135/9781452226552.n5

Malen, B., & Brown, T. M. (2020). What matters to mentees: Centering their voices. *Mentoring & Tutoring: Partnership in Learning, 28*(4), 480–497. https://doi.org/10.1080/13611267.2020.1793086

Prendergast, M. (2019). Generosity in performance. *NJ: Drama Australia Journal, 43*(2), 100–113. https://doi.org/10.1080/14452294.2019.1703207

Smith, T. D., & Hendricks, K. S. (2020). Listening to voices seldom heard. In T. D. Smith & K. S. Hendricks (Eds.), *Narratives and reflections in music education: Listening to voices seldom heard* (pp. 1–15). Springer.

Sverdlik, A., Hall, N. C., McAlpine, L., & Hubbard, K. (2018). Journeys of a PhD student and unaccompanied minors. *International Journal of Doctoral Studies, 13,* 361–388. https://doi.org/10.28945/4113

CHAPTER 12

Canadian K-12 Music Educators' Pandemic Teaching Experiences

The Silver Lining

Francine Morin

Abstract

The experience of teaching in K-12 school music programmes across Canada changed dramatically for music educators in March 2020 because of the emergency created by the COVID-19 pandemic. Results from *Singing in Canadian Schools: COVID-19 Impact Survey* (Morin & Mahmud, 2021) confirmed that music and choral programmes suffered significantly, but that positive outcomes also arose from the innovative music teaching approaches that evolved during this unsettling time. A full discussion of categorised data themes resulting from an analysis of the written comments of Canadian music teachers (N = 375) illuminates these positive outcomes – for music education and singing, and music educators and their students. Music teachers explored broader music content in classes and offered students more diverse musical experiences. They skillfully incorporated more technology into music programmes, emphasised individual musical development over that of ensembles, and built stronger personal connections with students. Moreover, music teachers benefitted from accessing an array of online professional learning opportunities. The theory of action learning (Brockbank & McGill, 2003; Revans, 1982, 2008) is posited as a possible explanation for music educators' adaptive and constructive responses to the pandemic crisis. The experiences of music teachers during the COVID-19 crisis provides the field with an opportunity to re-think school music education and rebuild it for the future.

Keywords

music teachers – music education – pandemic – COVID-19

1   Setting the Context

The onset and spread of COVID-19 significantly altered music teaching practices and student learning in K-12 schools across the globe. *Singing in Canadian Schools: COVID-19 Impact Survey* (Morin & Mahmud, 2021) was conducted to examine COVID-19 pandemic impacts on the use of singing in K-12/CEGEP school music programmes in Canada. Given that arts education researchers also had to adapt to the pandemic-related challenges of doing in-person field work, data for this study were collected using *Qualtrics* (2012), a secure online survey platform. When developing the online tool, I worked closely with an advisory committee comprised of representatives from Choral Canada and other national organisation partners funding the study. Using virtual meeting platforms such as Zoom, we were able to develop, nurture, and sustain the conversations necessary to guide the nation-wide study. The opportunity to learn more about online survey and meeting platforms provided me with the opportunity to grow as an arts education researcher. I now have an expanded repertoire of technology skills and tools that I am continuing to use in other research studies.

Overall, the survey results confirmed that the impacts of COVID-19 on Canadian school music programmes involving singing were severe and widespread. Due to rigorous health restrictions placed on singing, thousands of K-12 students no longer benefitted from participating in the rich range of regular and extra/co-curricular music programmes involving singing and choral experiences implemented through face-to-face interactions. Hundreds of music teachers identified some health and safety measures that were difficult for them to implement in adapted instructional settings in schools. Instructional time spent singing and the scope of singing experiences offered to students declined immensely, both in-person and virtually as teachers were suddenly required to find alternative pathways to teach music with little or no singing. It was not possible for most music educators to teach or assess many of the music learning outcomes mandated in official Canadian music curricula through singing, a situation that has led to significant music learning loss, especially related to singing, and incomplete profiles of students' musical growth. Working conditions declined for music teachers throughout the crisis and the majority worked without modified music curricula and/or assessment tools to accommodate for the mandatory restrictions on singing. Professional development for teachers was inadequate in helping them cope with swiftly changing music teaching protocols, especially for singing. They experienced the loss of designated music classrooms, opportunities to perform live with students, and were assigned additional non-teaching responsibilities. Teachers spent more time planning, and mostly without compensation. These factors, including feelings of having decreased support from division administrators and government authorities, negatively affected music teachers' mental health, well-being, and job satisfaction. Despite this dismal backdrop, I will turn to a discussion of some more luminous results.

In this chapter, findings for one provoking theme we investigated will be reported in more detail – positive outcomes and opportunities for music teachers and students. The open-ended question used to gather qualitative data for this theme was, what are the positive outcomes or opportunities that resulted for you and/or your students related to singing and music education at school during the pandemic? In asking teachers this question, the aim was to garner insights into whether a "silver lining" was emerging from this difficult and complex pandemic situation for them and/or their students. In other words, it is possible that some positives arose during the bleak months that followed March 2020, and if so, these positives should be identified. Rich qualitative data were generated in response to this question from 375 teachers. Teachers' written comments were analysed using Saldana's (2015) qualitative data analysis and interpretative techniques. The approach begins with coding or assigning meaningful labels to units of text, sorting similar units into thematic categories, and then generating concepts and theory. Overall, this process enabled me to summarise data, select key quotations, and make sense of what teachers were saying. Most music teachers who commented (319 or 85.07%) identified a range of positive outcomes for music education and singing, as well as benefits for both music teachers and their students which are worthwhile sharing with the arts education community.

2   Positive Outcomes for Music Education

2.1   *Broadening the Range of Essential Music Learnings*
Table 12.1 presents the six thematic categories that emerged from music teachers' comments referencing positive outcomes for music education more generally. By far, increased time to explore aspects of the music curriculum that teachers had limited time to address in their school programmes under normal circumstances was the most frequently cited positive outcome for music education within teachers' comments – "We have been able to concentrate on some other areas of music that are sometimes ignored due to a lack of time". For instance, one experienced high school choral teacher revamped their performance-oriented choir classes which reportedly "morphed into some wonderfully creative composition challenges, song writing workshops, and passion projects utilising a myriad of artistic forms of expression". Another

TABLE 12.1   Positive outcomes for music education

Thematic category	Frequency
Time to focus on a broader range of essential music learning areas	High
Virtual presentations and concerts	Moderate
Project-based learning	Moderate
New music education programmes	Low
Renewed appreciation for music	Low
Music still brings joy	Low

stated that after the crisis forced them to shift away from their predominantly performance-based teaching model, new areas of learning were fostered with students which will "make my programme more balanced in the long run". An elementary music educator was able to "focus more on aural melodic and rhythmic discrimination, reading rhythm patterns and playing them on instruments, learning about jazz and classical composers as well as learning new skills like bucket drumming and body percussion".

It was clear that additional time was at teachers' disposal because of the limitations placed on higher-risk music teaching and learning activities. Instructional time typically spent pre-pandemic singing and playing wind instruments during classes, engaging students in performance-based activities, and/or preparing for live music performances was now available to advance other music concepts and skills that did not involve these restricted activities. Two teachers summed up this perspective, "We have used the challenge of not singing to strengthen other music skills that will make us stronger when we sing again" and "I've been able to introduce students to a much larger variety of music and go more in-depth with topics I wouldn't be able to otherwise as many classes were spent in rehearsals". There was a sense that these additional learnings would "strengthen the foundation of singing" once music programmes return to normal.

Music teachers commented on how they studied a broader range of music styles, genres, and forms with their students, including non-Western musical practices. Additional active music learning through "body movement, gestures, and even sign language" was explored during the pandemic. Further instructional time was devoted to the development of music literacy skills, aural skills, reading music, theoretical concepts, and music vocabulary. For example, one teacher said, "I realise there are many other valuable skills that can be developed without singing. I taught more theory, practiced more ear training, and rhythm exercises each day". Another cited benefits from "having the class time to focus on theory, rhythm, reading notes on a musical staff, form, history, styles, listening, composition, instruments, symphonies, different performers, styles, and body percussion". Classes spent on composing music took a leap during the pandemic, as did studies of music history, composers, orchestral and world instruments. Comments like this one were common: "I had time to focus on things I normally rush through or don't cover as thoroughly, for example, the creative process and composing" or "Nous avons fait davantage de projets de création musicale".

Teaching modules on beat and rhythm were explored via various media such as: non-pitched percussion instruments, body percussion, and different types of drums (e.g., West-African drums, bucket drums). One teacher shared, "We have been able to study rhythms and rhythmic composition on a much deeper level". Teachers delved into studies of pitched percussion instruments (e.g., tone-barred instruments, tone bells, boom whackers, stringed instruments (e.g., ukulele, guitar), and even keyboard instruments as they were "pushed to explore instruments more".

2.2 Virtual Music Presentations and Concerts

The opportunity to involve musical guests in school music programmes through virtual presentations/workshops and/or sharing the results of music teaching and learning through producing virtual concerts that "reached wider audiences" than they did via in-person concerts were ideas raised at moderate levels by teachers as definite benefits of the pandemic to music education. An elementary teacher reported that "Each class learned a piece of music for a virtual Christmas concert using either instruments, movement with or without props, and performed songs with sign language. This month we were able to have a virtual workshop involving all 24 classes in the school with the National Arts Centre featuring two presenters". Another explained that doing performances online had been a "positive experience" and described one "amazing collaborative video performance", but with the caveat that performing online is "not nearly as fulfilling as live concerts". Regarding the chance to work with guests, one vocal choral teacher affirmed, "The biggest benefit is I can get high level virtual artists to stream into my classes that I could never have had into my classes in a face-to-face format". Another predicts, "We will surely continue to invite guest speakers (e.g., composers) living elsewhere to join us online".

2.3 Pedagogical Pilots, Appreciation, and Joy

Another positive outcome that came to light at moderate levels was the chance that students were given to undertake project-based learning in the music classroom, a form of learner-centred inquiry rarely used in pre-pandemic music classrooms. One teacher was excited about this work, "My grade 8's did a fantastic project called *My Musical Journey* that they reflected upon, researched, and recorded". A few teachers reported on how they had time during the pandemic to develop and pilot new music programmes – "I was able to use one-to-one Chromebooks to design a fully online PBL [project-based learning] music programme, which might have further applications after the pandemic". Small numbers also cited a renewed appreciation by students for music education as a positive outcome of the pandemic, indicated by statements like "The students have realised what they have taken for granted for so long and crave for a return to normalcy". Some also mentioned that despite the restrictions, "music still brings joy to my students". Students who participated in music during the pandemic continued to feel "very connected to each other" and maintained a sense of community.

These kinds of positive outcomes resulting for music education due to pandemic restrictions in Canada were observed by other music education researchers conducting survey research across the globe. Hash (2021) found that band teachers in the United States also reported covering a greater variety of music learning content in their instrumental school music programmes during the crisis and undertaking more arranging and composing with their students. Researchers from Germany, Greece, and Turkey described an extensive range of inventive and effective music teaching strategies developed and implemented during COVID-19 by music teachers in these European countries (Pabst-Kruger & Ziegenmeyer, 2021) which is like the range reported by Canadian music teachers. Parkes et al. (2021) discovered that K-12 music teachers in the United States increased their repertoire of teaching approaches and methods for engaging students in music learning. American music teachers acknowledged opportunities to expand their music curriculum goals, experienced increased self-efficacy, and became more proficient adopting a variety of helpful resources. The sense among Canadian music teachers that a benefit of the pandemic is a renewed appreciation for including music in the schools was echoed by music teachers in England (Daubney & Fautley, 2021).

3   Positive Outcomes for Singing

3.1   *Renewed Valuing of Singing*
Music teachers also reflected upon and delineated positive outcomes that related more specifically to singing which are summarised in Table 12.2. Most often they talked about how the absence of singing during the COVID-19 crisis resulted in a reawakened appreciation of singing and choral-related experiences in schools. This sentiment is represented by comments like these ones,

TABLE 12.2   Positive outcomes for singing

Thematic category	Frequency
Renewed appreciation for singing-related experiences	High
Learning to sing outdoors	Moderate
Production of recordings	Moderate
Learning to sing online	Low
New singing programme	Low
Time to focus on other vocal/choral topics	Low
Learning to use humming in vocal programme	Low
Online rehearsals	Low
Virtual choir	Low

"It has given me and my students a renewed sense of how important singing together and using our voices is to us. And how much it is a vital part of our community rituals and creating those feelings of togetherness and belonging" or "We realised just how much we LOVE singing. You don't know what you've got till it's gone", or "Maybe there is a new desperation to sing that sparks a singing revolution next year". A key message conveyed by Canada's music teachers is that the value of singing in schools and the contributions that vocal and choral programmes make to students' musical and social-emotional lives is something that may have been taken too lightly prior to the pandemic and it is now sorely missed. One teacher put it simply this way, "Absence makes the heart grow fonder". It seems clearer now that school music programmes that include singing and choral music ensemble experiences are critical to contributing to the overall musical development and well-being of students, as well as school cultures. Several teachers concluded that the pandemic has "reinforced how much we do value singing" and without a doubt they will be "so grateful to be able to sing again".

3.2   Outdoor Singing and Performing Using Technology

At more moderate levels learning to sing outdoors and to produce recordings of singing and choral performances were identified by teachers of singing as useful outcomes of the pandemic. Some discovered that they were "able to sing outside" with students and "outdoor teaching and learning is possible and effective" in a vocal music class. Vocal/choral teachers created many recordings during the pandemic including "videos of small group singing that were sent home to parents". One music teacher wrote happily, "Much more recording of performances has given us the opportunity to reach a wider audience and a trove of videos to share in future recruitment efforts". Likewise, another indicated, "We have been able to live stream performances from our music room which has allowed family and friends who would not been able to attend a performance at school to be a part of our concerts in real time". Video recordings were also considered helpful because they offered a permanent record or as one teacher noted "a souvenir of their [students'] music making".

3.3   New Course Development

Less frequently music teachers identified other benefits which can be shared. One explained, "If I go online, I can model singing and students can respond safely at home". Such comments showed that teaching and learning singing online was enabling and an important outcome of the pandemic situation for some students. This idea is substantiated by one teacher's efficacious report, "I've developed my 100% online vocal course from the ground up, and it's given me a boost of confidence that I can still teach what I love in new ways". Likewise, another teacher had the opportunity to be "piloting a new programme during the pandemic, and coincidentally it's having a positive impact on singing in [her] programme specifically". The musical needs of diverse student groups were also addressed during the pandemic in some Canadian schools. For example, one music teacher wrote about the chance to "offer a special music class for our special needs students in place of my choir slot ... something I hope we can keep".

3.4   Reimaging Choral Music Content and Practices

Teachers of singing devoted more time to topics like "vocal anatomy and vocal health" or they led studies on "solo performers who have continued to create through the pandemic", "song composition", or "the ethics of performing". One vocal choral teacher, "dove into listening examples in concert choir" and "scatting [vocal jazz] as individuals and the theory behind it, all without the time restraints of learning a few tunes for our next performance". An increased experimentation with non-singing approaches led some teachers to discover that "humming does have a place in a vocal programme". Others choral teachers commented on the usefulness of virtual rehearsals with one concluding that "Zoom rehearsals will be kept" in the future. A similar sentiment was echoed by this teacher, "Our new-found abilities to work online mean that we will be able to hold rehearsals virtually rather than cancel completely in case of bad weather". Evident in a few comments was the emergence of "virtual choirs" at some schools, which was also considered a constructive result of the COVID-19 teaching experience.

Music teachers from other countries also identified benefits for singing that resulted from teaching during the pandemic. European music education researchers found that teachers there made videos of singing for special school occasions which was valuable, as did Canadian music teachers (Pabst-Kruger & Ziegenmeyer, 2021). In one study within the European compendium, a useful practice for singing was developed during COVID-19 by teachers which involved requiring students to video-record themselves singing assigned parts of choral works. These individual recordings were collected by teachers and merged, and in this way, students could view videos of themselves singing pieces together. Music teachers in Europe, the United States (Parkes et al., 2021), and in Canada also assessed learning outcomes for singing using video and audio recordings when students could not sing in person at school. A noted benefit both in Canada and abroad was that students tended to practice more to perform their best on the recording. Music teachers in all three studies indicated they would continue to use this assessment practice in the future. As was found for music education in general, teachers of singing shifted the content of their classes to what was possible which increased and expanded instruction to include more listening to vocal and choral music, and interpreting it in relation to theory, history, and/or culture. Teachers of singing also discovered useful digital tools such as *Solfy*[1] which is an interactive programme for students to practice Solfege at home. Like some Canadian music teachers, those from the Netherlands, Romania, and Israel (Pabst-Kruger & Ziegenmeyer, 2021) viewed this singing programme as an AI-based solution for teaching and learning singing during the pandemic and in the future.

4   Benefits for Music Teachers

4.1   *Discovering Alternative Music Pedagogies and Resources*
Table 12.3 shows that one of the most highly cited benefits for music teachers resulting from their pandemic music teaching experiences since March 2020 was the exploration and discovery of a broad array of alternative music pedagogies, practices, and instructional resources – "I learned so many different ways to teach my students that I would have never considered before". This newly acquired repertoire of teaching approaches evolved from the need for teachers to "think outside the box", "push outside of [their] comfort zone", and "get creative". They had to work imaginatively and quickly to find new ways forward for continuing music programmes at school, in most cases under highly constrained contexts and without the use of singing, wind instrument playing, or their music classrooms and equipment. Because of the variety and novelty

TABLE 12.3   Benefits for music teachers

Thematic category	Frequency
Discovery of alternative music pedagogies, practices, and resources	High
Increased efficacy with virtual teaching and technology	High
Professional learning and development opportunities	High
Increased knowledge of students	Moderate
Time to focus on individual students	Low
Decreased performance-related stress	Low
Learning to adapt	Low
Increased versatility	Low
Time to reflect on role of music education	Low
Development of multi-level units	Low

that these pandemic teaching strategies provided to students, teachers also observed some increased student engagement. This connection is represented by this comment, "I really had to search for ways to teach as many outcomes as possible in a safe way. Many of these engaged my students more than ever and I will be continuing to use these ideas in the future".

4.2   *Virtual Teaching and Technology*

In response to this survey question, again and again music teachers identified increased knowledge of and efficacy with teaching using various technologies as worthwhile outcomes of the pandemic. It was common for teachers to state in a general way that they were simply "learning a lot about technology", "becoming more tech savvy", or "les résultats positifs sont ma capacité à enseigner la musique virtuellement". In other statements specifics were evident, such as this teacher who said they developed "a music technology curriculum that will benefit programming post-pandemic". Teachers identified a range of technology tools as advantageous: "I love *MusicplayOnline* – it saved me in classroom lessons", "I will keep my head-set mic after the pandemic", or "I discovered online theory programmes and using TEAMS to communicate and do assignments" as advantages. Some trialed other kinds of applications, "I have created a music website which has been well received and I discovered a plethora of online teaching tools". One teacher will continue to post classroom performances of songs on the school's website because this practice "increases awareness of the classroom music programme". Overall, music teachers benefitted from acquiring various technology skills such as: mastering online video teaching (Zoom, Microsoft TEAMS), rehearsing, and performing platforms, music software programmes, and video and audio recording and editing. Although cautious about using too much in the way of digital music-making moving forward, some music teachers indicated that "technology will remain part of [their] music classes".

4.3 Professional Learning Enhancements for Music Teachers

A third benefit raised many times by music teachers pointed to the expanded opportunities for professional learning and development that was afforded to them during the pandemic. One music teacher working in a rural community was thrilled to report, "I have participated in in more music-specific PD this year than ever before". Communities of music educators and various organisations locally, regionally, nationally, and internationally came together to support one another through networking in efforts to share instructional resources and pedagogies considered feasible for teaching music during the pandemic. Several respondents reported in this way, "Many music teachers have shared resources, tips, and ideas on digital platforms for free to help each other through pandemic teaching, and this has definitely helped my teaching and personal professional development". Others gave specific examples such as, "I was able to attend ukulele teacher training online" or "I have also taken part in lots of online webinars and self-directed courses that pre-pandemic I could never have afforded to attend or been able to travel to as they normally occurred across North America or halfway around the world. Being able to participate online has opened a whole new world of live and on-my-own time PD opportunities".

4.4 Learning More about Students

At more moderate levels, teachers commented on benefitting from learning more about their students as musical learners. To illustrate, this teacher said, "I have gotten to know my choir members on a deeper level, the connection has been truly meaningful". For one teacher, the QUAD system, "enabled me to get to know the students one-on-one better than the pre-COVID school timetable". While working online with students learning at home, another admitted to discovering that "some of the terribly shy students have beautiful voices". A few teachers said that they had time for "more deeper conversations with students" and "getting to know students individually and personally". This notion seemed to go hand in hand with another advantage of teaching during the pandemic, although mentioned less frequently, which was more time to give students individualised attention because class sizes were smaller during the pandemic.

4.5 *Other Important Gains for Music Teachers*

Less often but interestingly teachers mentioned that they experienced some relief from the "stress that comes with preparing for live performances" such as concerts, assemblies, and festivals. Teachers learned that they had the capacity to adapt to changing circumstances and said they gained versatility and resourcefulness. For instance, one teacher said that the pandemic, "made me a more versatile teacher with a quick ability to implement unique music lessons and units on the fly". Without the pressures of preparing for performances and the suspension of many extra-curricular music programmes, music teachers had time to reflect on their practices and re-think the role of music in education. For instance, one respondent wrote, "I have been able to focus on other musical areas and rethink lesson plans, which has resulted in some creative teaching ideas". Another said, I think we rely on singing too much and this has taught me to think more outside the box and consider the needs of students who do not like to sing". A more philosophical shift was contemplated by this teacher, "I believe that this [the pandemic] has also opened student learning beyond the *whiteness* of our existing performance-based programmes, and that is a good thing". And finally, because of teaching on carts, teachers developed their ability to create multi-level units of instruction for use with various grade levels. One teacher reported to be "rotating units through different levels" to create music without singing.

A consistent finding across pandemic-related survey research in music education examining positive outcomes is that music teachers benefited from exploring and expanding their pedagogical toolboxes for engaging students with music (Hash, 2021; Morin & Mahmud, 2021; Pabst-Kruger & Ziegenmeyer, 2021; Parkes et al., 2021). Other common benefits noted across these studies are that music teachers successfully adapted to remote teaching and learning when schools closed, increased their knowledge of technology, and were able to use various technologies for teaching in the virtual environment (e.g., video conferencing platforms, course management systems, music education software, audio, and visual editing software). Other research findings corroborating with our Canadian study suggest that music teachers acquired a deeper knowledge of individual students because they had more time to focus on them. For example, Spanish music teachers reported this same gain resulting from increased contact time with students during the pandemic and learning more about them as unique young musicians (Calderón-Garrido & Gustems-Carnicer, 2021). In the state of Illinois, Hash (2021) reported likewise that band teachers focused more on individual student achievement while teaching remotely during the crisis. Stronger connections between individual students, teachers, and music and important factors impacting relationality and student engagement in secondary instrumental teaching and learning contexts during the pandemic were uncovered by de Bruin (2021) in a qualitative study with Australian music teachers. These positive outcomes for music educators are essentially attributed to the reduction in time teachers typically spend performing with students and implementing co-curricular and extra-curricular music programmes, most of which were suspended during the pandemic.

5 Benefits for Students

5.1 Diverse Music Learning Experiences

Teachers identified some worthwhile outcomes for students in their responses to this question as can be seen in the categorical themes presented in Table 12.4. Most frequently, they indicated that students benefitted from experiencing music learning in more diverse ways or as one put it "adding SO MANY new activities" to music classes for students. To illustrate, teachers offered comments such as, "the pandemic allowed success for students who are not successful at performance-based tasks" or "the use of digital audio workstations (like *Soundtrap*) has greatly improved students' interest and capacity in music-making in older grades". Another teacher offered this explanation, "Learners who were previously reluctant to sing or move are benefitting from acquiring a comprehensive gesture vocabulary because I devote more time, detail, and attention to the use of gesture to communicate learning and understanding … I offer individual choice".

5.2 Less Performance Anxiety

At midway levels of frequency, teachers reported that students benefitted from experiencing less performance anxiety during the pandemic. "Students did not have to navigate that anxiety because singing is not being asked of them this year". To further illustrate this point one teacher wrote, "Some students felt more comfortable to record themselves singing and then have the recording played in class rather than performing in front of their peers. I will continue to use this method at times in the future". Similarly, this teacher observed, "When students upload performances, they have many chances to get it right. Normally, they used to perform live and did not always do as well. So, they like pre-recording their tests. Performance test marks tend to be higher this year".

5.3 Smaller Class Sizes

Also emerging more moderately, music teachers reported that their students benefitted from the chance to work with them in smaller sized classes, and in

TABLE 12.4   Benefits for students

Thematic category	Frequency
Increased diversity of music learning experiences	High
Decreased performance anxiety	Moderate
Smaller class sizes	Moderate
Opportunity to set music goals	Low
Opportunity for personal growth	Low
Opportunities for therapeutic music experiences	Low

some cases, they linked low enrollments to greater music learning. One teacher reported, "Working in smaller ensembles has certainly been motivating for our students, and I believe that most of them have become better singers this year". Physically distanced students and wearing masks "helped develop skills in projection and listening". There were "fewer classroom management issues" which provided more time for learning. For example, "Smaller grade level choirs have allowed for more music literacy, individualised instruction, exploration of more culturally specific songs, skill sets, and abilities". In smaller classes, quieter students were also engaging and interacting more comfortably. According to this teacher, "My ADD [attention deficit disorder] students were able to focus and engage more in class activities in smaller groups!!" When class sizes were 10–12 students, another noted that their music classes were "awesome for students' attention, engagement, and progress!"

5.4   *Learning Enhancements for Students*
Less frequently, teachers wrote about their ability to give students more individualised attention during the pandemic and set learning goals for them. There were opportunities for both musical and personal growth for music learners. "They are doing a lot of individual learning rather than in groups, so they are developing independence. They are developing their creativity and higher-level critical thinking skills. When we return to singing, they will be better equipped". Another teacher reported that "some students got a LOT more of my time and energy in a more one-on-one way". Music teachers had time to focus on students who did not always feel comfortable with music making in groups and were "able to explore some solo projects". In terms of personal growth during the pandemic, teachers noted increases in students' "patience", persistence", "respectfulness", resilience", "empathy", "social awareness", "mindfulness", and self-regulation skills".

At lower levels, teachers described offering therapeutic music experiences during the pandemic which was viewed as a benefit. Some used the music classroom to foster "positive mental health, belonging, purpose, a place to shine, a way to feel special and valued". One directly aimed to use "music as therapy" and "teach that learning an instrument does not have to be as studied and polished and can be more of an organic [process], using instruments and sound and patterns that sooth us, or help us celebrate the positive things in our lives and world". Others made comments like "I want music to ease burdens of worry amongst the children" or indicated that there has been "more time for reflection" during music classes in the pandemic context.

Across other survey studies like our Canadian one, music education researchers found that students generally benefitted from more diverse music learning experiences, greater individual musical achievement, and the development of musical independence (Hash, 2021; Morin & Mahmud, 2021; Pabst-Kruger & Ziegenmeyer, 2021; Parkes et al., 2021). In London, Daugvilaite's (2021) case study involving 10 instrumental students provides further evidence that students became more independent while learning online during the pandemic than what their teachers observed when working with the same students in face-to-face teaching contexts. The conditions under which students learned music during the pandemic such as smaller class sizes and reduced pressure to prepare to perform afforded the time for teachers to focus on individual musical growth rather than on group or ensemble musical growth.

6   Conceptual and Theoretical Insights

Teaching music in Canadian schools during the COVID-19 pandemic presented teachers with a unique set of challenges and problems to solve. The findings of the qualitative component of this Canadian study offer the arts education community a bird's eye view of how school music teaching and learning adapted and benefitted. K-12 music and choral teachers made efforts to continue implementing their programmes during the crisis even without the support, resources, and professional development they needed to modify their music curricula, undertake teaching music virtually, or teach in-person under highly restrictive health and safety protocols. The responses of teachers to the pandemic crisis bring to the fore their creativity, resilience, and ingenuity which can, at least in part, be explained by action learning.

With little to no music instructional resources or modified curriculum documents to guide music teaching and learning in Canada's school, teachers of music and singing were forced to assume an action learning stance. Action learning is a rich philosophy of learning and practice used in fields like education (Brockbank & McGill, 2003; Revans, 1982, 2008). The goal of action learning is pragmatic – to resolve a real-life problem, especially for critical ones defined by Grint (2008) as crisis situations that demand swift action, like the challenges music educators were confronting. As a job-embedded form of professional development; action learning is "outcome-oriented and problem focused … it enables people to learn by doing" (Coughlan & Coghlan, 2011, p. 6). It is undertaken by peers who share problems and have a need to do something about them (Pedler, 2011). Action learning is provoked by a dilemma that requires colleagues to work together and act.

The literature, including research, theory, pedagogical and curriculum publications, or consulting experts in the field is not relied upon in action learning in education because existing knowledge and resources may not sufficient, available, or applicable to a particular school context. It is for this reason that the theory of action learning offers a useful explanation for how music educators managed to find a way forward by formulating new teaching strategies and innovations to confront challenges and improve and resolve their dire situations at school. As action learners, Canadian music teachers addressed their own issues and problems, learning through the processes of inquiry, innovation, reflection, and collaborative networking and sharing.

7 Conclusions and Recommendations

Canadian K-12 music educators identified several positive outcomes of their pandemic teaching experiences for music education in general and for singing, as well as benefits for themselves and their students. As a result of the crisis, music educators came to realise that a more comprehensive and balanced music curriculum that includes all essential learning areas (music language and performance skills, composing and arranging, cultural and historical understanding, interpreting musical experiences, and so on) is important. They now understand that technology has value and a place in the music classroom as a teaching, learning, and assessment tool. Pre-pandemic Canadian music educators tended to focus on performance skills and ensembles such as band and choir, emphasising the music development of the group over the individual music student. This tendency shifted during the pandemic and therefore music teachers are provoked to rethink their philosophies of teaching music, programme content, and goals. Looking ahead, music teachers will take along a plethora of new music pedagogies, resources, and experiences that they can consider for enhancing school music programmes in the continuing or post-pandemic context. It is recommended that division/district administrators, music education leaders, and music teachers participate in professional conversations to discuss music pedagogy innovations and other positive outcomes that emerged from their pandemic teaching experiences and consider ways that these can be used to enhance school music education and singing-related programmes moving forward.

The experience of teaching during a crisis also raised pressing questions for music teachers such as: What is more important the individual music student or the ensemble? What music curriculum content and pedagogies are most effective for engaging students in music learning? How can the pressures of performance in our music programmes be relaxed? How can new learning relationships between teachers, students, and music be created and nurtured in our programmes? By sharing their perspectives and raising these kinds of questions, Canadian music educators are igniting critical reflection on practice and inspiring change within school music programmes for the future. It is recommended that leaders at all levels in the music and education system use the COVID-19 crisis as an opportunity to re-think school music education and the unique role it can play in education recovery and rebuilding efforts. The unique values of music and singing in education need to be shared in convincing, comprehensive, and compelling ways in ongoing advocacy initiatives to ensure that K-12 music programmes across the country are resurrected, strengthened, and championed.

Acknowledgement

This study was funded by Choral Canada and its national partners – Canadian Music Educators' Association, Coalition for Music Education in Canada, and Kodály Society of Canada.

Note

1 https://www.4solfy.com/solfy_home/

References

Brockbank, A., & McGill, I. (2003). *The action learning handbook: Power techniques for education, professional development, and training.* Routledge.

Calderón-Garrido, D., & Gustems-Carnicer, J. (2021). Adaptations of music education in primary and secondary school due to COVID-19: The experience in Spain. *Music Education Research, 23*, 139–150. https://dx.doi.org/10.1080/14613808.2021.1902488

Coughlan, P., & Coghlan, D. (2011). *Collaborative strategic improvement through network action learning.* Edward Elgar.

Daubney, A., & Fautley, M. (2021). U-turns in the fog: The unfolding story of the impact of COVID-19 on music education in England and the UK. *British Journal of Music Education, 38*, 3–12. https://dx.doi.org/10.1017/S0265051721000048

Daugvilaite, D. (2021). Exploring perceptions and experiences of students, parents and teachers on their online instrumental lessons. *Music Education Research, 23*, 179–193. https://dx.doi.org/10.1080/14613808.2021.1898576

de Bruin, L. R. (2021). Instrumental music educators in a COVID landscape: A reassertion of relationality and connection in teaching practice. *Frontiers in Psychology, 11*, Article 624717. https://dx.doi.org/10.3389/fpsyg.2020.624717

Grint, K. (2008). Wicked problems and clumsy solutions. *Clinical Leader, 1*(2), 54–68. http://leadershipforchange.org.uk/wp-content/uploads/Keith-Grint-Wicked-Problems-handout.pdf

Hash, P. M. (2021). Remote learning in school bands during the COVID-19 shutdown. *Journal of Research in Music Education, 68*(4), 381–397. https://dx.doi.org/10.1177/0022429420967008

Morin, F., & Mahmud, M. N. (2021). *Singing in Canadian schools: COVID-19 impact survey.* Final report. Choral Canada.

Norris, T. (2020). Pandemic pedagogy: Innovative strategies for uncertain times. *Brock Education: A Journal of Education Research and Practice. 29*(2), 1–5.

Pabst-Kruger, M., & Ziegenmeyer, A. (Eds.) (2021). *Perspectives for music education for schools after the pandemic.* Music Teacher Associations in Europe. https://www.researchgate.net/publication/350448529_Perspectives_for_music_education_in_schools_after_the_pandemic_A_joint_publication_by_authors_of_the_network_of_Music_Teacher_Associations_in_Europe_Perspectives_for_music_education_in_schools_after_t

Parkes, K. A., Russell, J. A., Bauer, W. I., & Miksza, P. (2021). The well being and instructional experiences of K-12 music educators: Starting a new school year during a pandemic. *Frontiers in Psychology, 12*, Article 701189. https://doi.org/10.3389/fpsyg.2021.701189

Pedler, M. (Ed.). (2011). *Action learning in practice* (4th ed.). Gower.

Qualtrics Labs. (2012). *Qualtrics survey software: Handbook for research professionals.* Qualtrics Labs.

Saldana, J. (2015). *The coding manual for qualitative researchers* (3rd ed.). Sage.

Underhill, J. (2020). *The heart of the school is missing:Music education in the COVID-19 crisis.* Incorporated Society of Musicians. https://www.ism.org/images/files/ISM_UK-Music-Teachers-survey-report_Dec-2020_A4_ONLINE-2.pdf

CHAPTER 13

The Provision of Art Education for Children in Kenya Using WhatsApp

Lucy Mugambi

Abstract

The many problems brought about by the COVID-19 crisis have affected children going to school in Kenya, both positively and negatively. The lockdown interrupted learning and produced mental and physical health challenges for the children and youth in Kenya. As an artist/researcher/teacher, I explored WhatsApp as a potential pedagogical tool to instruct some children from their homes in 2020/2021, and ultimately it has become the norm. The home and immediate environment of the learners have become a valuable resource for art education. The learners continue to explore the newly found approach to learning art, and finding the joy in creating with things and materials found within their environments. They learned to make art works as well as forms that are meaningful to them and that speak for them. They used various media to express their feelings and experiences during the COVID-19 lockdown. COVID-19 opened an avenue for the learners to pay more attention to things in their environment creating artworks that were meaningful and expressive. The WhatsApp art programme also amplified the voices of the students in an ever changing world.

Keywords

COVID-19 – art making – WhatsApp – immediate environment.

1   Closed Schools

In response to the COVID-19 crisis the Kenyan government unexpectedly closed all schools and colleges on March 15, 2020. Almost 17 million learners, parents, and teachers were unsettled by this sudden school closure without adequate planning for how to handle the situation. The government rushed to organise digital modes of learning that included radio and TV lesson transmission. However, these modes were not a viable solution since most students, especially those in the rural areas, have no access to radio and television. A study by Tipton (2018) showed that Kenya "needs increased digital access to the internet to support training, documentation, and disseminating local innovations" (p. 277). However, even those who have these devices found it difficult to grasp the concepts since the materials were new and hurriedly prepared. Moreover, the parents were not well equipped to homeschool their children as they lack the knowledge, time, and skills to do so. These shortcomings meant that parents could not reinforce their children's learning at home. The lockdown consequently produced mental and physical health challenges for the children and youth in Kenya.

2 The Programme Design

A few parents from the eastern region of Kenya where I have been an art teacher for several years reached out to me to instruct their children from their homes. Since I was away in USA pursing my studies, I thought of WhatsApp as an easy, accessible, and affordable potential pedagogical tool of communicating with students learning from their homes. WhatsApp is an internationally available freeware, cross-platform centralised instant messaging (IM) and Voice-over-IP (VoIP) service owned by American company Meta platforms (formerly Facebook).

For the programme to work, the parents, teachers, and I needed to contribute to its administration. The parents provided monitored access to cellphones, data bundles for WhatsApp operation, and provided permission for student participation. They also released any necessary individualised information about their children as the programme evolved. This information included the age of the students, school grade, ability or disability status of the child and home location. These details helped in addressing students' needs during planning and monitoring the teaching/ learning progress.

As an artist/researcher/teacher, I explored how and if WhatsApp can be used as a pedagogical tool to instruct children from their homes in eastern region of Kenya during the COVID-19 lockdown. This programme commenced in May 2020 and continued even after the schools reopened in late 2021. While organising the students' lesson plans, I was reminded by John Dewey (1934/2005) that it is no easy task to separate the art of human experience from the human experience of art. In other words, there is no work of art apart from experience. Dewey's ideas invited me to see physical pieces of art, such as drawings, paintings, mosaic, and songs as the "art product", and reminded me that the actual work of art "is what the product does with and in experience" (p. 3). In this process of instructing the students at a distance through WhatsApp, I viewed art as a process within a given experience and observed what this experience would bring forth.

3 Running the WhatsApp Course

The Kenyan education curriculum emanates from a curriculum and instructional framework where there is a notion that if we have good methods of teaching, automatically good learning will follow. It is a curriculum-as-plan (curriculum-as-text), that is planned by curriculum writers typically far removed from classroom practice. However, Aoki (1993) who is a renowned educator provokes my thinking, encouraging me to pay more attention to the many layers of practices and experiences of my students as well as my own. Aoki (1993) asks us to accommodate the wisdom offered by lived stories that emerge while teaching and "listening thoughtfully" (p. 255) to what the learners say. In this WhatsApp art education programme therefore, I was prompted by this notion to work with the curriculum-as-lived, which is often referred to as Currere. As noted by Aoki (2005), Currere, has to do with running the course, and is more interested in the doing, being, making, creating, and living qualities of learning experiences. Aoki (2005) asks us to be open to the view that learning, knowing and understanding occur in multiple ways. I wanted to leave open spaces during teaching and instruction for growing to occur allowing the stories that are part of the lived curriculum life to unfold. As reminded by Aoki, I needed to find a balance between the curriculum as a plan and the curriculum as lived experience. This freedom of implementation allowed the students and I to have autonomy and embody own experiences and situations. I was concerned about the students' different narratives and lived experiences that emerge in the process of making and learning art. In this case we were to follow a curriculum plan that is lived rather than a curriculum that is laid in a plan. The aim was to use a curriculum landscape that accommodates lived meanings and therefore legitimates the thoughtful everyday narratives of the students through art.

Greene (1995) also calls me to be open in this process of instructing students using a new platform while reminding me to communicate to students "the notion that reality depends on perspective, that its construction is never complete, and that there is always more" (p. 4). Consequently, in this world where nothing really remains constant, it is our duty as educators to encourage students to cultivate multiple ways of seeing and multiple dialogues in their world.

Since the students were learning and creating art from their homes, each student's situation was different in many ways and these differences cannot be ignored. Subsequently, the inquiries undertaken during the learning and teaching in this art programme are woven into the fabric of the world, "embedded and enfolded into the matrices of our day-to-day embodied existence" (Smits et al., 2008, p. 61). I kept in mind that knowledge is subject to situational contexts, hence providing better understanding. Being a teacher for a while has brought me to the realization that creating art requires students to reflect upon and access their own experiences, attitudes, and beliefs. This learning extends beyond one solution since the students solve their problems in their own context and in unique ways.

My goal was to engage the learners in art making and in learning art processes, hence I decided to follow Dewey's thought that education is contingent on experience and should be viewed as a continuous process of rebuilding of experience. Vecchi (2010), who has done vast research on children's education, emphasises the importance of the environment as an educating agent. She encourages art educators to welcome children's many ideas as they try to explore various ways of expressing themselves through art. Given that the students were at home in their own environment, then, it was only logical to direct them to use this environment as their source of inspiration. I asked them to explore the colour, texture, and shapes of things/objects that they use/see every day. They were free to explore things such as cups, plates, and animals within the home and even the vegetation around them. I believe through paying attention to materials/things in everyday experience and making art, the students in the WhatsApp programme as suggested by Dewey (1934/2005) could transform themselves as they actively adapt to external materials and conditions. My aim was to direct the students to observe and experience the world around them, in a new way as they created art. Learning to look more.

4   The WhatsApp Class

I have been working on average with a group of 12 students from the eastern rural region of Kenya. The students joined the art class because their parents were searching for an art teacher who could engage their children during the COVID-19 lockown. Most of the parents knew me since I had been an art teacher in the region for several years. The students' ages ranged between 3 and 17 years. Although the number of students has been fluctuating since the schools re-opened after the COVID-19 lock down, there has been a consistent flow of students attending the programme.

  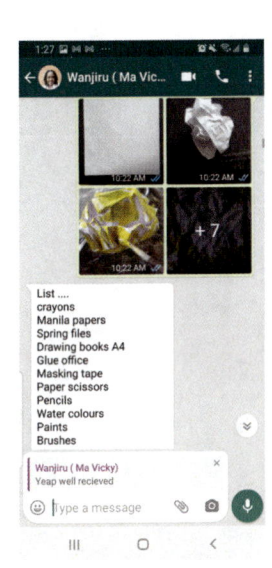

FIGURE 13.1   Communication through WhatsApp

I began by providing common instructions to students of the same age range through the WhatsApp (see Figure 13.1). I provided the younger children simple instructions that they could follow with the help of their parents/guardians. The instructions for the older students mostly depended on what they already knew.

However, this eventually changed due to the time difference dynamics between Kenya and US which made it difficult to follow the students' progress in time. Eventually, I decided to use an alternative method where I introduced a subject matter, and the students would find their own ways of approaching it. For instance I brought about the topic of making connections and reaching out to people that matter to us while in the COVID-19 lockdown. With this topic the students produced a variety of art works that ranged from postcards, drawings, paintings as well as music and poems (see Figure 13.6, example of a post card created for a friend by Jo).

This approach seemed to work quite effectively since the students reside in unique environments that offer different possibilities of creating art. In a way, this open-ended type of assignment encouraged the students to use their democratic rights to make choices about hands-on activities within the WhatsApp virtual mode of art learning. Through this way of learning and doing art, I came to understand some of the important intentions that children bring to their artistic activity, as well as ways that children make meaning through art making (Malin, 2013). For example, they used art to express what and how the COVID-19 situation made them feel. For example, Figure 13.2 shows Tutu aged

FIGURE 13.2
Alone (artist Tutu aged 5 years)

5 representing himself as lonely and alone during the COVID-19 lockdown. On the other hand Figure 13.3 shows Kaka's (aged 10) drawing depicting awareness of COVID-19 safety protocols that made her keep distance from her friends.

From these activities it was apparent that children will engage in and respond to art making according to their motivation as well as their artistic experiences. I acknowledge that clear instructions are crucial, but I agree with Nicoll and Oreck (2012), that "if we aim to make sure everyone understands everything and can anticipate exactly what is about to happen, we may deny students the chance to make their own discoveries and shape their own artistic experience" (p. 10). Therefore, the autonomy for the students to control whatever art creations they made was necessary.

5   Immediate Environmental Resources

Anning and Ring (2004) allude that aesthetic preferences that young children employ in their drawing activities are often rooted in their cultural surroundings, and therefore, we chose to work with materials within the students'

FIGURE 13.3   Social distancing during COVID-19 (artist Kaka aged 10, with permission)

environments. The postcard by Jo in Figure 13.4 was created using wastepaper that he collected from his home and created papier-mâché. He created a support for the card from a carton box and applied the papier-mâché on it. The flower on the postcard is created from real flower petals from his surroundings. He used grass to create the impression of the flower twigs on the picture. The idea was to allow students to create goal-directed activities within their cultural settings that would be intimate and meaningful to them. Cohee Manifold (2009) suggests that we ought to encourage students to develop long term, multi-layered projects based on their "own selected themes" (p. 269) that could result in individual and collaborative art making. These projects can be done as personal tasks that propel actions leading to individually-defined goals. The students were to use the immediate environment as the supplier of art-making resources, as well as the source of creative drive for them to achieve these goals. Time spent in this environment was therefore a crucial aspect of the art-making. It is important to note that most of the students I have been working with reside in the rural areas and hence the themes that were suggested below relate to this aspect of the project. The most important tool for the student was the environment that helped them access their senses and engage in their own dialogue. The aim was to create an environment for independence, allowing them to develop their own questions and problems and try to solve

FIGURE 13.4
My friend's postcard by Jo (14 years)

them on their own. Some questions that arose from the students related to the issue of isolation and when they would resume school to win their friends. For instance, Jo (Figure 13.4) created a postcard to send to his friend since they had not met for a long time.

I bore in mind that "children's experience with real objects and the art materials they use to represent them is significant in creative representation" (Savva & Trimis, 2005, p. 2). Ultimately, to enhance this process of art-making we gave prominence to environmental contexts, that is, space in its broad sense as well as time.

6   Themes Tackled

The main purpose of this WhatsApp learning was to engage students in making art constructively at home. I hoped that they could find the process of art-making relaxing and enjoyable, creating sense, and meaning in their lives. As I mentioned earlier, the students I worked with ranged between the ages of 3 and 17 years. This meant that the activities that they engaged in differed in difficulty, but the themes were broadly the same. Furthermore, the art resources and medium used differed according to the age and the surroundings of the student. I am aware that the teaching of art production usually focuses entirely on composition, artistic procedure, and skill development. Nevertheless, these areas were not the focal points in this programme.

We first explored the basic aspects of art such as use of colour, texture, forms, shapes, balance, unity and variety that can be used to compose any artwork. This content served to offer the basic skills required in making art. There was no limitation of the methods/processes and materials used by the students to create their artwork. Although I suggested broad topics to work on, I encouraged the students to create art that comes from within them. The topics explored included, but were not limited to, emerging issues such as isolation, loneliness, nature, or experimenting with materials. We agreed that there was no wrong or right in doing art and that the process was the most important part of the art-making and not the product. The rightness or wrongness within the art context is simply a product of practice and expectation. If the student was able to carry their idea through and make it into a visible form, then all the steps in the process were of importance. However, even those ideas that did not mature into complete visual art products, were as much works of art as any finished products. Hence, I advised the students to retain their visual thought processes in the form of scribbles, sketches, drawings, failed works, models, studies, thoughts, and conversations. These forms in themselves became narratives of their journey of art-making at home during COVID-19.

7   Talking about the Artwork

Zimmerman (1985) reminds me that aesthetic education increases a student's sensitivity to art and that "language is the vehicle through which awareness and sensitivity to art can be developed" (p. 45). This means that, talking about art is just as essential as creating art. Anderson et al. (2002) also recognise that engaging children in meaningful artwork conversations helps them to intellectually observe and reflect upon their own artworks and those of adults. Enlightening students on responding to their own art as well as that of others was therefore an important aspect of this WhatsApp virtual art learning. I urged the students to talk or write about their artworks pointing to what they liked most about it. I also asked them to share any frustrations that they may have encountered in their art-making process as well as in the art product. The WhatsApp group video calls with the students and parents served as an appropriate platform for this sharing. Since a work of art is always about something, then it calls for interpretation by the viewer who is apart from the original creator of the work. The student artist was free during the making of the artwork to interpret what he/she found of interest in the actual world. However, from the artist to the work of art is a process of discovery and the work of art to the spectator is a process of interpretation. Feibleman (1946) notes that the work of art is a thing existing separately both from process and from its creator. Consequently, the work of art is an impartial existent in the actual world, having its own worth and its own structure for which it is no longer responsible to the artist. In actual sense, once the artwork is out there, the artist does not have control of how it may be viewed. I encouraged the students to share their art works through WhatsApp photos and videos to review what others thought about their creations. Consequently, the art-making and talking about their work in a way helped the students to learn from each other, as well as discover materials in their environment that were useful in art making. Jo (Figure 13.4) for example, confessed that he had never processed papier-mâché or used it to create art like he did in this art programme (see Figure 13.6). It was something that he had not learned in school since art/craft is not given prominence. I believe this is because designers of the curriculum lay a stronger emphasis on the sciences than the art education in Kenya. Andang'o (2010) who carried out research on integrating the arts in early childhood education in Kenya noted that the arts are "one of the most effective ways of teaching children about humanity, life and the society in which they live" (p. 11). Some of these qualities were brought to bare through the conversations they had among themselves as they talked about their own and each other's artwork. For instance, during one of the WhatsApp video call sharing, a student in the programme advised Jo (postcard creator) to start a business of selling post cards.

Advising Jo, he said "This can be a good source of income, especially now that we have financial hardships brought about by this Corona virus".

8   Paying Attention to the Ordinary

The normal school art curriculum hardly affords students the opportunity to learn from their neighborhoods or surroundings. I believe art is not something that can be set apart for occasional pleasure, but should be pursued in all that we do, encounter, select, and interpret. It is difficult to detach ourselves from daily creative experience and production of art because creation is for everyone, and we all live with it. Even those who claim that they are not artists are engaged in art creation sometimes unconsciously as they undertake their daily living. Doing simple things, such as selecting what to wear, picking different flowers in the garden to put in a flower vase, or even deciding where to place items in the room or on the wall, is all art. Kuper (2015) notes that aesthetic values permeate our everyday life and we ought not think of them as "the exclusive province of museums and concert halls" (p. 1).

This WhatsApp programme encourages students to be keener in their surroundings as they carry out their art activities with the premise that everyday endeavors can be a source for self-directed learning and discovery. In terms of art education, paying attention to ordinary things in our surroundings prompts an inquiry into these places, and it allows us to indulge our inquisitiveness and learn from these sites with a renewed interest. Bey (2013) highlights that these sites facilitate creative processes for teaching and research. Students had the opportunity to learn from their surroundings through collecting and interpreting objects and images while making art through creative explorations. Tavin (2000) also explains that such places can generate possibilities for negotiating past and present experiences, hence deconstructing meanings. In this programme, the students' surroundings, therefore, became useful sites for teaching and learning while making artistic creations. The students were consequently consciously or unconsciously compelled to think outside the box about different ways of being in the world. Through art-making the students unified the separate elements of their everyday environment and explored various and creative ways that human beings, nature, and structures of their surroundings interconnect. This interconnection allowed the students to create concrete connections to their social reality during the COVID-19 lockdown. For instance, Kaka (see Figure 13.3) brought about the issue of social distancing and wearing masks whenever in social places. This ignited a debate about where to get masks cheaply since a mask was being purchased at a price of one hundred Kenyan shillings. May, one of the students whose mum is a seamstress explained how they were making their own masks at home using leftover fabric scraps. In this conversation May explained to the rest of us, "Mimi nimeshamake masks zangu za kumatchiza na nguo zangu [I have made my own different masks to match my dresses]".

In this programme, therefore, as the students responded to visual elements in their surroundings, they had the chance to conduct personal experiments and freely enquire creatively into various matters of their lives. These matters included the issue of COVID-19 that had affected their lives in varied ways and was depicted in many of their artworks. For example, the drawing shown in Figure 13.2 depicts Kaka's (10 years old) knowledge of the health mandate to maintain one meter distance away from others and the wearing of masks.

9   Art Mediums

The basic purpose of works of art is to communicate meaning, whether through the process of making or in the product. Luhmann and Roberts (1987) explain that we require a medium in or through which this communication will occur. An artistic medium, therefore, is the material used to create a work of art. Mediums depend on the type of art being created and hence contributing to the stye of art and its meaning. The art creator is normally the determiner of the medium to use since he/she understand their creation better. In this WhatsApp virtual education programme, however, the students were limited in the type of media they could use because some are expensive and out of their reach. They hence used locally available materials as they explored the following art techniques. I observed that the selection of media used in making the artworks was determined by age, location, time, and motivation of the students. Additionally, as the students worked with different media, for some it was just a way to explore the media, that sometimes led to accidental discoveries. For others, it was an impulsive representation of things going on within their lives. While for some of the older ones it was premeditated representation. Due to the scope of this chapter, I have only featured a few examples of media, techniques, and art works of the students in this WhatsApp programme.

10   Drawing

The students used various drawing media such as crayons, pencils, charcoal, and ink to produce interesting drawings while expressing multiple ideas, and feelings.

Figure 13.2 shows a drawing coloured with crayons by Tutu, aged five years representing his aloneness during COVID-19 lockdown. To describe his drawing, he noted that: "Siku hizi mimi hukaa peke yangu. Sina mtu wa kucheza ama kuongea naye [These days I am always alone. I don't have anybody to play or talk to]". Figure 13.3 shows a drawing on the theme 'emerging issues' by Kaka aged 10 years. She depicts social distancing during COVID-19 in relation to her own experiences. She is cognizant of the safety protocols and the need to stay safe.

11   Painting

In the technique of painting there is a variety of mediums that can be used to create pictures. Since watercolours are bright with assorted hues, they are always great for creating landscapes as well as patterns. Furthermore, they dry fast and students who are beginners can easily control them as they paint. The students in this programme used the painting technique to convey ideas, express emotion, use their senses, explore colour, explore process and outcomes, and create aesthetically pleasing works through watercolour. Figure 13.5 shows a self-portrait by Da who is age 6. Figure 13.6 is a marble pattern by Ma aged 7 years. They created the artworks by following the prompts I provided through the WhatsApp text as seen in Figure 13.1.

After Ma completed her piece, she was very excited about it, and this is what she remarked during our weekly WhatsApp video call: "I really love my artwork it looks very beautiful. I will put it on my bedroom wall!"

12   Natural and Found Objects

Jo, who is 14 years old, explored the woods in his environment, and later created the postcard in Figure 13.4 for a friend who he had not seen for a long time

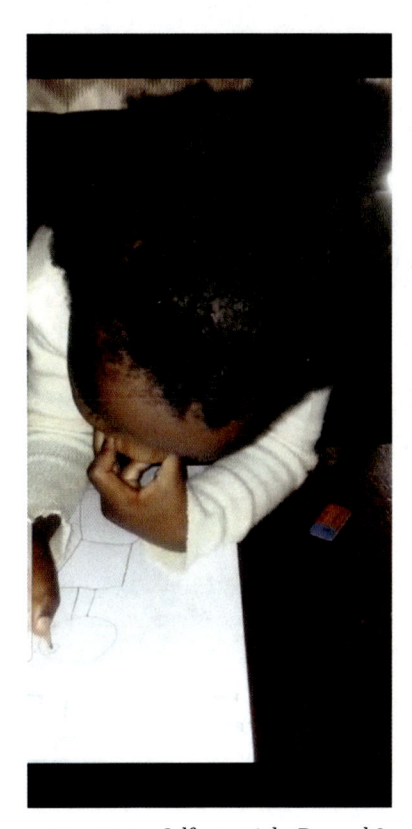

FIGURE 13.5   Self portrait by Da aged 6 years

FIGURE 13.6   Marble pattern (artist Ma 7 years old, with permission)

due to the COVID-19 lockdown. The card is made using real petals from wild-flowers, natural dyes from flowers, and papier-mâché made from wastepaper.

Figure 13.7 shows Jo's colourful abstract pattern, a wall hanging for his mum's bedroom created using salt, glue, and watercolours.

In a world that no longer remains the same, Kantawala (2021) urges us as educators to adapt, survive, and rely on "incredibly imaginative ways to find creative connections to our meaning-making" (p. 5). This WhatsApp virtual art programme continues to engage the students in art making as they cope with emerging issues in their lives. Since art experiences are not readily available in schools, I think more virtual art education should be provided to students.

FIGURE 13.7   Abstract pattern by Jo, age 14 (with permission)

References

Aoki, T. T. (1993). Legitimating lived curriculum: Towards a curricular landscape of multiplicity. *Journal of Curriculum and Supervision, 8*(3), 255–68.

Aoki, T. T. (2005). Curriculum in a new key. In W. F. Pinar & R. L. Irwin (Eds.), *Curriculum in a new key: The collected works of Tedd T. Aoki* (pp. 200–215). Lawrence Erlbaum.

Anderson, Piscitelli, B., Weier, K., Everett, M., & Tayler, C. (2002). Children's museum experiences: Identifying powerful mediators of learning. *Curator (New York, N.Y.), 45*(3), 213–231. https://doi.org/10.1111/j.2151-6952.2002.tb00057.x

Anning, A., & Ring, K. (2004). *Making sense of children's drawings*. McGraw-Hill Education.

Andang'o, E. A. (2010). Integrating the arts in early childhood education in Kenya: Possibilities for the creative mind. In *Educating the creative mind: Developing capacities for the future* (pp. 10–13). Kean University Press.

Bey, S. (2013). Excavating the cityscape through urban tales and local archives. *Art Education, 66*(4), 14–21.

Cohee Manifold, M. (2009). What art educators can learn from the fan-based artmaking of adolescents and young adults. *Studies in Art Education, 50*(3), 257–271.

Dewey, J. (2005). *Art as experience*. Penguin. (Original work published 1934)

Epstein, A. S., & Trimis, E. (2002). *Supporting young artists: The development of the visual arts in young children*. High Scope Press.

Feibleman, J. (1946). The psychology of art appreciation. *Journal of General Psychology, 35*(1), 43–57.

Greene, M. (1995). Art and imagination: Reclaiming the sense of possibility. *The Phi Delta Kappan, 76*(5), 378–382.

Irvin, S. (2008). The pervasiveness of the aesthetic in ordinary experience. *The British Journal of Aesthetics, 48*(1), 29–44.

Kantawala, A. (2021). Lived experience and knotty networks. *Art, 74*(1), 4–7.

Kupfer, J. H. (2015). *Experience as art: Aesthetics in everyday life* (pp. 1–3). SUNY Press.

Luhmann, N., & Roberts, D. (1987). The medium of art. *Thesis Eleven, 18*(1), 101–113.

Malin, H. (2013). Making meaningful: Intention in children's art making. *The International Journal of Art & Design Education, 32*(1), 6–17. https://doi.org/10.1111/j.1476-8070.2013.01719.x

Manifold, M. (2009). What art educators can learn from the fan-based artmaking of adolescents and young adults. *Studies in Art Education, 50*(3), 257–271.

Miller, B. (2001). The promise of after-school programs. *Educational Leadership, 58*(7), 6–12

Savva, A., & Trimis, E. (2005). Responses of young children to contemporary art exhibits: The role of artistic experiences. *International Journal of Education & the Arts, 6*(13), 1–23.

Sheringham, M. (2006). Checking out: The investigation of the everyday in Sophie Calle's *L'Hôtel*. *Contemporary French and Francophone Studies, 10*(4), 415–424.

Smits, Towers, J., Panayotidis, E. L., & Lund, D. E. (2008). Provoking and being provoked by embodied qualities of learning: Listening, speaking, seeing, and feeling (through) inquiry in teacher education. *Journal of the Canadian Association for Curriculum Studies, 6*(2), 43–81.

Tavin, K. (2000). Teaching in and through visual culture. *Journal of Cultural Research in Art Education, 18*, 37.

Tipton, T. M. (2018). Ethnographies from the field: The state of arts education in Kenya and Czech Republic. In *International yearbook for research in arts education 5/2017: Arts education around the world: Comparative research seven years after the Seoul Agenda* (pp. 274–277). Waxmann.

Vecchi, V. (2010). *Art and creativity in Reggio Emilia.* Routledge.

Zimmerman, P. (1985). Writing for art appreciation. In A. R. Gere (Ed.), *Roots in the sawdust: Writing to learn across the disciplines* (pp. 31–46). National Council of Teachers of English.

CHAPTER 14

A Pedagogy of Arts and Multiliteracies

Beryl Peters and Julie Mongeon-Ferré

Abstract

This chapter shares learnings from the first stage of a critical participatory action research study conducted during the global pandemic, which necessitated changes to the original research design and implementation to include virtual and hybrid spaces for teacher questionnaires, interviews, focus groups, and classroom learning.

The study reconceptualises understandings about arts literacies within a pedagogy of multiliteracies. Arts literacies are positioned as essential affordances for all learning. The goals of the study are to identify, analyse, and implement promising practices and models for designing with the arts in a pedagogy of multiliteracies.

The authors are two leaders in arts education, engaged in a research partnership between Université de Saint-Boniface, University of Manitoba, and the provincial Bureau de l'éducation française. This partnership was developed to gather diverse perspectives and to collaborate with Kindergarten to Grade 12 educators and administrators from English, Français, and French Immersion programmes regarding arts and multiliteracies teaching and learning.

The authors share themes emerging from questionnaire and interview data about arts and multiliteracies teaching and learning, and the challenges and solutions for implementation, including the shift to digital technologies. Study themes are illustrated through participant examples of authentic arts, digital, and multiliteracies design, concluding with an epiphanic event. Study data provides compelling evidence that arts, in a pedagogy of multiliteracies facilitated by digital technology, has the potential to create quality, equitable, diverse, inclusive, and engaging learning spaces now and for the future.

Keywords

arts education – arts literacies – digital technologies – learning literacy

1   Introduction

In this chapter, we share learnings from the first stage of a critical participatory action research study to identify and analyse promising practices for designing with the arts in a pedagogy of multiliteracies and to develop, evaluate, and implement recommended models. Because our research took place in the pandemic context, our learnings also include the resulting shift to digital technologies and the ways those digital resources facilitated multiliteracies learning.

We are career arts educators, researchers, and consultants leading arts education initiatives in Manitoba. Throughout our careers we have advocated for arts education and have been a part of many efforts to raise the profile of arts education. We read the authors propounding that the arts would make us smarter (Jensen, 2001) and we listened to Elliot Eisner (2002) exhorting us to move beyond the "arts makes you smarter" rationale for arts education and instead value the arts for their own sake. We worked with teacher teams to create our own rationale for the importance of arts education, as part of front matter in the current Manitoba Arts curriculum frameworks (Manitoba Education and Advanced Learning, 2015).

Despite decades of efforts and a wealth of compelling literature and research evidence for the importance of arts education, the gap between research and educational praxis is still enormous. We no longer struggle as much to make a case for the importance of arts education, but we struggle mightily to implement those beliefs. Our past research and practice has illustrated how arts literacies offer epistemological resources for arts education and all subject areas. Arts literacies are essential semiotic sign systems that afford a realm of unique and powerful resources for perceiving, for meaning making, and for communicating understandings about the self and world both in arts classrooms and those not explicitly arts-based.

We wondered if Eisner's (2002) beliefs in the importance of arts for arts' sake fused with the theory of multiliteracies (New London Group, 1996) could address the gap between research and praxis for arts specialists and non-specialists alike. Our study was designed to explore the potential of arts within a pedagogy of multiliteracies for Kindergarten to Grade 12 schools, and we developed a conceptual framework that positions all literacies, including arts literacies, as equal but unique. We undertake our research and practice guided in the belief that arts literacies are essential multimodal literacies that should be available to all learners.

This chapter stories the first part of our research journey and our emerging learnings about the arts, multiliteracies, and digital technologies. We share our conceptual framework and highlight key themes supported by study data including an epiphanic event. We conclude our chapter with our learnings to date and emerging answers to our central research question, "How can we design and transform K–12 learning spaces with the arts using a critical pedagogy of multiliteracies?" We begin with the unexpected context in which we undertook our study.

2   Pandemic Research Context

In March 2020, just as we completed recruitment and had begun planning with teacher participants in their classrooms, schools were abruptly closed with the onset of a global pandemic. For the next two years, we had no access to classrooms, and we adapted our research using virtual participant interviews, online and digital media resources.

Our interview data and the emerging literature indicated that existing barriers to arts education around the world were greatly amplified by effects of the global COVID-19 pandemic. While these pandemic effects did not cause all systemic issues in arts education, they highlighted and intensified many persistent challenges that existed independently of the pandemic context.

Impacts to arts education were so significant that many educators believed that arts education was placed in jeopardy (Joseph, 2022). Threats to arts education resulting from pandemic effects included new layers of inequitable access to arts education (Feindler et al., 2022), the floundering of performance and product-based arts programmes (Dik et al., 2022), the marginalisation of arts programmes due to the increased focus on literacy and numeracy and perceived achievement gaps (Aurini & Davies, 2021; Cunningham & Gibson, 2022; Joseph, 2022), the re-positioning of arts specialists to teach other subject areas (Parkes et al., 2021; Morin, 2021), cuts to arts programming and spaces (Morin, 2021; Tuttle & Hansen, 2022) and other threats.

Despite the many reported challenges, the pandemic context also produced remarkable examples of resilience, innovation, and even transformation in arts education (Dik et al., 2022; Hourigan, 2022; Joseph, 2022). School closures occasioned innovative digital and web-based approaches to arts instruction and ways to share students' creative work, and arts educators shifted from a focus on performance and product to process-based approaches (Feindler et al., 2022). New professional communities of support were established when arts educators had to quickly collaborate with others to find new ways of teaching arts education in changing, complex, and uncertain school environments (Grier, 2022).

These compelling examples of resilience, innovation, and transformation in arts education convince us that more than ever, arts learning is needed in our schools. Our beliefs in the essentiality of arts literacies and in the need for greater and more equitable access to arts learning provide the inspiration for the arts literacies/multiliteracies conceptual framework that informs our study and that we next describe.

3   Conceptual Framework: Arts and Multiliteracies

We place ourselves within the theoretical paradigm of bricoleur (Denzin & Lincoln, 2018) as we work "between and within competing and overlapping perspectives and paradigms" (p. 12). Our worldview is grounded in a complexivist ontology (Davis & Sumara, 2006) of multiple, emergent realities and assumes a critical complex, social constructivist, epistemological stance (Kincheloe, 2005).

We draw from critical pedagogy (Kincheloe, 2008), multiliteracies theory (New London Group, 1996), arts education (Eisner & Day, 2004), interdisciplinary studies (Brown & Bousalis, 2018), complexity theory (Davis & Sumara, 2006), curriculum studies (Hasebe-Ludt & Leggo, 2018), well-being and social-emotional literature (Edgar & Elias, 2021), transformative learning theory (Mezirow, 2009), and our own personal histories and experiences as arts educators.

3.1   *Arts Literacies*
Through millennia, the message that arts literacies are essential for learning has been argued from different perspectives. While the unevenness and quality of the research and literature on the benefits of arts education makes it challenging to navigate, four international handbooks on arts education (Barton & Baguley, 2017; Bresler, 2007; Eisner & Day, 2004; Fleming et al., 2015) and reviews of arts education research over the last twenty years indicate a range of positive relationships and effects for arts learning. Positive effects relate to academic achievement, learning motivation and engagement, personal skills, social and emotional well-being, confidence, self-esteem, and self-efficacy across grades, subject areas, and cultures (Bamford & Wimmer, 2012; Boyes & Reid, 2005; Deasy, 2002; Edgar & Elias, 2021; Fiske, 1999; Fleming et al., 2016; Saunders, 2021; Winner et al., 2013).

Influential, authoritative voices (Andrews, 2020; Bamford, 2009; Barton, 2020, Bolden & Jeanneret, 2021; Cornett, 2011; Davis, 2008; Dewey, 1934; Eisner & Day, 2004; Fineberg, 2004; Fowler, 1996; Greene, 1995; Pitman, 1998; Wright, 2003) permeate educational thinking about the importance and centrality of the arts. Their voices make a compelling case for the arts in education. But despite the depth and breadth of supporting literature and advocacy for the importance of arts literacies, we are still asking the same question Williams (1991) posed thirty years ago: "It seems fair to ask then, if the arts occupy such a central role in human life, shouldn't they have a central place in education?" (p. 3).

When arts literacies are not as valued as other literacies, learning is impoverished, and learners are denied important learning opportunities. Equitable access to the arts is repeatedly identified by educators and scholars as a key challenge for arts education (Bolden & Jeanneret, 2021); however, inequities only continue to increase. We take up the challenge to strive for equitable access to rich learning by designing with the arts in a pedagogy of multiliteracies. This challenge was not linked to the COVID pandemic but did gain importance during the pandemic context when existing inequities were accentuated, and new inequities were revealed.

3.2   *Multiliteracies*

While a pedagogy of multiliteracies has long grounded our research and thinking (Peters, 2011) and underpins this action research study, the unexpected crises and societal and educational demands during the global pandemic reinforced our beliefs in the need for rethinking literacy as multiliteracies, and for intentionally including and highlighting arts and digital literacies in a pedagogy of multiliteracies.

Literacy, narrowly defined as the reading and writing of print text, has undergone a paradigmatic shift towards a pedagogy of multiliteracies (Pullen & Cole, 2010) since the publication of *A Pedagogy of Multiliteracies: Designing Social Futures* (New London Group, 1996). The ten scholars of the New London Group believed that rapidly changing, multimodal information, communication, and media technologies in an increasingly connected culturally and linguistically diverse world, demanded a new more equitable approach to literacy pedagogy. Their ensuing discussions and consultations gave rise to a theory of pedagogy they described as "a pedagogy of multiliteracies" (New London Group, 1996). This alternative pedagogical approach to limited views of literacy was intended to enable a "full and equitable social participation" (1996, p. 60) in a "multiplicity of discourses" (p. 61).

The concept of multiliteracies has since evolved, resulting in different definitions and applications of multiliteracies (Kist, 2005). For this study multiliteracies are defined as a "range of literacies and literate practices used in all facets of life" (Bull & Anstey, 2019, p. 6). As learners move into the third decade of the 21st century,

> meaning is made in ways that are increasingly multimodal – in which written-linguistic modes of meaning interface with oral, visual, audio, gestural, tactile, and spatial patterns of meaning [...] the Multiliteracies approach suggests bringing multimodal texts [...] into the curriculum and classroom. (Cope & Kalantzis, 2015, p. 3)

The calls for expanded ways of knowing for diverse learners (Cope & Kalantzis, 2015) have never been more urgent as in the post-pandemic world. To navigate rapid unexpected changes, new multimodal ways of communicating, and increasing globalisation requires an even wider range of dynamic, complex, malleable, diverse, interrelated, multimodal literacies for meaning-making. We believe, like Kincheloe (2008), that a definition of literacy limited only to reading and writing print "is no doubt a blatant form of myopia. Such skills are necessary but insufficient in our larger effort to develop new critical ways of being" (p. 201).

4   Methodology

The central question of this critical participatory action research is: How can we design and transform K–12 learning spaces with the arts using a critical pedagogy of multiliteracies? We chose an action research design "that engages diverse groups of people in collaborative processes that produce practical, effective, and sustainable outcomes to real-world problems they experience in their work, community, organisational, or institutional lives" (Stringer & Aragón, 2021, p. XVI). To ensure equity and inclusion for all learners and study participants, to give research participants a voice, and to empower them to transform practice, this action research study is framed as critical participatory action research (Kemmis, McTaggart, & Nixon, 2014).

We developed 7 sub-questions for our research design and for this discussion, we focus on the following 2 questions:

1. What do K–12 educators identify as promising practices for arts and multiliteracies?
2. What do K–12 educators identify as their challenges, needs, and solutions for arts and multiliteracies?

We recruited arts administrators, K to 12 teachers, and students from English, French Immersion, and Français schools in Manitoba. We analysed data from 91 educators' responses to an anonymous online questionnaire posted on provincial and national arts education webpages and e-news communications, and from virtual interviews with 28 teachers and administrators. We distilled research data by reviewing, unitising, coding, creating categories, identifying themes, and analysing key experiences and epiphanic events (Stringer & Aragón, 2021). Data collection and analysis is ongoing as we continue to gather data from action research cycles of planning, acting, observing, refining, and re-planning.

In the following sections we share selected highlighted themes from online questionnaire and virtual interview data.

5   Highlighted Themes

In this section we highlight 3 key themes emerging from the 91 anonymous questionnaires and 28 participant interviews. Questionnaire and interview questions focused on participants' beliefs, understandings, experiences, and practices regarding arts and multiliteracies teaching and learning. Full questionnaire and interview results will be published elsewhere. Key themes included:

1.   Importance of Arts and Multiliteracies
2.   Systemic Challenges, Needs, and Pandemic Effects
3.   Success is Possible!

5.1   *Importance of Arts and Multiliteracies*

All participants contributed evidence that "beliefs about the importance of arts literacies and multiliteracies" was a significant overarching theme in this study, and one that our study participants engaged deeply with. Participants elaborated their beliefs and expressed them through different disciplinary lenses and perspectives. They were unanimous that arts and multiliteracy learning were essential for perceiving, making, and communicating meaning, for social-emotional learning and well-being, for student engagement and identity, and for equity and inclusion.

Study participant, "François", captured common beliefs about multiliteracies and their importance for equity and inclusion when they stated:

> I believe strongly that multiliteracies are essential to inclusion, engagement, and deep learning. While I don't believe multiliteracies are currently emphasised enough across the curriculums I teach, I make a concerted effort to integrate diverse multimodal texts in my classroom. These texts serve as tools for both acquiring and expressing understandings across disciplines.

Study participants stressed that although arts and multiliteracies were essential, it was important to ensure that the arts were not used in superficial ways. "Simone" noted that what's important is "moving thinking from how could I add some art (either cosmetically or superficially), to how can I discover the meaning potential that is already there".

Participants who identified as arts specialists largely supported arts learning as part of a pedagogy of multiliteracies, but also cautioned that this learning should not be at the expense of disciplinary arts learning. "Kyle" stated, "I believe that students should experience the arts in other subject areas, but they need to also have the benefit of having a dedicated specialist teacher for each genre such as music, visual arts, drama, etc.". "Louise" concurred, saying, "Agree, except that I believe that the arts are subjects that can and should also stand on their own".

5.2 Systemic Challenges, Needs, and Pandemic Effects

Participant data highlighted many significant systemic challenges to implementing arts and multiliteracies learning and a range of needs and support required for designing learning spaces with the arts in a pedagogy of multiliteracies. Common challenges and needs included:

- Lack of knowledge and understanding about the arts curriculum frameworks
- Lack of and need:
  - for administrative and other collegial support
  - for more funding, materials, and human resources
  - for time and opportunities to plan and collaborate with others
  - for more arts-based teaching and learning
  - for professional learning in the arts and multiliteracies
- Teaching isolation as a barrier
- Arts not viewed as a priority
- COVID-19 restrictions

Participants focused on the lack of support at multiple levels in the education system. "Lionel" identified lack of support "for arts education from other colleagues in the building". Another participant noted "reluctance/hesitation from teachers to properly integrate the arts ... teachers feel this is too much work". Others noted the lack of government support, for example, "the constant struggle with the possibility for losing my classroom and cuts to the arts", "the arts not being a priority in a strained and starved education system", and the need to "convince other teachers to develop a culture of the arts in the school".

The pandemic context posed additional challenges in particular for arts specialists. Although the original semi-structured interview questions did not include questions about the pandemic, negative effects resulting from the global pandemic was a prevailing theme across all interviews. Participants noted the same pandemic challenges described in the literature earlier in this chapter. As well, pandemic uncertainty made planning difficult for teachers. For "Peter" this was the biggest challenge: "And that's what was most challenging honestly, is just not knowing. And it was so difficult for us as a school to make any long-term plans".

Many participants expressed their lack of confidence in putting their beliefs about the importance of arts and literacies into practice. It was clear from interview data that these participants needed support to design and implement arts with multiliteracies learning spaces, particularly to adapt to new post-pandemic educational realities.

5.3   *Success Is Possible!*

Despite many systemic barriers, pandemic challenges, limited resources, and other constraints, a group of interview participants provided compelling data that successful design and implementation of arts with multiliteracies and facilitated by digital technologies was possible, even during a pandemic. Participants described using a variety of digital resources (e.g., SeeSaw, FlipGrid, Showbie, Edmodo, Edsby, Facebook Live and Facebook, YouTube, and various video-conferencing platforms, Google Classroom, Google Hangout, Google Meet, Microsoft Teams, game-based platforms, teaching videos, various apps, online blogs, websites, and video sharing and streaming services) as part of multiliteracy teaching and learning with the arts. Participants described ways of meaningfully infusing disciplinary arts learning with multiliteracies learning in all subject areas. Success was facilitated by rich collaborations, a sense of purpose and significance, deep and emergent learning opportunities, and by creative, flexible use of online learning and digital technologies. Brief illustrations of success are included in the following epiphanic event.

6   Epiphanic Event: "Elliot" School

Although interview data analysis revealed rich examples of successful design and implementation of arts with multiliteracies, one group of participants overcame systemic and pandemic barriers and challenges in momentous ways described by Stringer and Aragón (2021) as an epiphanic event.

An epiphanic event is defined by Stringer and Aragón (2021) as an event or experience that has a "marked impact on a participant" (p. 175) and where analysis reveals that participants have worked "exceedingly hard to accomplish something important" (p. 177). Our group interview with "Elliot" School is characteristic of an epiphanic event in which participants "divulge information about events that have special significance" (p. 177).

"Elliot" school was unique to our study in several ways. Most of our virtual interview participants were individual teachers from various schools, but several "Elliot" Kindergarten to Grade 5 teachers were keen to be interviewed. They asked to answer our interview questions as a group and prepared a hybrid in-person and virtual PowerPoint presentation. Their PowerPoint presentations and hybrid sharing then also served as a professional learning experience and way of celebrating their work with each other. Because the school had pivoted to virtual learning, they had the capacity to deliver hybrid professional development, and teachers who were home ill with COVID-19 were able to actively participate through Google Slides.

Our process of member checking with one of the organisers of the group presentation provided further data to confirm that indeed, this group interview and experience was "particularly significant" and had an "especially meaningful impact on respondents" (Stringer & Ortiz Aragón, p. 177). This significance and meaning was captured in the words of "Chris", a learning support teacher who spearheaded the school's multiliteracy conversations and co-organised the professional learning event:

> I was really really touched by the whole thing because it was the first time that I like got to sit, listen and hear people tell their story [...] It was [...] really special, because I saw some people who presented that they really found their voice as an educator in this way and it was such an important part of their, the construction of their identity [...] It meant a lot to a lot of people [...] a beautiful sort of rainbow of options [for multiliteracy learning with the arts].

Teacher participants described learning experiences using inquiry-based processes that included a variety of digital and online resources. Students used digital mentor texts, digital photography, video, digital tools and software such as GarageBand, internet searches, QR codes, and digital recordings to create and share their artworks and music compositions. We highlight two of the four projects described that day.

The inquiry project *Annie Pootoogook: Storytelling Through The Arts* explored Grade 4 curricular themes of Ways of Life in the North (Social Studies) and

Sound (Science). The internet gave access to a world that students would otherwise never have explored. Students first examined Annie Pootoogook's artwork online as inspiration for creating artwork that similarly shared their daily
life stories through visual art and was further transmediated through soundscapes. Students watched a video on the creation of soundscapes, chose and
recorded their sounds using GarageBand, tested them, and presented the artwork with soundscapes to their peers and community.

The project *The Snowy Day* began with Grade 2 and 3 students playing outside and exploring their snowy environment. Students connected to English
Language Arts, Science, Music, and Visual Arts curricular learnings. They created a storyboard around their selected snow memory and, in collaboration
with the music teacher, illustrated the story with soundscapes they created
with recorded environmental sounds, digital mixing, music loops, and a music
app. The students listened to a local radio/tv announcer for inspiration to create their own weather report audio recording as part of their storying. The
weather recording, winter story, and soundscape were uploaded as a YouTube
video made accessible by a QR code. Students included QR codes on posters
about their work posted throughout their neighborhood so that community,
family, and friends were able to listen to the student stories, view illustrations,
and hear the soundscapes and weather report.

Through digital technologies, students were able to share and celebrate their
work with others when families were not allowed to physically enter schools.
While the use of digital resources was not unique to the pandemic context, the
COVID-19 pandemic necessitated and influenced their use.

Visual arts literacies, music literacies, and digital modes were central and
critical for meaning-making in these inquiry projects. By representing experiences in their lives through artwork and music, supported by digital resources
and literacies, students engaged in a range of multimodal practices and literacies that reflected their particular cultural, social, and linguistic French
Immersion contexts, and explored curriculum learnings in deep and meaningful ways.

7   Our Learnings (for Now)

To answer the central question of this critical participatory action research
study, "How can we design and transform K–12 learning spaces with the arts
using a critical pedagogy of multiliteracies?" we began by asking participants,
"What are your beliefs about the importance of multiliteracies?" One participant succinctly captured the feelings of all study participants by responding,

"What is there to discuss here? Our students learn differently and so multimodal approaches and texts would only engage a wider population". "Chris" declared,

> the reality is that it's [multiliteracies] not a programme you deliver, it's not something you can learn to do … and I suppose the first part of that, that kind of connected everybody, was the co-constructed understanding that a multiliteracies approach is really a way of being. It's not a thing you do, if that makes sense, it's doing.

While participants in our study agreed with the literature supporting the importance of arts literacies (Saunders, 2021) and multiliteracies approaches for equitable access to learning (Zhang et al., 2019), a diverse range of needs and challenges emerged from our data that constrained implementation of those beliefs. Many of these challenges such as insufficient budget, space, and time, and devaluing of arts literacies, have long been noted in the literature (Lilliedahl, 2022). However, participants reported that the global COVID-19 pandemic exacerbated and created further hurdles in ways shared by educators around the world (Joseph, 2022).

The additional challenges affected many study participants' efforts to successfully design and implement a pedagogy of arts and multiliteracies. However, the restrictions of the pandemic also created opportunities for innovation and ways to creatively use online and digital resources for learning and for communicating and sharing learning. Many of these online and digital resources were already available to teachers and learners and part of arts and multiliteracies learning, but the pandemic circumstances shifted the use of these resources from occasional useful tools to everyday ways to create and communicate multiliteracies meaning for many participants.

"Elliot" School in particular, as described in the epiphanic event, infused online and digital technologies for creating and sharing students' multiliteracies work and for professional development. "Elliot" teachers not only adapted to new educational realities; they were empowered to be agents of change (Hattie, 2012). Teachers' learning designs in turn empowered their learners. The arts were not simply used as cosmetic enhancements or adjuncts to other learning; arts and digital literacies empowered "Elliot" learners to use the semiotic systems of the arts as sign systems and resources for perceiving, for meaning-making, and for communicating understandings.

Analysis of the "Elliot" School epiphanic event and other participant data points to two key factors that contributed to success: creating conditions for enabling transformative learning spaces with the arts and digital resources, and intentionally designing learning spaces and experiences in ways that occasioned rich, complex, multiliteracy learning with the arts. Conditions that enabled success included:

- administrative leadership, learning support teachers, and collegial support
- intentional teacher collaboration and questioning
- breaking down barriers between the isolated specialist and general classroom
- collective will, curiosity, and interest
- devoted teacher release time for planning
- opportunities for teachers to share and celebrate together

Successful intentional designs included:

- relevant and authentic connections to students' lives and interests
- inquiry-based cross-curricular approaches to teaching and learning
- learning designs with different entry points and trajectories for diverse learners
- multiple available modes and literacies including the arts and digital and online resources
- flexible, sustained time to deeply and critically explore multiliteracies learning for teachers and learners

These lessons learned are important for educators adapting to new realities in education. It will be necessary to resist post-pandemic efforts to "recover learning losses" (World Bank Group, 2021) by limiting teaching and learning to a narrow and tested view of literacy and numeracy and instead, to see the pandemic experiences as a catalyst for addressing educational inequities amplified by the COVID-19 pandemic (Cunningham & Gibson, 2022).

A limitation of this study is that examples of arts and multiliteracies learning facilitated by digital technologies learning described in the epiphanic event cannot be generalised to other educational contexts. However, study learnings to date may serve as inspiration for other arts educators and classroom teachers to become teacher change agents and not only design but transform learning spaces with the arts in a critical pedagogy of multiliteracies.

8   Conclusion

"Elliot" School asked,

> How do we continue to live out what we believe about children and what we believe about learning [...] How do we live that out in this climate?

And so that was the question for us. It wasn't how do we get by doing literacy, it was how do we live these beliefs out with these constraints.

If we believe in the potential for transforming K–12 learning spaces with the arts using a critical pedagogy of multiliteracies, then we must also ask how we can live out our beliefs despite constraints from pandemics, governments, and global and local pressures for standardised testing. Study participants showed us that both specialist arts educators and classroom arts learning are necessary and that digital technologies can support equitable access to that learning. Students need access to multiple modes, including arts and digital, to adapt to the new realities in education. They need the disciplinary language and tools of the arts to bring to multiliteracy learning. Schools need to ask how arts educators can break out of their specialist silos to collaborate and co-construct with classroom teachers. They also need to ask how classroom teachers can be supported to integrate arts literacies. Our participants have shown us that it is possible to create the conditions, context, and learning designs that feature the unique meaning-making systems of the arts as available affordances. Arts and multiliteracies, facilitated by digital technologies, can engage all learners to make and communicate meaning about themselves and the world.

Our data collection and analysis is ongoing as we continue to gather data from action research cycles of planning, acting, observing, refining, and re-planning. We hope to impact future classroom practice and to contribute to future research exploring ways to realise the potential of arts and multiliteracies teaching and learning.

References

Andrews, B. W. (Ed.). (2020). *Perspectives on arts education research in Canada. Volume 2: Issues and directions.* Brill.

Aurini, J., & Davies, S. (2021). COVID-19 school closures and educational achievement gaps in Canada: Lessons from Ontario summer learning research. *Canadian Review of Sociology/Revue canadienne de sociologie, 58,* 165–185. https://doi.org/10.1111/cars.12334

Bamford, A. (2009). *The wow factor: Global research compendium on the impact of the arts in education* (2nd ed.). Waxmann Verlag.

Bamford, A., & Wimmer, M. (2012). *The role of arts education in enhancing school attractiveness: A literature review.* European Expert Network on Culture (EENC). http://eenc.eu/en/publications

Barton, G. (2020). *Developing literacy and the arts in schools.* Routledge.

Barton, G., & Baguley, M. (2017). *The Palgrave handbook of global arts education.* Palgrave Macmillan. https://doi.org/10.1057/978-1-137-55585-4

Bolden, B., & Jeanneret, N. (2021). *Visions of sustainability for arts education: Value, challenge and potential.* Springer.

Boyes, L. C., & Reid, I. (2005). What are the benefits for pupils participating in arts activities? The view from the research literature. *Research in Education, 73*(1), 1–14.

Bresler, L. (Ed.). (2007). *International handbook of research in arts education.* Springer. https://doi.org/10.1007/978-1-4020-3052-9

Brown, S., & Bousalis, R. (2018). *Curriculum integration in contemporary teaching practice: Emerging research and opportunities.* IGI Global.

Bull, G., & Anstey, M. (2019). *Elaborating multiliteracies through multimodal texts.* Routledge.

Cope, B., & Kalantzis, M. (2015). *A pedagogy of multiliteracies: Learning by design.* Palgrave Macmillan.

Cornett, C. (2011). *Creating meaning through literature and the arts: Arts integration for classroom teachers* (4th ed.). Allyn & Bacon/Pearson.

Cunningham, M., & Gibson, R. (2022). Rethinking curriculum: A pandemic opportunity for re-engagement with the Arts? *Curriculum Perspectives*, 1–10. https://doi.org/10.1007/s41297-022-00170-y

Davis, J. H. (2008). *Why our schools need the arts.* Teachers College Press.

Davis, B., & Sumara, D. J. (2006). *Complexity and education: Inquiries into learning, teaching, and research.* Lawrence Erlbaum.

Deasy, R. J. (Ed.). (2002). *Critical links: Learning in the arts and student academic and social development.* Arts Education Partnership.

Denzin, N. K., & Lincoln, Y. S. (2018). Introduction: The discipline and practice of qualitative research. In N. K. Denzin & Y. S. Lincoln (Eds.), *The Sage handbook of qualitative research* (5th ed., pp. 1–26). Sage.

Dewey, J. (1934/2005). *Art as experience.* Penguin.

Dik, D., Morrison, R., Sabol, R., & Tuttle, L. (2022). Looking beyond COVID-19: Arts education policy implications and opportunities. *Arts Education Policy Review, 123*(3), 160–168. https://doi.org/10.1080/10632913.2021.1931603

Edgar, S. N., & Elias, M. J. (2021). Setting the stage for social emotional learning (SEL) policy and the arts. *Arts Education Policy Review, 122*(3), 205–209. https://doi.org/10.1080/10632913.2020.1777494

Eisner, E. (2002, February). *For the love of the arts: Arts and education 2002* [Conference session]. Alliance for Arts Education in Manitoba (AAEM), Winnipeg, Manitoba.

Eisner, E., & Day, M. D. (Eds.). (2004). *Handbook of research and policy in art education.* Routledge. https://doi.org/10.4324/9781410609939

Feindler, C. O., Mayo, W., Shaw, R., Sabol, R., Tuttle, L., & Weaver, J. (2022). Jumping into the virtual environment: Implications and possibilities for arts education. *Arts Education Policy Review, 123*(3), 117–126.

Fineberg, C. (2004). *Creating islands of excellence: Arts education as a partner in school reform.* Heinemann.

Fiske, E. (Ed.). (1999). *Champions of change: The impact of arts on learning.* The Arts Education Partnership and the President's Committee on the Arts and Humanities.

Fleming, M. B., Bresler, L., & O'Toole, J. (2015). *The Routledge international handbook of the arts and education.* Routledge.

Fleming, J., Gibson, R., & Anderson, M. (Eds.). (2016). *How arts education makes a difference: Research examining successful classroom practice and pedagogy.* Routledge.

Fowler, C. (1996). *Strong arts, strong schools: The promising potential and shortsighted disregard of the arts in American schooling.* Oxford University Press.

Greene, M. (1995). *Releasing the imagination: Essays on education, the arts, and social change.* Jossey-Bass.

Grier, S. (2022). Responding & rebuilding amidst dual pandemics: An interview with state fine arts coordinators Alysia Lee & Dale Schmid. *Arts Education Policy Review, 123*(4), 236–244. https://doi.org/10.1080/10632913.2021.2011516

Hasebe-Ludt, E., & Leggo, C. (Eds.). (2018). *Canadian curriculum studies: A métissage of inspiration/imagination/interconnection.* Canadian Scholars.

Hattie, J. (2012). *Visible learning for teachers: Maximizing impact on learning.* Routledge.

Hourigan, R. (2022). Post COVID-19: Access to an arts education for all students. *Arts Education Policy Review.* https://doi.org/10.1080/10632913.2022. 2059730

Jensen, E. (2001). *Arts with the brain in mind.* Association for Supervision & Curriculum Development.

Joseph, A. (2022). Arts education in jeopardy: Research reveals the challenges and resilience of arts education and arts educators during and following the pandemic. *International Dialogues on Education Journal, 8*(1/2), 51–83. https://doi.org/10.53308/ ide.v8i1/2.251

Kemmis, S., McTaggart, R., & Nixon, R. (2014). *The action research planner: Doing critical participatory action research.* Springer.

Kincheloe, J. L. (2005). *Critical constructivism.* Peter Lang.

Kincheloe, J. L. (2008). *Knowledge and critical pedagogy: An introduction.* Springer.

Kist, W. (2005). *New literacies in action: Teaching and learning in multiple media.* Teachers College Press.

Lilliedahl, J. (2022). Why the arts are not considered core knowledge in secondary education: A Bernsteinian analysis. *Journal of Curriculum Studies, 54*(2), 165–178. https://doi.org/10.1080/00220272.2021.1925971

Manitoba Education and Advanced Learning. (2015). *Grades 9 to 12 visual arts: Manitoba curriculum framework*. The Government of Manitoba. https://www.edu.gov.mb.ca/k12/cur/arts/visual/framework_9-12.html

Mezirow, J. (2009). Transformative learning theory. In J. Mezirow, E. W. Taylor, & Associates (Eds.), *Transformative learning in practice: Insights from community, workplace, and higher education* (pp. 18–31). Jossey-Bass/John Wiley.

Morin, F. (2021). *Singing in Canadian schools: COVID-19 impact survey final report.* https://www.omea.on.ca/wp-content/uploads/2022/01/Singing-in-Canadian-Schools-COVID-19-Impact-Survey-Final-Report-December-9-2021-1.pdf

New London Group. (1996). A pedagogy of multiliteracies: Designing social futures. *Harvard Educational Review, 66*(1), 60–92. https://doi.org/10.17763/haer.66.1.17370n67v22j160u

Parkes, K. A., Russell, J. A., Bauer, W. I., & Miksza, P. (2021). The well-being and instructional experiences of k-12 music educators: Starting a new school year during a pandemic. *Frontiers in Psychology*, 2837.

Peters, B. (2011). *A formative study of rhythm and pattern: Semiotic potential of multimodal experiences for early years readers*. University of Manitoba. https://mspace.lib.umanitoba.ca/handle/1993/4855

Pitman, W. (1998). *Learning the arts in an age of uncertainty*. Arts Education Council of Ontario.

Pullen, D. L., & Cole, D. R. (Eds.). (2010). *Multiliteracies and technology enhanced education: Social practice and the global classroom*. IGI Global.

Saunders, J. N. (2021). The power of the arts in learning and the curriculum: A review of research literature. *Curriculum Perspectives, 41*, 93–100.

Stringer, E. T., & Aragón, A. O. (2021). *Action research* (5th ed.). Sage.

Tuttle, L., & Hansen, D. (2022) Arts education in a virtual learning environment: An introduction to the lessons, policies, budgets and practices from the COVID-19 era. *Arts Education Policy Review, 123*(3), 115–116.

Williams, H. M. (1991). *The language of civilization: The vital role of the arts in education.* https://files.eric.ed.gov/fulltext/ED355133.pdf

Winner, E., Goldstein, T. R., & Vincent-Lancrin, S. (2013). *Arts for art's sake? The impact of arts education*. Educational Research and Innovation: OECD Publishing.

World Bank Group. (2021). *Mission: Recovering education in 2021.* https://www.worldbank.org/en/topic/education/brief/mission-recovering-education-in-2021

Wright, S. (2003). *The arts, young children, and learning*. Allyn and Bacon.

Zhang, Z., Nagle, J., McKishnie, B., Lin, Z., & Li, W. (2019). Scientific strengths and reported effectiveness: A systematic review of multiliteracies studies. *Pedagogies: An International Journal, 14*(1), 33–61.

CHAPTER 15

An Alternative Art Museum Engagement in the Era of COVID-19 Pandemic

A Pedagogical Experimentation

Elmira Sarreshtehdari and Yasaman Moussavi

Abstract

The social distancing measures during the COVID-19 pandemic impacted our lives in many ways, whether psychologically or physically. While the lockdown influenced our social existences, embodied interactions, ways of communication, and perception, it could offer an opportunity to think about the possibilities of alternate spaces. Provoked by the new normal, we adopted an a/r/tographical experimentation based on the following proposition: *Physically go to a museum by taking another person virtually*. For us, this proposition became an entry to discover an exploratory environment which led to re-examine our positionality as artist-educators while acting and reacting to the physical space of the museum and virtual spaces of our devices. In this a/r/tographical study, we ask: How does the process of knowledge-making vary between the online and physical space of the art museum? In what way do the teaching and learning approaches reshape from in-person to virtual and vice versa? And how does a/r/tography as methodology could accommodate activating the potential in-between spaces of the virtual and actual?

We explore our inquiry at the art museums located in Chicago and Vancouver. We visited each museum in-person and through video calls; then, exchanged documentation of our experiences through conversations and corresponding writings.

Although this co-generated aesthetic experience appears different from regular gallery and museum visits, in the ambiguity of this journey, our thinking proceeds and stretches the exhibition space to an inquiry in which we share our thoughts and perceptions towards new ways of learning. This creative scholarship has become an allegory for the relationality and communication between educators and learners. By relying on each other's bodies and perceptions, we adopted the way in which learners trust educators and educators become accountable for navigating physical and online spaces of learning.

Keywords

a/r/tography – art museum engagement – distance learning – performative pedagogy

1   **Prelude**

The socio-spatial phenomenon during the COVID-19 pandemic has significantly transformed our social existence, embodied interactions with the space
around us, modes of communication, and the way we perceive the world. While
the lockdown has impacted our mental and communal life, it inspired us to
look for emergent alternate spaces in our creative practices. To explore alternative ways of social bonding through embodiment, despite remote learning,
we designed a collaborative a/r/tographical walking experimentation based on
the following proposition: *Physically go to a museum by taking somebody else
virtually.* By fostering this stimulating query, we co-generate a communal pedagogical space by challenging our positionality as learners and artist educators
in relation to the actual (physical) space of the museum and virtual spaces of
our devices that disrupt the commonality of knowledge-making and learning.
Although we are both from Iran and are cohorts in the Ph.D. program at The
University of British Columbia (UBC), due to the pre-emptive restrictions, we
had never met in-person; however, we cultivated a close relationship through
our shared scholarship. We chose to do an a/r/tographical inquiry at the contemporary art museums in the cities we resided in, Chicago and Vancouver.
We visited each museum in-person as well as through a video call. Then set
the ways to document and exchange our experience of the visits through conversations and corresponding writings. A/r/tography as a performative and
creative methodology accommodated the foundation of this project (Irwin,
2003, 2013). In the word of Springgay et al. (2005), "a/r/tography dislocates
complacency, location, perspective, and knowledge. [It] becomes a passage
to somewhere else" (p. 909). Dwelling in the in-between spaces and the fluidity of this methodology shifts the fixed perceptions and predictions while
redefining the process of researching and creating meaning (Irwin, 2003). In
this chapter, we approach learning as a participatory act that co-evaluates the
knower and known while transforming both (Davis, Sumara, & Luce-Kapler,
2000). Disrupting the conventional way of interacting with the museum space
disclosed many hidden and unknown potentialities that art museums as an
"anomalous space of learning" (Ellsworth, 2005, p. 42) could offer. Throughout this performative project, we started proposing a few questions, such as,
How does the process of knowledge-making vary between the online and

physical space of the art museum? In what way do the teaching and learning approaches reshape from in-person to virtual and vice versa? And how does a/r/tography as methodology could accommodate activating the potential in-between spaces of the virtual and actual?

This rest of the chapter is divided into four sections plus the Conclusion. Each section narrates an individual at the same time mutual, physical, and virtual experiences that formed in the space of the museums. These reflections, rather than repeating or contradicting each other, intend to complement and correspond to one another in order to best illustrate different aspects of the project.

2   Physical Visit to the Museum of Contemporary Art Chicago (MCA)

On our trip to the MCA, I shared my physical presence in the exhibition space with Elmira by holding my phone in different positions to facilitate the process of perceiving the art for her. Although she was physically absent, she co-constructed a moving pedagogical space by expressing a virtual experience (see Figure 15.1). We co-curated our movement in the spaces of encounter and redefined the relationship between leader/visitor and teacher/learner through sharing thoughts and scholarly dialogues.

After discussing our a/r/tographical walking journey in the museum, I chose to take Elmira to the Museum of Contemporary Art Chicago because MCA builds upon the concept of advocating space to emerging and contemporary artists instead of collecting and showcasing old and traditional arts and artifacts. Following the Alfred H. Barr (1941) concept of the museum as "torpedo" (p. 7) MCA is a "laboratory" (p. 8) not a collection of archival objects belonging to the past; it is an educational site for experimentation. In 1964, a group of collectors, art dealers, artists, and art critics, came together and founded MCA, based on their shared belief in the new concept of museums as a creative space for artists and art educators to experiment and showcase artworks that belong to the current discourses of social life. In accordance with the Chicago city plan, the MCA building is built on a square grid (MCA, n.d.). To me, this characteristic of the building, besides the aesthetic logic behind it, alludes to the city as a communal, cultural, and artistic space. Using big windows on the face front of the building is an invitation for the public to connect to the art world. I believe, the formation date of MCA aligns with the Epistemic III era which according to Kerstin Smed (2012) defines as a dispersed regime of the display, non-fixed meaning, and becoming more idiosyncratic. This era emphasizes on curation – rather than scientific classification and artistic creation – as a provider of a context in which the visitors create their own meaning (Smed, 2012). Adapted

 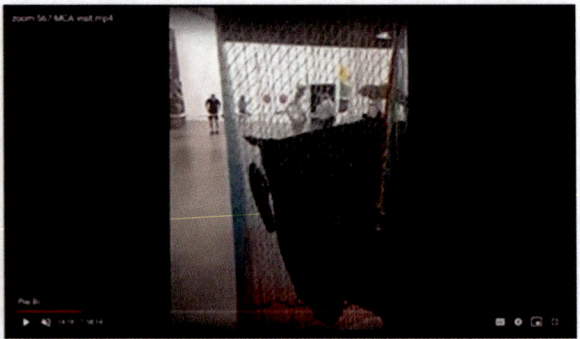

FIGURE 15.1   Left: Screen shot from the video call, Installation view, Carolina Caycedo: From
the Bottom of the River, MCA Chicago December 12, 2020–September 12, 2021.
Right: Installation view, Carolina Caycedo: From the Bottom of the River, MCA
Chicago December 12, 2020–September 12, 2021 (photograph by Yasaman
Moussavi)

to the challenges of capitalism and market economy, this museum – like many
contemporary art museums – targets "modifying the concept of 'stake holder's
value' into 'visitor's value' as a guiding principle of pedagogy and communication" (Smed, 2012, p. 66). For that reason, MCA offers many public and educational activities.

I video called Elmira. We, as if having one body and two minds, were moving
and extending ourselves to the space of the exhibition. The dialogue between
us reshaped and reformed the museum from the place of the display to a learning environment and blurred the boundaries of the physical distance between
us. The geographical distance is disrupted, scattered, and transformed by the
body's mobility in the in-between spaces. Through a virtual shared chat room
with my colleague, I travelled between space and time, here and there, virtual and actual. The mobility became a "practice, experience, embodied and
imbued with meaning and power" (Creswell, 2006, p. 2), which transformed
the spaces of encounter to an educative interval. John Dewey (1934/1958)
defines intervals "as periods in which one phase is ceasing, and the other is
inchoate and preparing" (p. 56). The continuity of the intervals, mobility of the
body and mind generate a learning environment in which we as scholars, educators, and learners communicate and exchange ideas.

When we reached the gallery space on the first floor, we noticed a huge
painting on the far left facing the outside window of the main entrance room.
I explained to Elmira the placement of the work and its possible view from the
outside. We wonder about the play of inside and outside, public and private
contexts in both museum and tradition of Iranian culture, while we unpacked
Orkideh Torabi's painting, a humorous representation of a public bathroom
(see Figure 15.2). The painting carries criticism of the patriarchy and the

FIGURE 15.2   Screenshot from the video call, Installation view, Atrium Project: Orkideh
Torabi, MCA Chicago. January 16, 2021–March 13, 2022. Work shown: Peach
House's 5 Bucks Morning Special, 2020. Fabric dye on stretched cotton;
85 × 54 in

narrowly structured space allowing only men to be visible to the public; at the
same time, it exposes a space of privacy – even subliminal homoeroticism –
within the tradition of Iranian miniature.

We discussed how the curator generates an assemblage of pedagogy and
architecture by positioning the artwork in a transitional space between the
inside and outside of the gallery (see Figure 15.3). Our collective experience led
us to expand our thinking beyond just observing the art object but stretching it
out to the environment and location of the work. While simultaneously raising
questions about the role of the external aspects regarding unfolding artworks,
we noticed how the collective conversation impacted our understanding. John
Dewey (1938/2015) discusses how interaction with the surroundings and continuity of the experience could constitute learning. Dewey argues that experience is both external and internal; that is to say, "there are sources outside of
an individual which give rise to experience" (p. 40). He stresses the importance
of interaction and situations by discussing that "an experience is always what
it is because of a transaction taking place between an individual and what, at
the time, constitutes his[/her] environment, whether the latter consists of persons with whom he[/she] is talking about some topic or event" (p. 43). In that
regard, the liminal positionality of us, the artwork, and the virtual space that
we communicate in, cultivate a mobile pedagogical site in which we share our
wonders and thoughts. In a way, we created a recurring mobile space in which
we think together yet physically apart.

FIGURE 15.3   Left: Outside view of MCA Chicago, 2021, center: Installation view, Atrium
                Project: Orkideh Torabi, MCA Chicago. January 16, 2021–March 13, 2022.
                Work shown: Peach House's 5 Bucks Morning Special, 2020. Fabric dye on
                stretched cotton; 85 × 54 in, right: Artist statement, Atrium Project:
                Orkideh Torabi, MCA Chicago. January 16, 2021–March 13, 2022
                (photography by Yasaman Moussavi)

3   Virtual Visit to MCA

Sitting behind my desk in Vancouver, I was waiting to meet my colleague at the
Chicago Museum of Contemporary Art (MCA). I had never been to Chicago.
My limited knowledge of the city was based on what I had heard, read, and
seen in the media. When I think of Chicago, I imagine a city by the water, beautiful but populated, a hub for art. When I think of Chicago the reflective image
of the bean-shaped sculpture, Cloud Gate, made by the artist Anish Kapoor
appears in my mind with a background song by Elvis Presley (1969) reciting:

> *As the snow flies*
> *On a cold and gray Chicago mornin'*
> *A poor little baby child is born …*

I did not know what exhibition I was going to visit. After back-and-forth
texting, we started the video call. Suddenly I was there, 3,540.0 km away from
home. We were in a spacious hall with wide window glasses and a high ceiling.
The sound of Vancouver rain was making a huge contrast with the sunny day
outside in Chicago. Our spaces were colliding. I felt disoriented. My consciousness was split between the two locations.

We turned to a large mural on the wall by Orkideh Torabi. I gathered my
attention. A painted image of the half-naked men bathing in an old Iranian

public bath (Hammam) covering the whole entrance wall. I was now travelling between four spaces, my hometown Tehran, Chicago, Vancouver, and the ambiguous space of my screen. I could not see the whole work at once. One fragment at a time, as much as my co-maker could fit into the frame of her phone camera. My brain was putting together the parts I had encountered to create a complete image of what I was supposed to see. I asked her to take me closer to the mural. After all, Yasaman was my metaphorical body. We got closer to the image and started probing together. While narrating the mural details, she generously moved her body around so I could have a better understanding of the painting's relationship with the space, light, and the people around it. She turned to another wall and quietly started reading the artist's statement for me. I was disembodied; however, I felt physically there. I was standing next to my colleague and conversing about the artwork. However, most of my perception depended heavily on my vision to translate and reconstruct other senses. While untangling this experience, I was curious to know if vision (to some degree) would be enough to understand the qualities of an artwork.

Elaborating on such a matter, Brian Massumi (2008) suggests that the act of seeing in itself is a form of an active movement. By seeing we not only perceive the relations between an object and the world surrounding it but also can imagine the object's volume and dimensionality without walking around or touching it. This lived relation, according to Massumi, is not passive but an active yet abstract experience. He further explains that objects within themselves carry numerous potentials that the act of seeing gradually unfolds and perceives these potentialities; in his words "seeing an object is seeing through to its qualities ... an object's appearance is an event, full of all sorts of virtual movement" (Massumi, 2008, pp. 4–5). Lovise Søyland (2021) adds to this notion by arguing that although vision plays an essential role in how we perceive through virtual materiality, our imagination, and past experiences, it also contributes to reconstructing the physical reality. Søyland (2021) says,

> We can experience [objects] through vision but not through touch, smell, or taste. To make sense of movement in virtual environments, humans use their experiential knowledge gained from moving in physical surroundings. When we experience virtual materiality or a virtual environment past our previous experiences of movement, we can re-enact material touch and other forms of sensory experience from the material world in this new experience. (p. 235)

By residing in a virtual space, I had to rely on somebody else's body to connect my mind with the surroundings and to accommodate a window for my vision to be activated. I was being carried toward and against the objects present around the exhibition without having any control. I had to ask to be repositioned. My body felt incomplete and depended on another person. This experience was not comparable to a regular online tour of a museum since our interaction was live and happening at the current time.

For Sara Ahmed (2006), to be orientated is to "know where we are when we turn this way or that way" (p. 1; O'Donoghue, 2020, p. 189). However, in this experience I could go anywhere, but not. I could see any object, but not. I felt strangely dis/oriented. Maxine Greene (2004) says, disorientation occurs "when what was once familiar abruptly appears strange" (p. 140). Founding myself dis/oriented, heightened my attentiveness; it became an active form of being. The unexpected dis/orientation happening throughout this experience made me more focused and curious to be engaged with the exhibition. I was seeking to find more information. Although being restricted, I was less passive. Dónal O'Donoghue (2020) points out that

> oftentimes it is only in moments of disorientation that we realize that we have been orientated all along and up to that point [...] In moments of dis-orientation, one most likely seeks clues to reorientate ourselves. (p. 189)

4   Physical Visit to the Vancouver Art Gallery (VAG)

At the time of writing this paper, many galleries and museums across Canada and the US were impacted by the COVID-19 pandemic. Museums were either closed or the opening hours were drastically reduced with strict regulations

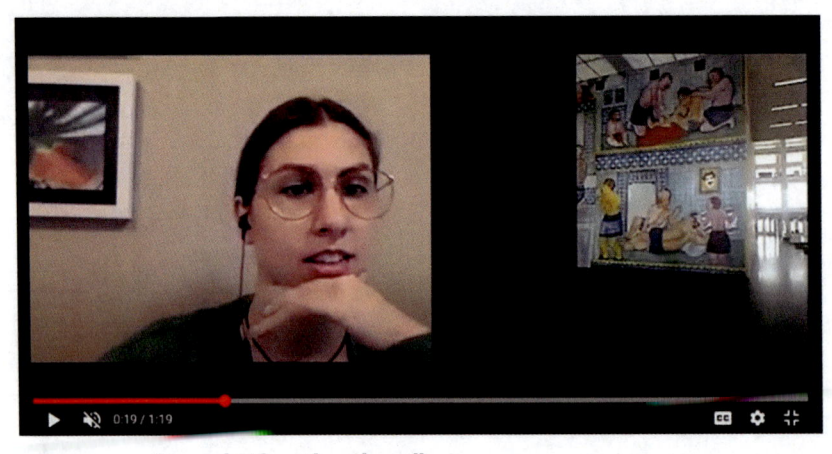

FIGURE 15.4   Screen shot from the video call, 2021

regarding attendance. A large number of exhibitions and shows were postponed, and those on display were not interactive or participatory and mostly belonged to the museums' collections. I had to decide to choose an art museum that was open and preferably exhibiting contemporary art as well as being significant for the Vancouver's art community. Ultimately, following our a/r/tographical proposition, I took my co-walker (virtually) to the Vancouver Art Gallery.

Since its initial opening in 1931, Vancouver Art Gallery has always been on the move, it has changed multiple architectural appearances and locations throughout the years. As this art institution's educational programs and art collections expand, it constantly demands a larger space. It is undoubtedly intriguing to follow how this non-for-profit organization has been adjusting to Vancouver's perpetual transformation and development. While this metropolitan city grows, expands, and gets populated, Vancouver Art Gallery, like an inseparable organ, has been reflecting and embracing the change. Moreover, each of the buildings that the museum has resided in embodies a significant history; being part of the museum's identity, these buildings could be counted as historical artefacts themselves. The current museum's edifice was initially used as a provincial courthouse, but in 1983 it was assigned to become the new home of the Vancouver Art Gallery (VAG, n.d.). Located in the center of downtown Vancouver, the architecture of the building, with its large neoclassical columns, expansive yard, and surrounding stairs, imitates ancient Greek and Roman communal buildings to create an inviting place for gathering. The architecture of the VAG fully reflects its institutionalized nature. Elizabeth Ellsworth (2005) explains that museums and galleries as educational spaces are designed to invite visitors to connect the outside with the inside. These designs not only allow our bodies to physically experience artefacts on display but also to construct an *affective* environment for going beyond one's self to unfold multiple possibilities for understanding and communicating (Ellsworth, 2005). According to her, the museum's architecture reinforces a particular way of moving by guiding us between the corridors, floors, and around the walls. All the signs and regulations in place police the ways in which we walk and pause around the museum's space. Therefore, if considering the museum as an "anomalous place of learning", physically being in the place directly contributes to how knowledge shapes and learning happens (Ellsworth, 2005, p. 42). Walking around the museum is part of the immediate pedagogical experience. Focusing on the pedagogical relationship between the body and space, a/r/tography has dedicated extensive scholarship to the educational aspect of walking. According to Rita Irwin (2013), "a/r/tography is concerned with the creative invention of concepts and the intensities experienced in relational, rhizomatic, yet singular, events" (p. 198), and it is walking that "activates [this] creation of concepts. To walk is to move-with thought" (Springgay & Truman, 2019, p. 131). A/r/tographical walking "opens spaces for ambiguity and multiple interpretations in meaning making; fosters connections and ruptures through conversations with people, texts, art, ideas, and one's surrounding environment" (Lee et al., 2019, p. 682). The ambiguity residing in the act of walking complicates the way in which one interacts with the surroundings. Walking by being temporal as well as spatial interrupts the ordinary form of perceiving and sensing one's ecology. Tim Ingold (2015) argues that "when we walk, we encounter sites in motion and in relation to one another ... things seem different depending on whether we are 'coming to' or 'going from'" (p. 48).

Pedagogical walking in museum spaces is activated and nourished by different curatorial approaches. The design and juxtaposition of each exhibition play a significant role in how we aesthetically experience what we encounter.

Although these aspects of the museum spaces open up multiple possibilities for meaning-making and learning, they also constrain the audience's experiences. Oftentimes, it is required that the body physically be in the space of the exhibition in order to embody the whole experience. Consequently, this limitation makes the museum to be perceived as temporal and only for a limited number of visitors. During the pandemic, many museums and galleries attempted to adjust to the unprecedented situation by exhibiting their shows virtually or providing virtual tours for visitors who no longer could have access to the collections or shows. Many scholars and educators adopted this approach in their classes and educational sites by turning to online alternatives. Although the nature of the exhibition engagement has been drastically compromised, this new way of looking opened up an unexpected opportunity to be exposed to a broader range of artworks, locally and internationally.

Although museums – with numerous regulations in play – had opened up, the possibility of travelling between countries remained unknown. This situation motivated us to create a performative project fostering the new-normal behaviour.

When I arrived at the museum location, I was not sure if I am allowed to hold any camera or phone throughout the exhibition visit. I waited in line about two meters apart from other visitors to get my card scanned and my name written down with the time of entry as part of the safety regulations. I felt extremely anxious since I did not know what we were about to encounter, who the artists were, what work of art we were about to engage with, or what materials and mediums were used for the exhibition. This approach was completely intentional; we both wanted to experience the exhibition together and firsthand.

There were a few shows, mainly from the VAG's collection. I could either go right, left, straight ahead, or upstairs. After scanning the hallway, I decided to enter the room on my right. I did not know if the large, curved painting picking out attracted my attention or the fact that, as Iranians, we read our surroundings from right to left. Before entering, I hesitated.

– *Do you usually read the statements before seeing the work or after?*
– *Either way works for me. Do however you like.*

Although I preferred reading the statement after visiting the artwork, I tried to show the large text on the wall, but the text appeared out of focus and unreadable on my phone camera.

– *I'll send you a photo of the artist's statement instead. I think it is more convenient.*

Across the room, on the front wall, an animated video was playing (see Figure 15.7). Diffusing rhythmic light and sound like a heartbeat all over the space. A painting was constantly brightening up, showing off the glowing neon and gold colours, then vanishing in the shadows. We sat on the bench in front of the video installation. I was worried if my colleague could hear the sound clearly and if the video was aligned with the edges of the phone screen. My vision was going back and forth between the two frames. I realized that the video was different with more contrast on my phone; the painted border around the projection was appearing and disappearing with the transition between light and shadow reflecting a new quality.

I immediately realized that our performative project immensely challenged the conventional way of engaging with the museum. My body was extended and bound to technology. I was not only looking at the art objects with my eyes, I had to become another person's eyes, ears and body as well. Although I was physically in the museum space, I was carrying my phone camera as a small window, a third communal space, to transfer what was happening around me. I was existing and moving between two spaces, an actual (physical) and virtual. Our emergent conversations were shaping and developing in a temporal and spatial in-between site. The liminality of our beings at that moment corresponded well with our a/r/tographical inquiry, since a/r/tography in nature activates the in-between spaces where the artist/researcher/teacher's being in the world enters the flux (Irwin 2003, 2013). In this tensional space, learning defines and redefines meaning through the course of aesthetic experience and interaction with other(s). The fluidity of the physical and virtual environment

served as a fertile in-between space for probing and discovery where one's
mobility could be translated into thinking, feeling, talking, making, and even
writing (Irwin, 2013). Rita Irwin (2003) elaborates,

> it is in this in-between space[s] that chaos is appreciated alongside order,
> complexity alongside simplicity, and uncertainty alongside certainty.
> These complex spaces are attuned to invention and the possibility of
> poetic wisdom. (p. 64)

The camera as our pedagogical tool became a creative prosthetic to expand
the possibility of communicating and existing in a place without actually
being there. Yasaman was active and present in the moment and in relation to
the space, to me, and the art surrounding her but without any physicality. She
was walking and moving through and with my body; therefore, I was looking
at all of the works *doubled*. Constantly comparing to see if what I am showing is being reflected similarly to another person. To read the texts, I had to
bend down and slowly read the writings on the wall. In this experience, I was
twice as attentive as usual. I had to constantly confirm with Yasaman if she
was seeing and hearing the works properly, describing missing details of what I
was encountering in person. I was both embodying the educator's identity and
the learner's. Although I did not know the exhibition myself, as a mediator, I
felt highly responsible to familiarize Yasaman with what I was extracting and

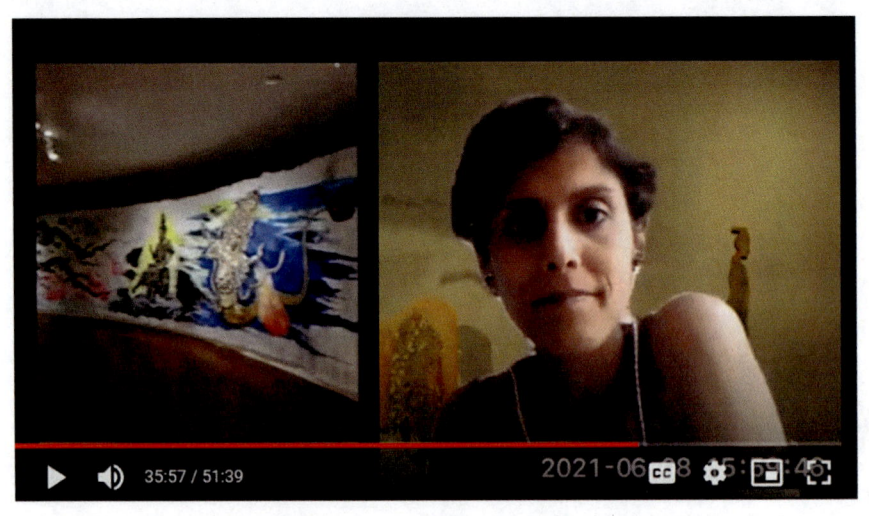

FIGURE 15.5   Left: Screen shot from the video call, Mythological Time by Sun Xun, February
              20, 2021–September 6, 2021 , exhibition at the Vancouver Art Gallery, work
              shown: Mythological Time by Sun Xun, 2016, Video animation. Right:
              Screen shot from the video call, 2021

FIGURE 15.6   Installation view, Mythological Time by Sun Xun, February 20, 2021–
                September 6, 2021, exhibition at the Vancouver Art Gallery, work shown:
                Mythology or Rebellious Bone by Sun Xun, 2020, ink painting, size 1181 in

learning at the moment of speaking. Learning and teaching were happening simultaneously.

5   Virtual Visit to VAG

I was sitting on a couch in my apartment in Chicago, waiting for my colleague to take me on a virtual tour of the Vancouver Art Gallery (VAG). My first visit to that museum was exciting. Imagining the gallery format, I wondered how different it would be to experience the gallery in-person than virtual. Drowning in my thoughts, suddenly, Elmira called. I pushed the green button; then my device virtually transfer me to the Vancouver Art Gallery.

Elmira, with care, moved her phone to accommodate my viewpoint while describing the inside and outside of the museum's layout and explaining our orientation. She showed me around while walking and quietly explained what was on view. I carefully focused on the screen of my computer and imagined my virtual body in the museum's space. Upon entering the gallery, I noticed a play of animated light on the wall. Elmira went closer to accommodate the view for me. A video animation was projected on the gallery wall and framed by an

FIGURE 15.7   Installation view, Mythological Time by Sun Xun, February 20, 2021–
September 6, 2021, exhibition at the Vancouver Art Gallery, work shown:
Mythology or Rebellious Bone by Sun Xun, 2020, ink painting, size 1181 in

ink drawing (see Figure 15.7). As the video began, the frame around it turned black and disappeared. I noticed each transition between the stop motion's frame followed by a shift from light to dark, and that transition influenced the tone of the frame around the artwork from white to black. The appearance and disappearance, the hidden and revealed, created an ambiguous space of wonder and curiosity. I thought about the meaning of a frame that is supposed to mediate the spectator's experience or as a structure, a rule, or a set of logical assumptions. The frame could also imply the lack of something, an absence of the body, or content. It could allegorically refer to the body and mind, object and subject, inside and outside, virtual and actual. It seemed that the frame and the content could be complementary components in constant dialogue. I questioned:

> Does the rectangular frame of the computer embody my virtual experi-
> ence? Does it limit my viewpoint? Or does my imagination and curiosity
> exceed the frame? How should I trust my disembodied experience that
> lacks sensory awareness? Does the frame give me a sense of orientation,
> a place to settle my thoughts? Or does it set a boundary?

My floating thoughts dissolved in the voice of Elmira, expressing her con-
cern about not being able to entirely focus the camera on both the frame and the video animation. My colleague explained that she was able to see both animation and frame at the same time. Our dialogue expanded on orienta-
tion/ disorientation, placement, and displacement and how these issues could impact our understanding. We talked about our positionality and its relation to how we perceive the artwork and understand our surroundings. Our orientation was constantly changing in relation to our roles as mediator/ teacher and learner/ visitor. We established relationships between concepts, experiences, and locations through exchanging information and thoughts.

6   Conclusion

This a/r/tographical inquiry was an exploration of embodied and disembodied experiences in which learning and understanding unfold through the process of thinking and experimentation. In the virtual walk that occurred through a video call, and in the absence of our bodily presence, the virtual experimentation rendered meaningful potentials in the proximity of the other person's physical experience. Our propositional stimuli, as each moment unfolds the present, awakens the realness of virtual, the tension between sight and seeing, feeling and thinking. Neither the physical nor the virtual experiences came across as full and complete, but as Dónal O'Donoghue (2020) mentions, "for things to appear ... something else has to withdraw from appearance" (p. 186). We explored the liminality of our experiences by activating it through collective thinking, walking, interacting, and perceiving, which led to creating knowledge through virtual and physical aesthetics of attunement. Moreover, the architecture of the museums and the curation of the exhibitions formed a hidden choreography for our bodies to move around the artworks in a particular manner which alluded to the way we co-constructed perception regarding the objects around us. Considering that, Ellsworth (2005) argues, "architecture becomes pedagogical, pedagogy becomes architectural when together they create a fluid, moving pivot place that puts inside and outside, self and other, personal and social into relation" (p. 38). We responded to the performativities that the space was offering by creating a performance of our own (Garoian, 2001). The process of this performance extended our way of learning beyond the museum space. We not only learned about the history of the museums that we took one another and the exhibitions happening in them but also learned about the social and cultural inclinations of the two cities as well as our own approaches to scholarship as artists and educators.

We based our project on the constant care and trust between the two practitioners. By relying on each other's bodies and perceptions, we followed the underlying reciprocal nature of education, the way in which learners trust educators and educators become accountable for hosting and navigating around the space of learning. The relational and collaborative foundation of this inquiry reminded us that learning could not happen in the void. Inevitably human body and its being in the world are fully relational; although being singular, our individuality is always defined by being *with*. In relation to the other, we do not become one with that individual nor meet as a result of commonality between the two, but this encounter in relation emerges from being vulnerable and open to *other* (La Jevic & Springgay, 2008). Consequently, by affecting and being affected, we co-construct "a network of relations" with the world and people around us (La Jevic & Springgay, 2008, p. 70) that potentially could be beneficial for both learners and educators.

This experimentation suggests opportunities for an innovative way of thinking and learning. In that regard, we found our proposition versatile and provocative that could be cultivated and used as creative pedagogy in many educational sites.

References

Ahmed, S. (2006). *Queer phenomenology: Orientations, objects, others*. Duke University Press.

Barr, A. H. (1941). *Papers in the Museum of Modern Art archives*. The Museum of Modern Art Archives. https://www.moma.org/research-and-learning/archives/finding-aids/Barrf

Creswell, T. (2006). The production of mobilities: An interpretive framework. In T. Creswell, *On the move: Mobility in the modern western world* (pp. 1–24). Routledge. https://doi.org/10.4324/9780203446713

Davis, B., Sumara, D. J., & Luce-Kapler, R. (2000). *Engaging minds: Changing teaching in complex times*. Taylor and Francis. https://doi.org/10.4324/9781410605467

Davis, M. (1969). In the ghetto [Recorded by E. Presley]. On *From Elvis in Memphis* [Album]. RCA Victor.

Dewey, J. (1958). Having an experience. In J. Dewey, *Art as experience* (pp. 35–57). Capricorn Books. (Original work published 1934)

Dewey, J. (2015). Criteria of experience. In J. Dewey, *Experience and education* (pp. 33–50). Free Press. (Original work published 1938)

Ellsworth, E. A. (2005). Pedagogy's hinge: Putting inside and outside into relation. In E. A. Ellsworth, *Places of learning: Media, architecture, pedagogy* (pp. 37–56). Routledge Falmer. https://doi.org/10.4324/9780203020920

Garoian, C. R. (2001). Performing the museum. *Studies in Art Education, 42*(3), 234–248. https://doi.org/10.2307/1321039

Greene, M. (2004). Curriculum and consciousness. In D. J. Flinders & S. J. Thornton (Eds.), *The curriculum studies reader* (2nd ed., pp. 135–149). Taylor & Francis e-Library.

Handel, A. (2018). Distance matters: Mobilities and the politics of distance. *Mobilities, 13*(4), 473–487. https://doi.org/10.1080/17450101.2017.1394681

History: Background on the Vancouver Art Gallery. (n.d.). Vancouver Art Gallery, Retrieved June 2, 2021, from https://www.vanartgallery.bc.ca/history

Ingold, T. (2015). Knowledge. In T. Ingold, *The life of lines* (pp. 46–50). Routledge. https://doi.org/10.4324/9781315727240

Irwin, R. L. (2003). Toward an aesthetic of unfolding: In/sights through Curriculum. *Journal of the Association for Curriculum Studies, 1*(2), 63–78.

Irwin, R. L. (2013). Becoming a/r/tography. *Studies in Art Education, 54*(3), 198–215. https://doi.org/10.1080/00393541.2013.11518894

La Jevic, L., & Springgay, S. (2008). A/r/tography as an ethics of embodiment. *Qualitative inquiry, 14*(1), 67–89. http://journals.sagepub.com.ezproxy.library.ubc.ca/doi/pdf/10.1177/1077800407304509

Lee, N., Morimoto, K., Mosavarzadeh, M., & Irwin, R. L. (2019). Walking propositions: Coming to know a/r/tographically. *The International Journal of Art & Design Education, 38*(3), 681–690. https://doi.org/10.1111/jade.12237

Massumi, B. (2008). Inflexions 1: The thinking-feeling of what happens. *INFLeXions: A Journal for Research Creation.*

Museum of Contemporary Art Chicago. (n.d.) MCA.

O'Donoghue, D. (2020). Orientations, dispositions, and stances in art education research and scholarship. *Studies in Art Education, 61*(3), 185–194. https://doi.org/10.1080/00393541.2020.1809216

Smeds, K. (2012). On the meaning of exhibitions – Exhibition epistèmes in a historical perspective. *Designs for Learning, 5*(1–2), 50–73. https://doi.org/10.2478/dfl-2014-0004

Søyland, L. (2021). Making sense of movement: A/r/tographic explorations of physical and virtual environments. In L. Søyland, *Grasping materialities: Making sense through explorative touch Interactions with materials and digital technologies* [Doctoral dissertation] (pp. 232–249). University of South-Eastern Norway, Norway.

Springgay, S., Irwin, R. L., & Kind, S. W. (2005). A/r/tography as living inquiry through art and text. *Qualitative Inquiry, 11*(6), 897–912. https://doi.org/10.1177/1077800405280696

Springgay, S., & Truman, S. E. (2019). A walking-writing practice: Queering the trail. In S. Springgay & S. E. Truman (Eds.), *Walking methodologies in a more-than-human world: WalkingLab* (pp. 130–142). Routledge.

CHAPTER 16

Hiroshima-Concordia

A Transnational Art Education Commons in Action

*Anita Sinner, Kazuyo Nakamura, Natalie Pavlik, Congmao Li,
Nao Kameishi and Motoki Wada*

Abstract

In this chapter, we share how and why virtual team projects in visual art education offer a distinct mode of exchange for teaching and learning. Kazuyo and Anita bring together graduate students, in this case, Natalie, Congmao, Nao, and Motoki, who participated in a recent collaborative project via our home universities of Hiroshima and Concordia, located in Japan and Canada, respectively. Our experiments with diversifying learning contexts have been an effort to respond to the ordeal of the pandemic; however, this initiative has evolved over two years to become an emerging transnational commons, which we continue to develop as an alternate form of coming to know with our diverse scholarly cultures. Such real-time global approaches to teamwork are somewhat unconventional in higher education, given different institutional structures, time zones, languages, and more, yet in our experience, these challenges serve as an invitation to rethink, remake, and reimagine art education as an expression of collectively creating knowledge together when forming a virtual community of practice. Living our inquiries beyond the restrictions of a physical classroom, we recognise that boundaries are porous and can be ruptured easily with digital technologies to generate possibilities to not only meet the demands of the current pandemic, but to equally take up sustainability as the future of our field of study.

Keywords

collaborative partnerships – online learning projects – short-term virtual engagement

1 Mapping Transformative Teaching Practices

We co-create this conversation through life writing where first person accounts of in-course collaborative partnerships help unpack the ways in which we are adapting curriculum design. Through commentary, we map some of the issues, challenges, and insights of significance when introduced to UNESCO's Global Citizenship inquiry through this project (UNESCO, 2015, 2016).

In the fall of 2021, Kazuyo and Anita bridged themes of globalisation and the United Nation's Sustainability Development Goals (SDGs) as a means of activating team engagement, where self-directed groups composed of members from both classes negotiated their parameters of practice with autonomy and discretionary decision-making at the heart of defining a project of importance to the group (see Nakamura & Sinner, in press). Our parameters were open-ended; we asked students to share an issue of local concern that had global educative significance and to collaborate to create artworks for a virtual exhibition in response to that issue. By ensuring that projects were uniquely 'glocal' in orientation, purpose, and structure, students as decision-makers in curriculum design undertook a host of logistical problem-solving tasks from institutional protocols to communication methods, alongside discrete art practices among team members, in relation to the local contexts of host cities, all mediated by technology.

Such diffractive movements refocus our attention from deductive interpretation to consider how we are 'becoming-with' ever-expanding conversations (Bozalek, 2017; Bozalek & Zembylas, 2016a, 2016b). Such practice generates entanglements that recur in the commentaries we share, mapping both the pedagogic moments and the ways we read our experiences relationally, suggesting "a new assemblage of possible entry points into this territory of research productions" emerged (Ringrose, Warfield, & Zarabadi, 2018, p. 1). The project as an encounter was initial, that is, it was intended to introduce activities that advance professional qualities as artists, researchers and teachers, from which students may take elements into their own practice. In turn, students embraced their subjectivity and agency, demonstrating situated knowledges, capacities of creative thinking, and collaborative partnerships as formative in developing a transnational learning commons.

2 Potentialities: Nurturing a Transnational Learning Commons

Aligning with a body of scholarship that advances the benefits of online learning in higher education (see Gokcora, 2021, among others), we push the parameters of engagement further at a transnational level. Much like other COIL projects (collaborative online international learning), we integrate modules that are designed to foster sociocultural and intellectual exchanges in relation to art education. Our intent is to diversify learning environments in our field beyond the prescribed studio classroom by expanding learning networks and generating habits of mind receptive to what Gokcora (2021) describes as pluralistic points of view and peer-to-peer learning and feedback on activities grounded in interdisciplinarity, global awareness, and digital literacies.

With this orientation, we envision movement toward a transnational commons, akin to Peters' (2021) notion of an 'intellectual commons' premised on an ethic of sharing and collaboration. A learning commons is a ubiquitous term in higher education for an open, inviting, generative space in which to communicate about ideas, often aligned with libraries (e.g., Lampert & Meyers-Martin, 2019), and learning spaces on campus (Cox et al., 2022). However, in our case, we are interested in extending this construct to COIL projects to nurture participatory, creative collaborations, making our emerging transnational commons a proposition to art education as a space and resource curated together by students and instructors to engage and deepen understandings of glocal issues through experiential knowledge. In this way, our transnational learning commons is predicated on life writing (micro-scripts) as a mode of intercultural engagement, encouraging flexibility in identity and an increasingly global understanding of self-in-relation, where learning is always in motion.

Drawing attention to 'ah-ha' moments in this commentary, we express wayfinding across cultures as processes, relationality, and events, where intuitiveness and responsiveness bring us into learning contexts that reside in the middle and move us in multiple directions concurrently to find new pathways and identify patterns of experiential practice in a different way. Our writing team is composed of students who participated in one of four different in-course groups – Group 3 included Congmao and five members from both classes, and Group 4 included Nao, Motoki, and Natalie, as well as three additional members – and each group undertook different projects. Our diffractive method of reading with, in, and through each other's life writing serves as an amplification of experience that draws out the essence of learning mediated by technology and the vitality of composing our responses. Our approach appertains to intra-actions, a cutting up and collaging of commentary on our experiences to denote when agency emerges in the co-constitutive forces inside and outside the event of learning (see Barad, 2007). As an experimental text, we weave our insights in ways that map movements within the groups, not to flatten the conversation to generalities but to keep the conversation open, to re-read the transformative moments differently, and to embrace diffractive practice in the dissemination of scholarly inquiry (see Murris & Bozalek, 2019).

The following micro-scripts serve as sources of information regarding evolving intercultural narratives and how we theorise education and art practice alongside learning and living together by expanding social and academic networks with sensitivity and tolerance to help students rethink preconceived notions about self, society, and perhaps even the global community more fully (Nakamura & Sinner, in press). Such participatory engagement sets the stage for reducing barriers in communication in an effort to articulate signature pedagogies as they happen (Reck & Wald, 2018). Our learning vignettes may be read thematically to account for more expansive, inclusive, diverse, and equitable modes of coming to know.

To set the scene, our universities are signatories to the UN's SDG mandate, and as such we integrate these guidelines in our curriculum. Hiroshima hosts a diverse international cohort of graduate students in education, and at Concordia, graduate students were mostly Canadian and in fine arts. Bringing together international-national, education-fine arts, multi- and single-language speakers, alongside the values and beliefs guiding the SDGs and Global Citizenship, begins with a respectful embrace of difference as a pedagogic opening, where different core skills and learning priorities inform collaboration, with a willingness to learn from one another – all needed skills for proficient global competencies.

Overcoming constraints inherent in learning at an international level required we 'put our teacher hat on' to attend to potential barriers through proactive deliberation, deep listening, facilitation and negotiation. Inspired by Rancière (1991), our teams were intentionally autonomous in this project. Students self-selected what tools they employed in making art, how they managed multi-language exchanges, and how discretionary decisions were made to balance team priorities as well as the dynamics of socio-cultural relations. This ensured students could individually direct learning supports that effectively facilitated their contributions to the collaborative process. For example, Zoom was an acceptable platform across both universities, yet real-time translations was not an available application through our universities, so students exchanged a host of language applications outside of the Zoom format to communicate together. Students adapted 'translanguaging' (see Cenoz & Gorter, 2022, among others) in their learning experience, including Mandarin, Farsi, French, Spanish, Japanese and English among their shared languages, with English as the most common language across both classes. Ensuring students had the latitude to set parameters further democratised learning beyond traditional course delivery, reflective of values of equity, diversity, inclusivity and accessibility. To render experiences authentically, and to bring the nuance and texture of individual insights to the fore, the commentaries which follow are shared verbatim, as written by graduate students. Such immersion places choice-based learning at the heart of conversations about curriculum.

3   Encountering Processes: Localities, Activations, and Translations
         as Making

Processes involve complex entanglements of the matrices of relations in the
learning equation created by links, places, things, and times. Our writing team
for this chapter explored processes through localities, activations and translations as making together.

3.1   *Congmao: Exploring Locality*

Initially, we spent a significant amount of time introducing ourselves and
exchanging information regarding our daily lives, personal experiences, and
interests in professional studies and research. We then brainstormed on the
topic and determined some relevant key terms to stimulate a more specific
discussion. During the first hour-long discussion, too many suggestions were
offered to decide on a specific theme; thus, we decided to hold another discussion. In the process of deciding when to meet, we noticed that the six people
on the team resided in three different time zones; hence, we created a timetable for each team member to make it easier to see everyone's time zone. During the second discussion, we felt the limitations of the meeting times and
online discussion and decided to express the keyword *locality* determined by
the group through the medium of video footage.

We posed questions, such as: What different sustainable development challenges exist in different localities? If we travel from one locality to another one,
what new perspectives do we gain? How can art help express these problems?
Over the course of a week, two students from the same locality paired up to
develop a project to address the sDGs in their context, filming their processes
and thoughts. We then shared the finished video and entered the second stage
of video production. Two students in one city sent their video documentation
to two students in another city, who created a relevant video response: from
Montreal to Hiroshima, from Hiroshima to Vancouver, and from Vancouver to
Montreal. Before the entire video was completed, we had an online discussion
in which we shared and reported on our progress. Additionally, we wrote a
brief summary of what we discussed, what we were going to do next, and what
we needed to prepare for the next week in our weekly log.

3.2   *Natalie: Sharing Activations*

I enjoyed the process of diving into the project together as a team without a full
plan or understanding of where it was going to go. It was an interesting experience to be virtually grouped with a diverse team of people and immediately
begin with the task of brainstorming. Our response to this challenge was to

start by learning about each other's day-to-day lives, personal histories, environments and research interests. Although we were able to connect through conversation, we decided that to better understand one another, we would take photos of our walking practices, however broadly this might be interpreted. Our following meeting consisted of a "show and tell" setup, through which we were able to learn about each other by seeing and hearing about the different walks, paths, and journeys of our past week. This activation was so successful that we continued this practice throughout the following weeks, each time bringing various photos that reflected our experiences and what we wanted to share with one another. This allowed us to get to know each other, reflect on our own environments, and assess similarities and differences among our team. Although we did not have a clear trajectory yet as a team, these weekly sharing meetings organically transitioned into our final project, during which we were able to connect our work with the SDGs and to one another thematically through the concept of *process*. In this way, everyone was able to share their visions within the collective composition of our video works.

Two aspects of our group communication in addition to our weekly meetings that I believe were integral to our success were an ongoing email chain with the group and a Google Doc where we added information and minutes. The email chain gave us all an opportunity to check-in with everyone after our discussions to see if there were any questions or things that needed clarifying. We also wrote weekly minutes with brief summaries of what we talked about, what we were going to do next, and what to prepare for the following week. This kept everyone on the same page and allowed people to translate the document if need be.

3.3 Nao: Walking as Translation

Our team held an online meeting once a week to advance the project. First, we introduced ourselves and our research contents to each other, and we shared what we were interested in. By examining them from the standpoint of the SDGs, we narrowed down the themes that the team members wanted to consider and gradually determined the direction of the plan. Next, based on a broad initial topic, each member went on an excursion to find something related to the SDGs in their surroundings, such as familiar art, and then we shared our findings at the meeting. *Walking* became an important theme for the team. Thus, we took a walk and photographed things we were interested in and scenes we liked. We recorded and shared how we felt at the time. Some members took pictures of familiar modern art, and our interest in each other's regions appeared to increase through art appreciation. Here, the visual medium of the photograph fulfilled an important role. Some members also created their artwork by combining natural materials and a piece of writing, and we could all connect with each other through the common theme, though we had different methods of expression. At the end of the project, we worked on producing a video piece and a written statement. The video, which traced the trajectory of each member walking, divided the process into three parts – morning, afternoon, and evening – and was considered to be helpful for people in tackling an issue and living a rich and healthy life.

In addition to an online meeting application, collaborative simultaneous editing apps (Google Slides, Google Docs) helped the team work more efficiently throughout the planning process. Moreover, by utilising a translation site, it was possible to instantaneously and accurately read what another member intended to convey. I found the email correspondence with other members to be the most important element of the project. We were able to establish a common understanding by repeating detailed communication by email regarding things we could not discuss or had missed in the meeting. Unlike a continuous stream of speech, the written documents are consistent and can be read repeatedly. By continually reviewing the statements of the members, we were able to understand what we each truly wanted to convey.

3.4   *Motoki: Making the Image Easier to Hold*

Although the theme of SDGs was given to us, our group launched a collaborative project with no set goals. We started by taking a walk in our surroundings and collecting photographic materials for our work. At that time, I had no idea what type of work I would undertake. However, after meeting with Canadian team members for collaboration and setting three themes for the SDGs – morning (input), afternoon (process), and evening (output) – the goals for the project became clearer. Moreover, the speed of our activities increased. It is not always ideal to fix everything, but it is important to set constraints to make the image easier to hold. This made it easier for each member to come up with original ideas and allowed us to work on our production. All of the images we produced were rooted in the SDG theme we first considered, and the originality was not self-constrained.

One reason for the collaboration's success was that we always visualised and summarised our thought and discussion processes. At the beginning of the project, we expressed our thoughts regarding our interest in art through a mind map called MindMeister. We also used Google Docs for documentation in meetings. This helped me recognise the nuances of words I did not hear or understand in a meeting and prepare for the next meeting. The results were organised by posting them to Google Slides to be viewed as a list. The slides were useful in organising the final product, a moving picture.

4   **Encountering Relationality: Sustainability, Relationships, Conversations, Immersion**

Relationality attends to how we stand in connection to one another during the event of learning, suggesting that a dynamic flow within communicative practices was underway; in this case, as sustainable relationships informed by immersive activities and informal conversations.

4.1   *Congmao: Sustainability Issues in Community*

I was very fortunate to be able to participate in this project with Canadian students living in a foreign country and involved in art or art education. As I majored in furniture design at university, I have been exposed to sustainability issues since that time. For the past two years, I have studied art education in my Master's programme. Recently, I have been able to discover the views and research of many scholars who are working on the SDGs from an educational perspective.

In this project, through group communication and video production, I learned more about people's thinking regarding various issues around the world and, specifically, sustainability issues in their communities. I learned, in particular, the differences in the visualisation of water resources by region and the importance of sustainable water use through the videos that were part of this project. I was able to intuitively understand the issues of migration and today's homelessness. Through this discussion and consequent learning experience, my understanding of the SDGs was also further diversified. At the same time, I was able to develop some ideas about the language in other people's videos. Although I do not speak English well, this project gave me the opportunity to express my thoughts in English with other team members. When I could not express myself sufficiently, the group members organised their thoughts as much as possible. We did not spend significant time together on this project, but we attempted to comprehend the personalities and ways of thinking of Canadian students. I consistently felt their enthusiasm, their admiration for us, and their willingness to express their ideas.

4.2   *Nao: Building Relationships*

Through collaborative production, we have been able to build a relationship through which we respect and enhance each other. As the theme of the team was *walking*, we were able to glimpse each other's thought processes as we worked on the project. Because of this, we were able to discern what types of things the members valued and what thoughts they had regarding the project. In spite of the short time period, we were able to maintain fulfilling relationships because of the theme, the SDGs, which helped us connect in a meaningful way.

I was able to improve my own communication skills through interactions with members. Although we used translation apps, language barriers often arose. In such instances, we made an effort to ask on the spot and to receive confirmation by mail when there was something that we did not understand. Furthermore, through the production of the work, we shared the lead role in a positive manner to efficiently advance the work, and we mutually confirmed the result. I believe that the power to advance the work smoothly was also improved through this process.

4.3   *Motoki: Sharing in Conversations*

When the collaborative project began, I was extremely defensive. The main reason for this was my fear of expressing an incorrect opinion in anticipation of formal and rigid discussions. However, when the meeting began, that anticipation and sense of anxiety changed. The atmosphere of the meeting with the Canadian students was more informal conversation than discussion. The Canadian students were receptive to what each other said, and they were also receptive to what I said, albeit in poor English. This allowed me to feel comfortable expressing my identity in co-productions and meetings.

Our team members wrote the Artist Statement in English and Japanese. At the time of its writing, I found that Canadian students' way of writing is artistic. I realised this aspect while translating the statement into Japanese. I was moved by the culturally different view of the world found in not only artwork but also artistically written texts. For example, the word "distance" may have multiple meanings, and when describing the time difference between Japan and Canada, the expression "beyond the time zone" may be used to evoke not only the time difference but also the geographical distance. Through translating the Artist Statement, I was able to experience the text from the perspective of an artistic world view.

During the production of the resulting video, not only English but also the Japanese language was respected. Both English and Japanese narrations were incorporated in the videos, which included both works and concepts; this was a testament to international collaboration. I was responsible for the proper, appropriate, and effective handling of the Japanese language from the perspective of communicating it to the world. This was the first time that I felt such a strong sense of responsibility and awareness of the Japanese language.

4.4　*Natalie: Immersive Learning*

Entering this project, I was fortunate to have had prior experience working with international teams of educators. I have taught English, art, and cultural lessons abroad in Germany and Switzerland in immersive learning environments, where learners would come to join a group of teachers from different parts of the world. I was working in a predominantly German environment while I was beginning to learn German, alongside other educators who were English language learners. Because of this, I related in some ways to the Japanese students, who were in a situation where they were communicating in a language they were not completely comfortable in. Upon hearing about the project, I was immediately impressed by how brave and adventurous the Japanese students must be to embark on this challenging experience, and upon meeting my Japanese team members and witnessing their dedication to communicating with our team, I was inspired by every interaction we had. A focus on mutual appreciation of language is one of my favorite things that came from my group's final videos, in which we included both an English and Japanese voiceover. It was so wonderful to hear my Japanese team members speaking in their first language, and they both expressed to me their enjoyment of the opportunity to share this aspect of their identities.

5　Encountering Learning as an Event: Connecting, Mediating, Differences, and Acceptance

Rogoff (2011) argued that the staging of the scholarly event creates a platform of action where intellectual exchange collapses the distance between theory and practice. In our case, we recognise that our reception of the event is contingent on the context, as demonstrated in the methods employed by teams, including connecting and mediating differences and how they came to understandings of acceptance.

5.1　*Congmao: Connecting Lives as Makers*

In recent years, video images have gradually reached the masses, with websites like YouTube and Bilibili showing people around the world documenting and sharing their lives, expressing their ideas, and visualising the lifestyles of different cultures. These vivid images seem to connect our lives as the makers even if we were not able to meet each other. The images are organically connected records of countless photographs, in which the intentions of the author collide with the reactions of the audience, generating even more ideas and curiosity. I became interested in other members' living environment through the videos they took.

I wondered: What do the sun, rain, and wind taste like across the broad Pacific and across the continents? How is the diet of those in other cultures balanced? What is their tone of voice when they spend time with their friends? How do customs and cultures born over the course of a long history materialise in every moment of life? These are things one cannot feel without experiencing them for oneself. Video images as a medium of art transmission are a language of communication, a reflection that moves our emotions and thus evokes thoughts regarding the world at large.

I deeply enjoyed participating in this project and felt connected to everyone by meeting with the team members each week. Receiving encouragement and praise from the Concordia team and learning new theories from their work was very rewarding. Moreover, this experience helped me build deeper relationships with my team members at Hiroshima University. We decided on the theme of the video together, went out in the city where the members live to find inspiration and materials, and completed the creation together.

5.2   *Motoki: Artworks as Mediators of Language*

First, the collaborative project gave me a chance to experience much of the visual appeal of art. At the beginning of the project, we took photos of our walks around our neighborhood and shared them together. The Canadian students seemed to find the scenery of Hiroshima and Japan, where we spend our daily lives, beautiful and unusual. On the other hand, the scenery in the photographs taken by the Canadian students was also beautiful and unusual for me as a Japanese person. As a common saying, "the darkest place is under the candlestick", reminds us, many attractive resources are lying around us, and whether we can utilise them depends on our observation and what we value. We need to look more closely at the towns we live in and the places we spend our time and recognise their value.

This project was also an opportunity for me to recognise that art has a role in promoting the understanding of language. I did not understand all of the English that the Canadian students spoke, nor would the Canadian students have been able to fully grasp the implications of my remarks. However, in the circumstances described in this essay, photographs and artworks became mediators between languages, and they played a role in facilitating the acquisition of information that language could not compensate for, thus promoting mutual understanding. Language acquisition is certainly among the most important skills for international collaboration. However, I have realised that language should not be singled out and that it is important that language and its meaning in connection to reality be linked.

5.3   *Natalie: Embracing Differences*

Visually seeing into each other's worlds was very powerful. I feel that we are often accustomed to photographs because of the internet, but when I pause to reflect, it is truly amazing to have this opportunity to visually engage with people across the world and learn about their perspectives through images and discussion. I learned a great deal from these shared images and the casual conversations that would follow, during which we asked each other questions out of curiosity. These moments led to laughter and further discussion about culture, society, and life that would not have been possible if we were not virtually face-to-face. Similarities amongst our worlds also became apparent as the weeks progressed, in particular, the changing leaves of autumn, our experiences with COVID restrictions, and our academic environments. We began to share a phrase throughout our different interactions, whether it be through email or zoom meetings: "Good morning and goodnight", alluding to the time change that separated us and how we were always disoriented by this difference. They were starting their days when we were ending ours, and both parties were often sleepy, some as the sun was rising and some as the sun was setting.

I sincerely enjoyed being involved in this project, and meeting with my team every week made me feel connected to our community. I learned a great deal from my Japanese teammates, their encouraging clapping, and their dedication to communication. I had previously never had a friend from Hiroshima before, so it was wonderful to get to know two individuals from there. This experience also led me to form deeper relationships with my Concordia team members, which can be difficult while only meeting virtually.

5.4   *Nao: Empathy and Acceptance*

Morning time in Japan is night time in Canada. Moreover, we use two different languages, Japanese and English. It was art, a universal language that connected us as individuals who were separated by distance and time. Art that appeals to us visually, aurally, and sometimes tactilely resonates directly with our senses and elicits in us the same emotions without involving language. Everyone reconfirmed the power of art through this collaboration. Each of us has a different sensibility, so we did not always share precisely the same thoughts. However, what is important is to attempt to understand the other person, and by having an attitude of empathy, we can accept and appreciate each other's thoughts and cultures.

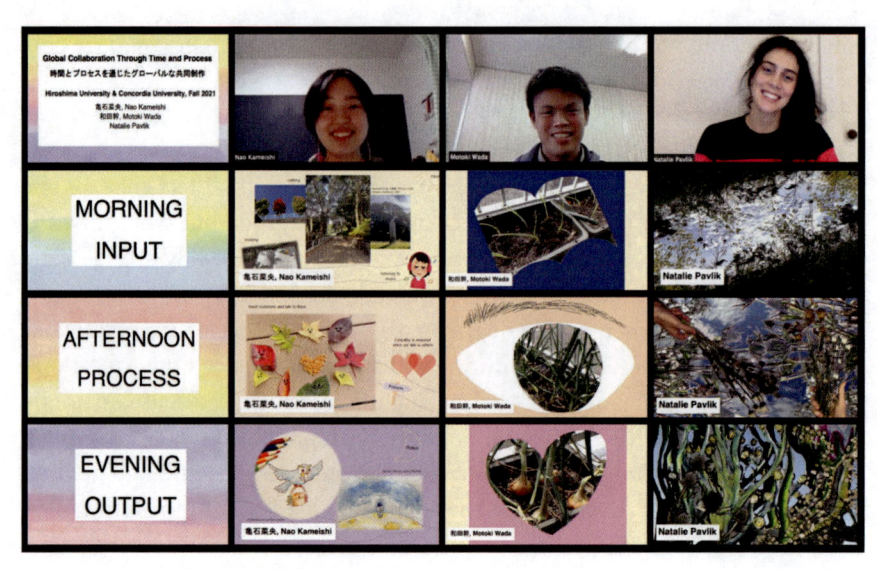

FIGURE 16.1 Making art together

The first thing that I noticed when viewing art was that the members were in different artistic environments. In Canada, it was possible to observe the abundant artwork even in the nearby park, which is surrounded by rich nature, and the scenery painted by the sunset becomes art in itself. In Japan, artworks cannot be seen easily in the town yet, and people go to museums to see them. The differences in the aesthetic environment provided various individual aesthetic perspectives. Art that we encounter in daily life and are familiar with creates differences in aesthetic sensations, such as how we experience colour, how we perceive form and our feelings related to an event, and how an idea is arranged and the methods of expression also differ across individuals. Our team's theme was that different people have different "ways of traveling" at different stages: Morning/Input, Afternoon/Process, and Evening/Output (see Figure 16.1). It was a very interesting event, although it was a matter of course that even if we were viewing the same object, how we looked at it was different.

Through this project, all members encountered art and considered the culture and life of those from the other culture. It was wonderful for me to imagine the temperature, the strength of the wind, and the voices of creatures while looking at Canada's scenery through the computer screen. I always gain new awareness when encountering other cultures, and I would like to use this awareness in my daily life. There are surely new discoveries that have not been noticed previously, and I would like to share these experiences with others and use them to drive further discovery and inspiration.

6 Thinking with Micro-Scripts: The Contours of Curricular Experiments

Micro-scripts offer another way of attending to the nuances of affective co-creation, revealing the contours of curricular experimentation that emerged in this case as bodily experiences, moving beyond language alone to embrace a spectrum of processes that shift learning from predictable standardised, individualised assignments to learning as an embodied intercultural reality. By emphasising and enabling student autonomy, we moved from a typical transmission approach to an emergent learning encounter that fostered trust, risk-taking, in-situ problem-solving, immediate feedback, responsibility in decision-making, and leadership in navigating team dynamics as an educative practice. The purpose of the assignment was not primarily to produce a product of art, but to activate provisional between spaces that generate contingent creative thinking. Opening higher education to different orientations and different criteria attends to the importance of exposing our future educators to different knowledge systems and to different global perspectives, issues, and questions as a living reality, in which thinking-doing-making transnationally becomes a disposition with cultural awareness. The commentaries suggest that collaborative practices evolved rhizomatically, connecting across, with, and through at distinct 'ah-ha' moments of convergence–divergence, and as our writing team demonstrates, our sense of self-in-relation became more fluid and affirming.

As evidenced in our commentary and in our textual strategy in this chapter, we elucidate how and why such modules encourage flexible learning environments that adapt to the needs of learners and encourage opportunities for success by emphasising diversified capacity building through collaboration. By co-designing activities together, student teams open up the scope of thinking-with, expanding the discussion to social, environmental, economic, political, and educational concerns as evolving ecologies of practice that form in collective team assemblages. Learning becomes reciprocal as an active process, in which the conditions of the environment generate new constellations of practice and identity, and arguably invoke good citizenship in the academy and beyond, where we come to hold a greater sense of security and tolerance across cultures, and where members are valued, respected and heard. As eloquently expressed by the writing team, such activities attend to discourses of caring, empathy, sensitivity to the environment, and how we all hold responsibility to find ways to work together in partnership by opening spaces of belonging where moments lost in translation are acknowledged with response-ability, and knowledge generation is verified in a question, issue, or phenomenon rather than only in the findings. The desire and will to learn becomes a habit of scholarly mind that then arcs beyond the course, the assignment, and the requisite institutional protocols to recognise that we are sustained in a complex condition of coming to know.

7   Shifting Horizons of Thought: Continuing Our Conversations with Impactful Practices

Creating spaces for alternate approaches to teaching and learning in higher education is a refreshing and invigorating way of living academically, and it is in this context that we invite continuing conversations with impactful practices through open systems of inquiry as those mapped among our writing team. Through-lines of processes, relationality, and events demonstrate how curricular decision-making and critical thinking about content, alongside meditative considerations, operate as learning with body-object-space. This approach commands different questions and can dislodge sedimentary and more traditional, predictive curriculum in higher education to shift horizons of thought, such as thinking-with SDGs.

Drawing on the notion of openness, our purpose in this experiment of transformative learning is grounded in "new spatialisation, interconnectivity, mobility, personalisation and globalisation of learning and education", where students are not restricted to learning only from one instructor but embraced a more decentralised, "many-to-many mode of interactivity" among peers, sources of information and, indeed, across space and time (Peters, 2014, p. 1). In this way, we foster learning contexts that attend to aspects of "post-digital openness" in an effort to explore how we co-create within nested human–technology–space dynamics and how we introduce "unlearning" methods and protocols of schooling in order to "relearn" in new ways – in our case, transnationally (see Jandrić, 2018). Underscoring our educative practices, we are advocating through our configurations for a greater emphasis on inclusivity and equal learning opportunities that transcend traditional institutional constructions and restrictions to redefine what constitutes knowledge and to imagine new architectures for teaching and learning as a creative and relational activity propelled by processes that are contingent on events, such as COIL activations. This adds to sustainability in curriculum in part by inviting projects that make a difference in the real lives of learners.

The dynamics of exchange within our emerging and still forming transnational art education commons are expansive and rich with potential and warrant further, more expansive inquiry and analysis to appreciate the scope of possibilities ahead. As we shift our orientation solely from content-driven courses and programmes to inclusive, artful forms of engagement that build capacities by attending to literary, performative, digital, and social platforms, we can speculate on how such incremental innovations may serve as templates for a reconceptualisation of higher education in the future. Perhaps modules and activations of specific interest to learners internationally, rather than courses only offered locally, may afford another kind of visual art education commons, manifest with the qualities and characteristics needed among our students in the future.

Acknowledgement

This chapter is supported in part by research that has been made possible by a grant from the Social Sciences and Humanities Research Council (SSHRC) of Canada.

References

Barad, K. (2007). *Meeting the universe halfway: Quantum physics and the entanglement of matter and meaning.* Duke University Press.

Bozalek, V., & Zembylas, M. (2016a). Diffraction or reflection? Sketching the contours of two methodologies in educational research. International *Journal of Qualitative Studies in Education, 30*(2), 111–127. https://doi.org/10.1080/09518398.2016.1201166

Bozalek, V., & Zembylas, M. (2016b). Critical posthumanism, new materialism and the affective turn for socially just pedagogies in higher education. *South African Journal of Higher Education, 30*, 193–200.

Cenoz, J., & Gorter, D. (2022). *Pedagogical translanguaging.* Cambridge University Press. https://doi.org/10.1017/9781009029384

Cox, A., Benson Marshall, M., Burnham, J., Care, L., Herrick, T., & Jones, M. (2022). Mapping the campus learning landscape. *Pedagogy, Culture & Society, 30*(2), 149–167. https://doi.org/10.1080/14681366.2020.1788124

Gokcora, D. (2021). Benefits of collaborative online international learning projects. *Academia Letters*, Article 202. https://doi.org/10.20935/AL202

Jandrić, P. (2018). Postdigital openness. *Open Review of Educational Research, 5*(1), 179–181. https://doi.org/10.1080/23265507.2018.1547943

Lampert, L., & Meyers-Martin, C. (2019). *Creating a learning commons: A practical guide for librarians.* Rowman & Littlefield.

Murris, K., & Bozalek, V. (2019). Diffracting diffractive readings of texts as methodology: Some propositions. *Educational Philosophy and Theory, 51*(14). https://doi.org/10.1080/00131857.2019.1570843

Nakamura, K., & Sinner, A. (in press). Inviting teacher candidates in art education to become global agents for sustainability. In R. Vella & V. Pavlou (Eds.), *Art, sustainability and learning communities*. Intellect.

Peters, M. (2014). Openness and the intellectual commons. *Open Review of Educational Research, 1*(1), 1–7. https://doi.org/10.1080/23265507.2014.984975

Peters, M. (2021). Knowledge socialism: The rise of peer production – Collegiality, collaboration and collective intelligence. *Educational Philosophy and Theory, 53*(1), 1–9. https://doi.org/10.1080/00131857.2019.1654375

Rancière, J. (1991). *The ignorant schoolmaster: Five lessons in intellectual emancipation* (K. Ross, Trans.). Stanford University.

Reck, B., & Wald, K. (2018). Towards a signature pedagogy for arts integration in educator preparation. *Pedagogies: An International Journal, 13*(2), 106–118.

Ringrose, J., Warfield, K., & Zarabadi, S. (2018). *Feminist posthumanism, new materialism and education*. Routledge.

Rogoff, I. (2011, July). *The implicated* [Keynote address]. International Visual Sociology Association conference, Vancouver, Canada.

Thiele, K. (2014). Ethos of diffraction: New paradigms for a (post)humanist ethics. *Parallax, 20*, 202–216.

UNESCO. (2015). *Transforming our world: The 2030 agenda for sustainable development.*

UNESCO. (2016). *Schools in action: Global citizens for sustainable development: A guide for teachers.* https://www.gcedclearinghouse.org/resources/schools-action-global-citizens-sustainable-development-guide-teachers

CHAPTER 17

Reflections on Research and Studio Teaching in an Online Environment

Michelle Wiebe

Abstract

This chapter records the experience of transitioning a studio class and a research project originally planned for an in-person undergraduate art education design class to an online environment. Pandemic scheduling resulted in 4 sequential offerings of the class, resulting in discoveries about teaching studio art and conducting research in an online environment. Not only was it possible to carry out a modified form of the research, but the scheduling also supported ongoing adjustments to instruction. As a result, it was possible to develop more viable approaches for art instruction outside of a physical studio while also gaining knowledge about the challenges students faced internalising the concept of empathic design. The timeline contributed to more effective class structures and exercises for introducing the concept of empathic design to each successive class. In a sense, the scheduling enhanced feedback to the extent that both the teaching and the research became situated in ongoing reflective action.

Much has been learned about online teaching in the arts. Some of what has been learned about connecting with students ultimately carries over to in-person instruction. These reflections also reveal the value of empathy instruction in art education because student work benefitted from the empathic focus both conceptually and aesthetically. An unanticipated outcome was that the classes were able to develop a sense of community and fruitful online critique discussions because of their growing ability to consider the views of others.

Keywords

empathy – design thinking – studio online – wicked problems

1 Introduction

> To be educated is not to have arrived at a destination; it is to travel with a
> different point of view. (Biesta, 2018, p. 30)

Following a compelling discussion about how politicised climate change and
global warming have become and the urgency of making changes to lower
emissions, a student wrote:

> To create an Infographic that can help lower emissions for someone
> skeptical about climate change. I have to be empathic about their val-
> ues, as "leaving a better place for our children" might not be as con-
> vincing. A more personalized message is needed. That is why I focused
> more on the benefits of renewable energy and lowering emissions than
> scientific data on global temperatures. I had also avoided phrases such as
> "climate change", "renewable energy", etc., as they might shut down the
> target audience due to their political affiliations. (Excerpt from student
> empathic statement)

The statement represents a portion of the written work and research documentation accompanying the student's infographic. The infographic itself
demonstrated that the student was considering their target empathically
and that it was having a visible impact on the resultant image. Both the statement and the design work resulted in satisfaction because they represented
advances in my teaching that arose out of ongoing research into teaching students to design empathically.

In the autumn of 2019, I conceived a study about teaching empathic design
to students enrolled in an undergraduate art education visual design course.
I planned to begin with a May offering of the course but prior to the start of
the class all teaching abruptly pivoted online. After a scramble, plans were
in place to begin the research albeit in the online environment. I consoled
myself that this would be akin to a pilot study to work out any glitches prior
to the September course offering, which I blithely assumed would be face-to-
face again. Of course, a full year of online teaching followed and successively
refined iterations of the research study resulted.

This discussion is situated on the learning that preceded the study, what
I have discovered through successive attempts to teach students to design
empathically in four consecutive online classes, and the unexpected discoveries about how students learning empathic approaches enhanced community.

2 The Study

This study sought to answer two connected research questions: 1) how students could learn to design empathically and 2) how learning empathic design would impact student design skills. To gain answers to the research questions, the study progressed as follows. Students were introduced to empathic design; students completed the Interpersonal Reactivity Index (IRI) self-assessment; students took on group or individual design exercises with an empathic focus; individual projects that included empathic focus criteria; and assessment of projects focused on the empathic understanding students displayed as well as the success of the design solution.

This was a multiple-case study with each successive class forming a case. In the online environment, the data did not include observation notes that would have arisen in a face-to-face setting but collection of student work, written statements, class exercises, and forum posts provided rich data.

3 Context

Students from across the University take our undergraduate art education classes, which results in diverse student populations and allows for rich class interactions due to the variety of student study foci. The classes discussed here ranged in size from 33 to 52 students and included students in all years of undergraduate study. In each class roughly 40% of the students were international. The course in which this study occurred is a combination of theory and studio practice with the studio work premised on learning design thinking as a means of problem-solving and working creatively. The course topic is visual design for persuasion and advocacy in art education. Design thinking is therefore introduced early in the course and students are required to follow the iterative process in each of their assignments. This is where the idea of teaching empathic design emerged because design thinking as popularised by IDEO and the Stanford School begins with empathy as a means to promote human-centred design.

4 Design Thinking

Design thinking is not new but has become increasingly popular across disciplines, resulting in the existence of many versions of the process (Heron et al.,

2022; Luchs, 2016). Despite many variations, however, Heron et al. (2022) say it is possible to understand design thinking as generally including empathising, defining, ideating, prototyping and testing (p. 3). The Stanford School model begins with empathy, which one gains through observation, whereas the IDEO model begins with observing to gain understanding. In essence both models begin similarly. This issue of empathy, however, is not the reason that design thinking has been an important focus of undergraduate design classes, rather it is the value of the iterative process as a means of approaching problems in art and design that makes it worthwhile for students to internalise the approach. Indeed, a central aim of design thinking is that it is a creative problem-solving process (Aflatoony et al., 2018; James, 2017; Luchs, 2016; Luka, 2019; Oxman, 2017; Todd & Norman, 2020).

From an art education perspective, the value of learning a design thinking process is more that it provides a context to question the status quo. Design thinking can help students learn to tackle problems without being over-whelmed by the knowledge that there is no clear solution (Watson, 2015). Because the process is iterative, students can also learn that it is valuable to revise, refine, and adapt their ideas as they sketch and plan without settling on their first concept. Graham (2020) does raise a cautionary note that art and art education should be about more than simply learning problem-solving within a process aimed at increasing creativity. Students are therefore encouraged to consider design thinking as an assistive approach used to refine their ideas or to get ideas flowing at the outset. Rather than blindly assuming that design will help solve problems, Biesta (2018) suggests that we need to pose 'what if' questions and query whether the "voice that expresses itself is racist' or the "creativity that emerges is destructive" (p. 14). From this perspective, framing the design thinking process in the context of beginning from an empathic stance, encourages students to consider the quality of what they are express-ing, which according to Biesta (2018), "has to do with how children and young people can exist *well*, individually and collectively, *in* the world and *with* the world" (p. 14).

Design thinking as introduced in class is not presented as a recipe for good design or as a problem-solving tool, rather it is taught as a means for students to explore ideas and to move beyond their previously held views. Students are encouraged not only to understand the rationale for each stage of the design thinking process but also to make it their own. They are discouraged from reducing the process to a step-by-step approach, which diminishes the capac-ity of design thinking to uncover 'the richness of the world' (Teal, 2010). When they can view design thinking wholistically as a means to contemplate their world rather than simply as a solution-based process (Chon & Sim, 2019), it becomes a meaningful element in both their artmaking and class interactions.

In an art education context, even in an art education design class, students should be in a place where they can break away from norms (Graham, 2020).

5 Empathy

As Editor in Residence at the Stanford School, Emi Kolawole suggested that engaging with a different worldview enlightens you because it provides new ways of thinking that are impossible if you cling to preconceived ideas (Kolawole, n.d.). While this is an incentive to engage in empathic thinking during initial planning, it is not the only rationale for empathic design. Design thinking is premised on initial observation and empathic understanding because design that is not connected to those for whom it is intended is unlikely to be appropriate (Heimgartner et al., 2011; Kouprie & Visser, 2009; Paron, 2020). In this class, students are presented with projects in which they must communicate ideas about social issues, and it is essential that they consider those for whom their message is intended, or the message will not be understood.

Designers have long considered the relevance of understanding the client's needs and wishes to design solutions that are suitable and therefore marketable, but this has not always included empathy. Kouprie and Visser (2009) suggest that the term empathic was introduced in the late-1990s as a way to develop more successful design solutions. In this context, empathic design meant that "designers should be more sensitive to users, be able to understand them, their situation, and feelings" (p. 438). Empathy has the capacity to shift the intent of the design from creating designs that seduce the audience into purchasing to creating designs that can address needs and improve lives (Devecchi & Guerrini, 2017; Kouprie & Visser, 2009; McDonagh & Thomas, 2011; Woodcock et al., 2018; Xenakis, 2017). From an educational perspective, learning about empathy while learning design is therefore valuable.

Developing a deeper understanding of what it means to begin the design process with empathy benefits from further discussion of the concept and also consideration of the limits that exist in terms of having a truly empathic understanding. It is, however, difficult to find theorists who agree on a standard definition (Cuff et al., 2016) because empathy research often refers to the ambiguity of the term (Cuff et al., 2016; Hall et al., 2021; Ickes, 2003). There are different disciplinary (DeVecchi & Guerrini, 2017; Jeffrey, 2016) and different theorist definitions (Konrath, O'Brien, & Hsing, 2011). Maibom (2014) believes, however, that the concerns with difference are overstated and says that even with varied uses of the term "almost nobody talks of an emotion as empathetic unless the agent is aware that it is caused by the perceived, imagined, or inferred emotion or plight of another, or it expresses concern for the welfare of another" (p. 2). Thus, for the purposes of my students, it was essential to develop a shared understanding of empathy and its role in their design planning (Hall et al., 2021; Maibom, 2014).

Although empathy can be explained simply as being aware of the subjective experiences of another (Wispé, 1986), empathy as integral to design is nuanced. For students, designing with empathy means that they consider how those for whom they are designing understand the world and how they live in the world. Viewing examples of messages that are aimed at a different audience often helps students realise how essential it is to think carefully about the feelings of those for whom they are designing. Understanding empathy as a construct is not enough, however, because becoming an empathic designer requires that students learn not only what empathy is but also how it impacts design decisions. As with other skill acquisition (Trninic, 2018), developing skill as an empathic designer also requires repeated practice.

6   Wicked Problems

Rittel and Webber (1973) proposed the concept of wicked problems to elucidate the difference between the definable or 'benign' problems of science or math. They were talking about planning issues where the problems were complex and there was never a solution. "Social problems are never solved. At best they are only re-solved–over and over again" (Rittel & Weber, 1973, p. 160). In a class that includes students from across campus who are trying to develop design 'solutions' this distinction is essential particularly as the students start to consider their design planning from an empathic stance. As students realise that a successful design for one group might not be successful for another, they see the value of empathic planning more clearly. This distinction also begins to address Graham's (2020) concern that art should be about more than a process for problem solving. In this context, design thinking becomes a process to assist students in developing approaches that address wicked problems using empathic understanding. In retrospect, discussing wicked problems early in the course also helped students cope with the online environment and its concurrent continual adjustments.

7   Empathic Design

In April 2020, it felt as if the world had shifted on its axis. I was scrambling to plan for a studio class that was now going to be online while also trying to adapt my planned research to fit the new delivery mode. Hurried investigations into the best ways to deliver classes online revealed plenty of sound advice but an absence of suggestions geared toward studio classes. Quinlan's (2010) *12 Tips for the Online Teacher* certainly helped with planning the basic structure of the course but left me scrambling for studio ideas. Adding to the pressure was my desire to begin research that had been conceived as a face-to-face study.

In addition, I realised that the pivot to online learning was causing distress for many students. Some were stuck in Canada and were longing to go home. An email from one student exemplifies what I heard repeatedly "since I live by myself in this time of unknown, my mental health went downshifted [sic]" (student email communication). My initial focus was on how to create a viable studio environment online and still follow my research protocol as closely as possible in the new setting, but I knew that my focus needed to include creating community for students who were "all in this time of unknown [sic]" (student email communication) and feeling that "it's a tough time for everyone" (student email communication). I did feel fortunate that the class I was about to teach in May of 2020, was a design class, which was structured such that students would be able to access necessary materials with relative ease. There was still concern about modifications that were necessary to make the studio learning workable and worthwhile.

As mentioned, the research I was hoping to do involved having students learn to design empathically and assuming that the online environment would be short-lived, the plan was to conduct the research as a pilot that would provide guidance for future interactions. Thus, with empathy in mind, I determined that the first thing I should do was model an empathic approach in terms of the class structure. Students were all sent a short questionnaire before the class started to determine the geographic location and time zone in which they were situated and their preferences in terms of synchronous versus asynchronous class times. The most compelling response was the student who said, "I am worried about how I will manage in a course that starts at one o'clock in the morning".

It was quickly apparent that asynchronous classes would be the most workable approach. Because many students also wanted regular check-in times, I made myself available during set periods that alternated between morning and afternoon. While this made the course material available for all students, studio environment became an even greater challenge. Additionally, there were students who had never taken an art class at university in the same class as students who were in their final year of Visual Arts studies. Class began with an exercise wherein students were required to respond to a reading by creating a visual definition of a key term. In an attempt to begin the process of creating a studio community, all students were required to post their visuals in an online forum. This first attempt was not a success, and I quickly learned that students also needed to respond to each other. This was accomplished by having students post reflective responses to the work of their classmates after each project. It was clear that the approach was working in the way that I always hope a studio critique will work when I received notes from students like this one:

> I am just wondering that if it is possible for me to change my previous assignment 1 to the new one that I created. because I really think that my previous is very bad. I had no clues when I was doing the first assignment, but after seeing others' work I was kind of enlightened. (Student email communication)

Other workarounds that contributed to community included team sign-up forums wherein students could indicate their desire to work with others. This resulted in students working in groups and meeting with me as a team. Face-to-face renditions of the class regularly include working in design teams and the group energy that students displayed while online was heartening. A second workaround was the hours spent taping video recordings of the class material. In Zoom meetings, students often commented that seeing and hearing me made them feel that I cared about them, which in turn made them not only more willing to experiment in their studio work but also to request meetings. Creating a balance of simple exercises and significant assignments also allowed students a safe zone for studio experimentation. The online environment made this more labor intensive for me because feedback took more time to communicate online than it would have orally in the studio but the payoff in terms of studio learning was worth it.

As we settled tentatively into the online environment, students were asked to complete the IRI (Davis, 1980) immediately after design empathy was introduced in class and the instrument's 28 statements served to highlight the concept of considering others. Because the IRI is written as a self-reporting measure, respondents rate their reactions to statements such as "I really get involved with the feelings of the characters in a novel" (Davis, 1980, qu. 5). The statements do not imply a hierarchy and respondents rate themselves using a Likert rating scale that accompanies each statement. The scale provides non-threatening choices ranging from not very like me to very like me. The IRI is self-reported, and concerns have been raised about whether the statements accurately measure the different dimensions of empathy (Baldner & McGinley, 2014); however, because the goal was to teach students to design empathically rather than focusing on their empathy globally, the IRI was useful as a prompt. I have continued to use the IRI even though it is not being used as a measure because taking time to respond to the instrument signals the importance of empathy and increases student understanding. As students navigated learning online, the empathic statements contained in the IRI were a reminder that the challenges they were facing were shared.

8   Learning Empathy

There is ample evidence that empathy can be taught (Bearman et al., 2015; Bullough, 2019; Casale et al., 2018; Helding, 2017; Patel et al., 2019). Empathy teaching varies in approach from simulations (Bearman et al. 2015), to reflections on art, literature, and history (Casale et al. 2018; Helding, 2017), observation (Hess & Fila, 2015) and empathic modeling (Altay & Demirkan, 2013). Each approach requires an investment of time and repetition because students do not develop empathy without practice. This was evident in my classes because in each class the students developed more empathic awareness as the course progressed. I realise that I also got more adept at providing experiences that increased understanding as well such that by the third class of the inquiry, students were much more successful at incorporating empathic elements in their designs.

Initially empathic design was introduced in a slide show with examples and followed immediately by the IRI. Then, each project contained the requirement that students include an empathic statement in their planning work and documentation. They were also required to demonstrate how their designs aligned with this empathic understanding. In the first instance, student work showed that they were not adept at thinking empathically. When students were exposed to exemplars (Ho, 2015) and the exemplars were the focus of online class sharing, their understanding grew. Development of understanding was exemplified by increases in student design responses. In the online environment, discussions were different than in person conversations because discussions occurred in online chats; sharing in the Zoom classroom; and via online discussion forums. The students adapted quickly and even appeared more willing to offer their ideas in the online discussion forums than they do in class, which is something worthy of further exploration.

9   Building an Online Community

After the limited success of the first forum post of their work on a studio exercise, students were required to respond to their classmates' work via the same forum. This began slowly and built as the discussions developed and confidence grew. The initial requirement was for a minimum of two comments, and this increased to a minimum of four comments. The value of our empathic study and discussions quickly grew apparent as students interacted with each other respectfully and sensitively.

> This poster is great! I love the playfulness of the imagery and how clean and clear the whole thing is. It's very easy to follow and certainly inspires the reader to appreciate the message. Great Job! (Student forum post)

Exclamation marks aside, the comment not only compliments the work but explains why the student feels the way they do. Even when students offered each other constructive feedback, they did it in a respectful manner.

This is a very interesting topic to pick, and I definitely learned from it, especially things I would have never questioned myself. You included good info for both sides of the infographic, but I think if you highlighted another benefit of keeping your old phone instead of saying not to get a new phone outright, it might be even more effective to the audience (student forum post) (see Figure 17.1).

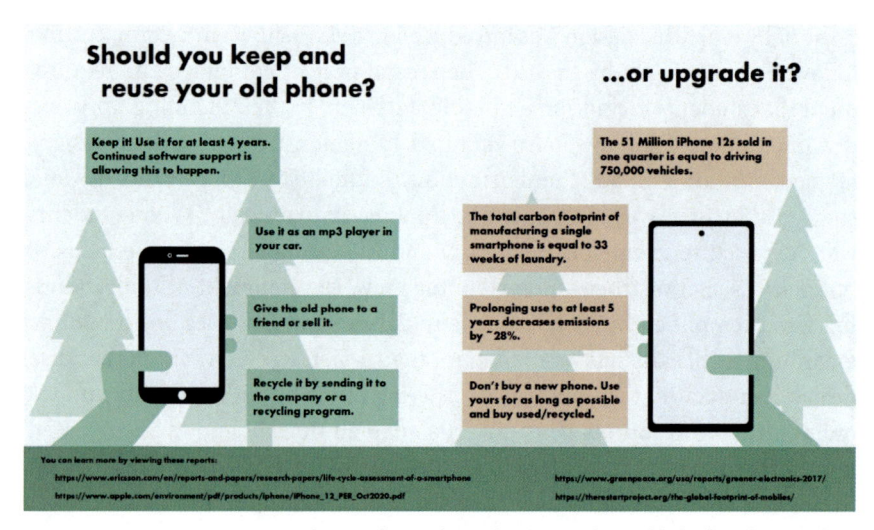

FIGURE 17.1   To reuse or upgrade – student infographic (copy of unpublished student work submitted for the infographic assignment, used with permission)

Not only were the comments thoughtful, but they also adhered to the project criteria, rather than being personal critiques. The online environment may have been a contributing factor although in a recent in-person class, the students demonstrated similar care during class critiques after comparable study of empathic design.

Instructions for posting were specific and designed to encourage gracious comments.

> Your comments may be in the form of questions about techniques, they may be affirmation for great ideas, and they may be comments about particularly successful responses to the assignment. (Forum post instructions)

The assignment progression also contributed to student learning because the first project simply focused on clear identification of audience and creating a visual that communicated with the audience through use of colour, typeface style (if type was used), and imagery. The goal was to encourage students to consider the empathic elements of their design as a focus. In the second project, students not only needed to consider their audience but also create an infographic that addressed a social issue by describing the problem and offering ways to address the situation. The impact of the focus on critique having a dual purpose both in identification of the perceived problem and potential approaches to ameliorate the issue also carried into online student interactions.

> I love how playful all the images and the typeface is [sic]. I also agree that the contrasting dark and yellow are very on theme with the sleep concept, it's just a weeee [sic] bit hard to read with the font, maybe bolding next time would work! (Student forum post)

It was clear that critique had been carefully considered and aligned with potential ways to address the perceived areas needing further work. The following comment refers to Figure 17.2:

> I really like the look and feel of the background as well as the 8-bit style. Both go well with what you're educating the audience about. I think that the style of the other graphics (ghost, ring, etc.) and the textboxes ("You can do it!", "Remember …", "Did you know that …") would have been more effective to follow the same 8-bit style. They appear out of place to me in the design. (Student forum post)

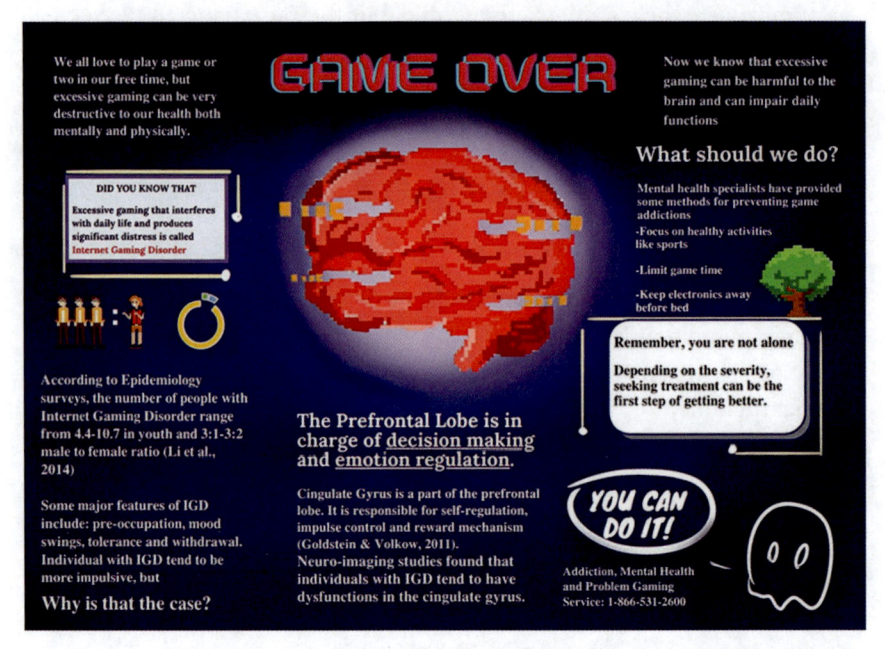

FIGURE 17.2   Game over – student infographic (copy of unpublished student infographic
                        submitted for class assignment, used with permission)

Student willingness to engage in discussion became more and more evident
as the course progressed. The first project, which focused solely on audience
identification included more questioning than suggestions. This fit with the
foci of class discussions and growing awareness of empathising with a specific
audience.

> I like how simple the colours are as well as how neat everything is. There
> is a little confusion on my own part when I first looked at it though that
> may due to me not being in the target audience. (Student forum post)

> Overall, I enjoyed your design and have only one question. Did you
> decide to use a layout for your design and, if so, what layout did you
> use? (Student forum post)

While I struggled to understand the question given that our layout sessions
had not discussed using no layout, the student who received the comment
clearly understood and answered.

> Thanks, for your feedback. I'm happy to hear that you enjoyed the poster
> and found many of the elements hopeful in understanding what the

project is. To answer your questions I did go with a layout design, in my thumbnails, I tried a couple of different layouts designs but was drawn into a 2 bar design with the bars being on the top and bottom with text within them. I then experimented with 2 columns. One of the columns being the main graphic and the other one containing important information about the product. Which you can see with the left side being my main graphic and the right side being my text with important information. (Student forum post response)

In this online exchange, I learned how the students were either understanding or not understanding the course material while the students were gleaning insights about their work because they were communicating with each other. It was heartening to realise that the vital element of discussion about studio work was occurring. Not only were students interacting and responding to each other's visual design work, but they were also doing so in a respectful and honoring manner that allowed learning to occur.

Thus, the forum post 'discussions' not only demonstrated that the students were becoming empathic but also contributed to creating the goal of an online studio. The online discussions also showed that the empathic approach was having an impact on student designs because they were remaining focused on the design goal. The class featured studio exercises as well as formal projects and the exercises were presented with the option of working in groups for the studio practice. Making this optional was important given the different time zones of the students and many did choose to work on their own. Others requested that a forum be created so that they could seek out classmates who would also like to complete their exercises in groups. The proviso that each group member was to create a minimum of 4 thumbnails prior to sharing their ideas resulted in rich discussions about approaches. Because I was invited to sharing sessions to offer guidance, I got to observe the students engaging and sharing their ideas. There were several instances in which students vocalised their delight about being able to build on ideas that were new to them.

10   Conclusion

Although teaching empathic design to help students be more aware visual designers was the initial inspiration, a realisation that there was a reported decline in empathy amongst undergraduate students (Dolby, 2014; Konrath et al., 2011) increased my interest in teaching students to consider empathy in their design planning. As classes moved online and stress mounted, including empathy development in the course appeared fortuitous. Students not only interacted with each other in online forums, but they did so kindly. The empathic focus increased consideration of design goals and this resulted in interactions that offered insight into what each was observing. In addition to glowing endorsements, the observational statements regularly included thoughtful suggestions about potential improvements. This response is one example:

> Thanks for the feedback! I didn't realize but the title could certainly be bigger and would be a small, but overall helpful change! (Student forum post)

Because students often responded to these suggestions with appreciation, it was apparent that the interchange was beneficial to learning.

This study has shown that students can learn empathic design and that this learning has an impact on both their planning and their final designs. While the online environment will not replace the richness of in-person studio learning, it is heartening to know that a combination of careful guidance and the provision of opportunities for posting and responding to visual work can result in an effective studio dialogue that supports artistic learning. As one student emailed, "I feel a lot more confident in my design and layout skills – and now I feel so much more aware of the need for empathy within all of my work, especially during such a difficult time".

References

Aflatoony, L., Wakkary, R., & Neustaedter, C. (2018). Becoming a design thinker: Assessing the learning process of students in a secondary level design thinking course. *The International Journal of Art & Design Education, 37*(3), 438–453. https://doi.org/10.1111/jade.12139

Altay, B., & Demirkan, H. (2014). Inclusive design: developing students' knowledge and attitude through empathic modelling. *International Journal of Inclusive Education, 18*(2), 196–217. https://doi.org/10.1080/13603116.2013.764933

Baldner, C., & McGinley, J. J. (2014). Correlational and exploratory factor analyses (EFA) of commonly used empathy questionnaires: New insights. *Motivation and Emotion, 38*(5), 727–744. https://doi.org/10.1007/s11031-014-9417-2

Bearman, M., Palermo, C., Allen, L. M., & Williams, B. (2015). Learning empathy through simulation: A systematic literature review. *Simulation in Healthcare: Journal of the Society for Medical Simulation, 10*(5), 308–319. https://doi.org/10.1097/SIH.0000000000000113

Biesta, G. (2018). What if? Art education beyond expression and creativity. In C. Naughton & D. R. Cole (Eds.), *Philosophy and pedagogy in arts education* (pp. 11–20). Taylor and Francis.

Bullough Jr., R. V. (2019) Empathy, teaching dispositions, social justice and teacher education, *Teachers and Teaching*, 25(5), 507–522. https://doi.org/10.1080/13540602.2019.1602518

Casale, C., Thomas, C. A., & Simmons, T.M. (2018). Developing empathic learners. *Journal of Thought*, 52(3–4), 3–18. https://www.jstor.org/stable/90026734

Chon, H., & Sim, S. (2019). From design thinking to design knowing: An educational perspective. *Art, Design & Communication in Higher Education*, 18(2), 187–200. https://doi.org/10.1386/adch_00006_1

Crawford, C. M. (2021). The unexpected online learning pivot: Faculty persistence through the swerve and dangle. In C. Crawford (Eds.), *Shifting to online learning through faculty collaborative support* (pp. 19–38). IGI Global. https://doi.org/10.4018/978-1-7998-6944-3.ch002

Cuff, B. M. P., Brown, S. J., Taylor, L., & Howat, D. J. (2016). Empathy: A review of the concept. *Emotion Review*, 8(2), 144–153. https://doi.org/10.1177/1754073914558466

Davis, M. H. (1980). Interpersonal reactivity index (IRI) – Measures empathy. *JSAS Catalog of Selected Documents in Psychology, 10*, 85.

Devecchi, A. & Guerrini, L. (2017). Empathy and design. A new perspective, *The Design Journal*, 20(Supp.1), S4357–S4364, https://doi.org/10.1080/14606925.2017.1352932

Dolby, N. (2014). The future of empathy: Teaching the millennial generation. *Journal of College and Character*, 15(1), 39–44. https://doi.org/10.1515/jcc-2014-0006

Gerdes, K., Segal, E., Jackson, K., & Mullins, J. (2011). Teaching empathy: a framework rooted in social cognitive neuroscience and social justice. *Journal of Social Work Education*, 47(1), 109–131. https://doi.org/10.5175/JSWE.2011.200900085

Graham, M. A. (2020) Deconstructing the bright future of STEAM and design thinking. *Art Education*, 73(3), 6–12. https://doi.org/10.1080/00043125.2020.1717820

Hall, J. A., Schwartz, R., & Duonga, F. (2021). How do lay people define empathy? *The Journal of Social Psychology*, 161(1), 5–24. https://doi.org/10.1080/00224545.2020.1796567

Heimgärtner, R., Tiede, L. W., & Windl, H. (2011). Empathy as key factor for successful intercultural HCI design. In A. Marcus (Ed.), *Design, user experience, and usability* (Pt II, HCII, pp. 557–566), Springer-Verlag.

Helding, L. (2017). Empathy and loving-kindness. *Journal of Singing*, 73(5), 547–551.

Heron, L. M., Agarwal, R., Greenup, J., Attong, N., & Burke, S. L. (2022): Leveraging the design thinking model to address campus accessibility challenges and assess perceptions of disability awareness. *International Journal of Inclusive Education*. https://doi.org/10.1080/13603116.2022.2041111

Hess, J. L., & Fila, N. D. (2016). The manifestation of empathy within design: Findings from a service-learning course, *CoDesign*, 12(1–2), 93–111. https://doi.org/10.1080/15710882.2015.1135243

Ho, K. (2015). Empowering learning and using student exemplars in teaching. *Teaching Artist Journal, 13*(4), 193–203. https://doi.org/10.1080/15411796.2015.1063878

Ickes, W. (2003). *Everyday mind reading.* Prometheus.

IDEO. (n.d.). Webpage. https://ideo.com

James, M. (2017). Advancing design thinking towards a better understanding of self and others: A theoretical framework on how Buddhism can offer alternate models for design thinking. *Art 1, 10*(2), 1–14. https://doi.org/10.7577/formakademisk.1649

Jeffrey, D. (2016). Empathy, sympathy and compassion in healthcare: Is there a problem? Is there a difference? Does it matter? *Journal of the Royal Society of Medicine, 109*(12), 446–452. https://doi.org/10.1177/0141076816680120

Kolawole, E. (n.d.). *Empathy* [Video]. Design Kit brought to you by IDEO.org https://www.designkit.org/mindsets/4

Konrath, S. H., O'Brien, E. H., & Hsing, C. (2011). Changes in dispositional empathy in American college students over time: A meta-analysis. *Personality and Social Psychology Review, 15*(2), 180–198. https://doi.org/10.1177/1088868310377395

Kouprie, M., & Visser, F. S. (2009). A framework for empathy in design: Stepping into and out of the user's life. *Journal of Engineering Design, 20*(5), 437–448. https://doi.org/10.1080/09544820902875033

Luchs, M. G. (2016). A brief introduction to design thinking. In M. G. Luchs, K. S. Swan, & A. Griffin (Eds.), *Design thinking* (pp. 1–11). Wiley.

Luka, I. (2019). Design thinking in pedagogy: Frameworks and uses. *European Journal of Education, 54,* 499–512. https://doi.org/10.1111/ejed.12367

McDonagh, D. (Guest Editor) & Thomas, J. (Guest Editor). (2011). Design + empathy = Intuitive design outcomes. *The Design Journal, 14*(2), 147–150. https://doi.org/10.2752/175630611X12984592779881

Oxman, R. (2017). Thinking difference: Theories and models of parametric design thinking. *Design Studies, 52,* 4–39.

Paron, A.J. (2020). Perspective design for all needs design empathy. *Journal of Interior Design, 45*(4), 3–9. https://doi.org/10.1111/joid.12182

Patel, S., Pelletier-Bui, A., Smith, S., Roberts, M. B., Kilgannon, H., Trzeciak, S., & Roberts, B. W. (2019). Curricula for empathy and compassion training in medical education: A systematic review. *PLoS ONE, 14*(8), e0221412. https://doi.org/10.1371/journal.pone.0221412

Rittel, H. W. J., & Webber, M. M. (1973). Dilemmas in a general theory of planning. *Policy Sciences, 4*(2), 155–169. https://doi.org/10.1007/bf01405730

Silva Pacheco, C. (2020). Art education for the development of complex thinking meta-competence: A theoretical approach. *The International Journal of Art & Design Education, 39*(1), 242–254. https://doi.org/10.1111/jade.12261

Stanford d.school. (n.d.). Webpage. https://dschool.stanford.edu

Teal, R. (2010). Developing a (non-linear) practice of design thinking. *The International Journal of Art & Design Education*, *29*(3), 294–302.

Todd, C., & Norman, J. (2020). Why is design thinking needed in art education? *School Arts*, *120*(3), 14.

Trninic, D. (2018). Instruction, repetition, discovery: Restoring the historical educational role of practice. *Instructional Science*, *46*(1), 133–153. https://doi.org/10.1007/s11251-017-9443-z

Watson, A. D. (2015) Design thinking for life. *Art Education*, *68*(3), 12–18. https://doi.org/10.1080/00043125.2015.11519317

Wispé, L. (1986). The distinction between sympathy and empathy: To call forth a concept, a word is needed. *Journal of Personality and Social Psychology*, *50*(2), 314–321.

Woodcock, A., McDonagh, D., Osmond, J., & Scott, W. (2018). Empathy, design and human factors. In T. Ahram & C. Falcão (Eds.), *Advances in usability and user experience*. Springer. https://doi.org/10.1007/978-3-319-60492-3_54

Xenakis, I. (2018). Reducing uncertainty in sustainable interpersonal service relationships: The role of aesthetics. *Cognitive Processing*, *19*(2), 215–229. https://doi.org/10.1007/s10339-017-0819-4

CHAPTER 18

The Arts Cure

Innovating Equitable Education and Research during and after the Pandemic

Kari-Lynn Winters, Catherine Hands, Snežana Obradović-Ratković and Julianne Burgess

Abstract

In 2020, face-to-face artmaking and artful sharing in education came to a grinding halt as people experienced global shutdowns due to the COVID-19 pandemic. Coronavirus-related disruptions and restraints contributed to feelings of confusion, isolation, and hopelessness. They also raised questions about how the arts could be transformed to create online communities for resilience, healing, and education. This research project explores how online artmaking could be an optimal approach for reshaping equitable education and research. Researchers, educators, administrators, students, and parents, participated in a year-long, online playbuilding process. Throughout their artmaking, the artists shared their teaching, learning, and life experiences during the pandemic, engaging in democratic decision-making related to scene development and the play's production. Data sources included COVID-related images, video recordings of rehearsal meetings, individual and focus group interviews, the online play, and a documentary film about the project. Using a narrative, vignette approach, we coded and categorized data based upon theoretical underpinnings of artmaking for resiliency and healing, as well as equitable teaching and research practices. The analysis process honed-in on the ways that the arts can promote resilience and healing during difficult times, as well as used to create collaborative, equitable online spaces in education. Findings demonstrate that the arts, regardless of being enacted face-to-face or online, can still offer innovative practices that contribute to equitable education and research, as well as artists' resiliency, learning, and wellbeing.

Keywords

drama – playbuilding – online arts research – online arts education – resilience

1 Introduction

As of March 2020, 80% of the world's learners were unable to attend school or university (UNESCO, 2020), with 138 governments closing their educational institutions (McCarthy, 2020). Globally, instructors continue to learn how to use online tools, such as *LifeSize* and *Microsoft Teams,* and become more proficient in using virtual learning management systems for their courses. The need for mastering online synchronous and asynchronous teaching was urgent, but the timeline was short, which endangered teachers' capacities and wellbeing (Fleming, 2020). These challenges opened participatory spaces for reimagining and transforming the arts (Jemal, 2020; Kraehe, 2020) into the vehicles of resilience, healing, wellbeing, and equity within online educational spaces.

In this chapter, we look closely at the ways in which educators can create such a community through playbuilding, which is both a conceptual framework and a participatory arts-based methodology. We address the following research questions:

1. How has the COVID-19 pandemic influenced equitable education?
2. In what ways might educators use artful practice virtually during and after a pandemic in order to build resiliency, inspire healing and a sense of wellbeing, and reimagine equitable teaching and learning practices?

We begin with an overview of relevant literature, discussing resilience, healing and wellbeing, and equitable teaching and learning in relation to arts education – themes that emerged from the data collected during the research study, and as a result of the COVID-19 context. Next, we describe playbuilding and provide examples from our study. Lastly, we summarize findings and provide concluding thoughts.

2 The Power of Arts Education

Social communities establish a sense of identity, inclusion, and belonging amongst their members (Strike, 2002), promoting wellbeing and resilience through equitable practices (Peppler et al., 2022). Participatory drama-based practices in face-to-face environments have been shown to create communities, where artists can develop shared educational goals and build relationships (Sinner & Conrad, 2015). For example, playbuilding is a form of applied theatre, constructed to address key social issues that are of collective importance. This artful approach encourages participation through collaborative leadership (Bishop et al., 2017). Every person involved is both invited to share their stories and to determine what gets included in the play script and its production. These collective practices enhance individuals' respect for one another and their sense of belonging, which in turn, support participants' social and emotional wellbeing (Canevari, 2022).

Shared educational projects are a hallmark of social communities in schools, acting as a "social glue", binding members together (Strike, 2002). However, it is unknown how these benefits transfer to participatory practices within online settings as moving the dramatic arts online may cause a loss of momentum and enthusiasm, collaborative opportunities, relationships, and empathy (Canevari, 2022). In such a context, educators would need to improvise, reframe, and re-imagine equitable education during and after the pandemic (Jemal, 2020; Kraehe, 2020), with the ultimate goal of building and sustaining social communities.

3   Building Resiliency through Arts Education

The global pandemic precipitated widespread instability through rapid and radical changes (Kraehe, 2020) particularly in the ways people teach, learn, and live. Additionally, uncertainties caused by COVID-19 challenged people's resilience. Creative, artful resilience often includes adversity and adjustment to changes and challenges (Gallagher et al., 2017). For example, Brown and colleagues (2017) found participatory drama contributes to knowledge-sharing, perspective-taking, problem-solving, and the adaptive capacity of study participants, who had been marginalized, and their communities with infrastructures negatively impacted by extreme weather events. Alongside community members, participants presented viewpoints, stories, hardships, and co-created possible solutions together (Brown et al., 2017). This kind of resilience is built in the arts through upholding a flexible mindset, strengthening emotional regulation, and understanding others' perspectives (Heise, 2014). Another study used drama methods to address poverty in a large, urban centre (Gallagher et al., 2017). Creative, artful resilience grew from the participants' efforts to theatrically improvise real-life situations and understand alternative world views (Gallagher et al., 2017). Through validating experiences, participants and audience members developed empathy for others and overcame uncertainties.

Both studies demonstrate that resiliency can be strengthened through participatory drama practices. Artful practices, such as these, build participants' coping skills, helping them to withstand hardships, suggesting that, "[t]o be an artist is to be resilient, adaptable, and flexible, while also committing to one's holistic wellness" (Davis, 2020, para. 8). At the same time, social communities are potentially developed as "artists do not operate in isolation" (Brown et al., 2017, p. 8).

4 Healing and Wellbeing through Arts Education

Like resilience, scholars suggest that arts-based practices offer physical, mental, and emotional wellbeing, lifting people out of darkness, isolation, and silence (Sinner & Conrad, 2015; Kivnick & Erikson, 1983). For example, American researchers used online scaffolded theatre workshops to engage with community members during the pandemic, with goals to process collective trauma, and promote dialogues of justice (Dixon et al., 2020). These workshops formed the basis of an online theatre production presented to a virtual audience. The project-built community amongst the participants and improved both their mental health and resilience (Dixon et al., 2020).

Strong communities evoke feelings of belonging and wellness; they have potential to treat and rehabilitate, while sparking individual and social change. For instance, a 10-month research project explored how the arts (and especially playbuilding) have the potential to build cultural bridges, resilience, and coexistence among Indigenous peoples, Canadian-born non-Indigenous peoples, and newcomers to the country (Winters et al., 2022). For the participants, drama, dance, poetry, music, and visual art opened doorways to collaboration, belonging, and healing throughout the shared project. In particular, one member, who was a refugee to Canada, reported her engagement helped repair the emotional traumas of forced migration and personal losses, allowing her to connect with others who also suffered from involuntary displacement. Creative activities can, therefore, enhance people's mental wellbeing and social connectedness. The arts nurture human beings and human relations and have the ability to foster equity, diversity, and inclusion (Ratković et al., 2019).

5 Fostering Equitable Teaching and Learning through Arts Education

An awareness of others and being responsive within communities can be a starting point for equitable education. Collaborative practices in the arts can oppose existing localized beliefs, blur boundaries, and challenge old assumptions (de Bruin et al., 2018). "Rather than one-size-fits-all approaches to designing learning environments, connected learning argues for culturally responsive programs that are tailored to specific interests and identities, and have an explicit emphasis on community connection" (Peppler et al., 2022, pp. 266–277). In one study, the participants fostered social justice and elevated the teachings of the ancestors, while healing through laughter, belonging, and applied theatre practices (Arteaga & Chavez-Arteaga, 2021). Their sociopolitical scenes provoked critical thinking for them and their audiences while honouring the Chicanx/Latinx peoples' histories and values and restoring equitable practices. In this and other studies, participatory drama adds to the quality of life of its participants by making them feel included and united in a common cause with a sense of purpose (Arteaga & Chavez-Arteaga, 2021; Rogers et al., 2015). These inclusive artful practices strengthen communities and offer members equitable spaces to learn and grow (Rogers et al., 2015).

Existing research demonstrates that face-to-face artful practices contribute to participants' equitable teaching and learning, healing, wellbeing, and resiliency. Owing to the pandemic's recency, little research has been published that examines whether online artful practices have the same potential impact. Bringing theatrical face-to-face learning principles to online teaching and community building may provide equitable opportunities for shaping people's self-expression and coping skills, promoting renewal and wellness for people in various communities. To achieve these goals, we examined the potential of online playbuilding in this chapter.

6   Conceptual Framework and Research Methodology

Playbuilding is an emergent, collaborative scripting, and performing experience (Tarlington & Michaels, 1995), as well as a profound and innovative arts-based research methodology (Norris, 2009). It uses a "build it, from the ground up" cumulative and inclusive approach (Taylor, 2020). Participatory drama practices, such as playbuilding, begin with an ensemble – the participants and their values, experiences, and relationships. Skills gained by the members include working collaboratively, listening to and valuing individual perspectives, developing confidence, building a sense of belonging, and engaging in a process fully to bring the project to fruition (Brown, 2014). Moreover, it highlights how people with diverse backgrounds and a common goal can collaboratively and creatively mediate data and re-shape understandings about a topic (Norris & Saudelli, 2018). Since the study context was (in part) determined by governing legislation regarding COVID-19 (e.g., self-isolation, physical distancing rules), our playbuilding approach became virtual.

We used purposeful sampling (Merriam, 1998). The criteria for recruitment required study participants to be members of the Brock community (e.g., faculty, students, alumni, previous research participants) or stakeholders in education (e.g., school administrators, principals, teachers). All participants needed to demonstrate an interest in arts education, have internet access, and be willing to be photographed/videoed and share these photos/videos. Fourteen study participants from across Canada took part in the study, ranging in demographic characteristics, such as age, gender, race, and ethnicity.

Throughout the playbuilding process, we worked individually and in small groups in Microsoft (MS) Teams or Lifesize discussing, co-writing, and performing scenes about the pandemic, exploring how it had affected our lives or the field of education. We wove together scenes, creating a 45-minute theatrical play and a documentary film about the project, bringing data to life through embodiment (e.g., movement, actions, facial expressions) and media applications (e.g., Jamboard). Next, we determined which scenes would be included and voted upon the order of the scenes. Every participant was included in this process. When scenes were ready, they were rehearsed, performed, and recorded, and later edited by a professional filmmaker. The collective viewed the final play and film before they were shared publicly, giving each member another opportunity to express opinions and feelings.

We collected rehearsal, interview, and focus group transcripts and video recordings, meeting notes, scripted work samples, screenshots, as well as artifacts about the COVID-19 pandemic. The researchers interviewed study participants, and each other, for 30–45 minutes – all were video recorded using MS Teams or LifeSize. Our research questions guided the data analysis. We coded data based on three theoretical underpinnings: resilience, healing and wellbeing, and equitable education. We first honed-in on these themes individually, identified sub-themes, and then came together to discuss and agree upon our findings. Except for the researchers (Kari-Lynn, Cathy, and Snežana), pseudonyms were used for all the participants.

7   Tales from Computer Screens

Hardships weaved their way throughout the COVID-19 pandemic, and hence, throughout our play. Participants had concerns about heavier workloads and stress, childcare, imposed restrictions, as well as isolation, illness, and loss. Alexa, for example, faced numerous setbacks during the pandemic:

> I was doing my masters thesis. I was grieving. My mother had died. My father was dying. Before the pandemic I was working as an actor. I could carve out my own space. Just before the pandemic, I was told that I had been exposed [to COVID-19] ... My husband lost his job. There was a lot

of unknown. A lot of losses. Schooling became troublesome. I wasn't a
teacher. [My] twins didn't want me in their classroom.

Nina, too, felt stressed because of the isolation she experienced being stuck
in a two-bedroom apartment in graduate student housing. Her children could
only get out on the balcony for fresh air. She did all the errands, including
grocery shopping, to protect her children from exposure to COVID-19. Others
faced additional challenges: home schooling, working from home, and building an online community. Themes of resilience, personal healing and wellbeing, as well as the impact of arts education on equitable education arose and
were touchpoints for participants' reflections during and after the project's
conclusion.

8   Enduring the Storm

For most, the pandemic deepened life's challenges. COVID-19 protocols
inspired unprecedented change and evoked feelings of confusion. And for
some, living a life without art left them bewildered. Kari-Lynn used an artful
approach to resiliency, she wrote scenes to maintain a sense of community
and help her cope during the pandemic. This scene is about when things first
began to change:

At First It Fell

Light like a snowflake.
A bit over there. Across the ocean. A bit over here. Closer to home.
News forecasted more of the same.
Coming our way.
More of the same.
Prepare for the storm ...

For Kari-Lynn, the pandemic fell slowly at first, with a foreboding sense that
things were going to get bad. Returning from New York city in late February
2020, she witnessed an empty airport. Never in her travels had she experienced
a sight like that!

Separation and isolation followed as government restrictions fell upon citizens world-wide. Confusion arose. And confidence dwindled as disruptions
bombarded us. A section from our *Kaleidoscopes* play demonstrates these
challenges:

Tug of War

(Is it real?!)
Dana: Look at the numbers!!
Alexa: It's a conspiracy!
Snežana: I don't believe this!
Rachel: My mother died.

Locked down in our homes, participants were divided physically and emotionally. Nina spoke of division – a wall between us. We were together, but separate. We thought about unity, while feeling alone. Dana missed face-to-face arts practices.

> I used to participate [in] playbuilding projects. I was also immersed in my undergrad in [the dramatic arts] program. When this phase of my life stopped and COVID started, I couldn't do it. I struggled ... I knew I needed the arts.

Dana joined the project to bring art back into her life. Nina agreed, saying playbuilding offered "a great opportunity" for her and her children "to re-engage in artful activities". Both participants realized the project helped them maintain social connectedness and overcome adversity. For others, the play offered new perspectives. Peter stated, "Before [the pandemic], I could only attach those types of [challenges] to individual experiences. And now I can see it more as a collective experience – a broader set of experiences". Some participants demonstrated resilience as parents and as students. Denise, a parent of two and a PhD student, states:

> Everyone was going to school at the same time ... [My] children were not showing faces – often talking to a blank screen ... but I can't let this bother me ... I do not want to police others in their space. If the screen is off or on, I can only control myself.

Denise regulated her emotions and thought rationally about the situation. She let go of what was beyond her control. Nina could relate. Also, a parent and a doctoral student, she experienced a lack of control due to the lockdowns:

> The children's schooling switched to online learning. I had reservations about online learning because it's not comparable to in-person learning [and it's] not healthy to watch a screen for hours.

To deal with her frustration, Nina relied on the project. It gave her an opportunity to dialogue with others, and also work alongside her children. Monika's parenting of twin kindergarten children during the pandemic reminded her to be more empathetic as an educator, "[I need] to stop and think where learners are coming from and what might be going on in their lives". Here, these parents built creative resilience to the hardships they were experiencing by reframing their thoughts, focusing on what was within their control, and understanding the perspectives of others. Additionally, the project promoted good stress management skills, including emotional regulation, so that they felt they could not only survive, but also connect, contribute, and prosper.

9   Pathways to Wellbeing and Healing

Living in isolation took a toll on participants' wellbeing. Cathy pondered about creating a community in times of physical distancing and isolation:

> It's so ironic. We're trying to create a community when actually our community is being segregated and compartmentalized, we are isolated to some degree. Even online we were not able to engage in a physical way with other people. And at the same time, we're trying to build a community.

Denise also recognized this conundrum of being together while being in isolation: "We cannot be brilliant nor sustain passion in isolation". These challenges jeopardized some participants' sense of belonging and wellbeing. The play and the playbuilding community, as disembodied as they were, ignited healing and wellbeing among participants. For example, Alexa appreciated connecting online:

> There is something about doing it online that makes it accessible ... In the old world, it would be hard to get all of us together. I wouldn't get to be in a room with people who bring so much ... Our project took some of the stress out of it.

Kari-Lynn agreed, "Being online allowed me to reconnect with friends from coast to coast". Monika too, loved the online community: "[The] project started in the thick of the pandemic, a reminder to weather the season and get through it ... [and] to reach out and connect with people". For some, the playbuilding increased feelings of renewal and belonging both inside and outside the project. Most participants also discovered joyful art activities at home, which increased their energy level and wellbeing. Peter shared his collaborative involvement in the arts at home:

> [W]e have two daughters, so we have done things that we have not done before. We have done some knitting ... a lot of painting ... colouring ... Seeing other peoples' creativity resonates with me.

For Cathy, the project reconfirmed her love for the arts:

> I really, really enjoyed the found poems. Pictures or audio files or video files inspire me ... I loved that the scene writing came quite easily to me ... The project itself was a breath of fresh air, a bit of a reawakening for me. I even started learning to play the guitar!

For Nina, playbuilding brought out the lighter side of everyone, promoting collaboration, respect, and community wellbeing. A few participants spoke of the need to heal. Sara, for example, stated: "The pandemic traumatized everybody ... and playbuilding gave us an opportunity to express how we experienced the pandemic". Additionally, several participants had endured deaths in their families. Snežana shared: "Some people are losing important people in their life. I lost my parents ... It just builds up". Alexa observed the power of community, "When people grieve, they need others". For some, our project was a "lifeline", offering them opportunities to stay connected. Alexa acknowledged the healing power of the arts:

> Artful practice [during COVID-19] is a form of self-care ... [U]ncovering self-knowledge and learning about others is healing. It is play. There is no necessary result. It feels more like community building – which is healing and social ... Everyone's personal stories are valuable and interesting.

For Alexa, the project's playfulness sparked her passion to help others heal:

> I am going to do some work in a hospice. I want to learn about facilitating support groups and educating ... I was thinking about how I could write stories about grief and help others ... I want to help others.

Watching final versions of the play and the film was healing for Snežana because it (playbuilding and life) did work out in the end. Some scenes made her laugh. Witnessing sadness and humor at the same time was cathartic and made Snežana proud of their play, their film, and their playbuilding community: "The laughter was healing despite and because of the long months of COVID-19, strain, and isolation".

10   Reimaging Equitable Education

All participants expanded their understandings of equitable education. Sara summarized: "Education is equitable when all students have access to the resources they need to build their skills. Equity is not the same as equality. Equity is providing what students need to perform at their best". Sara felt all students deserve access to learning opportunities regardless of their ability, age, gender, and cultural background.

The pandemic demonstrated that equitable education's parameters need to be broadened, considering children learning at home and being supported by their parents, affording the technology, and securing the infrastructures that support reliable internet access. For example, Nina spent most of 2021 in Pakistan, and saw unequal access to education across social classes and regions:

> Students did not have the opportunity to access online modules. Access to online learning is a privilege, and public schools' students didn't have access ... I could see the inherent inequality for marginalized students in impoverished or underserved communities.

Sara also observed the widening gap between marginalized and privileged students' academic achievement and wellbeing due to technology access. Even, in a Canadian context, Rachel had unreliable access to MS Teams during our project and Lana was unable to join regularly scheduled videoconference meetings due to bandwidth challenges. To illustrate their experiences, Lana wrote a scene, entitled, *Dis/Connected*, which Rachel and Denise performed.

Actor 1:   Sporrrrraaaaadddddddiiiic connection.
Actor 2:   Connection! Disconnection?
Actor 1:   Connection again! Can you hear me? Can you hear me now?
Actor 2:   Now?
Actor 1:   Uncertainty.
Actor 2:   New learning.
Actor 1:   For everyone.
Actor 2:   For everyone.

Similarly, Ana included a spoken word scene, in which she read a poem twice; the first time, she spoke only a few words in each sentence and then followed with a complete recital. Her scene demonstrated the challenges of communicating online due to weak internet connections. Access limitations decreased these participants' engagement and teaching/learning opportunities. Thus, different forms of participation and media (i.e., home videos, powerpoint slides, audio recordings) were offered by the researchers as ways to keep them involved in the project. Some participants suggested that some aspects of online playbuilding are inequitable due to the disembodied nature of the virtual practice, forcing them to re-imagine equitable drama education in cyberspace. Kari-Lynn observed:

> You don't see the full picture ... You can only see what the person holds up in front of the camera ... You cannot go through the screen. Whereas ... if there are two bodies standing side by side, you could go in between them ... It's unfair to those people who are kinesthetic learners or those with visual impairments.

Denise also found technology limiting, "we're not sharing in a way that's direct when online". Oppositely, some collaborators felt online playbuilding offered a structure for promoting equitable engagement in teaching and learning. Cathy observed:

> It's a very inclusionary equitable approach where everybody has an equal voice. It flattens out the hierarchy. You are not even an instructor, you are more of a facilitator or guide, bringing out the information and the knowledge and the connections amongst the people in the group.

Nina, and Sara agreed. They noted the online playbuilding process made space for everyone's contributions to the play, thus reducing the hierarchical structures typically found in a traditional Canadian education system. Within our study, power dynamics between faculty and students changed, and formal top-down authority was eliminated. Others, like Lana, acknowledged the need to "accept a different way of doing things". In this way the project "challenged how we related to one another, [our] ability to be aware and be reflective, and to come to a space with openness and humility". This mirrors the ideals involved in deconstructing colonization, according to Denise.

With a humble, resourceful mindset, the first step in creating an equitable and artful space in our project was getting to know the people. "Know who the audience is, what their needs are, [and] do they have access to the knowledge?" Sara noted, and Snežana agreed. In some cases, participants needed to supplement communication via computers with paper hardcopies and telephone conversations. For instance, Lana made short films and sent them to her colleagues before in-person, virtual and telephone meetings. Above all, this participant noted the importance of being perseverant in her efforts to communicate with others and ensure their ability to communicate as well.

11   Artful Practices and Their Application in a Post-Pandemic World

Throughout the pandemic and in its aftermath, participants reflected on how COVID-19 impacted their artful practice within educational contexts. All participants could imagine teaching in person in artful ways in the future, but some were still challenged to teach online, although they agreed it was possible. For the seven arts educators in the study, the pandemic did not change their passion for the arts, just the ways they engaged in their practice. Kari-Lynn observed:

> I've learned how to integrate technology, which is something that I'd never do; I was against using technology with the arts because I felt it took away from the visceral experience of the arts. I now see that technology can be integrated, and that online practices can help students.

Alexa noted that "[Online art] can assist us to stay in the moment and deepen our attention on the other people and react to the subtle details we get to see [close-up] on the screen". Not everyone felt the same as Kari-Lynn and Alexa. For instance, Rachel and Dana wondered if there was anyone engaged on the receiving end of their online drama classes. Dana did not enjoy online teaching, noting it was inappropriate because it was without embodiment (i.e., limited gestures, actions, facial expressions).

Participants noted the playbuilding process was transformational, impacting their teaching, research, and practices. It served as a personal affirmation of the importance to practice the arts, not only by producing it, but also by appreciating it in its various forms. Kari-Lynn noted the project opened her mind to what it means to be "creative in an online environment". She built her skills watching online plays, taking a variety of online writing courses, and co-chairing an online arts conference. Cathy shared, "The project was really an enormous reawakening ... I can see quite clearly what we can do with arts-based practice, regardless of whether we are online or not". For arts educator

Lana, our online playbuilding project was crucial for sustaining her career in arts education; it jump-started her application of online drama strategies. In the end, she felt offering both online and in-person components was the best way to engage in arts education. Monika changed her lessons, adding a variety of teaching strategies that not only met diverse learners' needs, but also took into consideration her students' learning environments. As a doctoral student, Nina felt inspired by the project and considered an arts-based approach in her research. Alexa wanted to collaborate more with others and work with those who are grieving, based on her positive experiences with our project. Denise realized that playbuilding "allows children to have a multiplicity of ways to access their inner feelings when they don't necessarily have the words". As an adult being introduced to the practices of playbuilding through this project, Sara stated, "it feels amazing to speak my thoughts through [the arts]". Lastly, Peter acknowledged that artful practice is "part of being human ... that we're all engaged with it at different times in our own spheres". Playbuilding confronts social, cultural, and educational divides and helps participants and their communities learn, live, and thrive together (Winters et al., 2022).

12   Thriving through Online Artful Practices and Equitable Education

For centuries people's lives have been enriched through in-person, interactive artmaking within institutional and community contexts. In 2020, though, face-to-face artmaking and artful sharing in education came to a grinding halt as communities confronted global shutdowns due to the COVID-19 pandemic. Coronavirus-related disruptions and restraints contributed to feelings of confusion, isolation, and hopelessness. In addition to uncertainties regarding the pandemic itself, there was also anxiety that came with remote teaching and learning, not to mention the stress of having to balance work, school, and family responsibilities while being locked down together. The pandemic has shown us that people need equitable art education opportunities that not only help them cope, but also thrive during difficult times. In this chapter, we examined the potential for online playbuilding to promote resilience, healing and wellbeing, and equitable teaching/learning opportunities.

Participants in our online community demonstrated coping mechanisms in response to adversity and uncertainties, demonstrating "creative resilience" (Gallagher et al., 2017); they displayed a flexible mindset and became sensitized to others' perspectives (Heist, 2014). Trusting the playbuilding process, participants found universal storylines and overcame setbacks (Winters et al., 2022) caused by COVID-19 and the government's restrictions. For example,

At First It Fell was a poem created in isolation, but through our playbuilding process, the participants concluded they had similar experiences. Peter acknowledged a change in his thinking. He explained that the participants' individual encounters now felt like a collective experience. Knowing that others have similar (and different) experiences, gave several participants a sense of wellbeing and resilience.

Regulating emotions is a protective "resilience factor" (Heist, 2014, p. 27) that makes collaboration and decision-making more productive. At times, participants represented opposing viewpoints. Often in the play, participants were asked to state a sentence about struggle or hope that could be reflective of the COVID-19 context. This was expressed in the scene *The Tug of War*. Statements made for the play were not necessarily participants' lived experiences. However, they resonated with true emotions that the participants had observed or heard about. This speaks to Heist's (2014) findings that participants need a flexible mindset to understand the perspectives of others and strengthen emotional regulation. Brown et al. (2017) and the participants in our play, remind us that resilience derives from inviting different perspectives. In drama, it is important to enact different characters, even those that may not reflect one's own feelings, ideas, values, or beliefs. This encourages the development of a collective and critical consciousness within communities (Sinner & Conrad, 2015). Learning how to express oneself (and to listen) inside our project helped build safe spaces for wellbeing and resilience.

Living through the lockdowns increased the stress levels among the project participants. Some participants found it especially difficult to build a supportive community online during isolation. For example, Cathy acknowledged the challenge of building a community, while being disconnected and compartmentalized. Denise agreed, "nobody can shine in isolation and sustain passion when alone". Dana also felt isolated and trapped without community: "It was hard to feel connected". However, mirroring Wilson et al.'s (2022) findings, some participants argued that online arts facilitated their social connectedness, community building, and belonging. This difference in participants' responses may have been rooted in their different personalities, life experiences, or concepts of community.

For most of the participants, our online artful engagement was a pathway to managing stress, increasing a sense of wellbeing, and experiencing joy. Monika and Alexa, for example, revealed that the play helped them relieve stress and maintain wellbeing. These findings concur with Rogers et al.'s (2015) and Winters et al.'s (2022) claims that artful practices provide an escape from life and its anxieties. Moreover, Peter – who experienced the playbuilding project (and the arts in general) as something uncomfortable – realized that the arts helped him reconnect with his daughters and enjoy other people's creativity. Cathy felt the same; the project reawakened her love for the arts.

For some participants, our online playbuilding project offered opportunities to connect, empathize, and heal during the lockdowns. For example, Snežana and Alexa acknowledged the healing power of the arts (Kivnick & Erikson, 1983) while experiencing deaths in their families. Alexa shared that collaborating with others in our project was a coping mechanism, "When people grieve, they need others". For Alexa, and as suggested by Arteaga and Chavez-Arteaga (2021), drama was a form of self-care, self-reflection, education, and healing because everyone's personal stories were valuable and interesting. Moreover, she highlighted that the arts are also about compassion; "I am taking a course about learning about grief, while grieving ... I want to help others".

Some participants found that experiencing the playbuilding process and watching the play and the film was cathartic and empowering. Witnessing sadness and humor, as well as struggle and hope, made the COVID-19 pandemic not only bearable, but also inspiring. Snežana shared: "The laughter was healing". Like Arteaga and Chavez-Arteaga's (2021) claim, the humorous scenes in our play provoked critical thinking, asserted cultural identities, and reaffirmed equitable practices within our playbuilding community. We experienced healing through laughter and belonging – united in a common cause.

Through our project, we explored how artful practices can be woven into teaching practices and learning opportunities online and in person. Similarly to Rogers et al. (2015), we found these practices to be a welcome addition to equitable education, contributing to the multiple ways of communicating and meeting students' diverse needs. Concurring with Sinner and Conrad (2015), Cathy described playbuilding as an "inclusionary equitable approach where everybody has an equal voice". Denise agreed and noted that online artful practice offered flexibility within the pandemic's "culture of rigidity".

Our practices were not entirely successful; they were limited by internet access and connection stability as well as the parameters of the medium itself – a lack of embodiment, limited contextual information, and the irony of creating a community in isolation. For example, Kari-Lynn observed: "You don't see the full picture ... You can only see what the person holds up in front of the camera. You cannot go through the screen". Concurring with Reynolds (2020), not all participants preferred the online medium for playbuilding. Yet, the online project provided learners with additional teaching and learning opportunities and ways of sharing knowledge. Moreover, the process of playbuilding was transformational for many participants – as Norris and Saudelli (2018) suggested – inspiring them to apply the arts in future face-to-face and online teaching/learning practices.

13   Recommendations for Practice and Policy

We highlight implications for policy and practice, offering several suggestions for enhancing resilience, wellbeing and healing, and equitable education through artful practice. The pandemic encouraged a broader conception of equitable education, casting a spotlight on socio-economic issues, family capacity, and connectivity as factors enabling or limiting children's equitable online learning.

Arts-based pedagogies, such as playbuilding, promote equitable learning opportunities for all. Playbuilding flattens the hierarchy, so that all students have a voice, engage in their education, and contribute to their and others' learning. The pedagogical structure of playbuilding ensures all learners are included. As a result, participants see themselves reflected in the work that is produced. Here, students' gender, age, cultural background, and socio-economic status are not obstacles to their engagement. Further, playbuilding strategies serve to increase the variety of ways people access and share information; it is done in an engaging and active manner that is driven by the interests of the participants, in both face-to-face and online environments.

During the pandemic, school districts were challenged to provide technology to all students. Students without appropriate technology still needed access to curriculum to avoid gaps in their learning. Policymakers and practitioners need to provide technological resources to create equitable and artful spaces in education. COVID-19 uncertainties raised questions about how the arts could be transformed and used for resilience, healing, and equitable education within online spaces. Addressing these questions, we gained a deeper understanding of the rapid shifts in education during the pandemic, imagined innovative forms of equitable education through the arts, and informed educational practice and policy. As we chart new territory with online playbuilding, we invite scholars and educators to further explore this arts-based pedagogy and research methodology.

References

Arteaga, M., & Chavez-Arteaga, A. (2021). Laughter, healing, and belonging: Cada quien tiene su lugar. In E. D. Cruz, L. S. Brenner, & C. Cerasco (Eds.), *Applied theatre with youth: Education, engagement, activism* (pp. 145–153). Taylor and Francis. https://doi.org/10.4324/9781003039419

Bishop, K., Weigler, W., Lloyd, T., & Beare, D. (2017). Fostering collaborative leadership through playbuilding. *New Directions for Adult and Continuing Education, 2017*(156), 65–75. https://doi.org/10.1002/ace.20260

Brown, H. (2014). *10 steps to collaborative playbuilding*. Sydney Theatre Company. https://d2wasljt46n4no.cloudfront.net/pdf/content-pages/community-pages/ STC_EBOOK_10STEPS_1.pdf

Brown, K., Eernstman, N., Huke, A. R., & Reding, N. (2017). The drama of resilience: Learning, doing, and sharing for sustainability. *Ecology and Society*, 22(2):8, 1–8. https://doi.org/10.5751/ES-09145-220208

Canevari, M. (2022). What we do doing theatre at school. An experience of social theater in Italy during the COVID-19 pandemic: An ethnographic research. *World Futures*, 78(6), 392–414. https://doi.org/10.1080/02604027.2022.2111963

Davis, T. C. (2020, Mar 23). *Teaching performing arts during the pandemic*. Howlround Theatre Commons. https://howlround.com/teaching-performing-arts-during-pandemic

de Bruin, L. R., Burnard, P., & Davis, S. (2018). *Creativities in arts education, research and practice: International perspectives for the future of learning and teaching*. Brill. https://doi.org/10.1163/9789004369603

Dixon, S. L., Gundersen, A., & Holiman, M. (2020). The# StayHome Project: Exploring community needs and resiliency through virtual, participatory theatre during COVID-19. *ArtPraxis*, 7(2a), 70–88. https://sites.google.com/nyu.edu/artspraxis/ 2020#h.p_3DTQw3g8Kzov

Fleming, N. (2020, May 8). *Curbing teacher burnout during the pandemic*. Edutopia. https://www.edutopia.org/article/curbing-teacher-burnout-during-pandemic/

Gallagher, K., Starkman, R., & Rhoades, R. (2017). Performing counter-narratives and mining creative resilience: Using applied theatre to theorize notions of youth resilience. *Journal of Youth Studies*, 20(2), 216–233. https://doi.org/10.1080/ 13676261.2016.1206864

Heise, D. (2014). Steeling and resilience in art education. *Art Education (Reston)*, 67(3), 26–30. https://doi.org/10.1080/00043125.2014.11519270

Jemal, A. (2020). Pandemic lessons. *ArtsPraxis*, 7(2a). https://sites.google.com/ nyu.edu/artspraxis/2020/volume-7-issue-2a/jemal-orourke-lopez-hipscher-pandemic-lessons?pli=1

Kivnick, H. Q., & Erikson, J. M. (1983). The arts as healing. *American Journal of Orthopsychiatry*, 53(4), 602–618. https://doi.org/10.1111/j.1939-0025.1983.tb03405.x

Kraehc, A. M. (2020). Dreading, pivoting, and acting: The nature of art curriculum in a post-pandemic world. *Art Education (Reston)*, 73(4), 4–7. https://doi.org/10.1080/ 00043125.2020.1774320

McCarthy, N. (2020, March 26). *COVID-19's staggering impact on global education*. World Economic Forum. https://www.weforum.org/agenda/2020/03/infographic-covid19-coronavirus-impact-global-education-health-schools/

Merriam, S. B. (1998). *Qualitative research and case study applications in education* (2nd ed.). Jossey-Bass Publishers.

Norris, J. (2009). *Playbuilding as qualitative research: A participatory arts-based approach*. Left Coast Press.

Norris, J., & Saudelli, M. G. (2018). Heating up online learning: Insights from a collaboration employing arts-based research/pedagogy for an adult education, online, community outreach undergraduate course. *Social Sciences, 7*(7), 1–23. https://doi.org/10.3390/socsci7070104

Peppler, K., Dahn, M., & Ito, M. (2022). Connected arts learning: Cultivating equity through connected and creative educational experiences. *Review of Research in Education, 46*(1), 264–287.

Ratković, S., Winters, K. L., Kitchings, S., Yang, S., Spratt, B., Ahmed, N., & Vinod, S. (2019). Five poems: Artistic pedagogy of the migrant soul. *Teaching and Learning Journal, 12*(1), 15–31. https://doi.org/10.26522/tl.v12i1.447

Reynolds, R. E. (2020). Theatre through a computer: A critical reflection of online teaching during the COVID-19 pandemic. *ArtsPraxis 7*(2a), 1–12. https://sites.google.com/nyu.edu/artspraxis/2020/volume-7-issue-2a/reynolds-theatre-through-a-computer?pli=1

Rogers, T., Winters, K.-L., Perry, M., & LaMonde, A.-M. (2015). *Youth, critical literacies, and civic engagement: Arts, media, and literacy in the lives of adolescents*. Routledge, Taylor & Francis Group.

Sinner, A., & Conrad, D. (2015). *Creating together: participatory, community-based, and collaborative arts practices and scholarship across Canada*. Wilfrid Laurier University Press.

Strike, K. A. (2002). Community, coherence, and inclusiveness. In P. T. Begley & O. Johansson (Eds.), *The ethical dimensions of school leadership* (pp. 61–76). Kluwer Academic Publishers.

Tarlington, C., & Michaels, W. (1995). *Building plays: Simple playbuilding techniques at work*. Pembroke Publishers.

Taylor, M. (2020). *Playbuilding for environmental literacy: A guidebook resource for secondary educators* [Unpublished Master's research paper]. Brock University.

UNESCO. (2020). *Education: From school closure to recovery*. https://www.unesco.org/en/covid-19/education-response

Wilson, C., Munn-Giddings, C., Bungay, H., & Dadswell, A. (2022). Arts, cultural and creative engagement during COVID-19: Enhancing the mental wellbeing and social connectedness of university staff and students. *Nordic Journal of Arts, Culture and Health, 4*(1), 1–13. https://doi.org/10.18261/njach.4.1.2

Winters, K. L., Obradović-Ratković, S., Longboat, C., & Dénommé-Welch, S. (2022). Building intercultural mentorship, wellbeing, and wholistic practice in graduate education: Scholarly reflections on playbuilding, storytelling, and the arts. In S. Obradović-Ratković, M. Bajovic, A. Pinar Sen, V. Woloshyn, & M. Savage (Eds.). *Supporting student and faculty wellbeing in graduate education: Teaching, learning, policy, and praxis*. Routledge. https://doi.org/10.4324/9781003268185

CHAPTER 19

What a Child Can Learn from Visual Arts

An Observation from a Math Education Researcher during the Pandemic

Xiong Wang

Abstract

We generally believe that children could benefit from art activities, but teachers or parents in particular might not be very clear about what a child can learn from doing art activities (Eisner, 1978/2002). As a parent and math education researcher, I expect a definite answer to that question. This called me to initiate an investigation on the growth of my son Colin in visual arts (e.g., drawing, painting, and crafts). During the pandemic, based on my observation of his online learning, I tried to understand what arts meant to him by using the epistemology of a whole person as the theory and interpretive inquiry as the methodology.

My observations and interpretations enabled me to reveal Colin's development in visual arts, including the changes in his affections for arts, the improvements in his art skills, and the influences of his growth in arts upon his school arts, writing, cultural awareness, science, mathematical thinking, and arts identity. The interpretations allow the emphasis of "goodness" of visual arts to be shown as grounded knowing rather than as "lofty but broad assumptions" (Kindler, 2010, p. 2).

Keywords

visual arts – growth in arts – art creation – children's art learning – learning from arts

1 Background

We generally believe that children could benefit from art activities. For instance, interactions with arts in the primary context can empower children's creative and emotive expression and their voice (Beachum & Gibson, 2019). Artistic themes are meaningful for the learning process in social interaction (Ramli & Musa, 2020). However, arts are often sidelined in school curriculum (Gibson & Larson, 2007; Tate, 2018). It might not be very clear for teachers and parents to know what a child can actually learn from arts (Eisner, 1978/2002;

Van't Hul, 2022). As a parent and math education researcher, I expect a specific answer to that question. As Rainford (2020) advocates that we should explore the role of creativity in enhancing children's development, I therefore initiated an investigation on the growth of my son Colin in visual arts (mainly about drawing, painting, and crafts). During the pandemic, I tried to observe and understand what Colin could learn from doing the arts through working with him at home.

I encouraged Colin to join a Sunday art class two years ago when he was 9 years old based on my judgement that he might be interested in drawing or painting. At the age of 2 years old, he was very fascinated by colours, very fond of recognising 200 colours of crayons. In Grade one, he always liked spending two or three hours in drawing pictures for his stories before writing the sentences. Unexpectedly, however, at the beginning of the art class, Colin did not enjoy drawing in the least as he did not feel the sense of accomplishment when he finished an artwork. This confused me so much that I was driven to think about what the arts meant to him. Such thoughts called me to initiate an observation of his art learning process. During COVID-19, as it happened that his art class was delivered online, I had an opportunity to be able to observe his whole learning process in and out of the class. This enabled me to have a deeper understanding of what and how he could learn from doing art activities. Encouragingly, my observation not only found an answer to my confusions but offered me surprises and even more insights into his art learning as well.

2   A Whole Person

When I decided to investigate Colin's growth in arts, my big concern was about what I should pay attention to. Theoretically, Indigenous pedagogies highlight the development of a child as a whole person (Antoine et al., 2018). But practically, our evaluation or understanding of their learning dominantly values their academic or cognitive knowledge disregarding the significance of a child's development in "self-awareness, emotional growth, social growth, and spiritual development" (p. 18). The broadened perspective of viewing a child's development challenges dominant ideologies which ignore emotional and spiritual domains in children's learning (Antoine et al., 2018). In essence, their emotional and spiritual developments in arts are crucial because the artistic process explores the object nature of things as well as the more subjective and spiritual aspects of life, nature, and culture (Zucker, 2019) and it can integrate mind, body, emotion, and spirituality (Lilly & Venukapalli, 2020; Lo & Matsunobu, 2014; Metzger, 2015).

I have had the experiences of adopting the epistemology of developing a child as a whole person in my research on students' mathematics learning. With such experiences, I decided to try the epistemology of a child as a whole person to observe Colin's learning process in arts. It is inspiring for me to see a child's learning beyond the dominate academic or cognitive knowledge.

3 Interpretive Inquiry

This study adopted interpretive inquiry as the methodology. Interpretive inquiry is conducted to develop an understanding that is more informed and sophisticated than the previously held one (Guba & Lincoln, 1994). It can help us perceive learning actions, expressions, or phenomena in a more intense, careful, and self-conscious way when we do not understand them very well (Smith, 1992). Furthermore, for interpretive inquiry, there is no meaning or knowledge out there waiting for being uncovered and it is the act of understanding that brings the meaning or knowledge into being (Ellis, 1998). In that sense, I used interpretive inquiry to understand Colin's learning from doing art activities and its meanings to him as a whole person in terms of the Indigenous wholistic view (Cull et al., 2018).

My background of math education research to varying degrees would impact my perspectives of observations and interpretations. For interpretive inquiry, our standpoints, experiences, pre-understanding, or prejudices are not taken as a concern but an asset, because these could help us see what makes sense to us (Ellis, 1998). My interpretations went through several interpretative circles (see Figure 19.1) derived from Davis and Renert's (2014) nested ecosystems. During my working with Colin, the first thing I noticed was his changes in affections for visual arts, which was taken as the first layer of my inquiry (Figure 19.1). The changes arose from confining himself in his own self-defined art world to connecting with an outside art space and to creating an art world beyond in his own way. This inspired me to question about what could make such changes occur. The inquiry directed me to examine the details involved in the process of Colin's doing his artworks, which brought forth another layer of investigation on Colin's growth in arts – the improvements in his art skills (Figure 19.1). The investigation revealed his improvements he made in pencil sketch, line drawing, still life drawing, figure drawing/painting, watercolour painting, oil pastel drawing, and artwork creation. It was evident that Colin could draw, paint, or make crafts better than before. However, I was curious about how these improvements impacted on him as a whole person. Thus, this further motivated me to expand my inquiry to another layer – the influences of

FIGURE 19.1
Interpretation circles

his growth in arts (Figure 19.1). This layer included enhancing his performance in school arts, reshaping the way of writing, experiencing the connections between culture and artwork creation, reinforcing science interests, presenting mathematical thinking, and reforming arts identity. Theoretically, the nested inquiry layers unfold from and are enfolded in one another. To understand one layer is to understand all the other layers. In nature, the inquiry layers are inextricable (Davis & Renert, 2014). In the following sections, I will illustrate the emergent interpretations from the whole inquiry.

4   Interpretation Results

4.1   *The Changes in Colin's Affections for Visual Arts*

Colin's changes in affection for visual arts had experienced the following process: a shift from confining himself to drawing his own favorite topics only (e.g., planets) in his self-defined art world (Early July 2020), first to trying the suggested topics by his teacher who encouraged him to jump out of his own world into an outer art space (Early September 2020), and then to creating an art world beyond in his own way (Early October 2020).

4.1.1   Self-Defined Art World

When he started his online art class, Colin merely immersed himself in drawing his own favorite topic – planets. In doing the art assignments, he only drew different forms of planets out of his mind (see Figure 19.2a) with complete

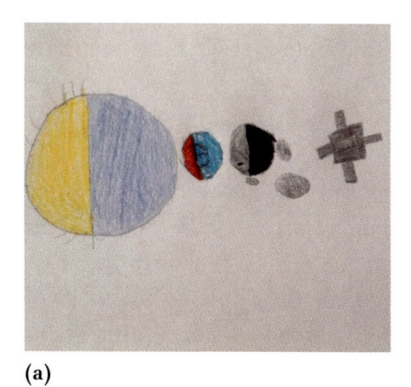

(a) (b)

FIGURE 19.2   Planet and jungle with aliens drawing: (a) March 23, 2020; (b) September 17, 2020

ignorance of his teacher's instructions and recommendations. Strategically, his teacher never criticised his artworks off the topics but appreciated them in terms of the dedication he made for his favorite subjects. In fact, each artwork he did was of great significance to him personally even though he did not practise or reflect the art skills taught by his teacher in the class. This kind of learning went on for nearly three months.

At that time, I did not know what would happen to him if it lasted longer, and I even took leave to doubt that he might not have the potential to do artworks. Meanwhile, I started to reflect on the meaning of learning visual arts for him. Afterwards, I felt it necessary to do something to let him make changes and get back on the "right" track – acquiring what was taught in the class. I persuaded him to try practicing the art skills taught a little bit in his artworks. Surprisingly, he did not reject my suggestion and followed suit. He applied the shading skills learnt from the class to his drawing of planets. This was a turning point at which he was willing to make changes for drawing his artworks.

Afterwards, I had thought that he might be ready to follow his teacher's suggestions to further improve his artwork, but he was reluctant to do so. I was anxious to push him to initiatively revise his artwork, so I straightforwardly erased the part of his artwork where he was suggested to make changes. But what I didn't expect was that he got so furious about my doing. He said that I had ruined his drawing because that part – the edges of the planet I wiped off could not join other parts together anymore. Actually, he drew the middle area in one stroke. Finally, he grudgingly shaded the middle part again. It was obviously inappropriate what I thought and how I did to push him to make some changes on his artwork because he was not ready to step out of his own world yet. I also came to realise whatever and however he drew were always meaningful to himself as the artworks originated from his own understanding and expression of the planets.

4.1.2   Connecting an Outer Art Space

Colin's self-identified world began to change from when he learnt to draw white clouds in one class. Drawing white clouds needs to mix multiple colours together. Although he still drew his own subject – a planet rather than clouds, he added snow to the planet by unexpectedly applying the skills of drawing clouds taught by his teacher. He also included aliens and fir trees to make his planet more interesting and imaginary. Later he presented his artwork before the whole class and he received much praise from his teacher and classmates for his creation and dedication. From then on, he was greatly motivated to begin building the connection between his own subjects and the outer art space under the guidance of his teacher. He brought his drawing techniques to a new level and he made possible the changes to his self-defined world.

4.1.3   Creating an Art World Beyond

Colin was willing to jump out of his self-defined art world and try to follow his teacher's instruction to draw or paint after he learnt about drawing a jungle based on Henri Julien Felix Rousseau's artworks (see Figure 19.2b). It was the first time that Colin had followed the teacher's instruction to draw the suggested topic during the class. In the drawing he included trees' leaves and stems, the sky, rocks, and a monkey. It was evident that he made a great progress in using colours and caring about the details. More importantly, this time, he based his drawing of the jungle on his observation rather than his own imagination. He also interestingly added his favorite alien figures to the jungle. Actually, the characters of those aliens had been designed for a novel he wrote in his spare time. He consciously included them in many of his later artworks. His attempt enabled himself to see an art world in which he could create various artworks presenting the suggested or proposed topics. Meanwhile, he could bring himself into the art world beyond by adding his favorite subjects (e.g., aliens) as a unique signifier of creation. He enjoyed such kind of creative process very much.

4.2   *The Improvements in Colin's Art Skills*

Colin made a dramatic shift in his affection for arts. This resulted from the improvements in his art skills. The improvements were reflected in such aspects as pencil sketching, line drawing, still life drawing, figure drawing/painting, watercolour painting, oil pastel drawing, and creating artworks.

4.2.1 Pencil Sketching

The skills of shading in pencil sketch were very challenging for Colin. He was impatient not only for making the subtle changes in the shading but also for shading the shadows layer by layer for creating the illusion of form, space, and light. However, he still made a great progress in sketching, first from refusing to do shading, then to making an attempt to shade a shadow very dark at once for example, and finally to being capable to shade an object layer by layer. If he came across a subject he really liked (such as 3-D shapes, especially with details of small pits on the surfaces), he could fully engage himself in its completion. Sometimes, he combined together the sketch and his favorite topic – space. He relocated his sketch of the 3-D shapes in the planetary system.

4.2.2 Line Drawing

Colin was very much willing to explore the line drawing as a way of creating artworks during his learning process. At the very beginning of drawing lines, he even could pay much attention to the details and he could demonstrate the line drawing in his scientific topics. He used different colour lines to create the landscape of exoplanets and the black lines to express his passion for planets and Periodic Table.

4.2.3 Still Life Painting

Drawing a still life was another challenging task for Colin. He refused to draw any still objects for a very long time. The turning point started from the moment when he assembled a planetary model, he was eager to draw it. Observing still objects was a great opportunity for him to practise drawing. In his drawing, he comprehensively presented the composition, proportions, background, positions of the components, the arrangement, shadows, and the light, especially very meticulous about all the details such as the tiny numbers and names on the model.

4.2.4 Figure Drawing/Painting

Drawing/painting people had been a long-standing challenge for Colin. At first, he just refused drawing or painting a figure. I guessed that he was perhaps not interested in drawing "people" as an art topic. But after I saw his first hard try of a figure – a lady (Figure 19.3a), I realized that drawing people was a really challenging task for Colin. Once when he was halfway through his drawing of the lady, he felt that his drawing looked horrible, so he didn't want to continue his drawing. As you can see from Figure 19.3a, the lady he drew was really out of shape. It was evident that drawing a figure was not an easy task for him. But to be honest, that artwork looked so funny that it made me laugh a lot. I gave

(a)   (b)

FIGURE 19.3   Figure drawing: (a) August 28, 2020; (b) October 23, 2020

him encouragement that even a famous artist might not be able to draw such a comic and interesting figure. Unexpectedly, my encouragement rendered Colin to be willing to go on drawing people.

For the second time, he drew a figure (Figure 19.3b) after learning from Jean Siméon Chardin's artwork *Boy with a Spinning-Top*. This time, he felt his drawing was pretty good. He seemed particularly satisfied with the little toy he drew – the spinning-top. Later on, he showed great interests in drawing cartoon characters. Once after learning from Johannes Vermeer's *Girl with a Pearl Earring*, he enthusiastically painted a very vivid cartoon girl.

4.2.5   Watercolour Painting
Of all the drawing or painting methods and techniques, watercolour painting was probably Colin's most favorite one. Only when doing watercolour painting, he was always enthusiastic and voluntary to complete an artwork. He could spend hours in mixing colours constantly to find "right" colours he needed. This might to some extent reflect his early years' fascination with colours. However, he was making colours this time rather than recognising them like before. He gradually became skillful at painting with watercolours: from painting over the pen lines at the beginning to painting precisely inside the pen lines. Meanwhile, he could creatively add his favorite topics (e.g., aliens or planets) to the paintings. When he painted Kafka, a character from *The Metamorphosis*, he

FIGURE 19.4   The lady in gold (December 12, 2020)

added aliens in his painting and let them swim with Kafka; when he learnt about Gustav Klimt's artwork *The Lady in Gold* (Figure 19.4), he painted planets to decorate the background and the dress. This made his paintings look very exotic and imaginary.

4.2.6   Oil Pastel Drawing

Colin very much liked oil pastel drawing because he had many colour choices. But at the beginning, to draw skillfully with oil pastels was very challenging for him, particularly drawing sharp lines or details. Fortunately, however, when he felt unsatisfied with his artworks, he was voluntary to make them revised over and over again. He was enlightened when he created an artwork about a magic banana – Alien's Space Station, including a spaceship, a platform, a power station, aliens and more (see Figure 19.5a). He presented his oil pastel drawing skills pretty well in terms of the colours, the shapes, and the creation. Later on,

(a)   (b)

FIGURE 19.5   (a) The magic banana, October 29, 2020. (b) Dusk in Venice, January 23, 2021

after learning about Claude Monet's artwork *Dusk in Venice*, he was in a great love for the fiery and multi-layered colours, and he was also in a bold attempt to use colours in his drawing. As you can see from Figure 19.5b, he mixed various colours together to present the yellow colour and used the blue to highlight the dusk scene. After learning from Giorgio Morandi's still life painting, he learnt to draw the light colours and the simple shapes of the objects. In fact, Colin has always been fascinated by the shapes of objects. I was not surprised to see that he loved drawing the bottles or boxes presented in Morandi's artworks, but that he liked such kinds of light colours from Morandi's. When doing his artworks with such interests, Colin did not add his favorite topics in his artworks but just showed his understanding of the artworks from Morandi and Monet. His interest in these colours may also be a response to his early years' fascination with colours.

4.2.7   Towards Creation

In the process of improving his art skills, Colin began to think about the combination in his artworks of his favorite themes, drawing or painting methods, and the requirements for the suggested topics by his teacher. Referring to the book *Alice in Wonderland* (assignment requirement), Colin created a character, Alice, in the wonderland of an outer space (Figure 19.6) by including a smiling cat, a magic potion, a card soldier, and a thinking rabbit, by adding his favorite topics such as floating planets, shooting spaceships, tiny aliens and more, and by using the pencil crayon drawing techniques he learnt from the class. This was a truly great change for Colin. His artwork not only satisfied the requirements of his teacher but also involved his favorite subjects as an element or background inside. Adding his favorite elements or backgrounds enabled his artworks to be full of the sci-fiction and exotic charm. This was representative of the bud of his creativity.

FIGURE 19.6   Alice in the wonderland of outer space (November 16, 2020)

4.2.8   Presenting Creation

Recently, Colin focused his artworks more on building the connections between the requirements by his teacher for the suggested topics in his art class and the subjects he always liked drawing in his artworks, and he was able to present the links as a whole instead of simply including his subjects as elements or backgrounds. When he was required to draw a character from the story of *The Nutcracker* for one of his assignments, Colin chose the character of Mouse King and made him as a planet Mouse King. In his drawing, the king was holding a planet cake and cane, wearing a crown with planet jewelry and a robe with planet buttons, and standing on a planet (Figure 19.7). The imaginary details of the Mouse King became indispensable parts of him as a planet king. He blended his favorite subjects and the suggested topic together as a whole.

4.3   *The Influences of Colin's Growth in Arts*

Colin's growth in arts influenced him as a whole person in many ways: his performance in school arts, writing, culture awareness, science, mathematical thinking, and arts identity.

FIGURE 19.7
The planet Mouse
King (March 5, 2022)

4.3.1   Enhancing the Performance in School Arts

For Colin, what he learned in the Sunday art class directly benefited his performance in school arts. He had not showed strong motivation for good performance in arts in his early years of school. However, he was recently able to apply what he learnt from the Sunday art class to his school artworks. This enabled him to perform better in his school arts course. After he learnt from the Sunday art class about how to draw flowers by using pencil crayons, he then used the similar techniques to finish his school art project about Asian Heritage Art – Blue and White Porcelain and Peony.

In addition, what Colin learnt from the Sunday art class extended his art horizons presented in his school artworks. When the Chinese New Year (the year of Ox, 2021) was approaching in 2021, he designed a greeting card for celebrating the Chinese Spring Festival by incorporating his favorite chemical elements with the Chinese New Year's signifier – the Ox. Upon his school celebration for the Chinese New Year, he was invited to present his greeting card before his schoolmates. This card completely surprised his schoolteacher because Colin had always refused drawing or painting animals in his school artworks for a very long time. The online art learning broadened his horizons of drawing and/or painting themes.

4.3.2   Reshaping the Way of Writing

Doing artworks also helped Colin improve his writing and reshape the way of his writing. In doing artworks, he went through several cycles of improving them under his teacher's guidance. Each completed artwork went by the following processes: first making a draft of an artwork, processing its details, and completing it, then revising it according to his teacher's comments, and finally revising it again till to the completion. Unexpectedly, Colin applied such processes of creating an artwork to his writing, facilitating his writing in a deep and sophisticated way. After he finished the first draft of one piece of his writings – A Door to Another Earth (a short suspense story) for a writing competition initiated by his school, he invited me to read it and give him some feedback, then based on my feedback, he revised it, and finally he revisited the revised draft over again until he felt nothing to be desired. His piece was voted as one of outstanding stories in his school. In particular, he was the only writer who created illustrations in the writing, which made his piece very special. Overall, the processes of doing artworks turned out to be an effective way of doing his writing and the capabilities of creating illustrations enriched his writing.

4.3.3   Experiencing the Connections between Culture and Art Creation

Colin's teacher from the Sunday art class carefully conceived the course contents with classic and modern artworks from the East and the West. The contents focused on the western artworks from the famous artists such as Alphonse Mucha, Gian Lorenzo Bernini, Giorgio Morandi, Gustav Klimt, Claude Monet, and you name it. The contents also included some eminent Chinese classical artworks and literature such as *Yungang Grottoes*, *Rivers and Mountains*, *Along the River during the Qingming Festival, Journey to the West*, and so on. These contents provided students not only with a space to understand these profound artworks but with the edification of culture and literature as well. In the art class, children were encouraged to integrate cultural understanding into art creation. After learning about Greek mythology in sculptures and stories in traditional Chinese paintings in the class, Colin created his artworks based on his understanding of these cultures. When he knew about Gian Lorenzo Bernini's god sculptures of Pluto and Proserpina, he immediately associated them with the planets named after these two gods and he created one piece of artwork (Figure 19.8) by putting together the gods in Bernini's sculptures and the two related planets. For another example, after he learnt about people's daily life and the landscape of the capital city during Song dynasty from the classic Chinese painting *Along the River during the Qingming Festival*, he created a 3-D artwork (Figure 19.9) presenting the astronomy phenomena – the occurrence of supernova and solar storm, the people's lives, and the street scenes at that time. The integration of cultural elements into his art creation deepened his viewpoints about those connections.

4.3.4 Reinforcing Science Interests

Colin's exploration in arts strengthened his interests in science. He blended his favorite scientific topics (e.g., planets or periodic elements) into almost his every single artwork. Actually, the blending process could be considered a presentation of his knowing about science. In his creative picture book, *the Unknown World through the Eye*, he based his drawing of the planets on the scientific knowledge including their names, colours, shapes, and positions. Creating artworks has become a way of expressing his passions, interests, and knowledge in science. In turn, his interests and knowledge in science enriched his personal creation of artworks.

FIGURE 19.8   Pluto and Proserpina (May 6, 2021)

FIGURE 19.9   3-D along the river during the Qingming festival (April 30, 2021)

4.3.5   Presenting Mathematical Thinking

Colin's creation of artworks also demonstrated his understanding of mathematical concepts, ideas, or thinking. In the art learning activity of imitating Leonardo da Vinci's artwork *Lady with an Ermine*, he used colours to do the imitation – the planets wearing the colours of *Lady with an Ermine*. This is a kind of conceptual imitation, very abstract and creative.

Another example is, in the activity of using the fruit of pear to create an artwork, he drew an imaginary asteroid with the shape of a pear. The pear-shaped asteroid showed that the connections he built between his artwork and the referent signified an important mathematical concept – equivalence. For instance, in mathematics, a fraction (e.g., $2/3$) in algorithm has the similar form of a rational expression (e.g., $(2x + 1)/(3y - 2)$) in algebra. This allows the properties of fractions to be applicable to rational expressions. The equivalence between fractions and rational expressions (e.g., the form and/or the properties) presents the advancement of mathematics from one area (e.g., algorithm) to another (e.g., algebra). In Colin's drawing of the pear-shaped asteroid, he created the asteroid by applying the form of the pear as a fruit to his favorite subject – planets. This advanced his art creation from one area (e.g., a real object) to his favorite topic (e.g., asteroid).

In addition, inspired by the structures of architectures, he adopted in his fashion design artwork (Figure 19.10) the concepts of transformations and patterns in geometry. Unexpectedly, his creation of artworks involving mathematical thinking also expanded my understanding about mathematics application. It inspired me to think about the reciprocal relationships between art creation and mathematics learning such as learning mathematics from creating arts and using mathematics to enrich art creation. Proudly to say, Colin's artworks have turned into great resources of my teaching for pre-service mathematics teachers. This is beyond what I had ever expected.

4.3.6 Reforming Arts Identity

At the beginning of his art learning in the Sunday art class, Colin refused drawing any topic assigned by his teacher but only used his own favorite ones to do the artworks in his own way. His logic behind that was that he felt it unnecessary to learn arts by exactly following the teacher's instructions because he did not intend to be an artist in the future. However, after he explored his own art world for a while, he was gradually able to integrate his favorite topics into the

FIGURE 19.10
Fashion design (January 30, 2121)

art creation and he began to enjoy the process of integration. As time went by, Colin changed his attitudes towards arts and reshaped his arts identity. Now he prides himself on his skillfulness at drawing, painting, and making crafts and he becomes very confident in his ability of creating an artwork like an artist as he considers himself as an artist. For Colin, arts have become a way of expressing his understanding of the world, generating new knowledge, and identifying himself.

5   Implications

During the art learning, Colin went through the following process: reviewing artworks from famous artists; appreciating peers' artworks; demonstrating and experimenting various drawing and painting techniques; and creating, sharing and revising artworks. The above process of his making an artwork presents a very profound recursive learning (Davis & Simmt, 2016) from the perspective of complexity thinking derived from my research interest in math education. Recursive learning is a contemporary learning concept that describes how people deepen their understanding about phenomena or concepts from different levels and perspectives. It is the occurrence of learning in pursuit of authenticity. For each artwork, Colin made several revisions according to his teacher's feedback and suggestions. The revising process presented evident effects on the improvements of his artworks.

In addition, Colin sometimes might not be very clear or did not know how to fully express his attitudes and aesthetics he held in his artworks. The recursiveness of reviewing artworks can facilitate him to reveal both the aesthetic rationality consciously or unconsciously implied in his artworks and the belief in his aesthetics. The following example demonstrated how his recursively reviewing helped him uncover the implied aesthetics in one of his artworks (referencing to Hayao Miyazaki's artwork *My Neighbor Totoro*). When he created the artwork of Mei and Totoro in an outer space, Colin first tried to darken the background and the ground of the space to highlight the castle and the figure according to his teacher's comments, but he found that the darkened ground was not what he intended to be. Then he erased the dark colour off the ground to keep it as what it had been. The revising process enabled him to realize the aesthetics implied in his original drawing of the ground. It was also considered a process how he revealed the meanings created in the artwork together with its aesthetics (Savva, 2003). The meanings were conceived as the soul of what he created.

6   Conclusion

Overall, Colin's growth in visual arts (drawing, painting, and making crafts) influences him in many aspects such as enhancing his performance in school arts, reshaping the way of his writing, broadening his understanding of culture, strengthening his interests in science, presenting his mathematical thinking, demonstrating his creative thinking, and reforming his arts identity. My unique role as a parent and math education researcher invites me to have distinguishing perspectives of viewing his learning in arts from the conventional perspectives of cultural contexts and cognitive development held in art education (Cunliffe, 2002; Eisner, 2002). And meanwhile, my views elaborate the specific benefits of visual arts for him as a whole person's growth. Certainly, his growth in the visual arts is unique and individual as Feldman (1994) advocates that a child's development in arts is not universal. However, my interpretations of Colin's growth in arts allow the emphasis of "goodness" of visual arts to be shown as grounded knowing rather than as "lofty but broad assumptions" (Kindler, 2010, p. 2).

References

Antoine, A., Mason, R., Mason, R., Palahicky, S., & Rodriguez de France, C. (2018). *Pulling together: A guide for curriculum developers*. BCcampus. https://opentextbc.ca/indigenizationcurriculumdevelopers/

Cull, I., Hancock, R.L.A., McKeown, S., Pidgeon, M., & Vedan, A. (2018). *Pulling together: A guide for front-line staff, student services, and advisors*. BCcampus. https://opentextbc.ca/indigenizationfrontlineworkers

Cuncliffe, L. (1999). Learning how to learn, art education and the 'background'. *Journal of Art and Design Education, 18*(1), 115–121.

Davis, B., & Renert, M. (2014). *The math teachers know: Profound understanding of emergent mathematics*. Routledge.

Davis, B., & Simmt, E. (2016). Perspectives on complexity in mathematics learning. In L. English & D. Kirshner (Eds.), *Handbook of international research in mathematics education* (3rd ed.). Taylor & Francis.

Eisner, E. W. (1978). What do children learn when they paint? *Art Education, 31*(3), 6–11.

Eisner, E. (2002). *The arts and the creation of mind*. Yale University Press.

Ellis, J. (1998). Introduction: The teacher as interpretive inquirer. In J. Ellis (Ed.), *Teaching from understanding: Teachers as interpretative inquirer* (pp. 5–13). Garland Publishing.

Feldman, D. H. (1994). *Beyond universals in cognitive development*. Ablex.

Guba, E. G., & Lincoln, Y. S. (1994). Competing paradigms in qualitative research. In N. K. Denzin & Y. S. Lincoln (Eds.), *Handbook of qualitative research* (pp. 105–117). Sage Publications.

Kindler, A. (2010). Art and art in early childhood: What can young children learn from "a/Art activities?" *Art in Early Childhood, 2*(1), 1–14.

Lilly, K. V., & Venukapalli, S. (2020). Aesthetic intelligence and aesthetic experience in children. *International Journal of Education* (*IJE*), *8*(4).

Lo, K. Y., & Matsunobu, K. (2014). Role of art and creativity in child culture and socialization. In A. Ben-Arieh, F. Casas, I. Frønes, & J. Korbin (Eds.), *Handbook of child well-being*. Springer. https://doi.org/10.1007/978-90-481-9063-8_185

Metzger, M. (2015). *The arts in early childhood: social and emotional benefits of arts participation*. Office of Research & Analysis, National Endowment for the Arts.

Rainford, J. (2020). Confidence and the effectiveness of creative methods in qualitative interviews with adults. *International Journal of Social Research Methodology, 23*(1), 109–122.

Savva, A. (2003). Young pupil's responses to adult works of art. *Contemporary Issues in Early Childhood, 4*(3), 300–313.

Smith, J. K. (1992). Interpretive inquiry: A practical and moral activity. *Theory into Practice, 31*(2), 100–106.

Tate. (2018). *Why study art?* https://www.tate.org.uk/art/talking-point/why-study-art#:~:text=Learning%20through%20and%20about%20the,a%20sense%20of%20individual%20identity

Van't Hul, J. (2022). The benefits of art for kids. *The Artful Parent*. https://artfulparent.com/the-benefits-of-art-for-kids/

Zucker, A. (2019, January 10). Art and education as a spiritual awakening. *Artfully Learning*. https://theartsandeducation.wordpress.com/2019/01/10/art-and-education-as-a-spiritual-awakening/

CHAPTER 20

The Genesis Project

An Investigation of Contemporary Music Composition

Bernard W. Andrews

Abstract

This study, entitled The Genesis Project: An investigation of contemporary music composition, examined the nature of current practice by professional composers composing orchestral works for major symphony orchestras. They completed four protocols – an online questionnaire, reflective journal, compositional analysis, and a video interview. There was a range of responses explaining why the composers composed, suggesting that it is very much an idiosyncratic process. Although the composers expressed an inner drive to create, the strongest motivator for composing was undertaking a commission. The composers commenced their earliest compositions from eight to twenty-three. Overall, they indicated a preference for being alone in a calm environment, preferably in the mornings. The conceptualisation of a piece and generation of musical ideas involved the imagination and feelings whereas the writing out of the music was a rational process, especially the final editing after a premiere performance. There was a focus on polychords and microtonality when discussing harmony, and Eastern scales and modes were integrated into their compositions. Among the male composers, gender was not an issue, although it was highlighted by the female composers as affecting their access to professional opportunities and mentoring. Experience gained with age was viewed as a significant factor, notably for developing compositional skills and increasing one's confidence. The composers identified several cultural influences, notably Eastern musical practices such as an emphasis on the horizontal (melody) rather than the vertical (harmony). They indicated that their compositional training assisted them in their practice, notably in the conceptualising and refining of their works.

Keywords

music composition – musical creativity – generative processes

1 Introduction

Music theorists in America (Adorno, 1980), Europe (Viera de Carvalho, 1999) and Australia (Walker, 1997) attribute the complexity of contemporary music to the dynamic changes in music throughout the twentieth century. Atonality and serialism, introduced by Igor Stravinsky and Arnold Schoenberg, respectively, represented a logical extension of the historical evolution of Western-European music beyond tonality (Pleasants, 1955). Technological inventions, such as the computer and synthesiser, transformed the ways in which musicians compose, perform and communicate their musical ideas (Collins & Dunn, 2011; Green, 2001). Mass media fostered access to world musics, introducing the intricate nuances of alternate modalities, vocalisations and tuning systems to Western composers (Folkestad, 2012; Lundquist & Szego, 1998). Despite these innovations there is limited knowledge of the nature of contemporary music composition.

2 Related Research

Studies by music theorists and researchers of composers' improvisational and compositional processes predominantly focus on the analysis of recordings, scores and sketch books. Complex schema, including linguistic and computational models, have been developed to explain how music is composed (cited in Lerdahl, 1988 and Krumhasl, 1991). Also, there has been speculation on the processes of well-known creative individuals (Gardner, 1993), and more recently brain scans by the researcher/musician Daniel Levitin (2006) undertaken on the well-known popular singer/composer Sting. Surprisingly however, few studies examine music composition with the creators themselves, although composers certainly have described the challenges of conceptualising and composing new music (e.g., Boulez, 1975; Rochberg, 1988; Sessions, 1970; Stravinski, 1947).

Early research suggests that there are essentially two types of composers: a working type (craft approach) and an inspirational type (Bahle, 1934); and composers engage in four basic stages – productive mood (preparation), musical conception (incubation), sketching (illumination), and composition (verification) (Graf, 1947). Major twentieth-century composers, such as Arnold Schoenberg, Carl Orff and Richard Strauss, participated in Julius Bahle's study (Auner, 2005). These stages have also been discussed and elaborated on by several other well-known composers, such as Igor Stravinsky (1947), Roger Sessions (1970), Pierre Boulez (1975), Morton Feldman (1984) and Elliot Carter

(1946/1994). The most comprehensive account of the composing process involved in-depth interviews with eight composers (Bennett, 1976). Bennett's research elaborated on Graf's categories but shifted the focus from feelings (productive mood) and thoughts (musical conception) to the writing process itself (i.e., sketches and drafts). He suggested that composing involves a process of discovering a germinal idea (preparation), a brief sketch (incubation), elaboration and refinement of a first draft (illumination), and revisions to a final copy (verification). Faultley (2010) updated Bennet's research and describes the creative process as: generation, organisation, revision, transformation, and development. More recent research suggests that composers make both conscious and unconscious decisions in their work (Sloboda, 1988; Trevarthen, 2012) and may not follow the stages in sequence but oscillate between them (Hung, 1998). They may also employ various strategies in conjunction with the stages (Fulmer, 1995). For some composers, improvisation is a key starting point in the process of composition (Folkstead 2012; Hsich 2012; Rusinek 2011). These findings suggest "that different composers use different strategies, and some composers use more than one strategy" (Radocy & Boyle, 1997, p. 10): it is "the idiosyncratic nature of the individual composing process" (Kennedy, 2002, p. 95).

In addition to the research findings on music composition, there are a substantive number of textbooks that have been used predominantly in university music departments and conservatories during the past several decades. Such works analyse the compositions of well-known composers and synthesise highly technical rules for writing music. This pattern appears consistent in both traditional classical music (e.g., Benward & Saker, 2015; Caplin, 2013; Gould, 2011; Huron, 2016; Tymoczko, 2011) and those in the more popular idioms (e.g., Bell, 2019; Denish, 2017; Mulholland & Hojnacki, 2013; Pease & Pullig, 2001). The rules for writing music, however, are not developed from direct contact with composers themselves, nor do they outline the emotional and environmental factors that facilitate composing (Collins, 2016). These rules reflect the highly structured socialisation musicians receive within institutional settings (Roberts, 1991). Such training does appear to effectively increase one's understanding of twentieth century innovations, such as twelve-tone music (Frances, 1992), and to more accurately judge emotional states (Nilsonne & Sunberg, 1985). However, this approach can result in highly stilted and mechanical writing (Cage, 1949; Stravinsky, 1947).

Researchers such as Emmons (1998) and Berkley (2001) have proposed non-sequential models of music composition. Emmons (1998) proposed a non-linear and non-sequential model that included formation, preservation and revision as its stages. Similarly, Berkley (2001) proposed a circular model that included generating, realising, and editing. Another model of creativity is the 'Genplore model' proposed by Hsieh (2012). This is a model of generative and exploratory creative functioning that "assumes that an individual would alternate between generative and exploratory processes, developing the structures according to the constraints of a specific task" (p. 154). Similarly, Konečni (2012) stated that there are two major phases of the creative process: the preparatory (an intense study of the newest developments of composition – what others have done) and the executive (the decision to begin work on a concrete piece). Composers, such as Johann Sebastian Bach, George Fredrick Handel, Josef Haydn, Wolfgang Amadeus Mozart, tend to use traditional forms (e.g., fugue, sonata, suite), whereas others have rejected conventional forms and created new ones, such as Richard Strauss (tone poem), Richard Wagner (music drama), Arnold Schoenberg (serialism), and Igor Stravinsky (atonality) (Kozbelt, 2016).

3   Theoretical Framework

Research on music composition derives from creativity research which adopts a multi-dimensional, socio-cultural approach. Mihaly Csikszentmilhalyi (1994) explains: "In order to understand creativity, one must enlarge the conception of what the process is, moving from an exclusive focus on the individual to a systemic perspective that includes the social and cultural context in which the 'creative' person operates" (p. 136). Creativity research focuses on four dimensions: the environmental conditions for promoting creativity; the creative process; creative products; and the characteristics of creative individuals (Amabile & Tighe, 1992; Woodman & Schoenfeldt, 1989). More specifically for music, these dimensions have been identified as the *pre-requisites* for composing (training, emotions, context), compositional *process* (strategies, techniques, sequencing), the *piece* itself (features, style, impact), and *person* (characteristics, pre-dispositions, motivation) (Andrews, 2004a, 2004b).

4   Methodology

This study, entitled The Genesis Project: An investigation of contemporary music composition, is based on the belief that an in-depth understanding of lived compositional practice can be achieved by collaborating with those professionals actively composing new music rather than through the traditional approach which involves studying musical scores and recordings post facto. It is based on the assumption that understanding the life experience of a musical artist involves sustained, reflective research of a complex and multi-faceted artistic phenomenon which involves a composer's personal and environmental conditions for composing, the compositional processes used in creating a new work, the work itself and the composer's perspectives on music. Roger Reynolds (2002) explains:

> A musical work is achieved gradually over time in a manner that doubtless varies for each composer: part discovery, part construction, even admittedly, part contrivance and ... also part sheer undirected bumbling ... There is a necessary (though by no means uniform) staging involved in the process of completing a musical composition. We can thus inquire into the process recognizing it as a multileveled search for ultimate integration rather than the unrolling of a scroll upon which has been inscribed in an already, mystical completed continuity that one needs only to receive. (p. 4)

This study employed Integrated Inquiry, a multiple-perspectives methodology (Andrews, 2008). This approach involves examining the complex and multi-faced phenomenon of composing by administering four research protocols congruent with the four dimensions of musical creativity and integrating the analysis/interpretation of the data. The overriding question of the study was: "What is the nature of contemporary compositional practice?" The four in-depth questions were: "What are the personal and environmental conditions required for composing music?" (*pre-requisites* – questionnaire); "How are generative processes, such as melodic development and modulation, employed in an extended composition?" (*compositional process* – reflective journal); "What are the musical characteristics of contemporary works?" (*piece* – compositional analysis); and "How is the role of the composer and contemporary music evolving in the twenty-first century?" (*person* – video interview) (refer to Figure 20.1).

The process of composing involves mediation between one's inner musical structure and the external musical notation. John Miller (2007) refers to this oscillation between the personal and universal as "transformational". The process of inquiry using Integrated Inquiry involves making explicit what is implicit in the mind of participants by identifying patterns and relationships of meaning (Moustakas, 1994). The role of the researcher is to understand these "lived experiences" (Creswell, 2003, p. 15). This means, that to study a particular phenomenon, a situation is sought in which individuals have first-hand

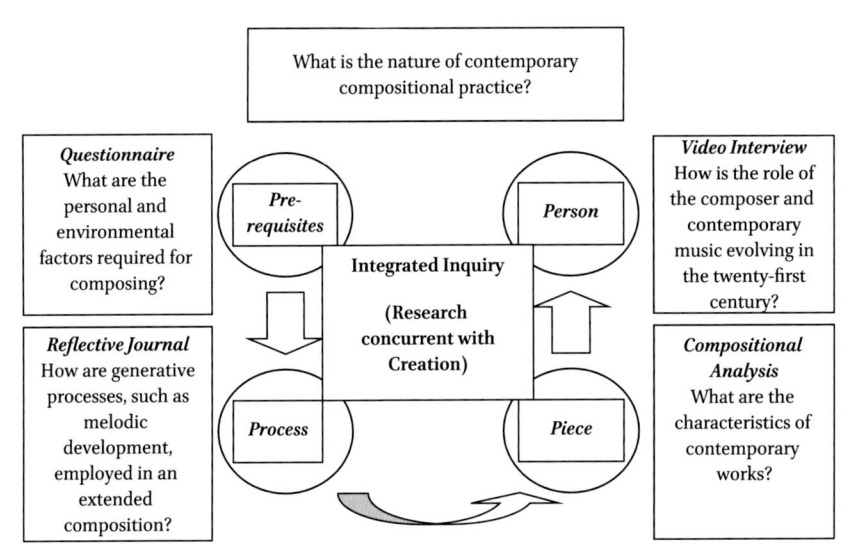

FIGURE 20.1   Integrated inquiry[1]

experiences that they can describe as they actually took place in their life. "The aim is to capture as closely as possible the way in which the phenomenon is experienced within the context in which the experience takes place" (Giorgi & Giorgi, 2003, pp. 27–28).

5   Instrument Protocols

In the preparatory stage for this study, a bank of interview questions on the four dimensions of music composition (i.e., pre-requisites/process/piece/person) were generated from the literature, elaborated on by composers and educators, and refined by researchers from the international community (Andrews, 2004a). For example, for compositional process, interview questions such as "What emotional states facilitate your composing?" and "Do you experience different emotions at different stages of the process?" were generated. The interview questions were then piloted in a taped interview with four of Canada's well-known senior composers. The pilot findings indicated the importance of early selection of composing as a career and the impact of new technologies, such as the synthesiser and computer, for composing and disseminating new music. Also, the findings indicated the importance of the "person" in music composition, especially of one's hopes and dreams, and of one's place in the Western tradition (Andrews & Wendzich, 2023). Consequently, a holistic approach, focusing on conceptualisation, creation and refining was deemed appropriate for The Genesis Project.

6   Participants

Twelve well-known professional composers, all composers-in-residence of major symphony orchestras, were commissioned to compose extended orchestra works.[2] Concurrently, they participated in this research/creation project throughout the conceptualisation, creation, and refining of the pieces. All composers invited to participate in the study are members of the Canadian Music Centre and they have received significant honours for their compositions, including numerous national and international composition awards. Together they represent the cultural diversity of Canada, old and young alike, and include highly successful women composers.

7   Analysis

7.1   *Online Questionnaires*

The composers indicated that mornings are the best time to compose "when the mind feels fresh and unhindered". They stated that "calm" is essential for composing new music. This is followed by determination and "concentration to the highest degree where one is so deep into the composition process that there is absolutely no distraction". Once the ideas are generated, the later stages involve more critical and reflective processes "to organise the ideas in a comprehensive and effective form and structure". The final stages of copy-editing and proof-reading can be undertaken with less regard for environmental conditions. One composer indicated that he found "additional inspiration working anywhere: at the airport, on the train, or in a hotel room in the centre of a city". Some of the composers stated that they experienced a 'flow' state, as one of them commented: "I find that once I slip into a relaxed state of mind, with little to no disruptions, time slips away, and the creative process unfolds". To achieve 'flow', five conditions were identified:
– be in a relaxed state of mind;
– avoid disruptions and distractions;
– suspend negative judgements;
– balance the intuitive and intellectual; and
– choose an environment that is comfortable and aesthetically pleasing

The composers also commented on the influence of gender, age and cultural background on their composing. Overall, there was a consensus that gender did not come into play for composing *per se*. However, it was a factor in access to commissions, notably by the female composers.

> There is a general cultural bias to demand expertise of women before allowing them access to high profile opportunities. By contrast, there is a general bias toward inviting young men to taking risks without necessarily having proven themselves first.

And also access to mentoring.

> Mentors tent to nurture younger artists who resemble the mentor ... gender acts as a barrier to those relationships, introducing the awkwardness of perceived sexual interest and other impediments to building trust.

Age mainly increased the composers' confidence level, skill level, and willingness to undertake more comprehensive works.

> Growing older, my compositions tend to grow larger in shape (longer pieces instead of shorter movements), and my materials are developed in a better, fuller way. This has to do with my growing knowledge in terms of building materials.

There was a general consensus that cultural background considerably influenced the composers' music. They mentioned Chinese, Greek, Jewish, Italian, Slavic, Georgian, French, Trinidadian, and Maori influences on their composing. For example:

> My background as a Chinese-Canadian makes me drawn to silences and slowly-folding materials, lyrical linear gestures and pentatonicism related to a Southern Chinese opera that I grew up listening to, and inspirations related to Buddhism.

And

> Growing up in a Greek household and as part of the Greek community of Montreal, I was deeply immersed in that culture throughout my

childhood and adolescence. This has certainly inclined me toward certain melodic and rhythmic preferences that permeate traditional folk and popular Greek music styles.

And

As for cultural background to some extent it does come through my compositions. Having had a Italo-Slavic early upbringing I would attribute my penchants for simplicity and clarity of melodic line and harmonic progression: a lyricism (Italian) with a fundamental bass (Slavic).

And

Being of French Canadian-European heritage, my music definitely has a post-Fauré aesthetic. In this composition, in particular, I use French Canadian themes with many French harmonic textures.

Finally, the composers commented on their compositional training and its impact on music composition. Essentially, their music was viewed as a balance between the rational (objective) and the intuitive (subjective); that is, "balancing one's understanding of instrumentation, formal and rhythmic procedures, notation, etc. with creativity, an innate sense of time, impact and emotion". Their training provided them with the skills to objectively organise and edit their work.

The training is much more helpful during drafting, orchestration, and post-completion assessment/editing. That's when a critical eye, honed aural skills, knowledge of existing repertoire, command of methods and techniques ... enable me to work more fluidly and efficiently. In essence, it enables me to effectively execute my vision (that was otherwise intuitively/emotionally arrived at).

7.2   *Online Reflective Journals*

For most of the composers, the composing process involved "a combination of emotional writing with rational activity". As one composer commented: "I find that my best work is the result of a process that strikes a balance between both of these qualities". Overall, there is more emotion involved in the generation of musical ideas. As these ideas are developed and orchestrated, a rational approach was utilised. One composer explained:

> At conception, I take the theme ... and imagine different possibilities ...
> When I start to write the music down in score form, I am using more of
> a rational process. I work my improvised material into a theme, texture,
> accompaniment, rhythm, and move it forwards by developing it
> rationally.

And another commented:

> Having drafted a great deal of emotionally-derived material in past
> composition sessions, today was very much about the nuts and bots of
> finding a way to make sense of it and figure out a way to have it progress
> logically.

The composers indicated that they moved through different stages in their
composing process. This involved the conception of "a specific mood and
image". Then it involved the "crafting and creating of a piece". Subsequently
the composers "typically draft the piece or movement of a larger work". Then
the composers "improve/refine/orchestrate the music into its near-final form"
by entering the music into a computer. The final stage consists of producing
the parts and editing the work". Generally, composing was viewed as a linear
progress with composers moving from one stage to another with occasional
movement back and forth between stages.

> There were occasional oscillating processes (going back for adjustments
> of ideas, articulation, details, etc.) before proceeding to the following
> stage, but the whole process points in direction in general.

Overall, there was a consensus that the musical decision-making was predominantly intuitive, especially when creating melody. Previous knowledge of
composing principles guided the creation of harmonies, the use of modulation, and the orchestration of the new piece. A composer's prior musical background also has an impact on musical decision-making.

> We study a lot of music, listen to a lot, spend a lot of time engaging with
> the music of great composers. Hopefully, this in some way informs our
> process and instinctual decision-making.

There was no indication by the composers that gender had an impact on
their composing. They did agree that cultural background had an impact

on their composing, especially for those trained in the Western-European tradition.

> I see older composers than myself ... being perhaps more rational in their process. This is tied to the style of composition in the mid 20th century as modernism had a strong hold on the composition world. Pieces had to be complex and exceedingly rational.

Another composer commented:

> As a Canadian-American male in his twenties who lives in North America, the set of influences on my music will most likely be different than someone who say, is not male, is in their 60's and has spent their entire life in Italy.

There was a general consensus that age was a major factor in affecting the compositional process. With age comes experience and increased organisational ability and writing skill. Also, one builds on one's previous compositional and musical experiences.

> I would say my process has improved and become more efficient/organised as I get older ... Now, I structure the time span of my creation process into differentiated stages and set myself weekly/monthly goals to reach. I think this change in compositional process has to do with growth in experience.

And

> I think age is a big factor, but only because with age comes experience. As much as this art is done through innate creative ability, it is also a learned art form that requires intense study, dedication and understating of what has come before and what is being created now.

7.3   *Online Compositional Critiques*

The composers used the traditional descriptive terms, such as melody, harmony, texture, and development, to describe their composing but in more varied ways in their comments.

> For example, harmony in a traditional setting can always be framed in terms of tonality and keys but in a contemporary setting might be descried in terms of intervals (what intervals make up the chord, such as

5ths), polychords (two chords on top of one another), microtonality, or even tonality used in an unconventional way.

And

> When describing stylistic features of a work, a composer would ask: "Does the work rely on linear (horizontal) motivic materials to develop from, or not?"; "Is the work based on notes, or based on sounds/noise?"; Are there extra-musical sources of inspiration or not?"

Composers alluded to the use of non-Western music, "particularly South-Asian and Middle-Eastern ... scales and modes from these cultures". Others spoke of the non-musical influences, such as the books, podcasts or movies consumed, that impacted their works. Still others described the stylistic features of their works in extra-musical terms; for example, "creating a shimmering musical texture inspired by iridescence" or "with each string pizzicato, they do a tiny glissando at the end of it to give it a melting feel".

Overall, the composers were unassuming about the impact of their compositions on contemporary music practice – that only time would tell the value of their works. There was also a sense that their compositions were but one in a series of new works that reflected the tenor of the times.

> I see the impact as something very small or imperceptible at the moment, at this point, but I do believe that what I compose might join forces with other works of creation by colleagues of past, present, and future, and eventually may transform into something greater that is probably out of my reach and understanding right now.

And

> It's very unlikely that anything I write will seriously impact or alter the course of contemporary music. Much of what we do is experimentation anyways, attempting to reconcile what has come before us with the trends, innovations and sensibilities of today.

Of the influences of gender, age and cultural background, gender appeared to be the least influential. Only one composer noted that gender was a significant factor.

> While trying to find my compositional voice in university, I deliberately avoided any sense of femininity or even vulnerability in my music ...

When I finally allowed this element into my music, my compositional voice changed, softened, relaxed, and very suddenly my career started due to winning prizes. I realised that I had tried to create tough, driven, masculine music to show that I was a good composer and fit in with my male colleagues.

Age was a significant factor as composers became more experienced over time. Compositional skills and a "more complete sense of the artistic self" were developed. The composers' confidence increased, and they became more efficient and effective in their writing.

As I become older, more life and artistic experiences are gained and I think they naturally influence my way of being as a person, and affect the way I think, perceive, and create, which ultimately transforms my creative work into something more complete in form ... more relaxed and reserved in a way, and more natural in terms of the flow of musical events throughout the piece.

The composers noted that their cultural background played a significant role in their writing, particularly those of French-Canadian heritage. Others mentioned the openness to cultural differences from living in a multicultural society and the influence of early experiences in other countries.

Growing up listening to Southern Chinese opera (featuring very lyrical, beautiful, soft and linear/horizontal melodic lines) before taking piano lessons and learning about Western music has somehow influenced my 'default' way of thinking about music – I tend to think and write in a horizontal/melodic mode, rather than vertical/harmonic. Also, silence and reserving energy are vital in my work ... East Asian cultures tend to value quietness and introversion a lot more than Western culture.

The structures of the compositions are quite varied and marked by complexity. The most common structure was the use of the ternary form but with several sub-sections. For example:

The structure of my composition is a 3-part from, with A section divided into three sections (A1, A2, A3), B section divided into 3 sections (B1, B2, transition, B3), a transition, and C section which essentially make up of materials from A and B sections, divided into 3 sections as well (C1, C2, transition, C3), followed by a Coda section.

All of the pieces are written in the acoustic mode with the exception of one of the pieces which opens with a computer-generated intro. Some of the compositions follow a traditional absolute approach, for example, a piano concerto in four movements. Others adopt a programmatic approach. For example:

> As I planned the piece, I realised that I could make this introduction of individual musical elements as an analogy to cooking. There is an introduction, five sections, and a summary. I have created a narration that occurs at certain breaks in the piece, allowing the piece to come together quickly without having to coordinate narrator and orchestra.

7.4   Video Interviews

The most common theme in response to the question "Why do composers compose?" was that composing was distinctly personal and not generalizable. Indeed, the composers provided a range of responses to the question. These included:
– Form of self-expression
– Connection to an audience
– Personal interest
– Curiosity
– Creative impulse
– Experimentation
– Extension of performance
– Commission to compose new music

Indeed, one composer even speculated on a range of possibilities:

> Some of them do that because they don't know to do anything else which is a pretty good reason, I would say ... For some people it's an extension of something that they do as a leisure that has taken all the place so it's a matter of enjoying yourself and the time that you've got. Some feel that they have a mission I guess, which is weird. What kind of mission can that be? ... And many do that because they've done music since they were little children, so they're programmed to do that. You do music because that's what you do.

With respect to the incentive to compose, both intrinsic and extrinsic motivators were identified. Composers mentioned that it was "an inner-drive to explore, create and discover" that intrinsically motivated them. It is a situation "where you write something you feel like writing and then the process becomes more interesting because then you imagine the musicians who are going to play it". There is the challenge, however, of addressing procrastination as one composer noted: "I have a project that's very long term, because when there's no deadlines, it just gets harder to define the time". In contrast, the commission represented the major external motivator. In this context major parameters are imposed:

> You're asked to deliver a product according to certain specifications It's almost like being a tailor where you have to do something tailor made for a group. And they have special specific measurement that you have to respect, and it has to fit the skill level and to fit the instruments.

Despite these restrictions, composers indicated that commissions provided a focus for their creativity. Moreover, aside from the financial implications, the limitations prompted the composers to extend their writing skills. They also enjoyed the variety of possibilities that commissioned engendered.

> I love that every project is different. It's written for a different organisation, for different musicians, for a different purpose, sometimes for different age groups … I feel lucky as a composer because my life is never the same. Each project has such a different focus and pushes me in a different direction or pushes me to connect with different types of people. And that is very exciting and motivating.

The predominant influence on the composers' early musical creativity was that of their parents. They provided music lessons at an early age, were supportive and encouraged musical development, and played music throughout their homes.

> My parents were very encouraging. I did also write pieces that sounded like, that were tonal and didn't sound like a child banging on a piano. But my parents were also not opposed to me banging on the piano, which I think was definitely influential. They also played a lot of music in the house – a lot of different kinds of music – especially Classical music – and I really liked it.

Another major factor was the influence of teachers who inspired to experiment and create new music.

> I studied piano with a very unusual man, really not a classical performer … We were in a small town outside of Calgary, and he was the only piano

teacher, and he intentionally lived off the grid, no electricity, he raised goats, he played Country and Western piano ... So I went to him with my piano pieces, and he said, 'why are you playing these? What's the emotion behind them? What is the story behind them?' And that started off my composing.

The age at which the composers wrote their compositions ranged from eight to twenty-three. University music programs provided the impetus for some of the composers as it provided an environment for them to experiment and create.

I was 17 where I felt like I felt my voice. I felt like a way of writing that I could call my own was when I was 17. And it was my piano sonata. I was this was my last year at Curtis ... I wanted to write something that celebrated my graduation.

And also

I said my first real composition I completed when I was twenty-one. And it was for saxophone and piano ... I was finishing up my undergrad in performance and I thought, OK, now I'm ready, I'm going to put one of my own pieces on my recital program.

Often the composers in the early stages would undertake exploratory compositions: "I was writing small things, not complete pieces". Then they would graduate to chamber compositions: "I wrote smaller works for saxophone and piano". Finally, they would undertake large-scale compositions as "the scale gets progressively bigger". These compositions were usually commissioned:

So the larger works I [am] usually commissioned to do because they take so long for me to do and edit properly that I'm doing for free doesn't make sense because in the time it takes me to write a large orchestral piece, I could write 20 smaller pieces.

Residencies with professional orchestras, choirs, or chamber ensembles provide some stability to the composers but these opportunities are quite limited. Most live from one commission to another. One composer stated: "It is a tough life because it's not a commercial product: the demand for classical contemporary composition is very rarified". Several of the composers supplement their incomes with teaching which generally is a positive experience. Another composer noted: "I find teaching to be very inspiring and it helps me to address weaknesses in my practice that I couldn't afford to address before as I was composing all the time with many, many deadlines".

Another factor which has a significant impact on a composer's career is winning prizes. This brings considerable media attention to the composer's works resulting in more performances. It also creates more commission opportunities:

> I got a call from the producer of Two New Hours at CBC, saying that he would like to submit that piece to represent Canada at the UNESCO International Roster of Composers ... Several months later, he called from Vienna and said "You've won, your piece won" ... It was broadcast in thirty-five countries ... I started getting professional commissions.

However, the landscape is changing for composers. The CD recording is passé – people have access to the internet so they don't have to buy it. As one composer noted: "I get my music recorded, it gets played on the radio ... and then I start collecting royalties. That's over". Composers have to modernise their thinking. The recording is now part of a cycle.

> The end game is another commission. The end is getting the recording, getting the recording listened to, getting people to like it, and looping it into another commission and another commission.

Overall, women are more involved in the workplace than in the early twentieth century and many have succeeded in their careers despite the many challenges of working in a male-dominated environment. It is only recently that more women have considered composing as a career.

> I think we've reached a point where it's much more feasible for women to become composers because there's less restriction to their role ... The expectation for women to get married and have children, that's kind of become not necessarily the norm. And we're more open-minded with this ... It does allow women to seek out much further musical instruction ... It's that we're not just seeing women composers, we're seeing more women in prominent roles in the arts in general as movie producers [and] as screenwriters.

However, despite these advances, the composers recognised that it was still more challenging for women to be successful in the composing profession. They lack ready access to commission and performance opportunities. "There's a whole network and it's very controlled by men". One composer noted that she had never had a women composition teacher, despite eleven years of university study in composition. There was a consensus by the composers that composing is a very demanding profession with very little financial stability. This situation is simply exacerbated for women.

> When you look at what it's taken, for example, female composers, what has taken them to be seen on equal footing as their male counterparts, definitely they've had a great struggle on their own accord to get to that place. And they're still struggling to assert their relevance right now.

The composers indicated that their cultural backgrounds, notably Chinese, Greek, Indian and Mauri (New Zealand), impacted their compositional style. As immigrants they were exposed to the music of their parents' mother country in their household. As one composer noted:

> The music that I first listened to was Chinese opera. It's obviously very different from Western Classical music. And that has had such a huge impact on how I think about music. It's like a default mode in the back of my mind. So, with that kind of built-in mindset, then I write my music and something different comes out. And it's just different from other people and it's fine.

Overall, many organisations "are looking a little more into diversity initiatives – voices that are not typically represented in concert music – represented in terms of performances and commissions". This is consisted with the Equity, Diversity and Inclusive (EDI) agenda of many Canadian institutions which is promoted by the federal and provincial governments. Further, music has become more globalised and more eclectic.

> I think because of the internet, we have a lot more access to a lot more information, so I think that the rate of development of music and how it's changed aesthetically over the year has sped up actually in the past ten years because of things like YouTube and social media ... I think that new music has probably developed aesthetically much quicker in the past ten years than it has in the past.

8   Discussion

There was a range of responses explaining why the composers composed, suggesting that it is very much an idiosyncratic process (Kennedy, 2002). Although the composers expressed an inner drive to create, the strongest motivator for composing was undertaking a commission. This provided a focus for their efforts and a means to hone their skills. Composers, such as Igor Stravinsky (1947) and Robert Sessions (1970) have commented on the importance of the commission for framing their work. The most influential persons on the composers' careers were their parents and their teachers. This consistent with the experience of well-known composers, such as Wolfgang Mozart who was influenced by his father (Kerst, 1965), and Anton Webern who was taught by Arnold Schoenberg (Hoskisson, 2017).

The composers commenced their earliest compositions from eight to twenty-three. None did so at a very early age such as Wolfgang Mozart (Kerst, 1965) or Felix Mendelssohn (Taylor & Spitzer, 2015). Residencies with orchestras or choirs represent an important source of income as do commissions. Many composers teach music to supplement their income, especially since CD sales have given way to streaming. Radio airplay, concerts and winning prizes have become very important as they result in public awareness and more commissions.

Overall, the composers indicated a preference for being alone in a calm environment with no distractions to commence composing. Most of them favour mornings over other times of the day, especially for the beginning and early stages of the composing process. Interestingly, Wolfgang Amadeus Mozart commented that he preferred a broader time frame:

> When I am, as it were, completely myself, entirely alone, and of good cheer; say traveling in a carriage, or walking after a good meal, or during the night when I cannot sleep; it is on such occasions that my ideas flow best and most abundantly. (cited in Zaslaw, 1994, p. 14)

The composers experienced both rational and emotional states when composing as commented on by Sloboda (1988) and Trevarthen (2012). The conceptualisation of a piece and generation of musical ideas involved the imagination and feelings whereas the writing out of the music was a rational process, especially the final editing after a premiere performance (Konečni, 2012). Generally, the composers moved through a linear process when composing consistent with Bennett's (1976) stages: discovering a germinal idea (preparation), a brief sketch (incubation), elaboration and refinement of a first draft (illumination), and revisions to a final copy (verification). However, they also moved back and forth among these stages as Hung (1995) noted.

Although the composers described their works with traditional labels, such as melody, harmony, texture, and development, they tended to expand the use of the terms themselves. For example, when discussing harmony, there was a focus on polychords or microtonality. Also, they integrated Eastern and mid-Eastern scales and modes into their compositions, which is indicative of the globalisation of post-modern music (Williams, 2019). There was no indication by the composers of a belief that their music would affect contemporary practice, although Andrews (2023) found that senior male composers tended to hope that this would be the case.

Among the male composers, gender was not an issue, although it was highlighted by the female composers as affecting their access to professional opportunities and mentoring. One women composer commented that she wrote "tough masculine music" to fit in with her male colleagues but was far more successful when she allowed her "sense of femininity" to emerge. In the field of composition, men dominate through the overwhelming number of their contributions. Indeed, there is a lack of value placed on women's works of art that has contributed to the denigration of their contributions. For example, the painting entitled Charlotte du Val d'Ognes was long thought to be a masterpiece by Jacques Louis David. The painting declined substantially in monetary value and critical esteem when it was discovered that it was the work of Marie Charpentier (Wolff, 1983). Other creative women, such as the pianist-composer Clara Schumann, became interpreters of their husband's works (Robert Schumann) rather than fully developing their own talents. As a result of this devaluing process, there is a continuing lack of awareness of women's creative contributions to the visual and performing arts and a need to actively promote women's musical works within the concert hall and classroom (Lindeman, 1992).

Women have a long and illustrious, although largely ignored, history of musical composition. Many of their works, unfortunately, are lost or destroyed, and those that are available need to be catalogued and annotated (Allen & Keenan-Takagi, 1992; Palmquist & Payne, 1992). Feminist scholarship in the 1970's and 1980's led to a resurgence of interest and research in women's creative contributions. In an extensive review of this literature, Edwards (1997) identified gender differences in relation to music, not only within the musical vocabulary, but also in relation to the musical canon. Women composers have consistently challenged notions of musical genius, Western European musical superiority, and musical forms related to gender (e.g., masculine and feminine themes in sonata-form). They also reject the mind/body split of the Western European tradition, acknowledge the physical response to music, link music with sexuality or pleasure more readily, and admit that physical experiences are significant to music's meaning (Peddle, 1991).

Ageing is a key factor in how composers develop, codify their practices, and view their place in musical history. There was a tendency towards higher efficiency in organisation and better use of time in the composing process (Kozbelt, 2016). Experience gained with age was viewed as a significant factor, notably for developing compositional skills and increasing one's confidence in music composition (Andrews, 2023). Time itself provides the catalyst for acceptance, and those who live long enough benefit from the acceptance of experts who must recognise and validate musical innovations (Csikszentmihalyi, 1996). Surprisingly, many composers come full circle and return to their roots. Composers, such as Olivier Messiaen, Paul Hindemith and Serge Prokofiev, ended their days as respectable members of the establishment as teachers, theorists and conductors, respectively. Moreover, many reverted to a conservatism reminiscent of the traditional conservatory approach, especially in their writings; for example, Paul Hindemith's harmonic treatise exemplified in the preludes and fugues entitled *Ludus tonalis*. Another example is Arnold Schoenberg who shocked the musical world with this twelve-tone method of composition. He ended his career as a well-known pedagogue at the University of California at Los Angeles – a teacher who imposed a rigid discipline on his students, very much in the traditional style:

> Whatever happens in a piece of music is nothing but the endless reshaping of a basic shape. Or, in other words, there is nothing in a piece of music but what comes from the theme, springs from it, and can be traced back to it. (Schoenberg in Rosen, 1975, p. 1336)

The composers identified several cultural influences in their work (i.e., Chinese, Greek, Jewish, Italian, Slavic, Georgian, French, Trinidadian, and Maori). These influences were seen as a significant influence on one's composing, notably with the influence of Eastern musical practices such as an emphasis on the horizontal (melody) rather than the vertical (harmony). None of them, however, mentioned composing outside the traditional Western canon. There was a desire to create large-scale complex pieces, such as symphonies and operas, for professional organisations. The most common structure was the ternary form with sub-sections (e.g., A1, A2, A3) with a mix of absolute and program music, which is consistent with Western-European practice (Konečni, 2012).

Many of the *enfants terribles* of the composing world, however, created national identities through their compositional styles. For example, Claude Debussy's use of flexible rhythm, vague tonality and fluid orchestral colours created the French Impressionistic School (Les Six); and Modest Mussorsky's use of bare harmonies, elliptical modulations and unorthodox orchestration gave rise to a Russian identity (The Russian Five). North American composers, however, have tended to study in Europe or in the Western European tradition, and integrated these traditions into their music. In the United States, this has given rise to the evolutionary "American School" of composition characterised by the music of Aaron Copland and Leonard Bernstein, in contrast to the revolutionary approaches developed by the Russian Igor Stravinski (atonality) and the German Arnold Schoenberg (twelve-tone). In Canada, the diverse cultural backgrounds of its composers have mitigated against a distinctive national musical style. Indeed, John Beckwith, well-known composer, scholar, teacher and former Dean of Music at the University of Toronto asks: "What is it like, that music? Are there any generalizations one can make about it that might connect with the Canadian composer's search for a character?" (Beckwith, 1997, p. 55).

In Canada, there are composers, such as Johan Weinzweig, who have integrated twentieth-century techniques into their music to make it truly their own, but this is not the norm. Most well-known Canadian composers have tended to exhibit diverse cultural influences. For example, one can detect the influence of Arnold Schoenberg in Istvan Anvalt's compositions, Paul Hindemith and Bela Bartok in Violet Archer's works, the sonic environments of Charles Ives, Aaron Copland and Virgil Thomson in John Beckwith's compositions, the principles of Claude Débussy and Gabriel Fauré in the music of Claude Champagne, the influence of Ralph Vaughan Williams on Jean Coultard and that of Igor Stravinski on Jean-Paul Couture, traits of Olivier Messiaen in the music of Talivaldis Kenins, and Anton Dvorak's influence in Osker Morawetz's works (MacMillan, 1975). In addition, there are those who adopted an eclectic approach, such as Murray Schafer and Harry Somers; others, such as Ernest MacMillan and Murray Adaskin, who based several of their compositions on folk material; and still others who affiliated their works with Canadian literature and art, such as Serge Garant, Bruce Mather and Norma Beecroft (Beckwith, 1997).

> Overt and conscious national and regional associations have been threaded through our repertoire for well over a century – evocations of winter's cold, of the northern lights or the loon's cry over the water – are an infusion of special Canadian timbre, as are also the frequent associations with the country's visual art, literature and history ... Diversity – multicultural diversity – is among the characteristic we often like to observe in our music. (Beckwith, 1997, p. 127)

Such cultural influences present a challenge to both composers and educators alike who must inform the public and students, respectively about contemporary music. Unlike the United States where similarities are emphasised, the focus in Canada is on diversity. The Canadian context encourages preserving the integrity of musical cultures within the Canadian mosaic (Elliot, 1990). This situation, however, creates tensions both in the concert hall and in the classroom where often conflicting conceptions of what constitutes music are proposed (Andrews, 1993). The situation is further exacerbated by technology where individuals of all ages have access to popular music on a global scale. Moreover, for most young people this represents their "personal music" in contrast to the "general music" of their parents and the "institutional music" of schools and the concert hall (Williams, 2019). For this reason, it is essential to encourage audiences and students alike to explore the diverse cultural traditions of the Canadian mosaic and avoid the controversies of what constitutes better music (Walker, 1990). Our efforts are put to better use by encouraging audiences and students to listen to all music more intelligently as only time will tell the merits of any new music in any particular idiom.

The composers indicated that their compositional training assisted them in their compositional practice, notably in the conceptualising and refining of their works (Ting, 2021). In contrast, many gifted composers, such as Hector Berlioz, Alexander Borodin, Emanuel Chabrier, Edward Elgar and Heitor Villa-Lobos, achieved a high level of artistic success without undergoing traditional compositional training; others had some limited exposure, such as George Gershwin, Francis Poulenc and Modest Mussorgsky; and still others left the conservatory system disenchanted, such as Claude Debussy and Erik Satie; or were expelled, notably Hugo Wolf. Indeed, the most respected traditionalists of the twentieth century, Edward Elgar and William Walton, and the greatest innovators, Igor Stravinsky (atonality) and Arnold Schoenberg (twelve-tone) were largely self-taught. As Igor Stravinsky (1947) wryly noted:

> Harmony as it is taught today in the schools dictates rules that were not fixed until long after publication of the works upon which they were based, rules which were unknown to the composers of these works. In this manner, our harmonic treatises take as their point of departure Mozart and Haydn, neither of whom ever heard of harmonic treatises. (p. 38)

9   Coda

The compositional landscape in Canada has changed significantly. Multiculturalism and more recently Equity, Diversity and Inclusion (EDI), both promoted by provincial and federal governments in Canada (Banks, 2019; OMEA, 2022), are factors in the allocation of arts council grants and commissions for music composition. The media has impacted on the globalisation of music as

Eastern and Western practices are integrated into contemporary music (Chan, 2021; Robinson & Friesen, 2021; Schippers, 2010). Above-all the internet has affected the distribution, performance and teaching of music internationally (Morrison, 2021). By examining the nature of contemporary compositional practice through the voices of professional composers, this online study has examined the personal and socio-cultural factors that affect the creation of contemporary Canadian music in the Western tradition. The Genesis Project i) extends the current research on music composition; ii) assists those who teach music composition in educational settings; iii) broadens our understanding of the generative processes of creativity in the arts; and iv) contributes twelve new works to the Canadian repertoire for performers and audiences alike.

Acknowledgement

The research for The Genesis Project was funded by the Social Sciences and Humanities Research Council (SSHRC), Canada, Grant No. 435–2016–0076.

Notes

1 Initially, The Genesis Project was conceived using traditional protocols; that is, there was to be a questionnaire, a reflective journal, compositional analysis, and an in-person interview. Due to the pandemic, it was necessary to pivot to an online format with the four protocols; that is, a website was organised for completion of the protocols by the composers, with the exception of the interviews which were undertaken by video conferences. Similarly, several of the premiere performances of the orchestral pieces were performed in an online format and streamed instead of the standard live performances.

2 One composer decided not to participate in the research component of the project after completing the questionnaire, thereby leaving eleven composers who completed the three remaining research protocols.

References

Adorno, T. W. (1980). Music and the new music. *Telos, 43*, 124–138.

Allen, S. F., & Keenan-Takagi, K. (1992). Sing the songs of women composers. *Music Educators Journal 78*(7), 48–51

Amabile, T. M., & Tighe, E. (1993). Questions of creativity. In J. Brockman (Ed.), *Creativity* (pp. 7–27). Simon & Schuster.

Andrews, B. W. (1993). Music in a multi-cultural context: Conflict in patterns of socialization. (Special Edition for research papers from the Pacific Sounds Conference). *Canadian Music Educator, 34*(5), 11–16.

Andrews, B. W. (2004a). How composers compose: In search of the questions. *Research and Issues in Music Education, 2*(2), 1–18.

Andrews, B. W. (2004b). Composing music in the classroom: The missing link in music instruction. *The Recorder, 46*(3), 12–19.

Andrews, B. W. (2008). Integrated inquiry: Transforming research perspectives. In S. Kouritzen, N. Piqemal, & R. Norman (Eds.), *Qualitative research: Challenging the orthodoxies* (pp. 169–180). Taylor & Francis.

Andrews, B. W. (2023). *How composers compose: An exploratory study*. In press.

Auner, J. (2005). Composing on stage: Schoenberg and the creative process as public performance. *19th Century Music, 29*(1), 64–93.

Bahle, J. (1934). Gestalt as applied to vocal compositions of contemporary composers. *Archive für die Gesamte Psychologie, 91*, 444–451.

Banks, J. (2019). *An introduction to multicultural education* (6th ed.). Pearson Education.

Beckwith, J. (1997). *Music papers: Articles and talks by a Canadian composer, 1961–1994*. The Golden Dog Press.

Bell, P. (2019) *Creating commercial music*. Berklee Press.

Bennett, S. (1976). The process of creation: Interviews with eight composers. *Journal of Research in Music Education, 24*(1), 3–13.

Benward, B., & Saker, M. (2015). *Music in theory and practice*. McGraw-Hill.

Berkley, R. (2001). Why is teaching composition so challenging? *British Journal of Music Education, 18*(2), 119–138.

Boulez, P. (1975). *Pierre Boulez: Conversations with Célestin Deliège*. Eulenburg Books.

Cage, J. (1949). Forerunners of modern music. In R. Samuels (Ed.), *The Boulez-Cage correspondence* (pp. 38–42). Cambridge University Press.

Caplin, W. E. (2013). *Analyzing classical form: An approach for the classroom*. Oxford University Press.

Carter, E. (1994). Surveying the compositional scene (collected essays and lectures). In J. W. Bernard (Ed.), *Elliot Carter: Collected essays and lectures, 1937–1995* (pp. 3–43). University of Rochester Press. (Original work published 1946)

Chan, H. (2021). Garage band's Chinese instruments: An overview and discussion of a virtual "ethnic" instrument. *Canadian Music Educator, 62*(3), 12–19.

Collins, D. (2016). *The act of musical composition: Studies in the creative process*. Routledge.

Collins, D., & Dunn, M. (2011). Problem-solving strategies and processes in musical composition: Observations. *Journal of Music, Technology and Education, 4*(1), 47–76.

Creswell, J. W. (2003). *Research design: Qualitative, quantitative and mixed method approaches* (2nd ed.). Sage.

Csikszentmihalyi, M. (1994). The domain of creativity. In D. H. Feldman, M. Csikszentmihalyi, & H. Gardner (Ed.), *Changing the world: A framework for the study of creativity* (pp. 136–158). Praeger.

Denisch, B. (2017). *Contemporary counterpoint: Theory and application*. Berklee Press.

Edwards, M. (1997). *Music discipline analysis: Women in curriculum series*. Towson University.

Elliot, D. J. (1990). Music in culture: Toward a multicultural concept of arts education. *Journal of Aesthetic Education, 24*(1), 147–166.

Emmons, S. E. (1998). *Analysis of musical creativity in middle school students through composition using computer-assisted instruction* [PhD thesis]. University of Rochester.

Faultey, M. (2010). *Assessment in music education*. Oxford University Press.

Feldman, M. (1984). Lectures 1984. In W. Zimmermann (Ed.), *Morton Feldman essays* (pp. 143–180). Beginner Press.

Folkestad, G. (2012). Digital tools and discourse in music: The ecology of composition. In D. J. Hargreaves, D. E. Miell, & R. A. R. MacDonald (Eds.), *Musical imaginations: Multidisciplinary perspectives on creativity, performance, and perception* (pp. 193–205). Oxford University Press.

Frances, R. (1992). Sociocultural artifacts in contemporary music. *Bulletin de Psychologie, 46*(410), 403–408.

Fulmer, D. (1995). *Composition as a generative process* [Unpublished paper]. University of Miami–Florida.

Giorgi, A., & Giorgi, B. (2003). Phenomenology. In J. A. Smith (Ed.), *Qualitative psychology: A practical guide to research methods* (pp. 25–49). Sage.

Gould, E. (2011). *Behind bars: The definitive guide to music notation*. Faber Music.

Graf, M. (1947). *From Beethoven to Shostakovich: The psychology of the composing process*. Philosophical Library.

Green, L. (2001). *How popular musicians learn*. Ashgate.

Hoskisson, D. (2017). *Anton Webern: A research and information guide*. Taylor & Francis.

Hsieh, S. (2012). Cognition and musical improvisation in individual and group contexts. In O. Odena (Ed.), *Musical creativity: Insights from music education research* (pp. 149–164). Ashgate.

Hung, Y. C. (1998). *An exploration of the musical composition background/experience, processes, and pedagogy of selected composers in Taiwan* [Ph.D. thesis]. Teacher's College, Columbia University.

Huron, D. (2016). *Voce leading: The science behind a musical art*. MIT Press.

Kennedy, M. A. (2002). Listening to the music: Compositional processes of high school composers. *Journal of Research in Music Education, 50*(2), 94–110.

Kerst, F. (1965). *Mozart: The man and the artist revealed in his own words* (H. Krehbiel, Trans. & Ed.). Dover Publications, Inc.

Konečni, V. J. (2012). Composers' creative process: The role of life-events, emotion and reason. In D. J. Hargreaves, D. Miell, & R. MacDonald (Eds.), *Musical imaginations: Multidisciplinary perspectives on creativity, performance, and perception* (pp. 141–155). Oxford University Press.

Kozbelt, A. (2016). Process, self-evaluation and lifespan creativity trajectories in eminent composers. In D. Collins (Ed.), *The act of musical composition: Studies in the creative process* (pp. 27–51). London, UK: Routledge.

Krumhansl, C. L. (1991). Music psychology: Tonal structures in perception and memory. *Annual Review of Psychology, 42*, 277–303.

Lerdahl, F. (1988). Cognitive constraints on compositional systems. In J. A. Sloboda (Ed.), *Generative processes in music: The psychology of performance, improvisation and composition* (pp. 231–259). Clarendon.

Levitin, D. (2006). *This is your brain on music: The science of human obsession.* Dutton.

Lindeman, C. A. (1992). Teaching about women musicians: Elementary classroom strategies. *Music Educators Journal, 78*(7), 56–59.

Lundquist, B., & Szego, C. K. (1998). *Music of the world's cultures.* International Society for Music Education.

MacMillan, K. (1975). Canadian music. *American Review of Canadian Studies, 5*(2), 66–81.

Miller, J. (2007). *The holistic curriculum* (2nd ed.). OISE Press.

Moustakas, C. (1994). *Phenomenological research methods.* Sage.

Mulholland, J., & Hojnacki, T. (2013). *The Berklee book of jazz harmony.* Berklee Press.

Nilsonne, A., & Sunberg, J. (1985). Differences in ability of musicians and non-musicians to judge emotional states from the fundamental frequency of voice samples. *Music Perception, 2*(4), 507–516.

Ontario Music Educators Association (OMEA) EDI Committee. (2022). OMEA equity, diversity, and inclusion resource creation project. *The Recorder, 64*(2), 19, 23–24.

Palmquiest, J. E., & Payne, B. (1992). The inclusive instrumental library: Works by women. *Music Educators Journal, 78*(7), 52–55.

Pease, T., & Pullig, K. (2001). *Modern jazz voicings: Arranging for small and medium ensembles.* Berklee Press.

Peddle, K. (Ed.). (1991). *Women and music: A history.* Indianna University Press.

Pleasants, H. (1955). *The agony of modern music.* Simon and Schuster.

Radocy, R. E., & Boyle, J. D. (1997). *Psychological foundations of musical behaviour* (3rd ed.). Charles C. Thomas.

Reynolds, R. (2002). *Form and method: Composing music.* The Rothschild Essays. Routledge.

Roberts, B. A. (1991). *Musician: A question of labelling.* Bookbinder's Press.

Robinson, K., & Friesen, K. (2021). Delivering a more global music curriculum: Challenges in Canada and China. *Canadian Music Educator, 63*(2), 32–40.

Rochberg, G. (1988). *The aesthetics of survival: A composer's view of twentieth-century music*. University of Michigan Press.

Rosen, C. (1975). Schoenberg and atonality. *The Georgia Review, 29*(2), 298–327.

Rusinek, G. (2011). Action-research on collaborative composition: An analysis of research questions and design. In O. Odena (Ed.), *Musical creativity: Insights from music education research* (pp. 185–200). Ashgate.

Schippers, H. (2010). *Facing the music: Shaping music education from a global perspective*. Oxford University Press.

Sessions, R. (1970). *Questions about music*. Harvard University Press.

Sloboda, J. A. (Ed.). (1988). *Generative processes in music: The psychology of performance, improvisation, and composition*. Clarendon.

Stravinsky, I. (1947). *The poetics of music*. Random House.

Taylor, B., & Spitzer, M. (2015). *Mendelssohn*. Routledge.

Ting, C. (2021). Composing for orchestra: A conductor's note. *Canadian Music Educator, 62*(3), 20–25.

Trevarthen, C. (2012). Communicative musicality: The human impulse to create and share music. In D. J. Hargreaves, D. E. Miell, & R. A. R. MacDonald (Eds.), *Musical imaginations: Multidisciplinary perspectives on creativity, performance, and perception* (pp. 259–284). Oxford University Press.

Tymoczko, D. (2011). *A geometry of music: Harmony and counterpoint in the extended common practice*. Oxford University Press.

Viera de Carvalho, M. (1999). New music between search for identity and autopoiesis: Or, the tragedy of listening. *Theory, Culture and Society, 16*(4), 127–135.

Walker, R. (1997). Visual metaphors as music notation for sung vowel spectra in different cultures. *Journal of Music Research, 26*(4), 315–345.

Williams, D. (2019). *A different paradigm in music education: Re-examining the profession*. Taylor & Francis.

Wolff, J. (1983). *Aesthetics and the sociology of art*. Allen & Unwin.

Woodman, R. W., & Schoenfeldt, L. F. (1989). Individual differences in creativity: An interactionist perspective. In J. A. Glover, R. R. Ronning, & C. R. Reynolds (Eds.), *Handbook of creativity* (pp. 77–91). Plenum Press.

Zaslaw, N. (1994). Mozart's European orchestras. *Musicology Australia, 17*(1), 13–18.

Printed in the United States
by Baker & Taylor Publisher Services